PALGRAVE MACMILLAN
GREAT DEBATES IN LAW

PALGRAVE MACMILLAN
GREAT DEBATES IN LAW

Series Editor
Jonathan Herring
Professor of Law,
University of Oxford

Contract Law
Jonathan Morgan

Criminal Law
Jonathan Herring

Employment Law
Simon Honeyball

Family Law
Jonathan Herring, Rebecca Probert and Stephen Gilmore

Property Law
David Cowan, Lorna Fox O'Mahony and Neil Cobb

Other titles are in course of preparation.

If you would like to comment on this book, or on any other law text
published by Palgrave Macmillan, please write to lawfeedback@palgrave.com.

PALGRAVE MACMILLAN
GREAT DEBATES IN LAW

GREAT DEBATES IN
PROPERTY LAW

DAVID COWAN

Professor of Law and Policy,
University of Bristol Law School

LORNA FOX O'MAHONY

Professor of Law,
Durham Law School, Durham University

NEIL COBB

Lecturer in Law,
Durham Law School, Durham University

palgrave
macmillan

This edition first published 2012 by PALGRAVE MACMILLAN

Palgrave Macmillan in the UK is an imprint of Macmillan Publishers Limited, registered in England, company number 785998, of Houndmills, Basingstoke, Hampshire RG21 6XS.

Palgrave Macmillan in the US is a division of St Martin's Press LLC, 175 Fifth Avenue, New York, NY 10010.

Palgrave Macmillan is the global academic imprint of the above companies and has companies and representatives throughout the world.

Palgrave® and Macmillan® are registered trademarks in the United States, the United Kingdom, Europe and other countries.

ISBN: 978–0–230–27890–5 paperback

This book is printed on paper suitable for recycling and made from fully managed and sustained forest sources. Logging, pulping and manufacturing processes are expected to conform to the environmental regulations of the country of origin.

A catalogue record for this book is available from the British Library.

10 9 8 7 6 5 4 3 2 1
21 20 19 18 17 16 15 14 13 12

Printed and bound in Great Britain by
CPI Antony Rowe, Chippenham and Eastbourne

CONTENTS

1. THEMES OF PROPERTY   1

2. TENURE AND ESTATES   21

3. THE 1925 LEGISLATION   41

4. LEASES   61

5. LAND REGISTRATION   85

6. UNLAWFUL OCCUPATION OF LAND:
SQUATTING AND ADVERSE POSSESSION   107

7. THIRD-PARTY INTERESTS IN THE USE AND CONTROL OF LAND   127

8. HUMAN RIGHTS AND PROPERTY LAW   145

9. LAW, EQUALITY AND HOUSING   165

10. MORTGAGES AND SECURITY INTERESTS IN LAND   186

11. COHABITATION: RIGHTS TO THE HOME   204

12. CONCLUSIONS: WHAT IS THE POINT OF PROPERTY?   226

PREFACE

The subject of property, and specifically of land law, has the potential to be an endlessly fascinating area of study. We all usually need to live somewhere, to be somewhere, and so to exist in some relationship with land. Yet, while its importance is in one way reflected in its status as a foundational subject for any LLB degree, for too long property law has been regarded by undergraduate students as a difficult, inaccessible and insufficiently relevant area of law to their everyday lives. This book seeks to change that, by introducing readers to property law as a fluid and ever-changing entity, developed over centuries of debate and cultural change; and by enabling readers to appreciate that to understand the current rules requires a sense of where those rules have come from, how they might change in the future, and why they matter in the real world. The book takes a contextual approach throughout, encouraging students to think critically about the nature of land law, its political, social, cultural and economic contexts, and the values which are inherent to the system as it has developed in England and Wales.

This book broadly follows the structure of most conventional undergraduate property or land law courses as they are delivered in UK law schools. However, we are seeking to provide something quite different from other books, which typically introduce the subject by providing an exposition of the principles from within the closed system of property law's logical and rationally ordered boundaries. Such approaches start from the law, work through the law, and often end with the law. While we have all taught land law courses that follow a largely conventional format in respect of the topics covered, we strongly believe that there is much more to discover in these foundational topics than doctrinal approaches alone can hope to reveal. Indeed, by placing the law as it is formally constituted at the centre of the picture, we would argue that such approaches conceal at least as much as they expose.

What we hope to have produced, therefore, is not just another land law book, but a searching volume designed to support the study of property law by uncovering the (often messy, frequently politicized and heavily value-laden) real-world environment in which real actual people negotiate their way around (and sometimes outside) legal principles; and how those principles interact with wider socio-economic contexts, policies and values. While the book is modelled around the key topics delivered on typical undergraduate courses, it seeks to engage readers in the 'why' of land law, as well as the 'what' and 'how' set out in traditional texts. Our rationale for writing this book, then, is to re-invigorate the subject for a new generation of readers, emphasizing the relevance of these debates for contemporary society. This is the approach that we ourselves adopt, as scholars and teachers of property, to engage with and understand our subject. We believe that, by capturing some of these ideas and perspectives, mapped onto the topic areas of the conventional land law course, our approach offers a new pathway through which to enhance and develop the ways that land law is understood by students and by researchers. Our bold aim in writing this book has been to enable and encourage others to see property as we do: as an attractive, exciting and valuable subject.

CASES

United Kingdom

*Abbey National Building Society
v Cann* [1991] 1 AC 56   33, 101

*Abbey National plc v Office of Fair
Trading* [2009] EWCA Civ 116   78

Aldred's Case (1610) 9 Co
Rep 57b   140

Allen v Seckham (1879)
11 ChD 790   43

Anderson Antiques v Anderson Wharf
[2007] EWHC 2086 (Ch)   222

Antoniades v Villiers [1990]
1 AC 417   69, 75–7

Ashburn Anstalt v Arnold [1989]
Ch 1   68

Ashley v Drum Housing Association
[2010] L&TR 117   180

Austerberry v Oldham Corp (1885)
29 CH D 750   130

Bachelor v Marlow (2001) 32
P&CR 36   140

Bailey v Stephens (1862)
12 CB(NS) 91   139

*Bank of Ireland Home Mortgages
Ltd v Bell* [2001] 2 FLR 809   57

*Bankway Properties Ltd v Pensfold-
Dunsford* [2001] 1 WLR 1369   75–7

Barca v Mears [2004] EWHC
2170 (Ch)   57, 146

Barclay's Bank plc v O'Brien [1994]
1 AC 180   191

Barnhard v Greenshields (1853) 9
Moo PC 18   43

*Barons Finance Ltd v Olubisi,
Mayor's and City of London
Court, 26 April 2010*   195

Beedles v Guinness Northern Counties
[2011] EWCA Civ 442   180–1

Begay v Keedah 19 Indian L Rep
(Navajo 1991)   120

*Berrisford v Mexfield Housing Co-op
Ltd* [2010] EWCA Civ 811;
[2011] UKSC 52   68, 70–2

Birmingham CC v Doherty [2009]
1 AC 367   150, 151, 153

Bolton v Buckenham (1891)
1 QB 278   196

Boustamy v Piggott (1995)
69 P&CR 298   194

Bradley v Carrit [1903] AC 253   194

Bristol & West Building Society v Ellis
(1996) 73 P&CR 158 (CA)   198

Browne v Flower [1911]
1 Ch 219   140

*Bruton v London & Quadrant
Housing Trust* [2000]
1 AC 406   68–9, 73–4, 149–50

Bryant v Lefever (1879) 4 CPD 172   139

Burns v Burns [1984] 1 Ch 317   211

*Camden London BC v Shortlife
Community Housing* (1992)
90 LGR 358   68

Carlton v Goodman [2002]
EWCA Civ 545   207

*Celsteel Ltd v Alton House Holdings
Ltd* [1985] 1 WLR 204   143

Central London Commercial Estates
    Ltd v Kato Kagaku Ltd [1998]
    4 All ER 948   107
Cheltenham & Gloucester Building
    Society v Norgan [1996]
    1 WLR 343   198
Cheval Bridging Finance Ltd v Bhasin
    [2008] EWCA Civ 1613   198
Chlokar v Chlokar [1984] FLR 313   100
City of London BS v Flegg [1988]
    AC 54   45, 102
Clark v Chief Land Registrar [1993] 2
    WLR 141   55
Clark v Novacold [1999] IRLR 318   178
Connors v UK (2004)
    40 EHRR 189   151, 152, 153
Cook v The Mortgage Business plc
    et al [2012] EWCA Civ 17   34
Copeland v Greenhalf [1952]
    Ch 488   140
Cowan v Chief Constable for Avon
    and Somerset Constabulary
    [2002] HLR 44   83
Crabb v Arun DC [1976]
    Ch 179   215, 219, 220
Crowe v Wood [1971]
    1 QB 77   139, 140
Croydon LBC v Barber [2010]
    HLR 26   151

Dalton v Angus (1881) 6 App
    Cas 740   140
DiPalma v UK (1988)
    10 EHRR 149   163
Director General of Fair Trading v
    First National Bank plc [2002]
    1 AC 481   78

Eastland Homes Partnerships Ltd v
    Whyte [2012] EWHC 695 (QB)   157
Edwards v Lloyds TSB [2001]
    1 FCR 139   58
Errington v Errington [1952]
    1 KB 290   69

Eves v Eves [1975]
    1 WLR 1338   210, 213
Ferrishurst v Wallcite Ltd [1999]
    Ch 355   101
First National Bank plc and Achampong
    [2003] EWCA Civ 487   57, 58
Forcelux v Sweetman [2001]
    2 EGLR 173   32

Garside v RFYC [2011]
    UKUT 367 (LC)   32
Ghaidan v Godin-Mendoza
    [2004] 3 WLR 113; [2004]
    2 AC 557   158, 165
Gillett v Holt [2001]
    Ch 210   215, 220, 221
Gissing v Gissing [1971]
    AC 886   210, 212, 217
Gladehurst Properties Ltd v Hashemi
    [2011] EWCA Civ 604   81
Goodman v Gallant [1986]
    2 WLR 236   207
Grant v Edwards [1086] Ch 638   210,
    213, 221

Hair v Gillman (2000)
    80 P&CR 108   140
Halifax plc v Okin [2007]
    EWCA Civ 567   198
Hall and Preddy v Bull and Bull
    [2011] EW Misc 2 (CC)   175
Hammersmith and Fulham
    LBC v Monk [1992]
    1 AC 478   24, 82, 148, 152
Hammond v Mitchell [1991]
    1 WLR 1127   210
Hill v Tupper (1863)
    2 H & C 121   139
Hodgson v Marks [1971] Ch 892   101
Horsham Properties v Clark
    & Beech [2008] EWHC
    2327 (Ch)   157, 158, 199
Horsham Properties v Clark [2009]
    1 WLR 1255   197

Hounslow LBC v Powell [2011]
  2 WLR 287   148, 154, 156,
  157, 199, 229
Hunter v Canary Wharf [1997]
  AC 655   140
Hypo-Mortgage Services Ltd v Robinson
  [1997] 2 FLR 71   101

In re North East Property Buyers
  Litigation [2010] EWHC
  2991 (Ch)   33, 34
In re Prestige [1984] ICR 473   182
Irani Finance Ltd v Singh [1970]
  2 WLR 117 (ChD); [1971]
  Ch 59 (CA)   54

JA Pye (Oxford) Ltd v Graham [2000]
  Ch 676; [2003] 1 AC 419   123
Jennings v Rice [2003] 1 P&CR 8   219
Jones v Challenger [1960]
  2 WLR 695   52
Jones v Kernott [2011] UKSC 53   206,
  208, 212–13, 216, 217
Jones v Smith (1841) 1 Hare 43   43

Kay v Lambeth LBC [2006]
  2 AC 465   149, 150, 151, 152, 153
Khodari v Al Tamini [2008]
  EWHC 3065   195
King v Jackson (1998) 20 HLR 539   83
King v Keston Properties Ltd (1985)
  49 P & CR 212   100
Kregliner v New Patagonia Meat Co
  [1914] AC 25   194

Lace v Chantler [1944] KB 368   72
Leeds CC v Price [2006] AC 465   148,
  150
Lloyds Bank plc v Rosset [1989]
  3 All ER 915; [1991]
  1 AC 107   101, 209, 212, 214
London & Blenheim Estates v Ladbroke
  Retail Park [1992] 1 WLR 1278;
  [1994] 1 WLR 31   139, 140

Mabo v Queensland (1989)
  166 CLR 186   23
Malcolm v Lewisham BC [2008]
  1 AC 1399   178–9, 180
Malory Enterprises v Cheshire
  Homes [2002] 3 WLR 1;
  [2002] Ch 216   100, 101
Manchester City Council v
  Pinnock [2010] 3 WLR 1441   146,
  154, 156, 157, 158, 199, 229
Manchester City Council v Romano and
  Sumari [2005] 1 WLR 2775   178
Mannai Investment Co Ltd v
  Eagle Star Life Assurance Co Ltd
  [1997] AC 749   71
McGlynn v Welwyn Hatfield DC [2009]
  EWCA Civ 285   151
McPhail v Persons Unknown [1973]
  Ch 447   107
Midland Heart v Richardson,
  Birmingham Civil Justice Centre
  (ChD), 12 November 2007   162–3
Mikeover v Brady (1989)
  21 HLR 513   69
Moncrieff v Jamieson [2007]
  1 WLR 2620   140
Mortgage Corp Ltd v Lewis Silkin
  (25 February, unreported)   57
Multiservice Bookbinding v Marden
  (1979) Che 84   194

Nash v Paragon Finance [2001]
  EWCA Civ 1466   194
National Provincial Bank Ltd v
  Ainsworth [1965] AC 1175   100
National Westminster Bank Ltd v
  Stockman [1981] 1 WLR 67   55
National Westminster Bank plc v Malhan
  [2004] EWHC 847   45
Nicholls v Lan [2006]
  EWHC 1255 (Ch)   57, 146
Nine Regions (T/A Logbook Loans) v
  Sadeer, Bromley County Court,
  14 January 2009   195

O'Brien v Robinson [1973] AC 912   78
Office of Fair Trading v Foxtons Ltd
   [2009] EWHC 1681   78
Oxley v Hiscock [2005] Fam 211   217

Palk v Mortgage Services Funding plc
   [1993] Ch 330   200
Paragon Finance v Pender [2005]
   EWCA 760   194
Pascoe v Turner [1979] 1 WLR 431   219
Perry v Phoenix Assurance [1988]
   1 WLR 940   55
Pettitt v Pettitt [1970] AC 777   212, 225
Phillips v Pears [1965] 1 QB 76   140
Pieretti v Enfield LBC [2010]
   EWCA Civ 1104   182
Polonski v Lloyd's Bank Mortgages
   Ltd (1997) 31 HLR 721   200
Prudential Assurance v London
   Residuary Body [1992]
   2 AC 386   68, 70, 71, 72
Purdie and Bellwod v Miller,
   High Court, 20 October 2011   33

Qazi v Harrow LBC [2004]
   1 AC 983   147, 149, 151, 152,
154, 157, 229
Quick v Taff-Ely BC [1986] QB 809   77

R (Khatun) v Newham LBC [2002]
   HLR 29   78
R (McIntyre) v Gentoo Group Ltd
   [2010] EWHC 5 (Admin)   157
R v CRE, ex p Hillingdon LBC
   [1982] AC 779   182
R v Horncastle [2009] UKSC 14   147
R v Martin (Anthony Edward)
   [2003] QB 1   10
Ramsden v Dyson (1866) LR 1
   HL 129   214
Re Citro (a Bankrupt) [1991]
   Ch 142   52, 55–6, 57
Re Ellenborough Park [1956]
   Ch 131   139

Re Mayo [1943] Ch 302   6
Redstone v Welch [2009] EG 98   33, 34
Rhone v Stephens [1994]
   2 AC 310   130
Ropaigealach v Barclays Bank plc
   [2000] QB 263   157, 197

Samuel v Jarrah Timber [1904]
   AC 323   194
Say v Smith (1530) 1 Plowd 269   68
Scrowther v Watermill Properties
   [2009] EW Misc 6   33
Sledmore v Dalby (1996)
   72 P&CR 196   220
Smith & Snipes Hall Farm v River
   Douglas Catchment Board
   [1949] 2 KB 500   129
Southwark LBC v Mills [2001]
   1 AC 1   78
Spectrum Investment v Holmes
   [1981] 1 WLR 221   107
Stack v Dowden [2007]
   2 AC 432   208, 210, 211, 213,
216, 217, 219, 222, 223, 224
State Bank of India v Sood [1997]
   Ch 276   45
Stokes v Brent LBC [2009] EWHC
   1426; [2010] EWCA Civ 626   153
Strand Securities Ltd v Caswell
   [1965] Ch 958   100, 101
Street v Mountford [1985]
   AC 809   65, 68, 69, 70, 72

Thamesmead Town Ltd v Allotey
   (1998) 30 HLR 1052   130
Thornborough v Baker (1675)
   3 Swans 628   194
Thorner v Major [2009] 1 WLR
   776   215, 221, 222
TSB Bank v Marshall [1998]
   39 EG 308   57
Tulk v Moxhay (1848)
   2 Ph 774; (1848)
   47 ER 1345   127, 129, 132, 140

*Voyias v Information Commissioner
& London Borough of Camden*
[2011] EA/2011/0007   114

Wandsworth LBC v Winder [1985]
AC 461   150
*Waver v London and Quadrant
HT* [2009] HLR 40   157
Westminster CC v Clarke [1992]
2 AC 288   65
Wheeldon v Burrows (1879)
12 Ch D 31   99, 143
Whittaker v Kinnear [2011]
EWHC 1479 (QB)   223
*Williams & Glyn's Bank v Boland
Ltd* [1981] AC 487   5, 55, 100,
101, 102, 200
Wright v Macadam [1949]
2 KB 744   140

Yaxley v Gotts [2000] Ch 162   221,
222
Yeoman's Row v Cobbe [2008]
1 WLR 1752   214, 215, 219, 222
YL v Birmingham City Council [2008]
1 AC 95   157–8

European Court of Human Rights
Belchikova v Russia, App No 2408/06,
25 March 2010   158

Blecic v Croatia (2004)
41 EHRR 185   150

*Case of JA Pye (Oxford) Ltd
and JA Pye (Oxford) Land Ltd
v UK*, App No 44302/02 see
Pye v UK

Jahn v Germany [2004]
ECHR 36   160
James v UK (1986)
Series A No 98   160, 163

Kay v UK (37341.06) [2011]
HLR 2   155

McCann v UK (2008)
47 EHRR 40   148, 152–3

Paulic v Croatia, App No 3572/06,
22 October 2009   148
Pye v UK (2006) 43 EHRR 2; (2008)
46 EHRR 1083   122, 123, 159,
160–2

Sporrong & Lonnroth v Sweden (1982)
Series A No 52   159, 163

Zehentner v Austria, App No 20082/02,
16 July 2009   158

LEGISLATION

UK statutes

Abolition of Tenures Act 1660 23
Administration of Estates Act 1925 41
Administration of Justice Act 1970
  s. 36 203
    (1) 198

Changing Orders Act 1979 55
Civil Procedure Rules 1998,
  Rule 55.8 109
Commonhold and Leasehold
  Reform Act 2002 133, 136
Commons Act 2006 135, 136
Consumer Credit Act 1974 194
Consumer Credit Act 2006 194
  s. 104A(1) 195
Contracts (Rights of
  Third Parties) Act 1999 140
Countryside and Rights of
  Way Act 2000 128, 131,
136
Criminal Justice and Public
  Order Act 1994 110
  s. 76 109
Criminal Law Act
  1977 115, 117, 118, 197
  s. 6 110, 111
  s. 7 111
    (3) 110
  s. 12A 110

Disability Discrimination Act
  1995 (DDA) 177, 178, 180
  s. 24

    (3) 178
    (5) 180

Equality Act 2010 (EA) 165, 173,
174, 176, 178, 179, 184
  Part 3 167
  Part 4 167, 170
  s. 13 166
  s. 15 177
  s. 19 166
  s. 20 167, 180
  s. 22 181
  s. 26 166
  s. 27 166
  s. 28
    (3) 167
    (4) 167
  s. 29(8) 166
  s. 32
    (3)(a) 167
    (3)(b) 167
  s. 33(6) 166
  s. 34(4) 166
  s. 35(4) 166
  s. 149 181, 183, 184
  s. 158 184
  s. 199 208
  sch. 4 167, 180
  sch. 5 para. 5 174

Family Law (Scotland) Act 2006 205
Forcible Entry Acts 110

Housing Act 1980 66

Housing Act 1985	65, 82, 98
s. 32(3)	73
s. 79	82
s. 86	81
Housing Act 1988	65, 66, 67–8,
72, 76, 82, 163	
s. 5	81
s. 21	68, 82
sch. 1	31
sch. 2 ground 8	31
Housing Act 2004	79–80
s. 21	80
s. 212(8)	79
s. 213	
(1)	79
(3)	79
(4)	79, 80
(5)	80
(6)	80
(6)(a)	80
s. 214	80
(1)–(2)	80
(4)	80
s. 215	80
Housing and	
Regeneration Act 2008	
s. 68	31
s. 70	31
Human Rights Act 1998	149, 151,
158, 165	
s. 2(1)	147
s. 3	147
s. 4	147
sch.	1, 145
Article 8	82, 199
Insolvency Act 1986	
(as amended)	57
s. 336	55
(4)	55
(5)	55
s. 335A	146
Land Charges Act 1925	41

Land Charges Act 1972	
s. 2	42
(2)	143
(5)	142
Land Registration Act 1862	85
Land Registration	
Act 1925	6, 41, 46, 55, 86, 96,
102, 137	
s. 3(xv)	5
s. 70	98
(1)(a)	143
(1)(g)	100
(1)(k)	97
Land Registration Act 2000	41
Land Registration Act 2002	9, 17,
46, 85, 88, 89, 90, 91, 92,	
93–6, 98, 101, 103, 104,	
105, 121, 122, 123, 124–5,	
138, 142, 160	
Part 8 sch. 5	92
ss. 2–8	97
s. 23(1)	194
s. 27	97
(1)	97
(2)(d)	143
(2)(e)	143
(7)	143
s. 29(4)	97
s. 58	97
s. 91	92
s. 116	221
sch. 2, para. 1	107
sch. 3	143
para. 1	98
para. 2	99
para. 2(c)	100
para. 3	143
sch. 6	
para. 5	108
paras 2–3	108
Landlord and Tenant Act 1985	
s. 8	77
s. 11	73, 77
s. 19(1)(a)	31

Landlord and Tenant (Covenants) Act 1995   65

Law of Property Act 1922   23

Law of Property Act 1925   6, 23, 41, 51, 53, 54, 56

  s. 1   23, 44

    (2)   44

  s. 2   45

  s. 25   52

  s. 27   45

  s. 30   52

  s. 35   51

  s. 52   68

  s. 53(1)(b)   207

  s. 54(2)   68

  s. 62   143

  s. 85(1)   194

  s. 87   194

  s. 91   200

  ss. 101–103   199

  s. 101(1)(i)   199

  s. 149(6)   71, 72

Law of Property Act 1969, s. 23   43

Law of Property (Miscellaneous Provisions) Act 1989,

  s. 2   68, 222–3

Leasehold Reform Act 1967   31

Limitation Act 1980   161

  s. 15   107

Localism Act 2011, s. 184   81

Mortgage Repossessions (Protection of Tenants etc) Act 2010   157

  s. 1

    (2)   187

    (5)   184

National Assistance Act 1948   201

Prescription Act 1832   139

Protection from Eviction Act 1977   68, 81–2, 197

  s. 1   83

s. 3

  (1)   82

  (2)   82

s. 5

  (1)   82

  (1A)   82

  (1B)   82

Public Health Acts   131

Race Relations Act 1965   167, 172

Race Relations Act 1968   173

Race Relations Act 1976   168, 174

  s. 78(2)   166

Rent Act 1977   67

Rentcharges Act 1977   44

Right to Light Act 1959   139

Settled Land Act 1925   41

Statute Quia Emptores 1290   23

Trust of Land Act 1996   143

Trusts of Land and Appointment of Trustees Act 1996   6, 46, 47, 55, 56, 60

  s. 3   57

  s. 14   200

  s. 15   57, 200

    (3)   57

  s. 30   57

UK rules and regulations

Consumer Credit (Agreements) Regulations 1983   195

Equality Act 2012 (Specific Duties) Regulations 2011/2260   183

Land Registration (Electronic Conveyancing) Rules 2008   92

Land Registration Rules 1925   87

Race Relations Act 1976 (Amendment) Regulations 2003/1626

  reg. 23(2)(b)   171, 174

reg. 24   171, 174
Unfair Terms in Consumer
  Contracts Regulations 1999
  SI 1999/2083   78, 195

European documents
Council Directive 2000/43/EC,
  29 June 2000 (EU
  Race Directive)   171, 174

European Convention on
  Human Rights   165
  Article 8   45, 145, 147, 148,
  150, 152, 155, 157, 158, 162, 164,
  175, 228, 230
  (1)   149
  First Protocol,
  Article 1 (A1P1)   45, 145,
  159–63

1

THEMES OF PROPERTY

INTRODUCTION

Books on property law sometimes begin with a discussion around the question: what is property? Such discussions are at different levels incorporating some or all of the following (and, no doubt, others): students are usually served up the 'bundle of rights' theory, best exemplified by Honoré's classic argument that, rather than focus on the thing itself, property law is focused on various rights in the thing and responsibilities which derive from one's ownership of the thing.[1] Students may also be served up the 'thin air' argument which broadly, and slightly more contextually, asks us to think about the relationships between people and space. Again, commonly but perhaps with less sophistication, we are enjoined to think about the difference between property and personal rights by reference to the ineffable characteristic of property rights (that they bind third parties). Property law then becomes a definitional struggle between property and the personal.

Our approach in this chapter and in this book is rather different. Rather than take issue with those starting points, we sidestep them because our search is for no less than the identification of certain key themes which govern property – the term 'govern' is used here to suggest that these key themes offer a certain mentality of property, or at least the way property is used in law. They produce what seem to be truths about property and these truths run deep so that, when they are brought out into the open and questioned, their logic seems, paradoxically, both unassailable but also assailable. We deal with this paradox below.

One such truth is about the value of ownership. Ownership is, in our sense, a governing function of property. It is imbricated in the fabric of liberal governance. It appears in various aphorisms and metaphors about property – owners live in 'homes', they are 'homeowners', investors, their home is theirs; renters are othered by that narrative, except that home ownership is assumed to be their ambition.[2]

---

[1] A. Honoré, 'Ownership', in A. Guest (ed.), *Oxford Essays in Jurisprudence* (Oxford University Press, 1961).

[2] C. Gurney, 'Lowering the Drawbridge: A Case Study of Analogy and Metaphor in the Social Construction of Home-Ownership' (1999) 36(10) *Urban Studies* 1705.

These aphorisms and metaphors have a striking importance in modern society in England and Wales, and, importantly, are replicated in government policy documents, which emphasize the 'naturalness' of home ownership.[3] As was suggested in 1976 (and is equally the case today):

> Even the use of English language is affected in government statements.... Owner occupiers have homes, tenants have dwellings. Council tenants have homes when they are being urged to buy them. The use of the emotive word in the one context rather than the other reflects the attitudes of those making the statements.[4]

In this introduction, however, we set out the governing themes of property law, as we see them. These themes are alienation, citizenship, exclusion, rationality, responsibility, and space.[5] They are not insulated from each other or, indeed, society. There is a complex interaction between them. They keep each other in check – problems are likely to result when one becomes dominant. They are intimately related with the ways in which property is viewed in society. We take each in turn below, but, before doing so, there is a further important point to make about the nature of our subject – indeed, one which goes to its root.

This is where we do take issue with the presentation of our subject. Perhaps because property law is a foundational subject for the professional bodies in the UK, it is somehow regarded by many as 'bounded'. Property law teaching exists to underpin conveyancing practice and is often geared in that way. For us, by contrast, property is a destination subject – it is certainly not the starting point. Property law exists in society (and vice versa), and it offers us a 'socio-legal object'.[6] That object – be it the land, the home, a map, or just paper – gets people to do things – sometimes extraordinary things – by association. Rather than focus on individual rights and responsibilities in the thing, we should approach property law by giving equal attention to humans and other objects; property law makes the objects 'speak'; it translates the land, the home, the map, the paper or whatever into its own language, and, perhaps because we don't quite have the language to translate it, we use metaphors.[7] This is a point which Margaret Davies makes, when she writes of property as a metaphor in the related discourses of knowledge, law and the person:

> Above all, the notions of exclusivity, boundedness, autonomy, immediate presence, and authority over the proper object (self, law, a field of knowledge), recur in the discussion. The property metaphor is one positive

---

[3] C. Gurney, 'Pride and Prejudice: Discourses of Normalisation in Public and Private Accounts of Home Ownership' (1999) 14(2) *Housing Studies* 163.

[4] A. Murie, P. Niner, and C. Watson, *Housing Policy and the Housing System* (Allen & Unwin, 1976) p. 171.

[5] Cf. the identification of 'traditional' key themes by Birks in 'Five Keys to Land Law', in S. Bright & J. Dewar (eds), *Land Law: Themes and Perspectives* (Oxford University Press, 1998).

[6] E. Cloatre, 'TRIPS and Pharmaceutical Patents in Djibouti: An ANT Analysis of Socio-Legal Objects' (2008) 17(2) *Social and Legal Studies* 263.

[7] A. Riles, 'A New Agenda for the Cultural Study of Law: Taking on the Technicalities' (2005–06) 53(3) *Buff L Rev* 973.

matrix for the construction of core Western values such as personal liberty and identity, the separation of law from politics and morality, and objective domains of knowledge. This is not to say that these values are *wholly* determined through the idea of the proper, but that as a metaphor it somewhat influences and reinforces specific notions of self, law and knowledge.[8]

Jennifer Nedelsky, in her classic work, draws on the same metaphors as Davies, arguing also that metaphors relate to the ways in which we experience our world so that it is not an option simply to avoid them.[9]

Autobiographical notes

In this book, we intersperse our analysis with ideas about, and metaphors of, property from within our own and our friends' lives to illustrate some of the central themes inherent in property (and scholarship about it), which are discussed above and below. This is the first such note.

Nailing it! A fragment of a housing history

When we bought our first place together in 1997, my then partner (who is a lawyer, but not a property lawyer) remarked that at last she was able to hammer nails into a wall. Up until that point, her housing pathway had been through renting either privately or from friends. Rather than entering into the spirit of that remark, it became chalked up as a possible framework for a paper.

This short biographical note seems important for a number of reasons. First, and most importantly, it speaks of property but in a rather complex and dynamic way. It does not just speak of property, it drips it, or, to put it yet another way, it *performs* property. This metaphor performs an appropriation of space, making something hers and, indeed, ours; it was designed to perform an ongoing ideal of belonging, making us belong to the space and the space belong to us. It constitutes an affective characteristic of property. The point, if you will forgive the pun, was about creating and performing 'home', a private space for us and a site of control.

The simple act to be performed illustrates a further element of property, one which has been said to be of the highest order of property, that is, exclusion. In making it hers and ours, she was also saying that it belonged to us and nobody else. It created a boundary between us and the rest of the world (although, strictly, our mortgage lender could have taken possession of the property at any time, subject to the terms of the agreement between us all, which we didn't read (!)). Stretching it a bit, her metaphor

---

[8] M. Davies, *Property: Meanings, Histories, Theories* (Routledge-Glasshouse, 2007) p. 39.
[9] J. Nedelsky, 'Law, Boundaries and the Bounded Self' (1990) 30(1) *Representations* 162, 169.

was also about the value(s) of private property against the social, whether that be the 'intentional community', group-based property principles, or publicly provided housing (sometimes now described as 'social housing').

Next, her comment performed not just property but a deeper sense of tenure. Ownership was counterposed in this comment to (formal and informal) renting relationships. Whether she was correct or not in asserting that she had been unable to hammer a nail in a wall when renting, a matter to be resolved in relational contract, the metaphor was designed to raise ownership to a different level over and above renting.

Property, then, is inherently political and it is the role taken by the various experts (including the self-constructed experts and lay persons), through which its voice is translated, that neutralizes that political element. Blomley's work on pavements provides a wonderful example of these moves, as he expertly demonstrates how there is a collision of understandings about use of the pavement across a range of expert, technical, and political logics although those logics have different inputs.[10] In these logics, pedestrianism is the unencumbered ability to move from point A to point B; it is simply about flow and circulation. This output is neutral as to the nature and type of obstruction, whether it is a beggar or a bus stop. To further this discussion, let us now introduce the core themes of this book.

ALIENATION

The first core theme of property concerns alienation – the flow of property within England and Wales, which connects with the global in a variety of ways, facilitates and furthers the dominance of the capital ideal. Property talks in this way through its monetary value. Much talk about land is about house price deflation or inflation – and, more broadly, about the worth of property; sometimes, it seems, property is only worthy when it is worth something.

The core of the system of property law in England and Wales is designed to facilitate the flow of money. Consider the following description of the 'epoch-making' legislation in the law of property:

> The main objects of the 1925 amendments are to assimilate the law of real and personal property whenever practicable, and to simplify and improve the practice of conveyancing, without interfering, more than is essential, with beneficial interests. For many years past the ideal of law reformers has

---

[10] N. Blomley, *Rights of Passage: Sidewalks and the Regulation of Public Flow* (Routledge-Glasshouse, 2011).

been to enable land to be dealt with as readily as stocks and shares, subject to the necessary modifications inherent to the subject-matter.[11]

That 1925 legislative settlement was primarily designed to achieve this purpose through an agenda which was founded on simplification; simplification would lead to certainty of title which, in turn, would lead to greater circulation and flow of property. It undercut the emergent problem of uncertainty as a result of the development of the doctrine of notice, through systems of registration of either interest or land or both (land charges or land registration). In doing so, it avoided what Lord Wilberforce subsequently referred to as 'the hazards' of the doctrine of notice:

> The system of land registration, as it exists in England, which long antedates the Land Registration Act 1925, is designed to simplify and to cheapen conveyancing. It is intended to replace the often complicated and voluminous title deeds of property by a single land certificate, on the strength of which land can be dealt with. In place of the lengthy and often technical investigation of title to which a purchaser was committed, all he has to do is to consult the register; from any burden not entered on the register, with one exception, he takes free. Above all, the system is designed to free the purchaser from the hazards of notice – real or constructive – which, in the case of unregistered land, involved him in enquiries, often quite elaborate, failing which he might be bound by equities. The Law of Property Act 1925 contains provisions limiting the effect of the doctrine of notice, but it still remains a potential source of danger to purchasers. By contrast, the only provisions in the Land Registration Act 1925 with regard to notice are provisions which enable a purchaser to take the estate free from equitable interests or equities whether he has notice or not. (See, for example, section 3(xv) s. v. 'minor interests'). The only kind of notice recognised is by entry on the register (*Williams & Glyns Bank v Boland* [1981] AC 487, 503–4).

This is a foundational statement of land registration, and it is one through which the triptych of simplicity-certainty-alienation (the core drivers of property law) seamlessly moves.

Importantly also, the 1925 legislation created the conditions which make the flow of money around property – through mortgages – possible. Again, the agenda was one of radical simplicity, creating a simple new form of mortgage (the charge by deed by way of legal mortgage) and facilitating multiple mortgages over the same property. The only thing stopping the lender is what might have been termed, albeit inadequately, 'prudence', and which has more recently been

---

[11] Sir B. Cherry, D. Parry, and J. Maxwell, *Wolstenholme & Cherry's Conveyancing Statutes* (London: Stevens & Sons, 12th edn, 1932) p. 12.

labelled 'responsible lending'.[12] The flow of capital also put the outright purchase of property practically out of reach for ordinary mortals.[13]

The centrality of alienation – and its corollary of ownership – was furthered by a rather mundane turn of events in the inter-war period which had quite dramatic consequences. The 1925 legislation, which is often ignored by housing scholars, was of central importance in the rise of ownership. Not only did it coincide with a rise in the proportion of owners but it also facilitated that rise. But it was not the only cause; indeed, its existence was entirely coincidental. Put simply, there were tight controls over the rents which private landlords could charge (and the mortgage interest they paid); there were multiple households living together; there was pent-up demand for alternative housing. Only part of that pent-up demand could be dealt with through the emergent public development of housing. Building societies, however, had a ready supply of money to lend and on terms favourable to ownership (rather than the then predominant tenure, renting). Building costs began to reduce. Major marketing campaigns were developed, which tied in with the prevailing social mores – ownership was said to be 'a bulwark against bolshevism and all that bolshevism stands for'.[14] The building society movement, which, at its heart, emphasized thrift and mutual self-help, offered a readily available supply of money for property purchase; it also offered an alternative to public subsidy and ownership. Such was the need for building societies to lend that they engaged in what we might now refer to as 'dodgy practices' – relationships with builders which produced jerry-built housing.[15]

Such is the stark power of the circulation of property implied by alienation that, even when legislation seeks to correct the assumptions of alienation, the juggernaut remains unmoved. The case study here is that of the Trusts of Land and Appointment of Trustees Act 1996, discussed in Chapter 3. In summary, this Act was designed to correct the position under the Law of Property Act 1925 which implied that, where property was held by two or more people in equity, there was an explicit duty to sell the property and a (lesser) power to postpone. The primacy of the duty to sell was reinforced by the practices of the law.[16] The almost pathological core theme of alienation, though, remains in the jurisprudence which has emerged under the 1996 Act. One might say, drawing on socio-

---

[12] The emphasis on 'responsibility' in respect of mortgage lending – both for lenders and borrowers – is discussed in Chapter 10.

[13] As one housing scholar put it, there is a 'magnificent contradiction': on the one hand, the construction of dwellings is fundamentally necessary for labour, but those who labour do not receive salaries or wages sufficient to purchase that property": S. Merrett, *Owner-Occupation in Britain* (Routledge, 1992) p. 72.

[14] H. Bellman, *The Building Society Movement* (Methuen, 1927) p. 54.

[15] The history of this can be found in a range of texts, but by far the most significant is P. Craig, 'The House That Jerry Built? Building Societies, the State and the Politics of Owner-Occupation' (1986) 1(2) *Housing Studies* 87; see also M. Ball, *Housing Policy and Economic Power: The Political Economy of Owner Occupation* (Methuen, 1983); D. Cowan & M. McDermont, *Regulating Social Housing: Governing Decline* (Routledge, 2006), ch. 8.

[16] See, in particular, *Re Mayo* [1943] Ch 302. Perhaps the most significant thing about this case is its brevity, which emphasizes just how obvious the outcome seemed to be.

legal understandings, that those remnants might have been anticipated – the past has a lengthy shadow on the present – but they are, nevertheless, significant.

CITIZENSHIP

T.D. Marshall's 'Citizenship and Social Class' remains one of the most influential scholarly treatises on Western liberal democratic conceptions of citizenship.[17] Liberal democratic citizenship in the West was conceived by Marshall in his 1970s essay as an almost inevitable progression towards the acquisition of civil, political and social or welfare rights. Accepting for a moment Marshall's construction of citizenship as synonymous with rights, it is quite clear that property has been one key site across which wider debates, about democracy, human rights and state welfare, have played out. The right to enjoyment of property, and the protected sphere of the home, have been central to past and present conceptions of liberal freedom.[18] The eventual extension of the franchise in the UK beyond the property-owning classes, and then universally, was pivotal to the democratization of Western citizenship from the late nineteenth century.[19] State provision of housing was part and parcel of the development of an approach to citizenship (although one which initially emphasized the differentiated nature of such citizenship).[20]

The role of property in citizenship discourse in the West remains fiercely contested, however, across each of these areas of rights acquisition. For instance, liberal citizenship through property rights and the privacy of the home has been subjected to a compelling critique for contributing to economic inequality and social exclusion. First, the rights of property acquisition and ownership form the bedrock of capitalist economic structures, and in turn their enforcement embeds political resistance to redistributive measures that one might argue are required to address the vast economic inequalities in society. Second, the conception of a protected private sphere of 'home', a space in which one has the right 'to be left alone', has often circumscribed the power of the state to protect the citizenship entitlements of the most vulnerable. The liberal private sphere has been especially problematic for those who understand the home as a site of exclusion. Freedom from state interference in the home has often meant control and unpunished violence by men over women within the private sphere.[21]

The social right to housing provides a further example of this politics of citizenship. Since the 1980s and 1990s an alternative construction of the

---

[17] T.D. Marshall, 'Citizenship and Social Class', in J. Manza & M. Sauder (eds), *Inequality and Society* (New York: W W Norton and Co, 2009).

[18] J. Waldron, *The Right to Private Property* (Clarendon, 1988).

[19] M. Ignatieff, 'Myth of Citizenship' (1987) 12(3) *Queen's LJ* 399.

[20] See D. Cowan & A. Marsh, 'From Need to Choice, Welfarism to Advanced Liberalism: Some Problematics of Social Housing Allocation' (2005) 25(1) *Legal Studies* 22.

[21] S. Walby, 'Is Citizenship Gendered?' (1994) 28(2) *Sociology* 379; R. Lister, *Citizenship: Feminist Perspectives* (Palgrave Macmillan, 1997).

rights of social citizenship has been powerfully evoked in Britain, both in the specific context of social housing and across all areas of welfare provision, tied to reconstructions of citizenship in terms of neoliberal individuality and self-responsibility, rather than collective needs-based state protection. The claimed solution to the perceived bureaucracy and dependency culture created by the welfare state has been self-reliance on the part of a new 'active citizen'. The 'right to buy', for instance, encapsulated Thatcher's aim to roll back the welfare state, while designed also to normalize home ownership as an expectation of good citizenship, in an attempt to tap back into the ancient Greek civic republican faith in an (inevitably conservative) property-owning democracy. Locating citizenship as at odds with the social provision of the welfare state also ensured a new division between citizens and 'anti-citizens', drawn on tenure grounds.[22]

The recent politics of citizenship suggests four things about the relationship between citizenship and property. First, Western citizenship is often understood to be synonymous with the acquisition of rights, but it is increasingly conceptualized in terms of the duties citizens owe to each other (and often the state). It is clear too that, while rights in and around property are usually seen to be progressive, they can contribute to the exclusion of others, by preventing access to the benefits of property, and exacerbating the powerlessness experienced by many within the constructed private sphere. Third, it might be said that the current model of citizenship employed in the law of property is one of differentiated citizenship. That is implied by the ever-increasing circuits of exclusion (and the different measures employed by the state to facilitate that exclusion) as against the increasingly circumscribed circuits of inclusion.[23] Fourth, we need to treat with caution claims that the progressive acquisition of rights of citizenship in and around property is irreversible. The recent politics of citizenship demonstrates clearly that our relationship to property, as citizens, exists in flux, and rights relating to property, such as housing, can morph in the face of new modes of thinking, whether feminism or neoliberal rationalities.

EXCLUSION

It has been said that exclusion – the right to exclude all comers – is of the highest order of property.[24] It is this right which enables the social construction of property as producing the autonomous, liberal and secure self; it produces inequality both inherently and as an outcome; it requires boundaries and, in

---

[22] J. Flint, *Housing, Urban Governance and Anti-Social Behaviour: Perspectives, Policy and Practice* (Policy Press, 2006).

[23] We are here employing the language of N. Rose, 'Government and Control' (2000) 40(3) *British Journal of Criminology* 321.

[24] J. Penner, *The Idea of Property in Law* (Oxford University Press, 1997).

mapping out those boundaries, it produces a governable territory (facilitating alienation).[25] This latter point is also foundational to our idea of government. Rose puts it like this:

> A telling picture hangs in the Australian National Art Gallery in Canberra. It shows traces of hills, rivers, trails, borders, overlaid by a vast eye. It is entitled 'The Governor loves to go mapping'. Cartography – the activity of mapping – exemplifies the ways in which spaces are made presentable and representable in the hope that they might become docile and amenable to government. To govern, it is necessary to render visible the space over which government is to be exercised. This is not simply a matter of looking; it is a practice by which the space is re-presented in maps, charts, pictures and other inscription devices. It is made visible, gridded, marked out, placed into two dimensions, scaled, populated with icons and so forth. In this process, and from the perspective of its government, salient features are identified and non-salient features rendered invisible.[26]

We look at the significance of mapping and space further below, and in Chapter 5 when we consider the project of title by registration in the Land Registration Act 2002.

Put another way, this right of exclusion is both definitional, in establishing the territorial boundaries, and also enabling in respect of the relationship of belonging between a person and their property. Because the drive of property law is alienation, property law misses out on a singular important facet of property, its affective capacity; what Cooper describes as 'belonging' – the 'core element of property at both a definitional and normative level' – which includes 'a relationship of connection, of part to whole'.[27]

Rights of exclusion also give rise to 'defensive homeownership', linked to the insecurity of everyday life. That insecurity '... has generated an imperative for the control and handling of domestic territory that seeks autonomy and refuge from dangers, as well as connecting to prevailing ideologies that celebrate personal autonomy and control'.[28] This notion of defensive homeownership territorializes risk and has, as its foundations, the link between property and crime control strategies. We are here confronted by '... the two major social facts of the last third of the twentieth century: *the normality of high crime rates* and *the acknowledged limitations of the criminal justice state*'.[29] Defensive home ownership is a response

---

[25] Nedelsky, n.9; cf. N. Blomley, 'The Borrowed View: Privacy, Propriety and the Entanglements of Property' (2005) 30(3) *Law and Social Inquiry* 661.

[26] N. Rose, *Powers of Freedom: Reframing Political Thought* (Cambridge University Press, 1999) p. 36.

[27] D. Cooper, 'Opening Up Ownership: Community Belonging, Belongings, and the Productive Life of Property' (2007) 32(3) *Law and Social Inquiry* 625, 629.

[28] R. Atkinson & S. Blandy, 'Panic Rooms: the Rise of Defensive Homeownership' (2007) 22(3) *Housing Studies* 443, 444.

[29] D. Garland, *The Culture of Control: Crime and Social Order in Contemporary Society* (Oxford University Press, 2001) p. 106 (emphasis in original).

to these social facts, one consequence of which has been the architectural and urban planning demand to enhance security.[30] Manifestations of this security are all around us (such as CCTV, lighting, etc.) but these techniques also implore us to act responsibly and, in effect, to self-police our space.

The 'gated community' is a particularly valuable example of the link between the understandings of exclusion at the root of property law and our everyday lives. The gate – both literal and metaphoric – operates as a defensive mechanism against the savage and barbarous exterior, a kind of safe haven and exclusion of the other.[31] McKenzie links their rise between developers, local government and middle- and upper-class consumers, in all of whose interests the gate exists. Although the term 'gated community' is a contested concept in itself,[32] one common thread is of interlocking legal rights and obligations, often through the use of covenants, to enforce community norms: '... a legal framework which allows the extraction of monies to help pay for maintenance of common-buildings, common services, such as rubbish collection, and other revenue costs such as paying staff to clean or secure the neighbourhood'.[33] As such, they represent the apotheosis of the logic of property law – a community divided off from the outside by its own relational local law and norms in which everything from allocation to security to refuse collection is private.

The limits of the exclusion thesis can be exemplified by, and in, the debate over the conviction of Tony Martin, a farmer who took it upon himself to shoot two burglars, one of whom died as a result. Martin was convicted of murder (which was subsequently reduced to manslaughter on the grounds of diminished responsibility).[34] The case became something of a *cause célèbre* for those who sought to apply the logic of property law (implicitly) by arguing, unsuccessfully, for the right to defend one's home. Radio 4's *Today Programme* held a poll of subjects to form a Private Members' Bill in Parliament in 2003–4 – the winning proposal (which attracted 37 per cent of the 26,000 votes) was to allow homeowners to use 'any means' to defend their homes.[35]

The exclusion thesis (for that is what it is), just like the citizenship thesis, should be broken down and problematized. Its assumptions are of sovereignty, security and self-governance in the home. As generations of family lawyers and social scientists would suggest, these assumptions do not reflect much of the

---

[30] See, for example, O. Newman, *Defensible Space: People and Design in the Violent City* (Architectural Press, 1972).

[31] See M. Davis, *City of Quartz: Excavating the Future of Los Angeles* (Verso, 1990); E. McKenzie, *Privatopia: Homeowner Associations and the Rise of Residential Private Government* (Yale University Press, 1994).

[32] See A. Bottomley, 'A Trip to the Mall: Revisiting the Public/Private Divide', in H. Lim and A. Bottomley (eds), *Feminist Perspectives on Land Law* (London: Glasshouse-Routledge, 2007).

[33] R. Atkinson & S. Blandy, 'Introduction: International Perspectives on the New Enclavism and the Rise of Gated Communities' (2005) 20(2) *Housing Studies* 177.

[34] *R v Martin (Anthony Edward)* [2003] QB 1.

[35] See <http://news.bbc.co.uk/1/hi/uk/3360765.stm>

reality of everyday life. Most violence occurs within the home; it can be seen as a site of oppression and abuse; the home is often the producer of homelessness.[36]

RATIONALITY

The fourth theme of property which cuts across law and governance is rationality. The emphasis on rationality pervades much of legal scholarship and education. For many legal scholars, the idea that law has an emotional dimension – that is, that legal doctrine and decision making is, or should be, influenced by emotional considerations – may seem surprising at least, and even antithetical or heretical. As students of the law, we are taught that law is objective, rational, impartial, that legal training teaches one to 'put emotions to one side' and to adopt purely rational analyses.[37] From this perspective, the idea that emotional responses and analyses might have a role to play in law conjures up the spectre of a subjective, irrational and partial system, which is anathema to our idea of 'what law is'.

Rationality is frequently presented as the unquestioned and unquestionable foundation of property thinking: property, and property law, must behave in ways that are rational if it is to achieve its other purposes (for example, alienability). Rationality is seen as necessary if the law is to achieve certainty, and to enable people to know where they stand in relation to property, so supporting the policy goals of trade in land and facilitating market transactions. In contrast, property law does not deal well with irrationality or with emotion. At the same time, although much legal analysis is posited on the presumption that law is and should be rooted in logic and rational choice (we speak of judicial reasoning), based on fact rather than feeling, there are many contexts in which (even) property law must respond to emotional phenomena – whether in the context of the emotional attachment that occupiers have to their homes as a special type of property based on its materiality as well as its emotional and psychological significance (see Chapter 5), or in the context of emotional relationships between property subjects (see Chapter 11). Indeed, it is the very emotional attachment to the thing which underlies our understandings about, and attachments to our own homes.

Rationality underscores property law in two important respects. The first is through the deep rationality that underpins the classical exposition of property law – and particularly English land law – as rational, logical, abstract and juridical in character. According to this view, the rules or doctrines of property law are based on deep logic, pure reason or strict rationality. Property law is treated as a

---

[36] See, for example, L. Moran, 'The Poetics of Safety', in A. Crawford (ed.), *Crime and Insecurity: The Governance of Safety in Europe* (Willan, 2002), who talks of an ambivalence at the heart of the notion of 'home'.

[37] See, generally, D. Sugarman, 'Legal Theory, the Common Law Mind, and the Making of the Textbook Tradition', in W. Twining (ed.), *Legal Theory and the Common Law* (Blackwell, 1986).

juridical category which must be internally coherent, and the rules of which are worked out only by reference to its internal logic. There is no role, in a system of pure logic, for external, policy-informed goals: rather, property law is viewed as non-instrumentalist, and its doctrine is judged according to consistency and coherence with its internal schema (for example, the meanings of the core juridical concepts of ownership, title, possession and so on). This view of property law supports a dispassionate, logical mode of reasoning; it is not concerned with the effects of rules or decisions on parties, or with the fairness of outcomes.

Non-instrumentalist approaches to private law emphasize its inner character rather than its external effects, seeking to find coherence in the internal characteristics of private law without external referents in the form of policy or social interests. In these accounts of private law, the theorists seek to detach the reason of the law from political and policy issues based on their conviction that private law is not a legitimate vehicle by which to achieve social policy goals.[38] The emphasis on deep rationality in such approaches to property excludes (re-)distributive considerations (for example, underlying inequalities). Those approaches are concerned with abstract rights rather than the welfare of parties. While they do not deny that other values (efficiency, welfare etc.) are persuasive within their own moral and political orders, those values are simply not relevant (so the reasoning goes) to the juridical order governing private transactions between individuals.

Critics of deep rationality approaches argue that they ignore reality – specifically, the reality that law, in theory and in practice, always has a subject, and a set of goals. The legal subject of property law is the notional person who is governed by the law. It is that person whose identity and characteristics are critical to the justificatory goals and values that inform the theory, that determine the rights and duties of legal persons (or subjects), and which in turn shape the expectations that inform legal doctrine, policies and practices, as well as the rights and remedies recognized by legal institutions. Deep rationality approaches generally exclude the subjective characteristics of the legal subject on the basis that formal equality requires that all subjects of property are treated equally in law (regardless of their relatively unequal social, economic or power resources).

A second meaning of rationality, prevalent in property discourse, is economic rationality. This view of property law admits that private law can have goals, but bases those goals on the values of economic efficiency. As such, it rejects socialwelfarist considerations in favour of the classical or neoliberal market-individualist model, which in turn reflects a particular model of (liberal) legal subjectivity. For the economic rationality model, the legal subject of property law – the imagined person who is expected to understand legal rules and procedures, as well as behave accordingly to protect their own interests – is conceived as an economically rational subject within the meaning associated with the classical economic theory of rational choice: that is, the subject of property is expected to behave in a self-interested, welfare-maximizing way.

---

[38] See, for example, E. Weinrib, *The Idea of Private Law* (Harvard University Press, 1995).

This conception of the legal subject is central to the autonomy-centred, deontological structure of property that emerged under the political ideology of liberal individualism. From this perspective, property transactions are viewed as opportunities for individuals to maximize their own welfare (i.e., profit), in an adversarial game from which each party – so long as they follow the rules of the game (which include respecting the autonomy and equal opportunities of others to do likewise) – aims to wrest as much as they can to their own self-interest. This perspective positions property within an adversarial transactional environment in which the parties' responsibilities are to their own self-interests and not to each other.

The economic rationality model of property law, and its construction of the legal subject as a rational agent aggressively pursuing his or her own self-interest, can be justified conceivably on several grounds. These include the need to ensure the security of long-term expectations, the reliability of investment strategies, the rationality of decision making about future land use, stable forward planning, the need to protect titles taken by purchasers and creditors, and the importance of ensuring that the substantial wealth tied up in land should not be rendered economically sterile. Economic rationalists emphasize the need to facilitate property transactions as smoothly and effectively as possible.

Critics of the liberal legal model of property challenge the ways in which the ideological constraints of liberal democracy have attempted to limit the reach of private law, demanding that it serve the liberal goal of autonomous rights, and not the competing aim of individual welfare.[39] One source of criticism is the emphasis on interpersonal justice – between the parties to the transaction, rather than social justice – which takes account of the wider implications of legal decisions and doctrines. The platform of neutrality on which the juridical legal subject is positioned is also critiqued in scholarship seeking to challenge the assumptions underpinning formal equality theories based on a liberal legal subject indifferent to the realities of need and advantage.[40]

The unreality of the stripped-down subject of classical liberal legal thought – which portrayed the subjects of law without revealing their actual socio-economic power – was exposed by the critical school of legal realism.[41] References to the stripped-down subject in justificatory theories of law were criticized on the basis that they operate as a shield for the implicit smuggling of (liberal) values into legal discourse, with (hidden) political consequences.[42] From this perspective, legal doctrine and institutions are not 'neutral' but have distributive consequences, perpetuating and reflecting political choices, social disadvantage and relations of inequality and oppression;

---

[39] For a discussion of the competing perspectives in contract law, see J. Adams & R. Brownsword, 'The Ideologies of Contract' (1987) 7 *Legal Studies* 205.

[40] J. Boyle, 'Is Subjectivity Possible? The Post-Modern Subject in Legal Theory' (1991) 62 *U Colo L Rev* 489.

[41] See, for example, E. Bonthuys, 'Accommodating Gender, Race, Culture and Religion: Outside Legal Subjectivity' (2002) 18 *SAJHR* 41 at 55; see also C. Smart, 'Law's Power, the Sexed Body, and Feminist Discourse' (1990) 17 *Journal of Law and Society* 194 at 210; M Mossman, 'Feminism and Legal Method: the Difference It Makes' (1986) 3 *AJLS* 30.

[42] Bonthuys, n.41.

law – including property law – affects distributions of risk, wealth and power. Critical perspectives have challenged the essentialist subject of formalist models of justice, arguing instead for substantive acknowledgement of inequalities and of the role of law in perpetuating or addressing substantive justice (or fairness) issues. For example, some feminist legal theory has argued that the presentation of legal doctrine as 'abstract', 'objective' and 'impartial' privileges what are perceived to be masculine values; and that legal methods which justify the contentless person of deep rationality approaches, or the economically rational subject of liberal property theory, claim to strip away the context in which transactions occur and the individual characteristics of the parties but in fact embed values which privilege the dominant (white, male, middle-class, Christian) paradigm.[43]

RESPONSIBILITY

As the discussions above have shown, property law, like areas of private law, tends to view the relationships between parties to transactions within particular frameworks of values. These framing values have direct, and sometimes explicit, implications for the ways in which responsibility for losses or harms is allocated in law. From a non-instrumentalist, deep rationality approach, questions about whether one party is *responsible* for the other's loss employ highly theorized and abstract concepts rooted in the rights and correlative duties (or responsibilities) of the parties. For the corrective justice theories that underpin such non-instrumental accounts of private law, the question of what it means to be responsible is a central concern. These modes of thinking take as their starting point a negative concep-tion of liberty: they posit that parties choose by their own free will to participate as subjects of private law, and so must bear responsibility for their own losses unless it can be positively shown that another party has *caused* that loss (and so is responsible for harming the losing party) in a legally significant way.[44]

For liberal theories of law – which acknowledge the role of property in achieving the goals of liberal/market individualism – the question is what our responsibilities to one another are as efficiency-maximizing liberal subjects. The economically rational, welfare-maximizing subject of the liberal legal model can be understood within Dworkin's account of responsibility. That account identifies autonomy and choice as key to law's strategy in achieving (formal) equality and justice holding individuals responsible, as rational agents, for the choices they have made based

---

[43] Ibid, n.41.

[44] See, for example, Ripstein's 'individual responsibility' thesis, which posits that '[a] society of equals – a just society, if you like – is also a society that supposes people are responsible for their choices': A. Ripstein, *Equality, Responsibility and the Law* (Cambridge University Press, 1999) p. 1; or Honoré's theory of 'outcome responsibility', which argues that being held responsible for the outcomes of our choices is 'central to the identity and character of the agent…our responsibility for what we do and for its outcome is inseparable from our status as persons': T. Honoré, *Responsibility and Fault* (Hart Publishing, 1999) p. 10.

on their own preferences. This is because (hypothetically, given fair circumstances and a level playing field) people are assumed to choose rationally according to what they value most.[45] That emphasis on self-responsibility to make binding choices is underpinned by the argument that the individual's (formally equal) capacity to make rational choices is the hallmark of the autonomous (i.e., free) subject. In summary, the privileged legal subject of liberal private law theories is an individualist, autonomous legal subject who takes responsibility for his[46] own actions and choices and whose free and equal moral agency must be respected by holding him to those choices, no matter how bad they are.

According to this model, the parties to property transactions have no positive duties or responsibilities towards each other or to the wider community. This proposition is challenged by competing theories which argue that the functions of property law include matters of distributive justice such as welfare policy and social context considerations.[47] Such theories adopt a more explicitly distributive perspective on how we conceive of our responsibilities in respect of property, not only between parties to the transaction as individuals but as members of a community within which property is a valued resource and private ownership of property is a privilege. The idea that property is privilege resonates with Hart's depiction of certain areas of law as 'power conferring legal doctrine',[48] expanding rather than contracting the scope of individual freedom by helping people to do certain things which are regarded as good:

> Such laws do not impose duties or obligations. Instead, they provide individuals with *facilities* for realising their wishes, by conferring legal powers upon them to create, by certain specified procedures and subject to certain conditions, structures of rights and duties within the coercive framework of the law. The power thus conferred on individuals to mould their legal relations with others by contracts, wills, marriages etc., is one of the great contributions of law to social life ... [49]

The idea that property has a social context broadens the meaning of responsibility for property law. If we accept that the state's role in respect of property is enabling, by which we mean facilitative, this raises important questions about the nature of the endeavours that are supported or privileged by property's laws. Should law's support for property be characterized (only) by the goals of economic efficiency, or should it be responsive to broader social and welfare considerations – which, if not accounted for in property's laws, become, by default, state responsibilities (funded

---

[45] See, generally, R. Dworkin, *Sovereign Virtue: The Theory and Practice of Equality* (Harvard University Press, 2000).

[46] Feminist scholars would argue that this legal subject is imagined as a 'he'.

[47] See, for example, J. Purdy, *The Meaning of Property: Freedom, Community, and the Legal Imagination* (Yale University Press, 2010); J Purdy, 'A Freedom-Promoting Approach to Property: A Revived Tradition for New Debates' (2005) 72 *U Chi L Rev* 1237.

[48] For a discussion of law as power-conferring, see H.L.A. Hart, *The Concept of Law* (Clarendon Press, 1961) pp. 27–38.

[49] Hart, n.48, pp. 27–28.

through general taxation), or, in the neoliberal state, the self-responsibility of the parties as 'autonomous consumers'?

Challenges to the limited conceptions of responsibility inherent to the deep rationality or liberal-individualist models adopt social constructions of property to emphasize the 'social' interest in property and the functions of property as a tool of egalitarianism. The relationships between property and community have also been dominant in the recent work of scholars such as Gregory Alexander and Eduardo Peñalver,[50] who have proposed a substantive (rather than procedural) conception of justice as it applies to property, built around the notion of 'human flourishing'. This scholarship, which challenges utilitarian and classical liberal theories of property, focuses on the social matrices necessary for the development of such human flourishing. It offers a rich basis for articulating alternatives to the individualist, negative rights conception of property as opportunity.

That school of thought (sometimes referred to as 'progressive property') tempers the individualism of classical property theory with the idea of society as an interconnected web, in which an ethic of mutual responsibility around property plays a central role in achieving the common good.[51] Progressive property emphasizes the social values of property, values of community, autonomy, personhood, environmental protection and security. Progressive property's portrait of the 'real person' as the subject of private property describes a model of 'just social relations' that encompasses the values of equality, dignity, respect and justice as well as freedom and autonomy. The community of rights invoked in this model of property emphasizes our shared commitment to the values of '... life and human flourishing, the protection of physical security, the ability to acquire knowledge and make choices, and the freedom to live one's own life on one's own terms';[52] and reasons that, to the extent that we (as members of communities that value private property) value property as necessary for us (as humans) to flourish, we have a moral obligation to support social matrices and legal strategies that promote human flourishing for others. The idea of community responsibility invoked in progressive property is based on a form of rationality, but not the self-interested economic rationality discussed in the previous section. Rather, in this context, we are held responsible for the wider community interest in property for human flourishing because we are rationally constrained 'to acknowledge the right of every other human being, as a rational moral agent, to develop the same capabilities'.[53]

---

[50] See, for example, G. Alexander & E. Peñalver, 'Properties of Communities' (2009) 10(1) *Theoretical Inquiries in Law* 127; G. Alexander & E. Peñalver (eds), *Property and Community*, (Oxford University Press, 2010); G. Alexander, E. Peñalver, J. Singer & L. Underkuffler, 'A Statement on Progressive Property' (2009) 94 *Cornell LR* 743.

[51] G. Alexander, 'The Social-Obligation Norm in American Property Law' (2009) 94 *Cornell LR* 745, 818–19.

[52] G. Alexander, E. Peñalver, J. Singer & L. Underkuffler, 'A Statement on Progressive Property', (2009) 94 *Cornell L R* 743.

[53] G. Alexander & E. Peñalver, 'Properties of Communities' (2009) 10(1) *Theoretical Inquiries in Law* 127, 142.

Law plays an important role in shaping the expectations of responsibility placed on property's subjects (as self-responsible liberal subjects, or as members of a community that value the property needs of others within the community). One manifestation of the notion of community responsibility for property subjects is the idea that being a private property owner carries some responsibility or duty in respect of the use of the property itself. This can be illustrated, by way of example, by the idea of an ethic of stewardship in respect of land, discussed in relation to the doctrine of adverse possession in Chapter 6. Traditional justifications for the doctrine of adverse possession included that stewardship justification[54] – the ethical argument that land ownership imposes a moral duty (or responsibility) of effective stewardship on the owner, to look beyond their own self-interest and to ensure that this limited and vital commodity is managed fairly on behalf of the community as a whole.

As the discussion in Chapter 6 demonstrates, the reform of adverse possession in the Land Registration Act 2002 marked a significant turning point (from a doctrine that required effective stewardship on the part of the land owner as a condition of retaining private ownership, on pain of potentially losing the right to recovery to a squatter) to a model of responsibility in which the state, through its bureaucratic system of title by registration, effectively relieved private landowners from those responsibilities in respect of land that may be occupied by squatters. This departure also has implications, discussed in Chapters 5 and 6, for how we conceive of land – as the material, organic and tangible physical entity that is used and occupied to satisfy material needs (for example, possessed by the squatter, or occupied as a home by the owner-occupier-subject to a mortgage), or as an abstract commodity (as an entry on the land register, or as securitization rights, to be traded on the secondary mortgage market). These distinctions – which can also be characterized as 'place' (the social, material manifestation of land) versus 'space' (the abstract representation of real property) – are considered further in the next section.

SPACE

Gray and Gray ask us to think about property using the notion of propriety – or the proper in property, 'a claim to the legitimacy of one's personal space in this land' – which they describe as 'pre-legal'.[55] This is an important claim, and one which links property law with parallel cross-disciplinary developments between law and geography on which this section focuses.[56] Space is an active participant

---

[54] See, for example, J. Karp, 'A Private Property Duty of Stewardship: Changing Our Land Ethic' (1993) 23 *Environmental Law* 735; L. Caldwell and K. Shrader-Frechette, *Policy for Land: Law and Ethics*, (Rowman & Littlefield, 1993) ch. 7.

[55] Gray and Gray, *Elements of Land Law* (Oxford University Press, 2009), para 1.5.43 and footnote 2.

[56] See the two important collections: N. Blomley, D. Delaney and R. Ford, *The Legal Geographies Reader* (Blackwell, 2001); J. Holder & C. Harrison, *Law and Geography* (Oxford University Press, 2003).

in property law, one which changes over time, according to disputes and the ways in which it is envisioned. We saw above how the crucial function of mapping out space enables government processes. One can take this further. The production of the map enabled land to be carved up and sold as free space, or *terra nullius*, through the doctrine of discovery – as Mawani puts it, 'They were here (once upon a time), but now they are gone'.[57] That is to say, the indigenous inhabitants were regarded as non-subjects and mapped out. In Palestine, according to Home, 'The mosaic of land parcels was plotted, a cadastral survey plan superseded verbal descriptions and the authoritative definition of land parcels, and new survey points were physically fixed on the ground'.[58] But the law-geography inter-action goes much further than this in thinking about boundaries and bringing alternative methodologies to its subjects.[59] It is, perhaps, trite to note here that property law seems to construct its own spatial boundaries through a series of apparent binaries – public/private, privacy/propriety, property/personal, community/outsider, inclusion/exclusion – which offer powerful descriptions through which space becomes place. Law/geography scholars often seek to disrupt such binaries.

Blomley, for example, in a study of gardening in Strathcona, Canada, disrupts the apparent binary between privacy and propriety – the garden was described as 'the public face of the family' – and pushes on to argue that '... the evidence here suggests that people live in a much more emulsive world when it comes to property' so that the boundaries of property are broken down. He argues that, instead of these binaries,

> ... we think of property as a way of being in the world. By this, I mean that it entails, at the very least, a set of beliefs, dispositions, and taken-for-granted norms, as well as embodied practices that relate to the world of things. Storytelling, lawmaking, mapmaking, adjudication, and fence building are all examples. Gardening, in part, is a symbolic and practical enactment of property. Property is put to work in multiple settings, of which the courtroom is only one.

By contrast, Layard, drawing on a case study of the regeneration of the city centre shopping area in Bristol, illustrates how these binaries were set up, how public was reduced to private through coalitions of expertise, resulting in the prohibition of certain 'spatial practices'.[60] Her rich theoretical analysis enables her to make some striking points about the effects of space becoming place. So, for example, she argues that '"good" or "anti-social" behaviour is determined by the vision of

[57] R. Mawani, 'Genealogies of the Land: Aboriginality, Law, and Territory in Vancouver's Stanley Park' (2005) 14(2) *Social and Legal Studies* 315, 324.

[58] R. Home, 'An "Irreversible Conquest"? Colonial and Postcolonial Land Law in Israel/Palestine' (2003) 12(2) *Social and Legal Studies* 291, 298.

[59] See, for example, N. Blomley, *Law, Space, and the Geographies of Power* (Guilford Press, 1994); D. Cooper, *Governing out of Order: Space, Law and the Politics of Belonging* (Rivers Oram, 1998).

[60] A. Layard, 'Shopping in the Public Realm: A Law of Place' (2010) 37(3) *Journal of Law and Society* 412.

place, most famously by the banning of wearing "hoodies" from some shopping centres. ... Currently, the signs that adorn the side of the buildings at the entrance to the retail-led developments make these prohibitions [dog-walking, guitar-playing, skateboarding, photography] graphically clear.'[61]

Perhaps never before has space played such a significant role in the everyday lives of property. Space has been globalized and the place is often the signals, the neurons, the bytes transmitted electronically (just as our chapters of this book have been electronically transmitted between us).[62] This global market and its national, and local, effects had a particularly significant impact on property at the time of the crisis from 2007–. The origins of this crisis lie in the US mortgage market and the importation of devices through which mortgages became transportable and bundled up as sellable commodities on the open market (devices collectively referred to as 'securitization').[63] The extra-territorial links created by the internationalization of capital lead to 'spillover effects' across nation states,[64] and which particularly impact on the individual in ways and for reasons that remain unclear at the margins (for example, the predicted rise in mortgage possession claims has yet to materialize).

Property law in England and Wales seems rather mundane when set against these kinds of international imaginations of space, but it nevertheless retains a salience by its apparent absence. Property law does not bat an eyelid at self-certified mortgages or 125 per cent mortgages or loan-to-income ratios that do not stack up. This is again the significance of the alienation frame, replicated in the commodification of the loan document itself, and a version of the responsibility thesis. Property law is indifferent to bad bargains (and some might say that those households caught in this trap were badly advised or just made an error of judgment).

CONCLUSIONS

In this chapter, our purpose has been to identify what, for us, are the key themes in property law. These key themes run through this book in diverse ways, sometimes obvious and seen, and sometimes lurking beneath the surface. Each of them is, or has, disrupting influences. Like a temperamental teenager, there is contrariness within each of these themes and some, frankly, are just rebellious.

---

[61] Ibid 436–37.

[62] See the brilliant analysis in A. Riles, *Collateral Knowledge: Legal Reasoning in the Global Financial Markets* (University of Chicago Press, 2011).

[63] See, generally, T. Wainwright, 'Laying the Foundations for a Crisis: Mapping the Historic-Geographical Construction of Residential Mortgage Backed Securitization in the UK' (2009) 33(2) *International Journal of Urban and Regional Research* 372; P. Langley, 'Sub-Prime Mortgage Lending: A Cultural Economy' (2008) 37(4) *Economy & Society* 469.

[64] S. Sassen, 'When Local Housing Becomes An Electronic Instrument: The Global Circulation of Mortgages – A Research Note' (2009) 33(2) *International Journal of Urban and Regional Research* 411, 420.

But that doesn't mean we should ignore them or not take them seriously. It can hardly be a surprise that there are tensions at the root of the principles of law governing such a finite, powerful resource. There are no easy answers – anybody who suggests there are is trying to get one over on you – but, if there is one key message to take from this chapter, it is that property law has a material reality which is obscured by a focus on doctrine; the way in which we use it and the law views it, and the problems which it causes all have their root in the 'social'.[65]

Further Reading

G. Alexander, E. Peñalver, J. Singer and L. Underkuffler, 'A Statement on Progressive Property' (2009) 94 *Cornell LR* 743.

N. Blomley, 'The Borrowed View: Privacy, Propriety and the Entanglements of Property' (2005) 30(3) *Law and Social Inquiry* 661.

M. Davies, *Property: Meanings, Histories, Theories* (Routledge-Cavendish, 2007).

N. Hopkins, 'Regulating Trusts of the Home: Private Law and Social Policy' (2009) 125 *LQR* 310.

A. Layard, 'Shopping in the Public Realm: A Law of Place' (2010) 37(3) *Journal of Law and Society* 412.

J. Nedelsky, 'Law, Boundaries and the Bounded Self' (1990) 30(1) *Representations* 162.

---

[65] Our sense is that each of us (the authors and you, the reader) have a different identity of the 'social' (and note the definite object which one might also question). So, for example, Latour argues '... the social is not a type of thing either visible or to be postulated. It is visible only by the *traces* it leaves (under trials) when a *new* association is being produced between elements which themselves are in no way "social"': B. Latour, *Reassembling the Social: An Introduction to Actor-Network-Theory* (Oxford University Press, 2005) p. 8 (emphasis in original).

2

TENURE AND ESTATES

INTRODUCTION

If all property is theft, then the doctrines of tenure and estates are a double theft. Not only do they legitimate (and define) the ownership of land as well as rights over it, but they also de-naturalize the law from experience. That is the great debate with which this chapter engages.

What we mean by de-naturalizing law from experience is that these doctrines, which are taught to most students in the opening classes of land law, take property law out of our ordinary everyday appreciation of our symbiotic relationship with land. Imposed aside from that relationship are a series of technical legal concepts which perform the double feat of apparent political neutering as well as introducing a technical character to legal, as opposed to ordinary, knowledge. This is what makes law 'law', so to speak: neutral, objective, and technical. As Riles suggests, 'This view of technical law as neutral and removed from the rough and tumble of fights over how to allocate scarce resources in society itself has political consequences'.[1] Students are taught that we cannot 'own' the land (that is the right of the Sovereign, the doctrine of tenure), and that what landowners own is merely what Gray and Gray refer to as an 'interposed abstraction'[2] between the owner and the land (the abstraction being time, the doctrine of estates).

What would property law look like, if rather than labelling it like that, we labelled it the 'law of the home' or 'the law of place'?[3] We would be forced to

---

[1] A. Riles, *Collateral Knowledge: Legal Reasoning in the Global Financial Markets* (University of Chicago Press, 2011) p. 67.

[2] K. Gray & S. Gray, *Elements of Land Law* (Oxford University Press, 2009), para 1.3.3.

[3] Both such terms are in regular usage in academic scholarship, giving rise to major conceptual advances – see, for example, L. Fox, *Conceptualising Home: Theories, Laws and Policies* (Hart, 2007); A. Layard, 'Shopping in the Public Realm: A Law of Place' (2010) 37(3) *Journal of Law and Society* 412. The understanding of property as 'proper' or as 'propriety' has similarly been a significant mine for understandings – see M. Davies, *Property: Meanings, Histories, Theories* (Routledge-Cavendish, 2007); N. Blomley, 'The Borrowed View: Privacy, Propriety and the Entanglements of Property' (2005) 30(3) *Law and Social Inquiry* 661.

think about the empirical question, what is a 'home' or a 'place', a more natural question rooted in the social realities of everyday life; and, although there might be temptation to essentialize, we would be forced to recognize that the doctrines of tenure and estates do radical injustice to our relationship with where we live, and indeed, to recognize that 'where we live' may well include nowhere, may be mobile, and/or a site of repression/oppression.[4]

All of this does not suggest that technical law should be overlooked – quite the reverse, for we need to appreciate its contours in order to understand the strategies it uses to govern everyday life without, in fact, being seen to govern, until one needs to engage with it. Let us unpack that comment a little. Law is not so much the tip of the iceberg but an abstraction through which we are governed, but we don't see it, and property law actually bears little relation to our everyday lives.[5] We talk about either owning or renting, living in a hostel or B&B, and, in so doing, elide unsatisfactorily property law with our everyday lives. Rather like the Borg,[6] we have assimilated property law into our talk but without some essential components. Captain Jean-Luc Picard escaped (just about);[7] can we? Nevertheless, property law is also all around us. It comes to the fore at certain crisis moments, tipping points which assimilate us as they force us to 'go to law' and result in some rather awkward conclusions.

After a brief description of the doctrines of tenure and estates, this chapter is split into three parts which are designed around these issues. In the first part, we outline research around tenure from the housing policy literature. In this research, various authors have considered the attributes of 'home' ownership as opposed to renting. This material enables us to frame our appreciation of the social reality of the doctrine of tenure and estates – or the way in which law is inadequately interwoven with, and translated in, society. We then develop these ideas through three case studies: long leaseholds, sale and rentback, and shared ownership. The great debate as regards long leaseholds can be summarized by the title of an important article, 'Owners yet tenants?'; with sale and rentback, it is as to the concerns with the 'reality' of the situation, although this exposes property law's peculiar appreciation of that reality. Lastly, the great debate as regards shared ownership, a modern creation (well, about 30 to 40 years old), is the way it passively uses the leasehold regime without amendment, causing considerable uncertainty for the 'owners'; what we find in relation to shared ownership is that the elements of the label 'shared' and 'ownership' are a nonsense in law; yet, this label is what is being peddled.

---

[4] See, for example, the highly suggestive discussion of the 'homeless vehicle' by Neil Smith: 'Contours of a Spatialized Politics: Homeless Vehicles and the Production of Geographical Scale' (1992) 33 *Social Text* 54.

[5] N. Rose and M. Valverde, 'Governed by Law?' (1998) 7(4) *Social and Legal Studies* 541.

[6] According to Wikipedia, 'The Borg are a fictional pseudo-race of cybernetic organisms depicted in the *Star Trek* universe associated with Star Trek' (http://en.wikipedia.org/wiki/Borg_%28Star_Trek%29, accessed 13.04.2012).

[7] http://en.wikipedia.org/wiki/Jean-Luc_Picard (accessed 13 April 2012)

TENURE AND ESTATES

The doctrine of tenure is an entirely incidental, historical anachronism in English law, although it can become the subject of intense debate even today.[8] In essence, it derives from the conquest by William I and his method of keeping hold of power. Sitting atop the feudal pyramid, he granted lands in return for services, the land being held of the monarch. Tenure in this sense merely means 'holding of' the crown. Put another way, it is said that the crown has radical title, that is, absolute ownership over land. But all of this simply explains the limits of what can be owned by us ordinary mortals, and what we can own is this abstraction called the estate. The doctrine of tenure provides that explanation; its lack of utility as a concept lies in the ways in which, and the reasons why, tenure itself became redundant following in particular the Statute Quia Emptores 1290 and the Abolition of Tenures Act 1660.

The estate being what is owned is of much greater importance and interest. The great success of the Law of Property Acts of 1922 and 1925 was to reach a position where the number of tenures capable of existing in land was reduced to two – the freehold and leasehold interest – and only two types were capable of existing as legal estates: the fee simple absolute in possession and the term of years absolute.[9] So important is this shift, and so dramatic, that it is contained in the opening words of the opening section of that great Act of consolidation in 1925, the Law of Property Act. These estates are translated into the colloquialisms of freehold and leasehold. The freehold (in this sense) is the best type of right which can exist in relation to land, for it is temporally finite only by being indefinite. In other words, its temporal limitation is that it lasts indefinitely. The leasehold interest is, as discussed in greater detail in Chapter 4, definite in duration, but it also implies a relationship between the grantor (the lessor, or landlord) and the grantee (the lessee, or tenant). Practically all flats are held leasehold for the simple reason that this was the only way of ensuring mutually interlocking obligations between those living horizontally (so to speak). Many houses are also owned in this way, although this is often for historical reasons due to the way in which various large landowners have carved up their property.

The more interesting estate is the leasehold, and here a little history is essential. Rather than being a property right, the historical derivation of the leasehold interest was as a chattel. It was convenient for it to be regarded as such at the time, but damages for trespass to a leasehold interest were not sufficient; so, in the ways in which lawyers have historically done, fictional mechanisms were devised to enable the leaseholder to recover possession. Over time, the fiction was able to be dropped so that the leasehold interest has a curious status in the law of

---

[8] See the discussion in *Mabo v Queensland* (1989) 166 CLR 186 concerning the prior rights of indigenous peoples over the Crown's radical title.

[9] Law of Property Act 1925, s. 1.

property, being defined properly now as a 'chattel real'. The notion of a chattel real is antithetical but conveys something hugely important about the lease: its basis lies both in contract and property law. For some of the time, this antithesis is hidden, for it may be neither relevant to a dispute nor relevant to our everyday lives. At times, though, it is productive of huge controversy, particularly when contract and property offer different solutions to a dispute or when the feudal status of the tenant becomes manifest.

As regards the former, consider Lord Browne-Wilkinson's analysis in the case of *Hammersmith and Fulham LBC v Monk*.[10] In this case, the question was whether a tenancy granted to two persons jointly could be ended by the unilateral service of a notice to quit by one of them. The House of Lords held that it could do so. Lord Browne-Wilkinson said:

> In certain cases a contract between two persons can, by itself, give rise to a property interest in one of them. The contract between a landlord and a tenant is a classic example. The contract of tenancy confers on the tenant a legal estate in the land such legal estate gives rise to rights and duties incapable of being founded in contract alone. The revulsion against Mrs. Powell being able unilaterally to terminate Mr. Monk's rights in his home is property based: Mr. Monk's property rights in the home cannot be destroyed without his consent. The other reaction is contract based: Mrs. Powell cannot be held to a tenancy contract which is dependant for its continuance on the will of the tenant.[11]

As regards the problems which arise when the feudal status of the tenant becomes manifest, consider the everyday situation of the tenant of a 99-year lease having to pay a ground rent to their landlord; a landlord seeking to levy a sizable service charge against their tenant; or where the tenant of what was originally a 99-year lease finds that the remaining term in the property is unmortgageable (because lenders will not lend against the remaining period of the term). There has been much law reform on the two latter issues but, in truth, the law has been poorly drafted and is complex, and disputes often arise.[12]

Debate 1

Transforming tenure in society

Compared to these legal meanings, tenure appears to be used in a completely different sense – and one which is driven to a large extent by housing policy – in society. Housing policy tenures are owner-occupation, private renting, local

---

[10] [1992] 1 AC 478.

[11] At 491.

[12] As one commentator put it, the law was 'too restrictive, too complex, and too expensive': D. Clarke, 'Occupying "Cheek by Jowl": Property Issues Arising from Communal Living' in S. Bright & J. Dewar (eds), *Land Law: Themes and Perspectives* (Oxford University Press, 1998) p. 400.

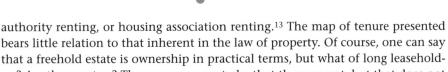

authority renting, or housing association renting.[13] The map of tenure presented bears little relation to that inherent in the law of property. Of course, one can say that a freehold estate is ownership in practical terms, but what of long leaseholders? Are they renters? The answer seems to be that they are not, but that does not really help us either because we then must ask: at what point does a long lease tip from being renting to owning? That is, however, to preface the next section. What is important here is to understand the ways in which housing policy has promoted ownership above all else, and the effects of that promotion on the ways in which tenure is viewed in society. There is now a bank of empirical work on the subject.

PROMOTING OWNERSHIP

The starting point is to note the massive evolution in tenure during the twentieth century. From a position in which practically all households rented (around 90 per cent), the latest statistics show that around 70 per cent of households are owners. Undoubtedly, one cause of that evolution was the failure of private renting and, although there are different ways of looking at the causes of that failure, the key period in this transition occurred during the inter-war years. It was during this period that diverse factors came together to push households into ownership. One factor was the economic climate which meant that building societies had considerable capital to lend for ownership and they manipulated mortgage law to make the cost of mortgages cheaper (such as increasing mortgage terms so as to reduce monthly repayments); another that construction for ownership became more profitable than building for rent; another that there was pent-up demand for accommodation; another that the introduction of security of tenure and rent control had limited the availability of property for rent.[14] As Ball puts it

> [Owner-occupation] became relatively cheaper, provided new comparatively spacious suburban housing attuned to the consumer goods that were beginning to come onto the market, and as all of the households that could afford to buy flocked into owner occupation it rapidly developed a social kudos. Conversely non-ownership began to become synonymous with the negative social status of being unable to afford house purchase.[15]

Studies of housing policy documents have also demonstrated the way in which owner-occupation became regarded rhetorically as both 'home ownership'

---

[13] See D. Cowan, *Housing Law and Policy* (Cambridge University Press, 2011), ch. 1.

[14] The best discussions of this period can be found in A. Holmans, *Housing Policy in Britain* (Croom Helm, 1987), ch. 3; and M. Ball, *Housing Policy and Economic Power: The Political Economy of Owner Occupation* (Methuen, 1983). For discussion of the ways in which the mortgage lending industry changed during this period, see P. Craig, 'The House That Jerry Built? Building Societies, the State and the Politics of Owner-Occupation' (1986) 1(1) *Housing Studies* 87.

[15] Ball, n.14, at 25.

and 'natural'. This promotion chimes with the neoliberal settlement of private, marketized relations creating bonds of obligation in private law.

As we saw in Chapter 1, the suggestion was that tenures other than ownership did not provide 'homes' and were somehow unnatural.[16] The zenith of this discursive formation was probably during the 1970s when ownership was paraded as 'a basic and natural desire' or as a 'deep and natural desire' for independent control over one's home.[17] Gurney's analysis of the 1995 housing White Paper makes a similar point:

> 'Home' as a normalising discourse is expressed in *Our Future Homes* through ideas of love, warmth, comfort, pride, independence, and self-respect. The chapter concerning home ownership is dripping with these ideas. This is normalisation through repetition and association. Significantly 'home ownership' is preferred to the more formal-legal terminology of 'owner-occupation' except in relation to specific proposals for legislation.[18]

These sentiments about ownership, and the moral and ethical values underpinning it, find their purest expression in the self-help literature of the nineteenth century and that deriving from the building society movement in the early twentieth century.[19]

The development of the welfare state did not really touch housing in the same way as it did other areas of social insurance – indeed, Cole and Furbey have suggested that 'Adolf Hitler proved a more decisive influence than William Beveridge in shaping the housing requirements of post-war Britain'.[20] The involvement of the state in the provision of housing, through local authorities, had always been regarded as contingent on the failure of the private sector; but it was anticipated that, as soon as the private sector was able to re-take the reins, the state's role would simply fall away.[21] As a retrospective, one can see that analysis holding good in the settlement of social housing after 1979, with

---

[16] A. Murie, P. Niner & C. Watson, *Housing Policy and the Housing System* (London: Allen & Unwin, 1976) p. 171; see also J. Kemeny, *The Myth of Home Ownership: Private versus Public Choices in Housing Tenure* (London: Routledge & Kegan Paul, 1981).

[17] Respectively, Department of the Environment, *Housing Policy: A Consultative Document* (London: DoE, 1977) p. 50, and *A Fair Deal for Housing* (London: HMSO, 1971) p. 4. It was at or about this time that the ghost was being given up on private renting: see F. Berry, *Housing: The Great British Failure* (London: Croom Helm, 1974) p. 123, and D. Cowan & A. Marsh, 'There's Regulatory Crime and Then There's Landlord Crime: from "Rachmanites" to "Partners"', (2001) 64(6) *MLR*, 831, 840–42.

[18] C. Gurney, '*Pride and Prejudice*: Discourses of Normalisation in Public and Private Accounts of Home Ownership' (1999) 14(2) *Housing Studies* 163, 173.

[19] See, further, D. Cowan and M. McDermont, *Regulating Social Housing: Governing Decline* (Routledge Glasshouse, 2006) pp.163–68.

[20] I. Cole and R. Furbey, *The Eclipse of Council Housing* (Routledge, 1994) p. 60.

[21] See the discussion in P. Malpass, 'The Wobbly Pillar? Housing and the British Postwar Welfare State' (2003) 32(4) *Journal of Social Policy* 589; and P. Malpass, *Housing and the Welfare State: The Development of Housing Policy in Britain* (Palgrave Macmillan, 2005).

various partial privatization mechanisms being employed (both individual and collective).[22]

UNDERSTANDINGS ABOUT OWNERSHIP

Although the evidence predates the current economic crisis and the major problems in the banking industry, as well as the attempt to revive the reputation of social housing, there is considerable evidence about the hierarchy of tenures in society. These largely mirror understandings in housing policy. Ownership is what is prized and aimed for, and anything else is somehow lesser. These findings have been controversial, though. The starting point is probably Peter Saunders' book, *A Nation of Home Owners*, in which he argues from his own survey data in three towns that home ownership provides ontological security. Rather than having petty and other rules imposed on the household by a landlord, the home owner has the power to create their own world through the lens of their home.

> Two principal motives are mentioned time and time again when people are asked why they prefer to own rather than rent their homes. One is financial – buying is seen as cheaper in the long run, or rent is seen as a waste of money, or rising prices are seen as a means of saving for the future or accumulating capital. The other has to do with the sense of independence and autonomy which ownership confers – the freedom from control and surveillance by a landlord and the ability to personalize the property according to one's tastes.[23]

Saunders argued that owners tended to associate 'home' with relaxation and personal possession, whilst renters defined it in terms of family or neighbourhood. The differences were most marked for council house purchasers. Tenants were 'much less inclined to develop attachments to their houses than owners'. Because of local authority control through the tenancy agreement, tenants were less likely to have personalized their homes (particularly because they had little or no choice over the property allocated to them).[24] However, the bigger point made by Saunders was that a 'consumption sector cleavage' had opened up between those who could afford to buy, and reaped the benefits of apparently inexorable capital gain, and those who could not, who then languished in the rented sector.

Saunders' work was hugely controversial, in part because it ascribed certain values to an apparently homogeneous class. It was the subject of an instant critique,

---

[22] Principal amongst these are the right to buy and the large-scale voluntary transfer of stock from local authorities to housing associations; see, in particular, H. Pawson and D. Mullins, *After Council Housing: Britain's New Social Landlords* (Palgrave Macmillan, 2010).

[23] P. Saunders, *A Nation of Home Owners* (Methuen, 1990) p. 84.

[24] See D. Cowan and A. Marsh, 'From Need to Choice, Welfarism to Advanced Liberalism: Problematics of Social Housing Allocation' (2005) 25(2) *Legal Studies* 22.

which emphasized the diversity of experiences and the fragility of the sector.[25] Further, Forrest and Murie referred to a 'paradox that, as owner occupation has expanded, it has become progressively what it is not supposed to be. It has become dependent in its present form on large-scale public support'.[26] Other studies noted that home ownership should be construed as a 'continuum' with a low-income end which is indistinct from renting – evidence from a study conducted in the late 1970s of areas of low-income home ownership in Birmingham and Liverpool suggested that home ownership was 'a squalid trap':

> Unlike many owners who might expect capital gains on their property and the possibility of movement to a different strata of the market, these owners may suffer real capital losses and far from being able to move they will be forced to stay in a deteriorating asset which will be in a deteriorating condition.[27]

There were studies of intersectional disadvantage in the housing system, which effectively forced certain households into ownership, and studies which suggested that, for some, ownership is a form of coerced exchange.[28]

Nevertheless, what comes out of Gurney's data is a rich picture of a social hierarchy of tenure, with ownership at the top and local authority renting at the bottom.[29] Gurney drew attention to the construction of tenure which came from his qualitative interviews through the use of well-known aphorisms and metaphors about home ownership, for example: 'an Englishman's home is his castle', 'it's yours at the end of the day' and 'renting's just money down the drain'. These aphorisms and metaphors formed part of the everyday understandings of his sample and were value-laden expressions of 'common-sense'; they constructed '... a housing tenure knowledge [which] is both stereotypical and prejudiced'.[30] His interviewees also constructed a morality about housing tenure through providing prejudicial accounts of renting and moral fables. Council housing was '... a metaphor for a stereotypical feckless class'.[31]

THINKING TENURE

Although housing policy researchers were once counselled to get rid of the fetishism of tenure,[32] there is little doubt that it retains a hold over researchers and soci-

---

[25] R. Forrest, A. Murie & P. Williams, *Home Ownership: Differentiation and Fragmentation* (Unwin Hyman, 1990).

[26] R. Forrest and A. Murie, *Selling the Welfare State: The Privatisation of Public Housing* (Routledge, 1990) p. 174.

[27] V. Karn, J. Kemeny and P. Williams, *Home Ownership in the Inner City: Salvation or Despair?* (Gower, 1985) p. 106.

[28] Summarized in Cowan, n.13, ch. 2.

[29] C. Gurney, 'Lowering the Drawbridge: A Case Study of Analogy and Metaphor in the Social Construction of Home-Ownership' (1999) 36(10) *Urban Studies* 1705.

[30] Ibid 1706.

[31] Ibid 1716.

[32] F. Gray, 'Owner Occupation and Social Relations', in S. Merrett, *Owner Occupation in Britain* (Routledge and Kegan Paul, 1982) ch. 5.

ety. Barlow and Duncan wondered aloud '... how the term [tenure] jumped the gap between this specialised, legal use and the much broader, quasi-scientific use by housing researchers. ... The process of transition between legal and quasi-scientific usage would be a useful subject for research in the sociology of knowledge, precisely because it seems unjustified'.[33] Now it is that very translation which is both interesting and uneasy. It is interesting because, as Cowan has suggested, it reflects a certain 'legal consciousness', a translation of the apparently neutral values of law into the political valves and values of society.[34] Perhaps that imperfect translation has occurred over time for policy reasons – it became important to know the numbers and proportions of households who are owners – or simply mirrored the way in which ownership was marketed as a homogeneous device. It is uneasy because, in its inaccurate rendering of the position in law, it is productive of major fault lines in the experiences of ownership. Housing policy finds this particularly hard to deal with; and, when faced with the cold reality of the apparently objective neutral position of property law, that imperfect translation of legal doctrines in policy and society becomes manifest.

Debate 2

Between ownership and renting (1): the problem of long leaseholds

This problem was set up in the introduction to the previous section. It concerns the fit of 'long leaseholds' with understandings of ownership and tenure both in law and in society. We do not need to set out what we mean by 'long' in this context – as was noted above, it is unclear when a leasehold interest becomes categorized as an ownership interest – but we should note the imprecision and inelegance in the use of such a term.[35] It is (of course) outside the realm of property law, which ascribes no such time period to the existence of a leasehold estate in land. But what the term leasehold does imply are the following characteristics: (a) a relationship between landlord and tenant; (b) the payment of a ground rent, often at a peppercorn or low value, and often a service charge; and (c) mutually enforceable obligations between landlord and tenant, with the consequences of non-performance potentially dire (including, in the case of tenant non-performance, the loss of their entire interest).

The growth of long leaseholds of property occurred at a number of key moments in time, each of which gives rise to quite separate sets of concerns.[36] First, during

---

[33] J. Barlow and S. Duncan, 'The Use and Abuse of Housing Tenure' (1988) 3(4) *Housing Studies* 219, 220.

[34] See D. Cowan, 'Housing and Property' in P. Cane and H. Kritzer (eds), *Oxford Handbook of Empirical Legal Studies* (Oxford University Press, 2010), drawing on P. Ewick and S. Silbey, *The Common Place of Law: Stories from Everyday Life* (University of Chicago Press, 1998).

[35] The idea of a long lease is probably one for more than 21 years, as that is the threshold beyond which certain statutory protections 'kick in'.

[36] See A. Stewart, *Rethinking Housing Law* (Sweet & Maxwell, 1996) p. 110 ff.

the nineteenth century, there were so-called 'building leases' usually of 99 years granted to build a property on a plot of land which would then be rented out. Second, in the period between the world wars, there was significant construction of mansion blocks. Third, during the 1950s and 1960s, a significant number of long leasehold properties were sold to 'sitting tenants'. Fourth, a significant number of flats have been sold since 1980 to former local authority tenants under the right to buy.

The research evidence suggests that long leaseholders' idea of themselves as 'owners', an idea which implies certain self-determining power over their physical accommodation, is not necessarily borne out by the reality of the relationships. And it can come as a real surprise to the 'owners'. As Cole and Robinson, drawing on their qualitative research with leaseholders, suggest:

> Leaseholders commonly balked at referring to themselves as tenants, preferring instead to consider themselves owner occupiers. Their legal status had been made clear to them, however, by the limited control and freedom they were able to exercise over significant aspects of their occupation. To many, unaware of or misunderstanding their legal position as leaseholders, this came as a surprise.[37]

The problems identified in that study '... were rooted in the freedom freeholders have to exercise authority without concern for the wishes of lessees'.[38] Inadequate repairs and maintenance, which were only reactive and not proactive (meaning costs eventually were higher and could not be offset); maintenance and service charges were high and increasing; and there were delays on the 'wasting asset' of the remainder of the term.[39]

Stewart considers the reasons for the growth of the market in the reversionary interest of the freehold. She makes the following significant point:

> The relationships between owners and occupiers have been transformed by the development of a market for the sale of flats. Once this market had emerged, there developed a dual market in flats...The value of flats for owner occupation became greater than their value to landlords for renting. In these market conditions, traditional residential investment companies are replaced by an aggressive breed of speculative break up companies who are not 'landlords' but asset strippers.[40]

The new breed of corporate freeholder sought profit from their investment. Profit could come in one of two ways: from waiting until the end of the lease (which was not long, of course, in relation to the nineteenth-century leases); or increasing

---

[37] I. Cole and D. Robinson, 'Owners Yet Tenants: The Position of Leaseholders in Flats in England and Wales' (2000) 15(4) *Housing Studies* 595, 608, citing one of their respondents as saying 'It was a shock really, to find out that your life wasn't really your own'.

[38] Ibid 602.

[39] Ibid 603.

[40] Stewart, n.36, 114.

service charges and administration costs. As Robertson puts it, the source of greatest resentment is that while the leaseholders live in the property and pay for the management and maintenance they are beholden to the freeholder who does neither.[41]

At the level of policy, the arguments range from 'pure' freedom of contract principles and 'pure' property rights to 'abuse' and 'exploitation' by 'neglectful' landlords.[42] One might suppose that party political lines would be clearly drawn on this issue – the Conservatives on the one side and Labour on the other – but that would be an inaccurate representation. Leasehold reform became a cross-party political issue. The Conservatives, during the 1980s and 1990s, saw leasehold reform '... as a natural and (vote-winning) extension of its ideological commitment to home ownership... [F]reeholders' control was seen as restricting the liberty of people to own their homes'; Labour supported leasehold reform as a social justice issue.[43] The London *Evening Standard* has also campaigned on the issue for some time.

Leasehold reform has come 'thick and fast' since the Leasehold Reform Act 1967.[44] There are now controls over service charges, insurance, management, consultation, enfranchisement (buying the freehold individually or collectively), right of first refusal, buying a further term of years, restrictions on the landlord's right to forfeit the lease for non-payment of service charge, a right to manage for leaseholders, and indeed an entirely new form of tenure, commonhold.[45] Amidst this welter of law, though, one thing is clear: in seeking to balance the principles of freedom with the rights of the users, the law is extremely complicated and it is more than easy to get lost in that complexity. The balance struck leaves the lease itself in place and there are many disputes which arise as a result of the poor drafting of those leases. Many disputes are the province of the Leasehold Valuation Tribunal and a brief reading of the reports of their judgments and appeals (to the Upper tribunal (Lands Chamber)) merely exemplifies that complexity.

A considerable number of everyday problems remain despite this welter of law,[46] and these can particularly impact on right-to-buy leaseholders (who often are the least likely to be able to afford to pay). Right-to-buy leaseholders will usually have properties which remain managed by the local authority (or possibly a housing association).[47] Other properties in the block are likely to remain as

---

[41] D. Robertson, 'Cultural Expectations of Homeownership. Explaining Changing Legal Definitions of Flat "Ownership" in Britain' (2006) 21(1) *Housing Studies* 35, 43.

[42] Cole and Robinson, n.37, p. 600.

[43] S. Blandy and D. Robinson, 'Reforming Leasehold: Discursive Events and Outcomes, 1984–2000' (2001) 28(3) *Journal of Law and Society* 384, 399.

[44] Robertson, n.41, p. 43.

[45] See, generally, S. Bright, *Landlord and Tenant Law in Context* (Oxford: Hart, 2007) ch. 13. As regards commonhold, this has not proved particularly attractive and is not discussed further here – for discussion, see D. Clarke, 'Long Residential Leases: Future Directions' in S. Bright (ed.), *Landlord and Tenant Law: Past, Present and Future* (Hart Publishing, 2006).

[46] See the Nearly Legal blog for a sample of these: <www.nearlylegal.co.uk/blog>.

[47] See H. Carr, 'The Right to Buy, the Leaseholder, and the Impoverishment of Ownership' (2011) 38(4) *Journal of Law and Society* 519.

social housing lettings. By virtue of government housing policy in the 2000s, social landlords were required to bring their properties up to the 'decent homes standard' by 2010.[48] Decades of underinvestment in the stock had left much of it in poor repair, and the programme did a great deal of good, but it also cost a lot (around £22 billion for housing and communities alone).

The costs of these works resulted in local authorities levying bills for thousands of pounds on largely unsuspecting long leaseholders. As the London Assembly put it:

> Preliminary discussions with stakeholders and leaseholders suggest that there are a number of factors surrounding the levying and payment of service charges that are proving problematic. These include:
>
> ▸ The level of services charges that are variable and depend on the level of work undertaken;
> ▸ Poor awareness of the need to pay service charges;
> ▸ Those on low incomes or struggling with mortgage/rent payments may not be able to cover large bills; and
> ▸ The transparency of the programming of repairs and the services charged for may not be great.[49]

The document notes that, of the 4,000 cases before the LVT, about 1,500 are service charge- related. The freeholder is only entitled to what is 'due' and 'reasonably incurred',[50] and it is usually the latter which causes the problem. What might seem 'reasonably incurred' to a landlord, however, might be regarded as unreasonable by a long leaseholder on the basis of cost.[51] However, it is perfectly open to the manager to take account of the means of the leaseholders to pay the service charge: 'the financial impact of major works on lessees through service charges and whether as a consequence works should be phased is capable of being a material consideration when considering whether the costs are reasonably incurred ...'.[52]

In summary, it can be said that the problematic of long leaseholders is that they 'buy into' ownership but are, as a matter of law, left in a subservient position. Ameliorating legislation has sought to redress the balance but only by tinkering at the edges and not at the fundamental issue, the lack of relation between ownership and leasehold. It is, then, an unfortunate clash between popular understandings of law in society and real, hard law in fact.

---

[48] DETR/DSS, *Quality and Choice: A Decent Home for All* (DETR/DSS, 2000) para. 7.7.

[49] London Assembly, *Proposed Review of Service Charges in London*, <http://www.london.gov.uk/sites/default/files/Service%20charges%20scoping%20paper.pdf >

[50] Landlord and Tenant Act 1985, s. 19(1)(a); *Forcelux v Sweetman* [2001] 2 EGLR 173, [39]–[40].

[51] Appendix 1 to the London Assembly document notes one local authority's '£13,275,183 service charge bill was then allocated respectively to 6,500 individual leaseholders on the basis of actual cost of work incurred'.

[52] *Garside v RFYC Ltd* [2011] UKUT 367 (LC), [14].

Debate 3

Between ownership and renting (2): sale and rentback

Sale and rentback transactions in relation to homes tend to be relatively common at times of economic hardship and as part of mortgage rescue programmes. They involve tenure shifting – the owner sells the property and the buyer, usually a property company, grants that former owner a tenancy of the property instead. These transactions should not be entered into lightly and, at least in relation to those transactions executed before the Financial Services Authority (FSA) began to regulate them in 2009, cause some major problems for property law. The FSA now require the seller to be given clear warnings about the consequences of the transation and its inadvisability.[53] One would have hoped that would cure the significant problems which have arisen and lead to professionalism in the sector. That professionalism was, as the cases recount, lacking at least in some firms. As a result, the cases raise questions about unconscionability, construction of tenancy agreements, breach of contract, proportionate evictions and overriding interests.[54] In short, they have become property law's growth area and are likely to be the next 'big' thing.

The most significant issue in these cases for our purposes here derives from the most difficult part of the decision of the House of Lords in *Abbey National Building Society v Cann*.[55] In that case, the House held that, in an 'ordinary' property transaction involving a mortgage, where the buyer could not proceed without the aid of the mortgage, there is not a moment in time (*scintilla temporis*) between the buyer's purchase and the grant of the mortgage. If there was, then it would have been perfectly possible for rights adverse to the buyer to arise in that moment. The significance of this is that, in principle, those rights would bind the mortgage lender in certain circumstances because the rights were created prior in time (a moment) before the grant of the mortgage. That made sense in those transactions which involved an acquisition mortgage.

The question raised in the sale and rentback cases is as to the applicability of that doctrine in those transactions. The usual way they are done is that the seller sells, the buyer buys with the aid of a mortgage and subsequently the buyer obtains a tenancy agreement (and often that tenancy agreement is poorly constructed and of limited utility). Often, the buyer makes representations concerning the enforceability of the tenancy agreement as part of the negotiations leading to the sale (e.g. that the buyer will be able to stay in the property for a set period or their life, rent will be reduced for a period or such like matter), sufficient in certain circumstances to give rise to a proprietary estoppel (see Chapter 11). The question in these sale and rentback scenarios is whether those

---

[53] See, generally, FSA, *Sale and Rent Back (Full Regime)* CP10/04 (FSA, 2010).

[54] *Scrowther v Watermill Properties* [2009] EW Misc 6 (EWCC); *Redstone v Welch* [2009] EG 98; *Purdie and Bellwood v Miller*, High Court, 20.10.2011; *In re North East Property Buyers Litigation* [2010] EWHC 2991 (Ch).

[55] [1991] 1 AC 56, esp at 92, Lord Oliver, and 102–3, Lord Jauncey.

rights by estoppel (or some other mechanism) bite before the grant of the mortgage (most commonly, the buyer has become bankrupt or gone into liquidation leaving the mortgage lender to obtain possession). If they do, then they will bind the mortgage in certain other circumstances which are not relevant here; if not, the mortgagee takes free. In *Redstone*, Judge Worster found that the sale was so dependent on the grant of the tenancy as to make it indissoluble from that transaction so that the property interest that was the subject of the sale was subject to those equitable rights. Now that seems to run against the position taken in *Cann*; and in the *In re North East Property Buyers Litigation* ('the NEPB litigation'), HHJ Behrens found that Judge Worster was wrong, and that *Cann* was binding and could not be distinguished.[56]

The NEPB Litigation was appealed to the Court of Appeal.[57] The facts of these cases for present purposes, because they are largely assumed, are that a number of owner occupiers entered into an agreement with the NEPB. The terms of the agreement were that the company would buy the property and, on sale, would then rent the property back to the sellers. NEPB's agents were not particularly well-versed in either property or landlord and tenant law. They promised different terms to each of the buyers and different rent levels, but many were told they could stay in the property for as long as they liked provided they kept to the terms of the tenancy. NEPB financed each transaction with a buy-to-let mortgage. Crucially, they did not disclose to the lender that the seller/s would remain in the property or the terms of the tenancy agreement (something which the FSA guidance now explicitly requires). Exchange of contracts and completion, including the execution of the charge, took place on the same day. NEPB then became insolvent and vanished. The lenders wanted possession.

The overarching question was whether the representations and agreements made between NEPB and the sellers created rights which bound the lenders. That, in turn, raised the question whether *Cann* was distinguishable on the facts. Etherton LJ, who gave the leading judgment and with whom Lord Neuberger MR and Rix LJ agreed, held that *Cann* was not distinguishable and, indeed, its policy driver was just as relevant to these cases. Possession was ordered as there were no other issues left to be decided.

The argument on which the parties sharply divided was whether, after exchange of contracts and before completion, there was sufficient equity in NEPB to grant the sort of estoppel/constructive trust/rectification type of interest which the sellers claimed. HHJ Behrens had held that the sellers' rights at that stage were purely personal. Detailed arguments were provided to the CA on these points, but, although attracted by the lenders' arguments, Etherton LJ sidestepped them by saying they were too technical (although he was attracted by the lenders' submissions on the point). As he put it, the question was whether the commercial and legal nature of the transaction was that there was a sale

---

[56] At [52].
[57] *Cook v The Mortgage Business plc et al* [2012] EWCA Civ 17.

subject to a reservation or two separate transactions (a sale of the freehold and a separate leaseback on completion). And 'the way the documentation was prepared points firmly in favour of the latter' ([34]). None of the sale contracts referred to the leaseback arrangement – indeed, they were all sold with vacant possession:

> The clear impression created by the contracts, therefore, was that the vendors would be selling without reserving any beneficial interests or other rights in the property. That was how any third party, including mortgagees lending money to fund the purchase, would be entitled to view the matter: comp. *Abigail v Lapin* [1934] AC 491. The contracts disclosed no basis for a qualified report on title to the respondent lenders by their solicitors which would have alerted the respondent lenders to the possibility that the appellant vendors expected to remain in possession after completion or that the purchasers would obtain anything less than the entire legal and beneficial interest in the properties.[58]

He went on to say, though, that even if an equity had arisen in favour of the sellers at that point, the *Cann* principle applied so that the lenders' interest prevailed. The question put to the Court of Appeal was whether the policy underlying *Cann* was still relevant and relevant to these particular transactions. In a nutshell, the sellers argued that '... unlike *Cann*, where the 'driver' of the transaction was to find a new home, the driver in the present cases, without which they could not and would not have proceeded, was the leaseback to the vendor',[59] that these cases involved different social and economic factors in which the need/desire of people (of modest means, advancing age as well as limited legal knowledge and experience) to stay in their homes was the uppermost consideration.[60] Further, and this is clearly crucial, the lender is in a better position to take the risk of fraud and carelessness in such schemes and should make appropriate enquiries.

Etherton LJ disagreed. Daisy Cann was in no less an unfortunate position to the sellers here;[61] in substance and reality, the driver for the sale in the NEPB litigation was the sellers' need/desire to sell their properties to discharge their mortgage and get some cash, and there was no reason for them to suppose that NEPB would not obtain a mortgage; and finally it was not for the lenders to make direct enquiry of the sellers, which may be inappropriate, but to ensure that the contract of sale contained all the details of the transaction.[62] The stage is now set for the Supreme Court to decide whether *Cann* was correct on the moment in time point, should they decide to grant permission to appeal.

---

[58] At [35].
[59] At [50].
[60] At [51].
[61] At [55].
[62] At [54]–[56].

Debate 4

The fit of shared ownership

BACKGROUND

In the 1980s, ownership was heavily promoted by the Thatcher governments; as we have seen, this continued a pattern of preference established by preceding governments, but the Thatcher governments also did rather more to promote it than others. They introduced a range of what were known as 'low cost home ownership' initiatives, ranging from the right to buy to providing cash payments for purchase. Shared ownership was initially developed as one of these initiatives, but it became heavily promoted in the period after the 1980s. The policy reason was relatively simple; it became a tenet of government housing policy that ownership had reached its sustainable limit (as was shown by the crash in the early 1990s) and alternatives were required beyond the mere bolstering of private renting. At the same time, it was also clear that many people were being priced out of ownership and affordability became a major issue.

Shared ownership provided a convenient mechanism through which sustainable low-cost ownership could be achieved. The policy model was relatively simple: the buyer bought (and buys) a percentage share in the property; over time, they can buy a greater percentage share, if and when they can afford it; eventually, they would end up owning the whole thing. It was a model which could also be delivered by the then government's preferred provider of social housing, housing associations, and it is fair to say that they were relatively keen to do so because, in an era of fiscal constraint, they would receive a decent proportion of public funding for this purpose; all of which still holds true.

Successive governments have promoted shared ownership as not just the solution to a problem but also as a policy priority. It is regarded as fulfilling the home ownership aspirations of households. This was the original aim of the shared ownership programme, enabling households to progress to full ownership;[63] and it has remained the case.[64] The 2010 Coalition government's agreement specifically contains a promise in the following terms: 'We will promote shared ownership schemes and help social tenants and others to own or part-own their home'. This rationale for the programme has developed over time so that its purpose is now to facilitate access to *sustainable* home ownership by increasing the supply of *affordable* home ownership.[65] In fulfilling the promotion of this policy, a huge

---

[63] Department of the Environment, *Shared Ownership: A Stepping Stone to Full Ownership* (HMSO, 1982) p. 21.

[64] DETR/DSS, *Quality and Choice: A Decent Home for All*, The Housing Green Paper (DETR, 2000) para. 4.2; Office of the Deputy Prime Minister, *HomeBuy – Expanding the Opportunity to Own*, Consultation Paper (ODPM, 2005) para. 1; Department for Communities and Local Government, *Homes for the Future: More Affordable, More Sustainable*, Cm 7191 (DCLG, 2007) p. 70.

[65] Home Ownership Task Force, *A Home of My Own*, The Report of the Government's Low Cost Home Ownership Task Force (Housing Corporation, 2003) para. 6.1 (a suite of recommendations largely accepted, or accepted in principle, in the Government's response: Office of the Deputy Prime

amount of public funding has been ploughed into its development, accounting for a proportion of total capital spend on social housing by housing associations of between 11 and 25.[66] The National Audit Office noted the following in relation to shared ownership and equity loans:

> In 2004–05 the Government spent almost £470 million on these two products. The products are absorbing a growing proportion of the support made available to the affordable housing sector, from 13 per cent in 1999–2000 to almost 30 per cent in 2004–05.[67]

The benefit to housing associations has been that they are able to recycle the receipts paid by the borrowers into certain of their other housing activities.

Although not one of the original key aims of the schemes, a significant objective now is that shared ownership is designed to meet housing need in one or both of two ways – buyers are most usually either on local authority or housing association waiting lists for housing (many of which are now held jointly or in common) or occupying social rented housing.[68] In purchasing a property (which they are not currently occupying), the buyer will be removed from the waiting list or move out of their social rented accommodation into their property. In this way, the length of the waiting list is reduced and/or a unit of social rented accommodation is freed for another household.[69] It is also regarded as a method of preventing homelessness[70] and contributes to the development of mixed-tenure estates, regeneration and sustainability, as well as enabling more people to share in asset wealth.[71] That identity of shared ownership as meeting housing need, and provided by social housing organizations, also creates a tension in the nature of the product itself – for the product is both social housing and, in policy terms, ownership.[72] The protection of the public investment in the property is also a telling factor against the power of

---

Minister, *Government Response to the Recommendations of the Home Ownership Task Force* (ODPM, 2003) pp. 6–7).

[66] G. Bramley and S. Dunmore, 'Shared Ownership: Short-Term Expedient Or Long-Term Major Tenure?' (1996) 11(1) *Housing Studies* 105, 109–10; S. Hills and A. Lomax, *Whose House is it Anyway? Housing Associations and Home Ownership* (Housing Corporation, 2007) p. 15;

[67] National Audit Office, *A Foot on the Ladder: Low Cost Home Ownership Assistance*, HC 1048 Session 2005–06, (NAO, 2006).

[68] See, for example, the eligibility criteria for such schemes: Office of the Deputy Prime Minister, *HomeBuy*, n.64, para. 1.4; Housing Corporation, *Capital Funding Guide* (Housing Corporation, 2006) para. 2.1.

[69] See A. Clarke, 'Shared Ownership: Does It Satisfy Government and Household Objectives?' in S. Monk and C. Whitehead (eds), *Making Housing More Affordable: The Role of Intermediate Tenures* (Wiley Blackwell, 2010), who describes this is as the 'double whammy' effect. The empirical basis for the success of this objective is less clear, partly because of the need for buyers to have financial security (in order to obtain a mortgage on the part they are buying) and partly because some social housing occupiers may well have left the sector at some point in the future in any event: National Audit Office, n.X, paras 44–47.

[70] DCLG, *Homelessness Code of Guidance for Local Authorities* (DCLG, 2006) para. 1.28.

[71] See, generally, Office of the Deputy Prime Minister, *HomeBuy*, n.64, para. 2.1.

[72] A. Wallace, *Achieving Mobility in the Intermediate Housing Market: Moving up and Moving on?* (Joseph Rowntree Foundation/Chartered Institute of Housing, 2008) p. 1. Shared ownership falls within the definition of 'social housing': Housing and Regeneration Act 2008, ss. 68 & 70.

the buyer as owner.[73] For example, the model leases generally require the buyer to give the provider a right of pre-emption so that the property can be recycled for other households in need.

That having been said, there are a large number of private schemes, usually run by building companies and particularly marketed during economic down-turns (when the market for 'normal ownership' is less secure). There is limited knowledge of these schemes, but what is known is that in some areas there are issues over competition between housing associations and these private companies.[74]

TRANSLATING THE MODEL

If shared ownership at the level of policy ticks all the right boxes, it creates a considerable headache for the lawyers implementing it. The problem is that shared ownership does not appear in our property law lexicon. It does not exist except in the minds of housing policy experts who dreamt it up and those who have turned that dream into a reality. Like Frankenstein's monster, the lawyers have fashioned the different bits of tenure available to them at the time into the shape of something equivalent to shared ownership, and, with a jolt of electricity, it came to life. And, continuing the Frankenstein theme, they are having consider-able difficult controlling it, for it has taken on a life of its own.

The mechanism used to deliver it is our friend, the long leasehold, or through a mortgage relationship (see Chapter 10). As Bright and Hopkins have suggested, the trust of land would have been a much better device to use (see Chapter 3),[75] but that device was not available until 1997 by which time the leasehold relation-ship was cast in regulatory stone. The conventional form is the long leasehold, which accounts for the majority of such properties. The buyer, then, takes a lease usually of 99 or 125 years over their share in the property. The lease contains standard provisions and some unusual ones. One of the latter is a clause which gives comfort to the buyer's mortgage lender if they have to claim possession of the property, for the housing association agrees to pay their costs. Such a provision was designed because shared ownership, as a new 'product', needed to be sold to lenders as well to make them willing, first to lend money, and second at affordable rates. Strangely, it might seem, the shared owner also takes responsibility for all the repairs, maintenance and service charges; so, even if they buy (say) a 25 per cent share, they are responsible for 100 per cent of those costs. The buyer pays a sub-market rent on the share they haven't bought, which *must* be set at no more

---

[73] The buyer, under the model leases, is not entitled to make physical alterations to the property without the landlord's written consent and cannot make structural alterations.

[74] G. Burgess, F. Grant & C. Whitehead, *Low Cost Home Ownership and the Credit Crunch: A Report on Regional Markets and Competition with Private Developers* (TSA, 2009).

[75] S. Bright and N. Hopkins, 'Home, Meaning and Identity: Learning from the English Model of Shared Ownership', (2011) 28(4) *Housing Theory and Society*, 377, 380.

than three per cent of the open market valuation of the provider's share with strict limits on the level of rent increases.[76]

Although the lease is long, it will usually attract the protection of the Housing Act 1988 and is usually an assured tenancy.[77] This can create a major problem because the buyer can be evicted if they fail for whatever reason to make two months' payment at the date of the relevant notice and they are still two or more months in arrears at the date of the hearing of the claim for possession.[78] The court has no discretion to refuse possession; it must make an order on this particular ground for possession.[79] The effect of such an order is the equivalent of forfeiture: the buyer loses not just the property but also their financial stake as well as any increase in value. It is an outrage, but, once the provider has chosen this route, the die is cast; there does not seem to be anything which can be done about it other than through the use of human rights law (as to which, see Chapter 8 for discussion in this context). Bright and Hopkins observe:

> Shared owners are, therefore, less secure than traditional owner-occupiers. They have to pay rent in respect of the 'non-owned' share, and (usually) will also have mortgage payments to make. Default in either can lead to loss of possession. Where default relates to rent, loss of possession may be mandatory, thus denying the purchaser the final procedural protection (available on mortgage default) of recourse to the court's discretion. Given the relatively low comprehension of how shared ownership 'works' it may be that purchasers are not conscious of this higher level of risk.[80]

What we have with shared ownership, then, is the marketing of a relatively innovative product as something which palpably it is not: ownership. Property lawyers are conventional and law is traditional (a fact emphasized by the use of the doctrine of precedent), and the doctrines of tenure and estates too powerful to escape. Again, Bright and Hopkins provide a powerful critique, arguing that their study of shared ownership demonstrates '... the inadequacies of tenure classification: it is ill-suited to acknowledge the heterogeneity that exists within housing; or to provide a meaningful account of the rights and responsibilities that exist between people and their housing'.[81]

CONCLUSION

The doctrines of tenure and estates retain a powerful hold over property lawyers. Their translation in law and society, in policy and lay terms, inadequately reflects their nature and effects. The belief of, and in, ownership as having a set of

---

[76] HCA/CML/NHF, *Shared Ownership: Joint Guidance for England* (HCA/CML/NHF, 2010), para. 15, p. 11.

[77] The exclusions to security of tenure in Housing Act 1988, sch. 1 are unlikely to apply because of the high rental element.

[78] Housing Act 1988, ground 8, sch. 2.

[79] *North British HA v Matthews* [2005] 1 WLR 3133.

[80] Bright and Hopkins, n.75, p. 389.

[81] Ibid p. 393.

underpinning values is easily exposed by the problematic of the long leasehold and shared ownership relations. The problems of long leaseholds are well-known in practice but they continue to cause real heartache precisely because the legislative 'solutions' have not particularly impacted on the root cause of the problem, the continuing landlord and tenant relationship. As regards shared ownership, there is a mismatch between the rhetoric of policy and the legal mechanisms designed to bring it into effect. There is, of course, a crossover between the two – both use long leasehold relationships – but the significant difference is that in respect of shared ownership, policy-makers are directly implicated in the problematic.

There is a further theoretical point to be made by way of reflection on the material in this chapter. A simple analysis, which focuses on the rationalities and techniques of government, needs to be supplemented here with an understanding of jurisdiction.[82] The ability of the provider in the leasehold relationship to obtain possession on a mandatory ground, thus cutting the long leasehold interest and capital payment away from the buyer, as a result of a simple jurisdictional choice (viz. the security of tenure implied by the Housing Act 1988) creates the conditions within which this policy and set of practices is extremely likely to cause major problems.

Further Reading

S. Bright, 'Of Estates and Interests: A Tale of Ownership and Property Rights', in S. Bright and J. Dewar, *Land Law: Themes and Perspectives* (Oxford University Press, 1998).

H. Carr, 'The Right to Buy, the Leaseholder, and the Impoverishment of Ownership' (2011) 38(4) *Journal of Law and Society* 519.

I. Cole and D. Robinson, 'Owners Yet Tenants: The Position of Leaseholders in Flats in England and Wales' (2000) 15(4) *Housing Studies* 595.

C. Gurney, '*Pride and Prejudice*: Discourses of Normalisation in Public and Private Accounts of Home Ownership' (1999) 14(2) *Housing Studies* 163.

A. Wallace, *Achieving Mobility in the Intermediate Housing Market: Moving up and Moving On?*, (Joseph Rowntree Foundation/Chartered Institute of Housing, 2008).

---

[82] See M. Valverde, 'Jurisdiction and Scale: "Legal Technicalities" as Resources for Theory' (2009) 18(2) *Social and Legal Studies* 139.

3

THE 1925 LEGISLATION

INTRODUCTION

There is no clearer illustration of the themes discussed in Chapter 1, or of the tensions that have shaped the development of English land law in the twenti-eth and twenty-first centuries, than the great debates that informed the 1925 legislation.[1] In 1925, a set of legislation was introduced in England and Wales that reshaped the system of land law and formed the basis for the system of land ownership and transfer until the introduction of the Land Registration Act 2002. Although most of the central concepts of property law are common law-based, the 'Englishness' of English land law is often identified by reference to this 1925 legislation, a collection of statutes which sought to modernize and simplify conveyancing, with the explicit objective of making land a more marketable commodity.

Debate 1

How can, or should, the property framework be structured to support the market in land?

The 1925 legislation represented a decisive break from the past for English land law. In seeking to place the law on a modern footing, it swept away many of the features of land law associated with the old system of aristocratic rule stemming from feudal times. The basis of the reforms was the promotion of the free-market philosophy identified by the early economist Adam Smith:[2] the 1925 legislation was designed to create a free market in land. The policy by which it sought to achieve this was:

---

[1] The Law of Property Act 1925, Land Charges Act 1925, Land Registration Act 1925, Settled Land Act 1925, Administration of Estates Act 1925.

[2] See, for example, A. Smith, *An Inquiry into the Nature and Causes of the Wealth of Nations*, ed. E. Cannan (Methuen and Co Ltd, 5th edn, 1904, first published 1776).

...to assimilate the law of real and personal estate and to free the purchaser from the obligation to enquire into the title of him from whom he purchases, any more than he would have to do if he were buying a parcel of stock.[3]

The main strategies of the legislation were to reduce the number of legal estates and interests, as discussed in Chapter 2, with other estates and interests taking effect only in equity; to introduce a system of registration of land charges (for *unregistered land*) to cope with the increased number of equitable interests flowing from the reduction of legal estate and interests;[4] to introduce a system of title registration; to extend the concept of overreaching; to reform the law relating to co-ownership; and to reform the law relating to mortgages. Some of these aims will be explored later in this book. This chapter focuses on the 'shape' of the system first – the reduction in legal estates and interests – before going on to consider the reforms in respect of overreaching and co-ownership.

Before the 1925 legislation, a greater number of different types of legal and equitable interests were capable of existing in land. When land was transferred from one person to another, purchasers had to investigate the title to the land to make sure of what they were buying. However, with a wide range of different legal and equitable interests potentially capable of binding purchasers, the process was complex, slow and expensive. Before 1925, the range of legal estates that could exist in land was wide-ranging (examples of now defunct estates included the fee tail and the life estate, which can no longer exist *at law*); there were also various subsidiary interests which could exist in the land, as legal interests; in addition to this various equitable estates and equitable interests were capable of subsisting in the land. The priority of these legal and equitable estates was determined according to the rules of notice. The core principles of the notice rules were that legal rights bind all the world, and equitable rights bind all the world *except* a bona fide purchaser of the legal estate without notice (equity's darling). Notice could be actual (the purchaser knew about the equitable interest), constructive (the purchaser could have discovered the existence of the equitable interest if they had made reasonable inspections and enquiries) or imputed (an agent of the purchaser – e.g. solicitor – had actual or constructive notice of the equitable right).

Legal rights presented a major obstacle for purchasers, as they were always binding. Equitable rights were potentially binding on purchasers, if they had actual or constructive notice of the right. The real problem was with constructive notice, as purchasers were *treated* as if they knew about the burden on their land, even though they did not *actually* know about it. The courts were wary of

---

[3] Lord Birkenhead in a letter to *The Times*, 15 December 1920.

[4] One consequence of *reducing* the number of *legal* estates in land was that the volume of *equitable* interests *increased*. The land charges system sought to deal with these equitable interests by enabling the interest holder to register their interests as a land charge. The land charges register introduced a system whereby certain equitable interests had to be registered as a land charge if they were to bind purchasers. These interests were classified in six categories, labelled A to F. The list can now be found in section 2 of the Land Charges Act 1972.

constructive notice, since it treats a third party purchaser or creditor as having knowledge which he did not in fact have.[5] However, a purchaser is not affected by notice of any interest if that interest could not have been discovered by carrying out reasonable inspections and inquiries. Consequently, the doctrine of notice places an onus on the purchaser to protect his or her title by making the necessary inspections and inquiries prior to accepting the property as security. This created more work for the purchaser, took more time and generated more expense.

The standard of reasonable inspections and inquiries depended on the individual case, and while it was generally sufficient if the third party satisfied the standard conveyancing practices appropriate for such a case, it was hard for a purchaser to know for sure if they had done enough to protect themselves. The limited guidance which purchasers had to go on emerged from the courts, which judged what was 'reasonable' on a case-by-case basis. It was established, for example, that '...if a person purchases an estate which he knows to be in occupation of another than the vendor, he is bound by all the equities which the party in such occupation may have had in the land.'[6] The fact of occupation constitutes notice to third parties that the occupier might claim an interest in the land.[7]

Under this system, in order to establish a clear title the purchaser (i.e. someone who buys the land, a bank who takes security over the land or a tenant) had to ensure that the seller had good title to the land. The purchaser also had to find any hidden rights and interests that might exist in the land and affect the title. In order to establish good title, the purchaser had to investigate a range of different types of factors, including:

Possession – the fact that someone was in possession of land was usually (but not always) an indication that they had some estate in the land. Common law presumed that the person in possession had a fee simple estate *unless and until the contrary was shown* (i.e. unless someone showed a relatively better title through documentation).

Documentary evidence – purchasers also needed to inspect the deeds to the property (this is a collection of all the documents that provide evidence about the seller's title). Purchasers needed to trace title back through the documents to follow the history of the title. This was described as showing a 'good root of title'.[8] The root of title was usually indicative of legal title only, although documents would sometimes show the equitable estates or interests existing in relation to the land. A purchaser was also deemed to have constructive notice of anything they could have discovered from the title documents.

---

[5] '[T]he doctrine is a dangerous one. It's contrary to the truth. It is wholly founded on the doctrine that a man does not know the facts, and yet it is said that constructively he does know them'; *Allen v Seckham* (1879) 11 ChD 790 at 795, per Lord Esher.

[6] *Jones v Smith* (1841) 1 Hare 43 at 60.

[7] *Barnhard v Greenshields* (1853) 9 Moo PC 18.

[8] Statute has limited the requirement for a good root of title from 60 years, to 40 (1874) and now to 15 years (Law of Property Act 1969, s. 23).

Physical inspection of the property – this was also necessary in order to discover some interests, especially equitable interests which might not have been created in writing and might not have been apparent from the title deeds.

Enquiries – the purchaser also had to make enquiries from the vendor to discover interests that might not have been apparent from the title deeds or on physical inspection (for example, an easement). The purchaser also had to make enquiries from other persons in occupation of the property. If a purchaser failed to make reasonable enquiries, they would be deemed to have constructive notice of any interests that could have been discovered from making enquiries.

The need to make these enquiries created significant time delays and considerable expense. Even if there had been a recent sale, the purchaser could not rely on the previous inspections and enquiries but had to re-do the whole process. The entire system hinged on the doctrine of notice. Purchasers could find themselves bound by hidden interests even though they did not have actual knowledge of the interests before buying the land. On the other hand, if you were the person with an equitable interest, you could not always rely on the doctrine of constructive notice to ensure that your interest survived the transfer of the land to the purchaser, since there was no clear rule about what had to be done to avoid constructive notice. This created considerable uncertainty for all involved in land transfer, and uncertainty causes delays and expense.

As we saw in Chapter 2, section 1, Law of Property Act 1925 limited the types of legal rights (those which bind purchasers automatically) that can exist in land to two legal estates (fee simple absolute in possession, and the term of years). Section 1(2) listed the other interests (not estates) which are available at law: easements, rentcharges,[9] charges by way of legal mortgage, similar charges not created by an instrument (this covers statutory charges) and certain rights of entry.[10] Any other interests in land that fall outside the statutory list can be *equitable* only. One consequence of this is that a wide range of equitable interests in land are vital to the working of the modern law of property. For example, as we will see below, the 1925 legislation made extensive use of trusts to regulate co-ownership of land. Another important aspect of the new system was the emphasis on registration of rights and interests, to ensure that so far as possible, purchasers would know what they were buying.

Yet, while the reduced categories of legal estates and interests and the introduction of systems of registration to protect certain interests went some way to protect the purchaser from undiscovered claims against the land, some gaps in the protection of purchasers were created by unregistrable interests: interests that do not fall within any of the categories of registrable interest and so are not *capable*

---

[9] A right to a money payment from land. Like rent, but paid by a freeholder. Increasingly unusual, and its creation was severely limited by the Rentcharges Act 1977. They can only be created now where there is a trust of land, or for an estate rentcharge, imposed to ensure the performance of covenants by the owner of land.

[10] The right to enter on breach of covenants in a legal lease, and a right of entry attached to a legal rentcharge.

of being registered. The most significant and substantial unregistrable interest was the interest of a beneficiary under a trust of land. The framers of the 1925 legislation were aware of this flaw in the system and the risk it could present for purchasers. They sought to manage that risk by drawing on the concept of over-reaching as a method by which purchasers could protect themselves against the undiscovered, unregistrable interests of beneficiaries under a trust.

Sections 2 and 27 of the Law of Property Act 1925 provided that, where there are two or more trustees, and the money from any sale is paid to all trustees, the equitable estates of any beneficiaries under a trust would be overreached. The purchaser would acquire a clear title to the land, with the equitable interest detached from the land, and attached to the proceeds of sale in the hands of the trustees.[11] Overreaching took place regardless of any notice of the beneficiaries' interests on the part of the purchaser. This principle protects creditors by providing that, so long as the purchase price is paid to two legal owners, the legal title acquired by the purchaser overreaches any equitable interests under trusts subsisting in the property.

Overreaching illustrates one of the central pillars of the 1925 property legislation: that land, including a person's home, was to be treated in the same way as other forms of property, with the goal of making land as easily and securely transferable as possible. Land was deliberately designated as merely another form of capital, as a commercial asset, as readily exchangeable as any other asset. It provides a useful illustration of the values that underpinned the 1925 legislation, discussed in the next section. It also demonstrates the difficulties which subsequent reformers have faced in displacing the ethos of the 1925 legislation: while the doctrine has been heavily criticized by both the Law Commission[12] and the Court of Appeal,[13] and the decision in *National Westminster Bank plc v Malhan*[14] suggested that it amounted to a discriminatory interference with the occupier's right to respect for home under Article 8 of the European Convention on Human Rights and/or the right to peaceful enjoyment of possessions under Article 1 of the First Protocol, the strength of land law's commitment to alienation has enabled the doctrine of overreaching to withstand – so far – these challenges.

Debate 2

What types of value does the private property system recognize with respect to land?

In addition to its significance in formulating the structures and systems of today's land law, the 1925 legislation embedded a particular perspective and way of

---

[11] The classic illustration is contained in *City of London BS v Flegg* [1988] AC 54.

[12] Law Commission, *Trusts of Land: Overreaching*, Working Paper No 106 (London: HMSO, 1988); and Law Commission, *Transfer of Land – Overreaching Beneficiaries in Occupation*, Law Com No 188 (HMSO, 1989).

[13] *State Bank of India v Sood* [1997] Ch 276.

[14] [2004] EWHC 847.

valuing land which, despite subsequent developments, continues to have a major impact on contemporary land law. It offers the first clear example of the strength of *policy* in land law, as expressed in the rise of protections specifically oriented towards purchasers, and designed to facilitate and build confidence in land transactions. Even where aspects of the 1925 legislation have been replaced (for example, much of the framework for land registration, originally set out in the Land Registration Act 1925, has been updated by the Land Registration Act 2002), the values that inform the current law remain heavily influenced by the explicit policies of the 1925 legislation.

This section introduces the idea of *value* in land, focusing particularly on the tensions between land as an asset for occupation and use (use value), and land as an investment asset (exchange value). It then demonstrates how and why the 1925 legislation embedded the idea of land as an investment asset, valued according to its financial exchange value, in a legal system that emphasized alienability. The law regulating co-ownership provides a useful case study for this discussion, and the chapter will chart the shifts in values, as reflected in the language of policies, from the 'trust for sale' to the emergence of the 'trust of land' in the Trusts of Land and Appointment of Trustees Act 1996 (TLATA). Yet, as the case law applying TLATA has demonstrated, the strength of the underlying core principles put in place by 1925 was such that – even after the parliamentary debate was resolved in favour of a more occupation-oriented conception of co-owned land – it has been extremely difficult to displace the values of the 1925 regime.

As the discussion in Chapter 1 has noted, English land law, particularly following the 1925 property reforms, has been dominated by an ethos of logic and rationality. Gray and Gray have claimed that, in relation to dealings between strangers, for example, landlords and tenants or creditors and occupiers:

> ...relationships are strictly commercial, bargaining is hard-nosed, social bondings are minimal and the value attached to land is primarily, perhaps even exclusively, an 'exchange value'. Altruism is in very short support; we are talking money.[15]

It is important to recognize that this characterization of land law is the result of a very clear policy agenda – primarily, the legislative commitment to the theme of alienation – rather than being inherent to the subject. The idea that land, including a person's home, should be valued as a piece of exchangeable capital (rather than for its subjective value to the occupier who used the land, for example) was one of the central pillars of the 1925 legislation. The 1925 legislation sought to make land as easily and securely transferable as possible, as readily exchangeable as any other asset, and to deny the idea that land had any special meaning just because it was occupied as a home. As such, it clearly emphasized the *exchange value* of land over its *use value*.

---

[15] K. Gray and S. Gray, 'The Rhetoric of Realty' in J. Getzler (ed.), *Rationalizing Property, Equity and Trusts: Essays in Honour of Edward Burn* (LexisNexis UK, 2003) p. 241.

Land, as an item of property, holds many different values, but in political, economic and legal discourses, the focus has often been on its use value and exchange value. Adam Smith (whose moral philosophy is often identified as the foundation for neoclassical economics) described 'value' as having '... two different meanings... [It] sometimes expresses the utility of some particular object, and sometimes the power of purchasing other goods which the possession of that object conveys. The one may be called "value in use"; the other, "value in exchange"'.[16] The contrast between use value and exchange value is also highlighted in Marxist critiques of political economy, which distinguish between 'use value', based on the intrinsic, material characteristics of the product and its usefulness in terms of satisfying a human want or need, and the 'exchange value' that can be realized in the market on sale. Land provides a paradigmatic example of both of these characteristics: it has inherent use value as well as a strong exchange value in the market. It has a complex array of: '... organic human uses... within a complex, interactive web of life ...',[17] while at the same time representing a significant financial resource, whose value is not consumed by use.

The ways in which these competing functions are recognized and given effect in property theory and law has not been constant, but has evolved over time as the demands that policy goals have made on property law have changed. As the discussion in Chapter 1 has demonstrated, the themes of property, particularly themes of alienation and economic rationality, have fuelled a strong tendency in law for commercial and economic values to be exaggerated in relation to all other values in land. The scene for this tendency to value land in terms of commercial alienability was set by the 1925 legislation. The 1925 legislation explicitly set out to treat land as a commodity, and to ensure that rights in land would be readily exchangeable in the market. The idea of land as material, organic property was superseded by an understanding of land as 'wealth', according to the abstract economic value it could generate on exchange. The 1925 legislation established an ideology of exchange in land law which has become a default setting, to the extent that even explicit attempts to override it – for example, by TLATA – have had marginal success.

THE HISTORICAL BACKGROUND TO THE 1925 LEGISLATION

The debate concerning the idea of *value* in land focuses particularly on the tensions between land as an asset for occupation and use (use value), and land as

---

[16] A. Smith, *An Inquiry into the Nature And Causes of the Wealth of Nations*, ed. E. Cannan (Methuen and Co Ltd, 5th edn, 1904, first published 1776), Book One, Of the Causes of Improvement in the Productive Powers of Labour, And of the Order according to which its Produce is Naturally Distributed among the Different Ranks of the People; see chapter IV, 'Of the Origin and Use of Money'.

[17] L. Caldwell and K. Schrader-Frechette, *Policy for Land: Law and Ethics* (Rowman & Littlefield Publishers Inc, 1993) p. 5.

an investment asset (exchange value). In *The Historical Foundations of the Common Law*, Milsom wrote that:

> From the earliest settlements until the Industrial Revolution the economic basis of society was agrarian. Land was wealth, livelihood, family provision, and the principal subject matter of the law... [land] was also government and the structure of society.[18]

In this agrarian society, peasant farmers 'owned' the plots of land on which they lived and worked, under the system of feudal tenure.[19] These original owner occupiers valued the land primarily in terms of its use value rather than its exchange value. There was a strong material connection between the peasant land owners and their properties (the soil which supported them).[20] These land owners were unlikely to use their land as a financial asset, either by selling or mortgaging the land.[21] This reluctance to trade with land was rooted in the symbolic importance of the land for peasants, as well as the belief that transacting in land would transform it to an item of exchange, and so dissipate its symbolic value.[22] Peasant land owners regarded their land as having a unique, social, use value, which they did not wish to lose by treating the land as an exchangeable item.

The idea that each piece of land has a unique value was explicitly swept away by the 1925 legislation, which set out to remove most of the remnants of the feudal system of land owning and to place the law on a modern footing. The economic agenda of the reforms was clear. The functions of property in land were fundamentally transformed by the rise of commercialism following the Industrial Revolution. Atiyah described this new commercialist society as effecting:

> ...transition from a law of property to a law of contract relating to property... the now familiar process by which the significance of property rights changed from their use value to their exchange value.[23]

The growth of credit as a means of doing business in a commercial society also impacted on the institution of property. Where property ownership had previously

[18] S. Milsom, *Historical Foundations of the Common Law* (Butterworths, 1981) p. 99.

[19] MacFarlane claimed that, using its commonsense meaning, England was a 'peasant society' between the thirteenth and eighteenth centuries: A. MacFarlane, *The Origins of English Individualism* (Blackwell, 1978) p. 9.

[20] W. Ashley, *An Introduction to English Economic History and Theory* (Vol. 1) (Longmans, 3rd edn, 1901), see pp. 33–38.

[21] MacFarlane, n.19, p. 23. Although MacFarlane recognized some evidence that English peasants were involved in the market and transacted on the land as a commodity, he argued that the land retained a special status until long after private property as a basic concept had been accepted: 'Although small pieces of land may be bought and sold to even out demographic differences between households or in crises, it is very clear that an extensive and open market in land, which treats land as just another commodity, is absent in traditional peasantries.' (p. 23).

[22] Ibid.

[23] P. Atiyah, *The Rise and Fall of Freedom of Contract* (Clarendon Press, 1979) p. 103.

been rooted in the tangible fact of *possession*, the role of property in the credit society was centred on the contractual *obligation*. Where property ownership in the pre-industrial society revolved around physical, tangible things, the rise of credit the commercial society revolved around the exchange value of property as wealth. Kahn-Freund argued that the object of property – the thing itself – became so insignificant that it no longer mattered: '...it may be a block of flats, an agricultural estate, a factory, or so many South African gold shares. The property object has become capital.'[24] The 1925 legislation sought to further this transformation, and to encourage transactions in land, through an explicit policy of treating land as capital or wealth. In the process it denied the proposition that each piece of land is unique as a thing. The goal was to render land more readily exchangeable in the market, and to achieve this goal, it was necessary to substitute the traditional conception of land as symbolic property with the modern representation of land as capital.

The development of the theme of alienation in land law was also associated with the emergence of the theme of (economic) rationality and a liberal market-individualist political orientation – what Atiyah described as an ethos of: '... newer individualism, stressing risk-taking, free choice, rewards to the enterprising and sharp and devil take the hindmost'.[25] As the discussion in Chapter 1 has noted, English land law, particularly following the 1925 property reforms, has been dominated by an ethos of logic and rationality. Gray and Gray have claimed that, in relation to dealings between strangers, for example, landlords and tenants or creditors and occupiers:

> ...relationships are strictly commercial, bargaining is hard-nosed, social bondings are minimal and the value attached to land is primarily, perhaps even exclusively, an 'exchange value'. Altruism is in very short supply; we are talking money.[26]

It is important to recognize that this characterization of land law is the result of a very clear policy agenda – primarily, the legislative commitment to the theme of alienation – rather than being inherent to the subject. The idea that land, including a person's home, should be valued as a piece of exchangeable capital (rather than for its subjective value to the occupier who used the land, for example) was one of the central pillars of the 1925 legislation. The 1925 legislation sought to make land as easily and securely transferable as possible, as readily exchangeable as any other asset, and to deny the idea that land had any special meaning just because it was occupied as a home. As such, it clearly emphasized the *exchange value* of land over its *use value*. Indeed, the strength of the underlying core principles put in place by 1925 was such that – even after

---

[24] O. Kahn-Freund, 'Introduction' in K. Renner, *The Institutions of Private Law and Their Social Functions* (Routledge & Paul, 1949). p. 28.
[25] Atiyah, n.23, p. 176.
[26] Gray and Gray, n.15, p. 241.

the parliamentary debate was resolved in favour of a more occupation-oriented conception of co-owned land – it has been extremely difficult to displace the values of the 1925 regime.

Autobiographical note

A legal journey: Lorna's perspective on property

There can be no doubt that the 1925 legislation pursued a particular policy agenda, and according to many of the conventional land law texts, the merits of this agenda are taken as read. Unlike those who are reading this book as students, my first encounter with land law was not through the medium of the English system. Studying, and later teaching, in Northern Ireland, a number of important differences characterized both the detail and (it seems) the underlying philosophy of land law. One of these differences is that the 1925 legislation never crossed the Irish Sea. While modern Northern Irish land law has developed as a hybrid of English and Irish influences, as well as including some particular approaches that are all its own, the absence of this behemoth of commercialist, pro-purchaser policy may (alongside other cultural differences) go some way to explaining the very different stances which the Northern Ireland Law Commission has taken on some key contemporary property law debates, compared to its English counterpart. For example, in its recent report and recommendations for the reform of land law, the Northern Ireland Law Commission not only declined to follow the English approach of effectively abolishing adverse possession, but proposed strengthening the position of the squatter in some significant respects (see Chapter 6).

The effect of a different starting point in the way I think about land law was recently brought home to me when writing about the Northern Ireland proposals. Reviews of the articles suggested that the readers (presumably anchored in English land law) thought it necessary to unpack the reasons why the Northern Irish approach neither presumptively followed the English approach, nor found it necessary to explain this 'departure'. The NI Law Commission did not apply a strong pro-purchaser/ legal title holder agenda, but appeared to approach key issues from an arguably more open initial position. There are technical and perhaps also philosophical reasons for this – for example, registration has not advanced at the same pace in Northern Ireland as it has in England and Wales – but there are also observable ideological differences. Most notably, perhaps, the Northern Ireland proposals appear to swim against what in England has been a fairly relentless tide towards a tighter system of registration, strongly focused on protecting legal title holders against informal claims such as those brought by squatters or the off-title interests of persons in occupation of land.

The fact that others found it necessary that the reasons for this should be explained, where I had thought them obvious (there are practical, political and philosophical reasons which potentially explain why the NI Law Commission did not take the English approach as its starting point) served as a useful reminder of one of the first lessons of legal research: that we all carry baggage in the way that we perceive, define and approach the questions that we set ourselves to analyse. Sometimes (perhaps often) we are not aware of that baggage (or researcher bias), yet the values that we bring to the project of legal analysis implicitly influence what we choose to write about and how we make our arguments. The same argument can also be made in relation to judges and the way that they understand the law and adjudicate disputes. Stepping back from the 1925 legislation to reflect on its remarkable success in setting an agenda and defining the values with which we think about property law in England brings this process of value acquisition, and its consequences for legal analysis and argument, into sharp relief.

Debate 3

What does English law regard as the purpose of co-owning land?

One key respect in which the machinery of the 1925 legislation sought to achieve the goal of transforming land into a capital asset was through the statutory 'trust for sale', imposed on all jointly owned property under the Law of Property Act 1925.[27] For most of the twentieth century, applications for the sale of co-owned land were governed by the statutory framework set out in the Law of Property Act 1925. The provisions concerning co-owned land in the 1925 legislation were very much in keeping with the overall policy goals of the reforms. Prior to 1925, problems had existed in relation to co-owned land, particularly equitable co-ownership – for example, under an implied trust, since these interests did not appear on the face of the title to the property, they were more difficult for purchasers to discover. The drafters of the 1925 legislation sought to facilitate the transfer of co-owned land by two principal means: first, all interests in co-owned land would be held behind a trust, with the trustees – identifiable from the legal title – empowered to execute transactions affecting the land; thus, purchasers could be confident that by dealing with the trustees, they would obtain good title. Secondly, the trust imposed on co-owned land by the legislation would be imbued with a presumption in favour of sale.

---

[27] LPA section 35 stated that: '... land held upon the "statutory trusts" shall be held upon the trusts and subject to the provisions following, namely, upon trust to sell the same and to stand possessed of the net proceeds of sale'.

THE TRUST FOR SALE

The statutory trust for sale, which imposed a legislative presumption in respect of all co-owned land, that the primary object of property ownership – for example, between spouses or partners – was investment and sale rather than use and occupation, had major implications for the meanings and values associated with co-owned land. As the Law Commission noted:

> The defining feature of the trust for sale...is that the trustees are under a duty to sell the trust land. Implicit in this is the notion that this land should be held primarily as an investment asset rather than as a 'use' asset.[28]

Co-owned land was valued as a capital asset only, and meanings associated with the personal use and occupation of the land – for example, as a home – were excluded. One of the features of this trust was the duty that was imposed on all legal owners of the co-owned land (the 'trustees for sale') to sell the property immediately. Although this mandatory obligation to sell the land was accompanied by a power to postpone sale,[29] in cases where the trustees chose to exercise this power to postpone sale, 'any person interested' could apply to the court under section 30 of the Law of Property Act 1925 for a judicial order forcing the sale of the property, such order to be granted at the discretion of the court.

The impact of the trust for sale was not merely ideological, but highly significant in practice. Section 30 was often used by creditors seeking to force the sale of a jointly owned property. The court exercised its discretionary power to order sale by balancing the creditor's interest in realizing the debtor's assets against the interest of the parties who opposed sale. When sale was opposed, this was usually on the grounds that the occupiers wanted to retain the property for their own use, for example, for occupation as a home. However, the object of the 1925 provisions was to facilitate the alienability of real property. That legislative policy characterized the judicial approach towards granting orders for sale under section 30 of the 1925 Act, as well as a natural concern for creditors' rights on bankruptcy. When balancing the competing interests, the court did not start from a neutral position but by asking whether it was inequitable *not* to allow the applicant to realize his capital share of the property.[30] Although the power to order sale was discretionary, the legislative policy in support of alienability, and the presumption that land – including the home – was merely another form of capital, created a presumption of sale to give effect to the purpose of the trust. In practice, this resulted in a clear tendency for the creditor's interest, which lies in the sale of the debtor's property, to prevail over the co-owning occupier who wished to retain the land for occupation and use as a home.[31]

---

[28] Law Commission, *Transfer of Land: Trusts of Land,* Law Comm No 181 (HMSO, 1989), para 3.1.
[29] Law of Property Act 1925, s. 25.
[30] *Jones v Challenger* [1960] 2 WLR 695.
[31] *Re Citro (a Bankrupt)* [1991] Ch 142.

As we have remarked in Chapter 1, in 1925, owner-occupation accounted for a small but growing proportion of the housing sector in the United Kingdom, although the government had already embarked upon a home-ownership campaign which aimed to encourage citizens to buy their own homes.[32] The broad outcome of these policies was that by 2009, around 69 per cent of households in the UK either owned, or were in the process of buying their own homes.[33] One of the objectives of government strategy in promoting home ownership in the United Kingdom was to promote a culture of citizenship: it believed that the expansion of owner-occupation would encourage owners to acquire a stake in the nation.[34] Yet, while these government policies promoting ownership sought to *encourage* occupiers to invest – economically, socially and emotionally – in their homes through owner-occupation, the 1925 legislation – which set the scene for the legal framework of property law that governs owner-occupation – was '... neither premised upon the existence of mass owner-occupation, nor aimed at providing a legal framework to govern such a pattern of ownership ... [the drafters of the 1925 legislation were] not concerned to provide a conveyancing regime tailored to the needs of the modern owner-occupied sector.'[35]

In fact, the policy of treating real property as capital in the 1925 legislation was geared to meet the needs of the commercial, industrialized society of the late nineteenth and early twentieth centuries.[36] As the Law of Property Bill passed through the House of Commons, it was clear that its object was to treat land as a commercial asset. The broad aim of the legislation was said to be '... to assimilate the law of real and personal estate and to free the purchaser from the obligation to enquire into the title of him from whom he purchases, any more than he would have to do if he were buying a parcel of stock.'[37] The focus on co-ownership was based on the particular hazards that undiscovered interests in co-owned land could present for purchasers. The LPA sought to protect purchasers from the risks associated with buying co-owned land by placing any beneficial interests behind the statutorily imposed trust for sale.

This had obvious, potentially adverse, consequences for any co-owners, whose interests were transferred to the proceeds of the sale: a co-owner, who may have thought they had an interest in the land itself, could find the property sold, and their claim applied against the purchase money. In fact, this 'conversion' of the co-owner's property interest took place long before the point of sale: from the point of acquisition of co-owned land, any equitable interest was designated as an interest in the capital value, rather than an interest in land. This doctrine of

---

[32] The role of the government in promoting the 'owner-occupier mortgaged to a building society' society is discussed in Chapter 10.

[33] C. Randall, *Housing*, Social Trends 41, London, Office for National Statistics, 2011.

[34] See further, D. Cowan and M. McDermont, *Regulating Social Housing: Governing Decline* (Routledge-Glasshouse, 2006) ch. 8.

[35] W. Murphy and H. Clark, *The Family Home* (Sweet & Maxwell, 1983) pp. 18–19.

[36] See 155 HL Deb (5th Series) col 709–710 (16 June 1922), Sir Donald McLean.

[37] Lord Birkenhead in a letter to *The Times*, 15 December 1920.

'conversion' gave practical effect to the policy of treating property in land as mere capital, rather than a specific interest in a particular item of real property. By the time the Bill was enacted, it was arguably already out of sync (or nearly so) with the ways in which householders sought to use land in the post-war period.

THE DOCTRINE OF CONVERSION

The parliamentary debates preceding the Law of Property Act attested to the government's policy of assimilating land with other forms of property, so that land would carry no special meaning. Some members of the House of Commons opposed the policy, arguing that '[y]ou cannot compare the transfer of stocks and shares with the transfer of property',[38] and that

> You may want one special piece of land…no one wants one special stock certificate…There is no magic in one stock certificate…[on the other hand] land is a special property. A man may want one particular piece of land, and it may be that no money can compensate him for the loss of it.[39]

These arguments were unsuccessful. The provisions of the 1925 legislation – specifically, the trust for sale and the doctrine of conversion – ensured that land would be valued according to its exchange value rather than its material and organic use value. This was achieved through the trust for sale, the defining feature of which was that the trustees were under a duty to sell the land, with the implicit assertion that the objective of this form of ownership was investment rather than use. The doctrine of conversion operated to ensure that, from the outset of the co-ownership – not merely on the point of sale – the beneficiaries' interests were interests in the proceeds of sale only: they were not interests in the land.

The effect of the doctrine of conversion was to treat the land itself as 'perfectly replaceable' by money. For example, in *Irani Finance Ltd v Singh*,[40] the court recognized that while '… In a non-technical use of language, the beneficiary may be said to have a real interest in the land …',[41] in legal terms:

> …the beneficial interest of a person whose interest arises under a trust for sale…is not one which is appropriately described as being 'an interest in the land'…[so that] he has no estate or interest in the land itself.[42]

The application of conversion to all interests in co-owned land in the 1925 legislation attracted considerable criticism, and, in a series of cases following *Irani Finance Ltd v Singh*, the courts wavered between the idea of property interests in co-owned land as interests in the land itself, on the one hand, and interests in

---

38 154 HC Deb (5th Series) col 145 (15 May 1922).
39 Ibid., col 124.
40 [1970] 2 WLR 117 (ChD); [1971] Ch 59 (CA).
41 [1971] Ch 59 at 69; per Buckley J.
42 Ibid.

its capital value, on the other.[43] In *Williams & Glyn's Bank Ltd v Boland*,[44] Lord Wilberforce described the proposition that an interest in co-owned land under a statutory trust for sale was an interest in the proceeds of sale only – through the operation of conversion – as 'just a little unreal' in the case of a *home* that had been purchased for the purposes of occupation. The use of conversion was ultimately altered by TLATA, although, as the discussion below will show, that theme of alienation had been so firmly entrenched in English land law that the ideals of TLATA had little practical effect.

BANKRUPTCY

The 1925 property reforms provided the courts with the ideology, the language, the tools and the justification to adopt a presumption in favour of sale, to value land as a capital asset only, and to disregard the non-financial interests of occupiers in their homes. This ethos was so strongly embedded in legal discourse that even when section 336, Insolvency Act 1986 was enacted, with a view to attaching greater weight to use and occupation of property as a *family home* in the context of bankruptcy proceedings at least for a limited period, the commercial interests of creditors continued to prevail. Section 336 of the Insolvency Act 1986 required the court, when exercising its discretion to order the sale of a family home, to have regard to a range of factors, including:

> ...the interests of the bankrupt's creditors, the conduct of the spouse or former spouse...the needs and financial resources of the spouse or former spouse, the needs of any children, and all the circumstances of the case other than the needs of the bankrupt.[45]

Yet, while this provision purported to provide the court with grounds on which to recognize the interests of the debtor's family in retaining their home, it was tempered by section 336(5), which required the court, once a year had passed from the instigation of bankruptcy proceedings, to: '... assume, unless the circumstances of the case are exceptional, that the interests of the bankrupt's creditors outweigh all other considerations'. The court's policy with regard to section 30 applications by trustees in bankruptcy was epitomized by the decision in *Re Citro (a Bankrupt)*,[46] in which Nourse LJ considered what factors were not exceptional circumstances. As he put it:

---

[43] In *National Westminster Bank Ltd v Stockman* [1981] 1 WLR 67 the interest was construed as an interest in land for the purposes of the Charging Orders Act 1979, to enable an interest in a trust for sale to form the subject matter of a charge). *Perry v Phoenix Assurance* [1988] 1 WLR 940 held that it did not amount to an 'order affecting land' under the Land Charges legislation; however, in *Clark v Chief Land Registrar* [1993] 2 WLR 141, the order was allowed as one where 'the interest was to charge the land not the proceeds of sale'. In *Elias v Mitchell* [1972] Ch 652, an interest in the proceeds of sale under a statutory trust for sale was described as a 'minor interest in land' for the purposes of the Land Registration Act 1925.

[44] [1981] AC 487, at 507.

[45] Insolvency Act 1986, s. 336(4).

[46] [1991] Ch 142.

What then are exceptional circumstances? As the cases show, it is not uncommon for a wife with young children to be faced with eviction in circumstances where the realisation of her beneficial interest will not produce enough to buy a comparable home in the same neighbourhood, or indeed elsewhere; and, if she has to move elsewhere, there may be problems over schooling and so forth. Such circumstances, while engendering a natural sympathy in all who hear of them, cannot be described as exceptional. They are the melancholy consequences of debt and improvidence with which every civilised society has been familiar.[47]

THE 'TRUST OF LAND': FROM SALE TO HOME?

The alienation focus appeared to change with the enactment of TLATA. The basis for that Act was to re-introduce the idea of use value in the home within the legal framework of property ownership by recognizing that home owners do not, in reality, regard their property as merely an investment asset, but value it also as a home. TLATA technically transformed the nature of co-owned interests in land. The 'trust of land' which is applied to co-owned property (in place of the trust for sale) was intended to re-establish the *use value* of the land itself, so displacing what had become an overwhelming emphasis on exchange value, while retaining the protections for the purchaser in the 1925 Act (overreaching, and indeed strengthening, the powers of the trustees). The basis for this shift appeared to be that home owners do not, in reality, view their property as an investment asset only, and that sale is usually the last outcome intended by co-owning occupiers in relation to their home. As the Law Commission put it, '[A] system devised for one set of social circumstances is being used for very different circumstances'.[48]

It was the unreality of the trust for sale in the new context of widespread ownership which propelled the reform.[49] The Law Commission recognized that, in most cases, the purpose of home ownership was the use and occupation of the property *as a home*, not (solely) investment in property as an asset pending the realization of its capital value on sale.[50] The fact that most co-owners acquire their owned home for the purposes of use rather than (merely) investment was reflected in the new trust of land. The main purpose of such a trust was to hold and use the land, not to realize its capital value on sale. The Law Commission recognized that land – especially the owned home – was likely to bear particular meaning and value for occupiers as '... the place where the beneficiaries live, or want to live in the future'.[51] As such, the trust of land reasserted the material, organic value of property in land, recognizing that property in land can be specific, unique, and not substitutable with capital. This approach to the value of property in land (use

---

[47] n.X, at 157.
[48] Law Commission, Trusts of Land, Working Paper No 94, (HMSO, 1987), para. 3.17.
[49] Law Com No 181 (1989), para. 1.3; Law Com WP No 94, paras 3.2, 6.4.
[50] Law Com WP No 106, para. 3.2.
[51] Ibid., para. 3.10.

value rather than exchange value) was described by Lord Browne-Wilkinson as being '... at last ... a little bit of common sense ...'.[52]

TLATA sought to address both the preference for sale at the heart of the trust for sale, and the implications of the doctrine of conversion. By abolishing the doctrine of conversion, the proposition that a co-owner's interest in land was limited to the proceeds of sale was re-shaped to establish the right as an interest in land.[53] TLATA also removed the duty to sell, thus seemingly diminishing the *prima facie* advantage previously enjoyed by parties applying for an order for sale of co-owned land. The Law Commission claimed that the section 30 discretion had been unduly governed by the 'duty to sell' and that this had 'confined the development of judicial doctrine to the formulation of reasons why sale should not take place'.[54] TLATA introduced (in section 15) new criteria to guide the court's discretion to make orders affecting the land, including the order for sale. These included regard for the intentions of the person who created the trust, the purpose for which the trust was formed (for example, occupation as a home), and the welfare of any minor occupant, as well as the interests of any secured creditor. Section 15(3) also directed the court to consider the interests of persons of full age entitled to interests in possession – that is, adult co-owners – with a consideration of the value of their interests. It is to be noted that the provisions of the Insolvency Act 1986 remain in force and the jurisprudence under that Act has followed *Re Citro (a Bankrupt)*.[55]

Yet, although these guidelines were intended to displace the presumption of sale, they have seemed to have little practical impact as the courts have remained largely faithful to the ethos of the 1925 legislation, continuing to order sale in most cases.[56] So, for example, in *Bank of Ireland Home Mortgages v Bell*, the court was particularly concerned in a situation where the bank had received no interest payments from the occupier beneficiaries for some time. If an order for sale were refused, that would have '... condemned the bank to go on waiting with no prospect of recovery [of their money] and with the debt increasing all the time, the debt already exceeding what could be realised on a sale'.[57] The factors to be balanced the other way were slight by comparison: the house had originally been bought as a matrimonial home and there were children. Yet, the male partner had left and thus the purpose was no longer relevant, and the son was not far short of 18 years old.

---

[52] 569 HL Deb (5th Series) col 1725 (1 March 1996).

[53] TLATA, s. 3.

[54] Law Comm No 181 (1989), para 3.6.

[55] [1991] Ch 142. Although there may have been a slight softening following on from the Human Rights Act – see *Barca v Mears* [2004] EWHC 2170 (Ch) at [40]–[42]; cf. *Nicholls v Lan* [2006] EWHC 1255 (Ch), at [43].

[56] See for example, *TSB Bank plc v Marshall* [1998] 39 EG 308; *Bank of Ireland Home Mortgages Ltd v Bell* [2001] 2 FLR 809; *First National Bank plc v Achampong* [2003] EWCA Civ 487; *Mortgage Corporation Ltd v Lewis Silkin* (25 February 2000, unreported).

[57] [2001] 2 FLR 809 at [31], Peter Gibson LJ.

The point about the bank waiting for its money was applied in (quite remarkable) circumstances in *First National Bank plc v Achampong*, in which the bank had been dilatory in bringing a claim for possession. As the judge in the county court had put it, 'The fact remains that the bank started these proceedings in 1993 with a debt of some £63,000 which because of their own inaction has allowed it to rise to some £180,000'.[58] Blackburne J however, argued that delay was neither here nor there because, in the meantime, Ms Achampong had received the use of the property,[59] and so had not been prejudiced. The further argument for Ms Achampong was that, although her husband had left her so that the immediate purpose of the trust to use the property as a home for them had failed, she was living in the property with her grandchildren, one of whom was severely disabled. That argument was brushed aside, partly on an evidential ground, and partly because

> Insofar as the purpose of the trust – and the intention of the Achampongs in creating it – was to provide a family home and insofar as that is a purpose which goes wider than simply the provision of a matrimonial home, I am unpersuaded that it is a consideration to which much if any weight should be attached. The children of the marriage have long since reached adulthood. One of them is no longer in occupation. It is true that the elder daughter, Rosemary, is a person under mental disability and remains in occupation but to what extent that fact is material to her continued occupation of the property and therefore to the exercise of any discretion under section 14 is not apparent.[60]

The only exception to this line of authority seems to be *Edwards v Lloyds TSB*,[61] in which Park J refused to make an order for sale. He regarded two particular facts of that case as salient: first, there was sufficient equity in the property to pay the debt; and second, the actual property itself was relatively modest and Ms Edwards would not be able to afford adequate alternative accommodation. Even so, he postponed sale for five years, until the youngest child was 18 years old.[62] The ethos of the 1925 legislation has clearly proven resistant to reform.

CONCLUSIONS

The impact of the commercial ideology and the theme of alienation that informed the 1925 legislation has been identified in many other contemporary contexts. For example, Hunter and Nixon's analysis of judicial attitudes in mortgage possession actions emphasized the significance of the market ethos in respect of owner-

---

[58] [2003] EWCA Civ 487 at [55].

[59] Ibid at [62].

[60] Ibid at [65]

[61] [2005] 1 FCR 139.

[62] He also ordered that no interest was to be paid in the meantime and that the parties had liberty to apply to vary the length of the postponement – an order which might be regarded as at the margins of discretion.

occupation. They found that, in cases involving default, both legal principles and judicial decision-making processes have been influenced by the idea that while:

> [f]or lenders their primary interest is in the commercial/exchange value of their property rights... [while s]ocial landlords have primarily been seeking, within certain constraints, to provide use value rights... the way in which judges exercise their discretion provides evidence of the dominance of market forces and the primary importance of the exchange value of the dwelling... judges take a very different view of the rights which have to be protected in cases against tenants from those involving borrowers.[63]

As such, the values put in place by the 1925 legislation continue to shape property law's ideological orientation, particularly in its emphasis on alienability and exchange.

The 1925 legislation commodified land. Its value

> ... is defined as an exchange value, often referred to as market value, when it is traded in a laissez-faire market... all commodities are fungible and commensurable – capable of being reduced to money without changing in value, and completely interchangeable with every other commodity in terms of exchange value.[64]

This has significant consequences for the way that we think about our owned homes. Dovey argued that:

> In the modern world, the house is a commodity involving substantial economic commitment. It is an investment of economic resources that yields profit and power. As such, the house has become increasingly similar to other products – being bought and sold, used and discarded like a car or washing machine.[65]

In England and Wales, the commodification of land is a direct result of the assimilation of land with other types of property in the 1925 legislation. The particular example used in this chapter concerns the trust for sale and the doctrine of conversion, both of which explicitly rejected the idea of land as a special or unique type of property, and valued it only in terms of its exchange value. In addition to closing out considerations of use, this also excluded consideration of the emotional dimension of property in land. As a mere commodity, a capital asset to be traded in the marketplace, the owned home was reduced to a house, and its owner regarded as a property investor. Not even the clear shift in legislative policy

---

[63] C. Hunter and J. Nixon, 'Better a Public Tenant Than a Private Borrower Be: The Possession Process and the Threat of Eviction' in D. Cowan (ed.), *Housing: Participation and Exclusion* (Ashgate, 1998) pp. 94, 95, 98.

[64] M. Radin, *Contested Commodities: The Trouble with Trade in Sex, Children, Body Parts and Other Things* (Harvard University Press, 1996) p. 3.

[65] K. Dovey, 'Home and Homelessness' in I. Altman and C. Werner (eds), *Home Environments* (Plenum Press, 1985) p. 53.

which was brought to bear in TLATA could displace the ethos and ideology of land law set in place by the 1925 legislation.

Further Reading

S. Anderson, 'Land Law Texts and the Explanation of 1925' (1984) *Current Legal Problems* 63.

S. Anderson, 'The 1925 Property Legislation: Setting Contexts', in S. Bright & J. Dewar, *Land Law: Themes and Perspectives* (Oxford University Press, 1998).

L. Fox, 'Creditors and the Concept of Family Home: A Functional Analysis' (2005) 25(2) *Legal Studies* 201.

4

LEASES

INTRODUCTION

In the previous chapter, we discussed some of the issues arising from co-ownership of property. In this chapter, we deal with a set of issues deriving from a different type of property right – the lease, also known as a tenancy. Part of the consideration here is about the dividing line between property and personal rights, to be sure, but the relationships created out of, or because of, a tenancy agreement are just as significant to our discussion. The themes outlined in Chapter 1 are equally relevant here, both as foreground and background.

There is a tendency – a real temptation – to get sucked in by the law, to over-privilege it, and miss your own perspective. The law is a backstop which is irrelevant in most agreements. With that in mind, the opening section asks you to think about your own experience as occupier and draws on landlord perspectives to illustrate the significance of respect and responsibility, which underlie the relationship between occupier and the person/s or bodies to whom these responsibilities might be owed. This is Debate 1: the everyday life of tenancy law. The following section looks at the dividing practices of the technical law, which divides off property from personal rights, paying particularly close attention to the notions of intention and exclusion. This is Debate 2: property rights versus personal rights. The next section discusses the law's construction of tenant's rights, noting the narrow constructions given to those rights. This is Debate 3: rights and their amelioration. The final section considers problems arising when the landlord seeks to determine a tenancy agreement. That is Debate 4: determining a tenancy. One significant omission from that final section is the intervention of human rights law, which is considered in Chapter 8.

Debate 1

The everyday life of tenancy law

We used to begin tutorials on leases by asking our students whether they had read their tenancy agreement. Most had not done so. Some, particularly those living with non-law students, had been asked by their fellow occupiers to read the agreement. None appreciated the extent of their rights and responsibilities in the property. The observation follows that, if they do not read the document or understand their rights and responsibilities, they cannot necessarily expect others to do so.

In a study of harassment and unlawful eviction in the late 1990s, one of the comments from a landlord that stood out was that they regarded the tenancy agreement as an entirely secondary, consequential aspect of the relationship between themselves and the occupiers.[1] They believed that leaving a bottle of wine (for male tenants) or a bunch of flowers (for female tenants) in the property at the start was a far greater control on the behaviour of the occupiers than the formality of the tenancy agreement. On the other hand, some social landlords now engage in tenancy signing ceremonies with their future occupiers, the aim of which is to make occupiers appreciate the extent of their obligations under the agreement so that enforcement of the tenancy agreement might become less necessary.[2]

These observations of landlords and tenants are, in fact, two sides of the same coin of legality and lead on to a broader point. Both the private landlord and the social landlords were seeking, in different ways, to get the occupier to take responsibility for the property; the social landlords have an extended meaning of the property here, to encompass the neighbourhood and community to whom the obligations of the tenancy agreement can also be said to be owed, a matter of less significance to the private landlord who is likely to be more concerned with the internal state of the property.[3] The students were enacting their everyday understandings of the extent of their agreement with the landlord, whether or not they read their agreements, through the payment of a sum of money and (we have no doubt, from personal experience) varying approaches to respecting the internal condition of the property. In sum, the versions of legality in these relationships are often extra-contractual but enact and perform assumptions about respect and responsibility.

The tenancy continues not because of the contract but because of the relational assumptions of respect and responsibility which underlie it.[4] These can, however, break down. Research into harassment and unlawful eviction usually finds, in relation to private landlords, that the landlord does not necessarily think about using due process of law to evict the occupier, but, rather, bases their decision-making

---

[1] A. Marsh, P. Niner, D. Cowan, R. Forrest, P. Kennett, *Harassment and Unlawful Eviction in the Private Rented and Park Homes Sector* (DETR, 2000).

[2] See, in particular, J. Flint, 'Reconfiguring Agency and Responsibility in the Governance of Social Housing in Scotland', (2004) 41(1) *Urban Studies* 151; J. Flint & J. Nixon, 'Governing Neighbours: Anti-Social Behaviour Orders and New Forms of Regulating Conduct in the UK', (2006) 43(5/6) *Urban Studies* 939; J. Flint & H. Pawson, 'Social Landlords and the Regulation of Conduct in Urban Spaces in the United Kingdom', (2009) 9(4) *Criminology and Criminal Justice* 415.

[3] See D. Cowan & H. Carr, 'Actor-Network Theory, Implementation and the Private Landlord' (2008) 35(Special Research Issue) *Journal of Law and Society* 149.

[4] See, generally, I. Macneil, 'Economic Analysis of Contractual Relations: Its Shortfalls and the Need for a "Rich Classificatory Apparatus"' (1981) 75(3) *Nw LR* 1018; P. Vincent-Jones, *The New Public Contracting* (Oxford University Press, 2006); H. Collins, *Regulating Contracts* (Oxford University Press, 1999).

processes on the understanding that the property is 'theirs'.[5] That understanding is often also shared by police officers who, it is found, sometimes unwittingly assist landlords in their unlawful activity.[6] In such circumstances, and others where resort to law is necessary, it is only at that point when the actual agreement takes on a presence and is translated into and through the process of 'going to law'.

This leads on to a further problem about the limits of law. A tenant who complains to the landlord about the state of the property (because there is damp or no central heating, for example), or about the landlord's broader management role, does so at their own risk. They may have every right to do so, but they may also recognize that a complaint often leads to eviction. This is the unquantifiable problem of 'retaliatory eviction' which arises when the landlord feels, for example, that there is a breakdown in trust with the occupier.[7]

It all depends on how long the occupier thinks they have left in the property – which may not necessarily correspond with their rights to remain in the property after the expiry of a fixed term – but it tends to reflect what has become known as the 'status of moveability' of occupiers.[8] Most private rented tenancies take effect under an assured shorthold tenancy, which only lasts for at least six months (or such period as the parties agree). In brief, such a tenancy can be terminated by means of a notice giving the tenant two months; such notices also require the court to make an order for possession (although this is not usually something of which many tenants are aware and, in any event, they may find themselves liable for court costs of the possession claim). It is easier for the tenant to move on to alternative accommodation. The relational nature of the tenancy agreement is rarely acknowledged in property law, nor in landlord and tenant law – it appears that merely putting the word 'law' after 'property' and 'landlord and tenant' neutralizes the relational understandings which are translated into legal rights and remedies – but it is clearly significant to everyday life.

The above points are further illustrated through the work of Diane Lister on the governance of tenancy relationships in the private sector. Lister's data consisted of qualitative interviews with younger tenants and their landlords. She demonstrates how the formal contract between landlord and tenant gave way to informal sets of understandings developed at the outset through the interactions between landlord and tenant. Neither party expected to negotiate about terms and rents. If the tenant sought to negotiate, '... it was perceived [by the landlord] as denoting financial insecurity and a potential risk'.[9] Lister's point was that by focusing on legal requirements, '... social

---

[5] See D. Nelken, *The Limits of the Legal Process: A Study of Landlords, Law and Crime* (Academic Press, 1983); D. Cowan, 'Harassment and Unlawful Eviction in the Private Rented Sector: A Study of Law (in-)Action' [2001] *Conveyancer and Property Lawyer* 249.

[6] See, for example, <http://nearlylegal.co.uk/blog/2010/07/illegal-eviction-and-the-police/>.

[7] See D. Cowan, *Housing Law and Policy* (Cambridge University Press, 2011) ch. 11.

[8] See, for example, J. Morgan, 'Housing Security in England and Wales: Casualisation Revisited' (2009) 1(1) *International Journal of Law in the Built Environment* 42.

[9] D. Lister, 'The Nature of Tenancy Relationships – Landlords and Young People in the Private Rented Sector' in S. Lowe and D. Hughes (eds), *The Privately Rented Sector in a New Century* (Policy Press, 2001) p. 99.

factors of relationships are overlooked which are significant and have a greater impact on behaviour than at first credited ...'.[10] Thus, social expectations of the relationship, combined with the emotional or sentimental attachments (including to the property) should be regarded as significant. Lister emphasizes the role of trust, which might be regarded as a central aspect of all ongoing relations. When trust breaks down between the parties, attachments can become more evident through unlawful action. Alternatively, and using language more associated with criminology, she refers to the overt and covert surveillance techniques used by landlords both inside the property and outside.[11] That being said, though, national landlord associations often draw distinctions between what they see as the landlord's proper role – controlling behaviour inside the property's boundaries – and that outside the property, which is the proper province of the public police.[12]

Lister's findings chime also with the critique of the anti-regulationists – the economists who assume that regulation of the market, and particularly rent, is a moral and practical hazard, causing declines in property quality and availability.[13] Margaret Radin argues against the idea that housing should be treated as an ordinary market commodity.[14] From the individual tenant's perspective, 'The intuitive general rule is that preservation of one's home is a stronger claim than preservation of one's business, or that noncommercial personal use of an apartment as a home is morally entitled to more weight than purely commercial landlording'.[15] As opposed to the landlord's commercial interest in the property, the tenant's personal interest in the property becomes bound up with their selfhood. Now, this dichotomy may well not hold good in this jurisdiction, where most landlords own or manage a portfolio usually of only one or two properties, which they regard as their 'own'; but what it does emphasize are the reciprocal obligations and, perhaps most importantly, the polyvocality of 'home'.

Debate 2

Property rights versus personal rights

Conventionally, in property law, one distinguishes a lease – a proprietary right – from a licence or other personal right. That proprietary right, however, obscures

---

[10] 'Controlling Letting Arrangements in the Private Rented Sector?' in D. Hughes and S. Lowe (eds), *The Private Rented Housing Market: Regulation or Deregulation?* (Ashgate, 2007) p. 72.

[11] 'Controlling Letting Arrangements? Landlords and Surveillance in the Private Rented Sector' (2005) 2(4) *Surveillance and Society* 513.

[12] See H. Carr, D. Cowan and C. Hunter, 'Policing the Housing Crisis', (2007) 27(1) *Critical Social Policy* 100.

[13] See, for example, Institute for Economic Affairs, *Verdict on Rent Control* (IEA, 1972); and the sophisticated analysis by B. Turner & S. Malpezzi, 'A Review of Empirical Evidence on the Costs and Benefits of Rent Control', (2003) 10 *Swedish Economic Policy Review* 11.

[14] M. Radin, 'Residential Rent Control', (1986) 15 *Philosophy & Public Affairs* 350; see also the sophisticated account provided by D. Cooper, 'Opening Up Ownership: Community Belonging, Belongings, and the Productive Life of Property', (2007) 32(3) *Law and Social Inquiry* 625.

[15] Radin, n.14, p. 360.

the complex nature of the relationship between landlord and tenant, which exists both contractually and as a matter of property. The reason for that division is largely historical but its enduring power remains. The dual nature of the relationship becomes particularly significant at different moments, when one or the other becomes pre-eminent. It also causes problems, such as in the enforcement of covenants between the parties when the original landlord or tenant has transferred their interest so that there is no 'privity of contract'.[16]

There has been considerable case law on the distinction between leases and licences, although it has diminished (both in scale and importance) since the implementation of the Housing Act 1988 because of the decline in security of tenure and rent regulation/control which had been in place previously; and, as regards council tenants, the Housing Act 1985 provisions concerning security of tenure apply equally to leases and certain licences.[17] The lease was a powerful right; now less so (as discussed above). These shifts have effectively neutralized the power of the law so that this law might be regarded almost as a passive bystander in most disputes.[18] That does not mean it is unimportant – a body of law which is largely symbolic remains important for what it represents (and it is not symbolic all the time). In this case, it represents a struggle both outside the law and inside the law as to the significance of different types of intention; or, to put it another way, different versions of truth.

A BRIEF DIVERSION

It is impossible to get a handle on the complicated law in this area unless account is taken of the parallel rise and fall of security of tenure and rent control/regulation.[19] As originally conceived in 1915, security of tenure (by which is meant that a landlord required a court order before the tenant could be evicted, such order only to be made on certain grounds of possession) and rent control (rent rises being set centrally) were linked to control over the levels of mortgage interest payable.[20] In the short term, this made sense,[21] but the conjunction was subsequently disturbed so that central control over mortgage interest was stopped.

It was assumed also that when wartime controls were no longer necessary, the rent control provisions at least would be discontinued. There was a succession of official reports, each of which was tasked to consider not only the technical law but also whether the provisions should be continued. As Cowan and McDermont

---

[16] Issues largely resolved by the Landlord and Tenant (Covenants) Act 1995.

[17] *Westminster CC v Clarke* [1992] 2 AC 288; Housing Act 1985, s. 79(3).

[18] Vincent-Jones describes the leading case in the field, *Street v Mountford* [1985] AC 809 as a 'shallow victory' as a result: P. Vincent-Jones, 'Exclusive Possession and Exclusive Control of Private Rented Housing: A Socio-Legal Critique of the Lease-Licence Distinction' (1987) 14(4) *Journal of Law and Society* 445, 455.

[19] Security of tenure and rent control/regulation have usually gone hand-in-hand, one being regarded as impossible without the other.

[20] The history of these provisions is set out in Cowan, n.7, ch. 1.

[21] Indeed, it was not wholly disadvantageous to landlords: A. Holmans, *Housing Policy in Britain* (Croom Helm, 1987) p. 388.

suggest, 'what is apparent in these reports is that the private sector should be made as free as possible and, when it is, it was thought that it should be able to cater for the population. The evident belief was that the free market would provide decent quality housing at an affordable rent, if it was given the chance. It was a belief in the value of enterprise, conceived as a "social service".'[22] The wavering commitment to rent control can be shown by the process of allowing 'creeping decontrol' – new lets being exempted from the rent control provisions – and, from the mid-1960s, a shift to rent regulation. Security of tenure remained largely in place until the Housing Act 1980 allowed landlords, under certain restrictive conditions, to grant less secure tenancies; by the Housing Act 1988, however, that limited form was given freer rein through the creation of the assured shorthold tenancy. The latter allows occupiers a minimum of six months' security. It is now the default tenancy arrangement in the private rented sector. Rent control/regulation is limited, in essence, to a market-based regime.

What the previous paragraph does not convey, however, is the *politics* of private renting. Until the 1990s, there appeared to be sharp divides between the Conservative and Labour parties, and debates about security and rent were conducted with considerable fervour.[23] Those debates seem like an age ago and are rarely stimulated today.[24] There is also what seems (if anything) a distant memory of judicial antipathy to rent control/regulation legislation regarded as ill-fitting,[25] and problematic relations between landlords and tenants. These latter points are best encapsulated in the bitter start of an article written by Roger Street, the principal protagonist in the law considered below:

> The Rent Acts are grossly unfair to landlords. A stranger obtains a weekly tenancy of a house: half a century may pass before the owner can have his property again. In the meantime he can only charge a so-called 'fair' rent which in many cases does little more than cover the cost of keeping the property in repair. As a result of all this, the capital value of the property drops to between one-third and one-half of the vacant possession value. Little wonder that over the years landlords and their legal advisers have sought various ways of avoiding the potentially horrendous consequences of being caught by the legislation.[26]

Street's concerns were tempered by the well-known knowledge that there were other well-worn routes through which landlords could avoid the security of

---

[22] D. Cowan & M. McDermont, *Regulating Social Housing: Governing Decline* (Routledge, 2006) p. 147.

[23] There is a full discussion in P. Kemp, *Private Renting in Transition* (CIH, 2004).

[24] Although the rules regarding the tenancy deposit regime did do so – H. Carr '"People Will Say We're in Love": Talking Dirty about Tenancy Deposits', paper presented to the Socio-Legal Studies Association annual conference, 2005, on file with the authors.

[25] See C. Hand, 'The Statutory Tenancy: An Unrecognised Proprietary Interest?' [1980] *Conveyancer and Property Lawyer* 351.

[26] R. Street, 'Coach and Horses Trip Cancelled? Rent Act Avoidance after Street v Mountford' [1985] *Conveyancer and Property Lawyer* 328, 328.

tenure and rent regulation legislation – for example, the grant of 'holiday lets' and 'winter lets'.[27]

However, the essential point of this section is that the debates about the distinction between proprietary and personal rights are shot through with considerations which are both extraneous and politicized. At their heart, as Roger Street discursively demonstrated, the distinction offers a far greater appreciation of our core themes of ownership, alienation and exclusion than is suggested by the apparently neutral case law discussed below.

Autobiographical note

Renting in the halcyon days

When I was a law student in the distant past, I had no idea about such matters as security of tenure or the like. We students were expected to move out of halls and into the private rented sector. That was what everybody did. That was in the halcyon days of student grants and free tertiary education. So, I moved out with my then partner and a couple of other students into a rented property. The landlord was a sweetie (more about him in a moment). Our rent was set by the rent officer at £14 per week each and we each received housing benefit to pay for it. I didn't know that this was a regulated tenancy under the Rent Act 1977, which granted us considerable rights to security. The following year, however, housing benefit vanished and my rent seemed to increase exponentially to £40 per week or thereabouts. And our landlord insisted on us signing something called an 'assured shorthold tenancy' contract.

I couldn't work it out at all – why should my rent jump by such an amount and why should my housing benefit disappear? I was less concerned by this new tenancy agreement. To be honest, in those days there were other more pressing concerns such as where my next drink was going to be had, and the questions soon disappeared in an alcoholic and cigarette haze.

But it is now clear to me after all these years that my legal education took place on the cusp of major shifts in security of tenure and towards market rents for properties. In that year, the impact on me of the deregulation of the private rented sector was felt most strongly at the local pub and tobacconist. My landlord clearly expected us to stay for the whole academic year and then move out (under both types of tenancy), and we did so.

Under the Rent Act tenancy, however, we could have stayed until a ground for possession emerged. Under the Housing Act assured shorthold tenancy, if it was properly granted, the landlord could have got us out

---

[27] At 335; see also House of Commons Environment Committee, *The Private Rented Sector*, HC 40-I (HMSO, 1982).

with a simple two-month notice under section 21, Housing Act 1988, and a court order.

And back to my lovely landlord. We regularly used to come home after a day at the library (or wherever) to find him in 'our' place, making a cup of tea. He used to make me one too, which I thought was very nice of him. I didn't appreciate that this was wrong (Protection from Eviction Act 1977), nor that it was a breach of the implied covenant of quiet enjoyment. Such things didn't bother me then.

Knowing what I know now, as a lawyer, I suspect that I might have approached matters rather differently then; but, as a socio-legal academic, I recognize the relational quality of the relationship between landlord and tenant, so that formal law may well be less relevant than the ongoing, day-to-day experience of our interactions. However, I am also acutely aware that my experience is not necessarily shared by students and other renters, for whom harassment and unlawful eviction together with terrible conditions in rented property can be an everyday affair. The day-to-day experience of barristers specializing in housing law is often precisely these types of cases. I hope it doesn't happen to you, but, if it does, talk to your local authority tenancy relations officer about it and get their help. They are a fantastic resource.

GENERAL PRINCIPLES

It is of the essence of a lease that it conveys the right to exclusive possession on the tenant; that is, the right in the tenant to exclude all comers from the property, including the landlord.[28] That is now regarded as so trite that it almost needs no authority in support. There must also be a term, one which is certain at the outset.[29] It is said that there must also be a rent, but this assertion is, in most cases, incorrect.[30] As it confers a property right on the occupier, it must also be properly granted at law or in equity.[31]

Certain agreements which confer on an occupier exclusive possession for a term may, however, not be leases: where there is no intention to enter into legal relations; where the landlord has no power to grant a tenancy;[32] or where the

---

[28] *Street v Mountford* [1985] AC 809; note that the reservation by the landlord of limited rights of entry confirms the exclusivity of the tenant's possession for, otherwise, there would have been no need to make such a reservation: at 818C.

[29] There is a line of authority going back to *Say v Smith* (1530)1 Plowd 269, affirmed by the House of Lords in *Prudential Assurance v London Residuary Body* [1992] 2 AC 386; for the effects, see *Berrisford v Mexfield Housing Co-operative* [2011] UKSC 52.

[30] *Street*, cf. *Ashburn Anstalt v Arnold* [1989] Ch 1, pointing out that the definition of a term of years absolute in the Law of Property Act 1925 does not require a rent; note, however, s. 54(2), which requires a proper rent for informally created legal leases.

[31] Law of Property Act 1925, ss. 52 & 54(2); Law of Property (Miscellaneous Provisions) Act 1989, s. 2.

[32] Compare *Camden London BC v Shortlife Community Housing* (1992) 90 LGR 358 and *Bruton v London &*

occupation is referable to some other relationship (e.g. employment, seller/buyer, tolerated trespasser).[33] These were regarded as 'exceptional categories' in *Street v Mountford*[34] but their exceptionalism is an empirical question, the answer to which is likely to depend in part on the reception of the prevailing statutory regulation.

Where there is more than one person who takes under the agreement (or agreements), the question also arises whether they are joint tenants, in the co-ownership sense.[35] If there is no express joint tenancy created, then the question is whether one can be inferred from the surrounding circumstances. Here, one needs to find the 'four unities' – possession, interest, time, title – but there appears to be a fundamental disagreement on the authorities. The problem usually arises where the occupiers take under separate agreements containing separate obligations in relation to the rent. How can one nevertheless get unity of interest and title from those facts? In *Antoniades v Villiers*,[36] the House of Lords felt able to engage in a process of legal alchemy by reading two separate agreements together, Lord Templeman regarding them as interdependent (as opposed to independent of each other). By contrast, in apparently similar circumstances, the Court of Appeal in *Mikeover v Brady* were unable to read the two separate agreements together '... because the monetary obligations of the two parties were not joint obligations and there was accordingly no complete unity of interest'.[37] The judgments appear irreconcilable (and it is no answer to that irreconcilability to say that one of the occupiers moved out subsequently in *Mikeover*, because the relevant date for determining the nature of the agreements is the date on which they were entered into).

The body of law described above proceeds by reference to the actual agreement itself. The agreement rules, although the labels the parties give to the agreement are irrelevant – it is the effect in law of the agreement which is crucial.[38] By contrast to that line of authority is another line which requires a rather different evaluation which goes beyond the tenancy agreement. Here, the question is whether the agreement itself (or clauses in it) is, in fact, a 'pretence'.[39] Originally, Lord Templeman had referred to the need for the courts to be '... astute to detect and frustrate sham devices and artificial transactions whose only object is to disguise the grant of a tenancy and to evade the Rent

---

Quadrant Housing Trust [2000] 1 AC 406. In the latter, although L&Q had no relevant estate, a tenancy by estoppel was created from the fact of a grant of exclusive possession for a term to an occupier who accepted it.

[33] *Errington v Errington* [1952] 1 KB 290, 297.

[34] [1985] AC 809 at 821.

[35] It is unclear, at best, why it was assumed that the parties were either joint tenants or licensees, and no consideration was given to whether they might be tenants in common – see the classic article by Peter Sparkes, 'Co-Tenants, Joint Tenants and Tenants in Common' (1989) 18(2) *AALR* 151; for further discussion, see S. Bright, *Landlord and Tenant Law in Context* (Hart, 2007), p.99.

[36] [1990] 1 AC 417.

[37] (1989) 21 HLR 513, 523.

[38] *Street* at 819E-F.

[39] *Antoniades*, 462H.

Acts'.[40] The problem with the latter formulation was the excessively narrow formulation of the doctrine of 'sham' developed in a different context.[41] The shift to 'pretence' was, one might infer, a recognition that this doctrine was designed to be more wide-ranging.

THE QUESTION OF 'TERM'

It is of the essence of an estate in land that it exists for a certain period. If there is an uncertain term, it will be void in law. The rule is that one needs to be able to tell, at the outset of the term, the maximum possible duration. Thus, in *Prudential Assurance v London Residuary Body*,[42] a term which allowed the occupier to take the property until the landlord required it for road widening was held to be void. A periodic tenancy, which rolls on from one period to the next, is valid only because the period itself (be it weekly, monthly or yearly) is certain, even though the tenancy may run on for an uncertain period until it is determined. However, 'A power for nobody to determine or for one party only to be able to determine is inconsistent with the concept of a term from year to year.'[43]

In *Berrisford v Mexfield Housing Co-Operative Ltd*,[44] the Supreme Court was able, on ancient authority, to circumvent this strict rule. The problem arose because Ms Berrisford (like many other tenants of a co-operative) had entered into a tenancy which provided that the term of the tenancy was to be from month to month. If it had stopped there, then that term would have been valid. However, it did not do so. Clause 6 of the agreement provided that the co-operative could 'ONLY' determine the tenancy by exercise of a right of re-entry on four limited grounds. Mexfield served notice to quit on Ms Berrisford after she fell into rent arrears (although those arrears were paid off). Mexfield did not purport to exercise their right of re-entry under clause 6, but to argue that, as the contractual term was void due to uncertainty as a result of the fetter on their right to determine the monthly tenancy, it became a periodic tenancy.

In the Court of Appeal, Ms Berrisford's defence was that the agreement retained its validity in *equity* when the original contracting parties remain in place.[45] The arguments here were finely balanced – should equity follow the law and hold that the restriction on the landlord's right to determine has no effect, or does equity have some life beyond the law, so that the contract can be given effect by way of specific performance?[46] The Court of Appeal, by majority, accepted the former proposition, on the basis that, in the absence of a trust or estoppel or

---

[40] *Street*, 825H.

[41] *Snook v London & West Riding Investments Ltd* [1967] 2 QB 786, 802, Diplock LJ.

[42] [1992] AC 386.

[43] At 394F.

[44] [2011] UKSC 52. For an excellent commentary, see K.Low, 'Certainty of Terms and Leases: Curiouser and Curiouser' [2012] 75(3) MLR 401.

[45] *Berrisford v Mexfield Housing Co-Operative Ltd* [2011] 2 WLR 423; the point being that in *Prudential*, the House of Lords were concerned with successors in title and not the original contractors.

[46] Of interest is that proprietary estoppel has not, hitherto, been relied upon by Ms Berrisford.

unconscionability, equity should normally follow the law (a reading which may well be too narrow).

Before the Supreme Court, however, the focus for Ms Berrisford's argument shifted, and decisively so, in her favour. Her argument was that the contractual term was void; that it was incapable of being a tenancy as a matter of law; but that prior to the LPA 1925 it would have taken effect as a tenancy for life (determinable earlier on the events in clause 6 of the agreement); and, after 1925, it became a tenancy for 90 years determinable earlier on the basis of the contractually agreed methods of termination (as a result of section 149(6), LPA 1925). The Supreme Court accepted this analysis. The majority also held that, in any event, as the parties were the original contracting parties, either way the contract into which they had entered was enforceable between them. This point serves as a warning to us property lawyers never to forget that property rights bite when issues of durability arise, but that the contractual obligations between the original contracting parties are enforceable in the ordinary way.

Nevertheless, it is the process of reasoning by which the Supreme Court, Lord Neuberger giving the leading judgment, reached that conclusion which is important. Mexfield first argued that, on a proper construction of the agreement, it created a monthly tenancy, determinable by one month's notice in accordance with established common law principles. This argument was rejected on the basis of principles of ordinary contractual interpretation: what would the reasonable person think that this agreement created as a term?[47] It was clear on the face of the agreement that Mexfield could *only* determine the agreement in accordance with clause 6. Furthermore, '...given the circumstances in which the Agreement was entered into, it seems unlikely that Ms Berrisford's security was intended to be so tenuous as to be determinable by Mexfield on one month's notice at any time from the day the Agreement was made'.[48] On the second question, whether the agreement could constitute a tenancy as a matter of law, Ms Berrisford conceded that it could not, following a line of authority culminating in *Prudential*. That gave rise to many comments about the unsatisfactory state of the certainty rule in leases, although the Supreme Court felt that, on the facts of this case, they could not overrule such a long-standing principle. That was for Parliament. They expressed their opinions in characteristically forthright terms, as had Lord Browne-Wilkinson in *Prudential*.[49] On the third proposition, there was plenty of authority to demonstrate that, before 1925, a tenancy with an uncertain term would have been regarded as a tenancy for life. Furthermore, that seemed to have been the intention of the agreement in this case, subject to earlier determination on the basis of clause 6 (as well as Ms Berrisford's right to determine the tenancy earlier, in clause 5). However, importantly, the same rule would seem to apply even if

---

[47] See, for example, *Mannai Investment Co Ltd v Eagle Star Life Assurance Co Ltd* [1997] AC 749.
[48] [19]. The agreement was entered into as part of a mortgage rescue scheme – Mexfield re-paid the mortgage which Ms Berrisford could not afford and granted the tenancy to her.
[49] [34], Lord Neuberger; [80], Lord Hope; [93]–[96], Baroness Hale; [105] & [111], Lord Clarke; [115] & [119] Lord Dyson.

the parties did not intend for such an outcome.[50] On the fourth ground, section 149(6) LPA 1925 clearly rewrites tenancies for life into terms of 90 years which are determinable on the same bases as the previous common law allowed. The fact that such arguments were not pursued in the leading cases of *Lace v Chantler* and *Prudential* was neither here nor there because the point was not argued in those cases.[51] It now appears, as Lord Neuberger (who was the unsuccessful counsel in *Prudential*) put it, 'Some of the statements about the law by Lord Greene and Lord Templeman can now be seen to be extravagant or inaccurately wide, but it is only fair to them to repeat that this was, at least in part, because the tenancy for life argument was not raised before them'.[52]

This does raise an oddity, though: the rule only applies where the tenant is an individual and not a corporate entity. As Lord Dyson put it, 'To treat an individual and a corporate entity differently in this respect can only be explained on historical grounds. The explanation may lie in the realms of history, but that hardly provides a compelling justification for maintaining the distinction today.'[53]

THE USES OF INTENTION

The previous section was neutral on the uses of intention in the creation of proprietary interests. However, intention is *the* central consideration. In the opening question of whether, on the face of the agreement, exclusive possession for a term has been granted, the intention is not the subjective intention of the parties. That is why the labels the parties give to the agreement are irrelevant. The question is whether, as a matter of law, the occupier has been granted exclusive possession on the face of the agreement. Here, it is also said, the regulatory protections of the Rent and Housing Acts are also irrelevant ('... they must not be allowed to alter or influence the construction of an agreement')[54], although perhaps the whole basis for the judgment in *Street* was to halt the practice of landlords contracting out of those very protections (certainly, that was the reason why the case was so significant at the time).

As regards the exceptional categories, intention is being used rather differently. Here, the courts are encouraged to look at the identity of, and relationship between, the parties in considering whether there was an intention to enter into legal relationships. If the parties are friends or relations, one might begin to wonder whether they really did intend to enter into legal relations, with the consequences which might subsequently occur. If a lease is created, then the Rent/Housing Acts become relevant – did they really mean to convey those protections (a less relevant question after the Housing Act 1988 assured shorthold tenancy regime). Rent

---

[50] See, for example, Baroness Hale, [94].

[51] [1944] KB 268, [53]. It is to be noted that this point would not have saved the tenancy agreement in *Prudential* in any event, as the original lessee was probably dead and a company cannot take a tenancy for 'life' as it has no 'life'.

[52] [53].

[53] [119].

[54] *Street*, 825H.

becomes an important, albeit not decisive, indicator. If no rent is paid, again one might wonder whether they intended to enter into legal relations. The key point, though, is that we are moving into the realms of subjective intention.

A tenancy by way of estoppel, however, offers an odd conjunction of both objective and subjective intentions. In *Bruton v London and Quadrant Housing Trust*,[55] the House of Lords were faced with this problem of intention. Lambeth council had a property in Brixton which they wanted to re-develop into flats. In the meantime, they entered into a licence agreement with L&Q for use as short-term accommodation for homeless persons. It was clear that Lambeth had no power to do more than that.[56] The licence agreement explicitly stated that L&Q could only grant licences to those homeless households to occupy the property. L&Q could not grant tenancies. The licence agreement between L&Q and Mr Bruton accordingly said

> As has been explained to you, the above property is being offered to you by [L&Q] on a weekly Licence from 6 February 1989. The Trust has the property on licence from [Lambeth] who acquired the property for development...and pending this development, it is being used to provide temporary housing accommodation. It is offered to you on the condition that you will vacate upon receiving reasonable notice from the Trust, which will not normally be less than four weeks. You understand and agree that while you are living in the property, you will allow access at all times during normal working hours to the staff of the Trust, the owners and agents for all purposes connected with the work of the Trust.

Mr Bruton also agreed 'To permit the Trust or its agents, surveyors or consultants to enter the property for the purpose of inspecting the state of repair and cleanliness of the property or any purpose connected at all reasonable hours of the day'. Mr Bruton was to pay £18 per week for his occupation of the property.

The question arose for the House as to whether, despite these clear circumstances and facts, Mr Bruton in fact was entitled to the benefit of certain statutory repairing covenants.[57] He would only have been so entitled if he had, in fact, a tenancy. How could a tenancy be manufactured from such unpromising facts? The starting point is the objective intention of the parties: did Mr Bruton have exclusive possession for a term at a rent? It was held that he did. Lord Hoffmann said '... [T]he classification of the agreement as a lease does not depend upon any intention additional to that expressed in the choice of terms. It is simply a question of characterising the terms which the parties have agreed. This is a question of law.'[58] The reservation of the right of entry to inspect the property for the state of repair and cleanliness merely emphasized that Mr Bruton had exclusive

---

[55] [2000] 1 AC 406.
[56] Housing Act 1985, s. 32(3).
[57] Landlord and Tenant Act 1985, s. 11.
[58] See also Lord Hobhouse's pithy observation: 'The relevant question is simply one of ascertaining the effect in law of the agreement which the parties made'.

possession.[59] The argument that L&Q had no power to grant a tenancy and did not represent that they had such a power was irrelevant (which surely meant that one of the essential elements of the estoppel (the representation) was absent) was met by Lord Hoffmann with the observation that

> ... it is not the estoppel which creates the tenancy, but the tenancy which creates the estoppel. The estoppel arises when one or other of the parties wants to deny one of the ordinary incidents or obligations of the tenancy on the ground that the landlord had no legal estate. The basis of the estoppel is that having entered into an agreement which constitutes a lease or tenancy, he cannot repudiate that incident or obligation.

The House was forced to emphasize the contractual element of the landlord–tenant relation.[60] Leases usually convey property rights, and L&Q had no property rights to convey to Mr Bruton – that is, as an ordinary application of the rule, *nemo dat quod non habet* (you can't give what you don't have). But here, Lord Hoffmann circumvented that rule with the observation that '... it is the fact that the agreement is a lease which creates the proprietary interest. It is putting the cart before the horse to say that whether the agreement is a lease depends upon whether it creates a proprietary interest.'[61]

Counsel for L&Q argued, however, that, even if the agreement had all the attributes of a tenancy, it was an example of an 'exceptional' case so as to take it outside the domain of landlord and tenant. Attention was drawn to the socially valuable functions of L&Q, and the circumstances of the case – all parties including Lambeth had never said or agreed that Mr Bruton could have a tenancy. Furthermore, at least Lords Slynn and Jauncey recognized that their judgment would cause problems in terms of future provision for homeless households as these types of arrangements would be curtailed by the effect of their judgment.[62] However, this was not one of the exceptional cases because the character of the landlord and the agreement with Mr Bruton was irrelevant. As regards the latter, the key point was that 'one cannot contract out of' the security of tenure legislation by claiming the agreement was something that it was not.[63] So, Mr Bruton was left with a very odd type of right – he could enforce the landlord and tenant covenants, especially of repair, against L&Q, but it was a tenancy by estoppel, a type of non-proprietary lease which would have limited effect, if any, on third parties. Indeed, it could be defeated by L&Q doing what they, in fact, did: surrendering their interest to Lambeth. That led to another story, about human rights, which is discussed in Chapter 8.

---

[59] Following Lord Templeman's remark to the same effect in *Street*, at 818.

[60] For discussion, see M. Wonnacott, *Possession of Land* (Cambridge University Press, 2006) pp. 15–17; cf J.-P. Hinjosa, 'On Property, Leases, Licences, Horses and Carts: Revisiting *Bruton v London & Quadrant Housing Trust*' [2005] *Conveyancer and Property Lawyer* 114.

[61] At 415C.

[62] At 410D, 412B.

[63] At 414D–E.

The same point about the relevance of subjective intention is equally relevant in co-ownership cases. It is significant that, in *Antoniades v Villiers*,[64] Lord Templeman quotes from the evidence given by Mr Villiers and Ms Bridger, the occupiers:

> He [Antoniades] kept going on about it being a licence and not in the Rent Act. I didn't know either but was pleased to have a place after three or four months of chasing. I didn't understand what was meant by exclusive possession or licence. Signed because so glad to move in. Had been looking for three months.[65]

Antoniades clearly intended both subjectively and on the face of the agreement to grant a licence. That was what the occupiers took and knew that they had taken. There was a clause in the agreement which allowed Antoniades to introduce further occupiers into the property, should he so wish. However, the property was only suitable for those living in 'quasi-connubial bliss'.[66] The reservation of that right was inconsistent with the Rent Acts and could not be enforced; separately, though, it was clearly not a genuine reservation of the right and it was, therefore, a pretence. In order to ascertain its genuineness the evidence extended beyond the agreement to the surrounding circumstances as well as the parties' subsequent conduct.[67]

The significance of the evidence of the occupiers is that the basis for the doctrine of pretence is the same as that for the Rent/Housing Acts – a broad-based jurisdiction concerned with inequality of bargaining power, premised on an assumption of disequilibrium between landlord and tenant in a situation of over-demand for a limited supply of accommodation.[68] The empirical basis for that justification is questionable. It is clear that the private rented sector is made up of a number of heterogeneous sub-sectors, such as the student market, the housing benefit market, the 'top end', etc.[69] Different considerations apply in each sub-sector. There are also geographical differences between areas as to the supply of private rented housing.

The key issue on the nature of intention in 'pretence' cases regards the subjective intentions of the parties. In *Antoniades*, the clause clearly was not genuine. However, in *Bankway Properties Ltd v Pensfold-Dunsford*,[70] there was a genuine clause which the parties clearly intended would be enforced. At the outset, the rent was £4,680 per annum payable by equal monthly instalments of £390 per month. Mr Pensfold-Dunsford was in receipt of housing benefit, a fact known to

---

[64] [1990] 1 AC 417.

[65] At 462.

[66] *Street*, 825G.

[67] At 475.

[68] J. Hill, 'Intention and the Creation of Proprietary Rights: Are Leases Different?' (2000) 16(2) *Legal Studies* 200, 214.

[69] See, for example, J. Rugg & D. Rhodes, *The Private Rented Sector: Its Contribution and Potential* (Centre for Housing Policy, 2008).

[70] [2001] 1 WLR 1369.

Bankway (a company owned by the mega-wealthy Pears family). After 12 months, however, clause 8(2)(iii) of the tenancy agreement said that the rent would rise to £25,000 p.a., a figure which all parties knew would not be paid by the housing benefit authority. This was a genuine clause in the sense that Bankway expected it to be enforced. However, its enforcement would also (at that time) take the agreement outside the protection of the Housing Act 1988 because it was outside the rent limits. The agreement had been intended to create an assured tenancy by Bankway.[71] The Court of Appeal held that this rent increase 'device' was not genuine. In part this was based on the surrounding circumstances – the clause had not been individually negotiated and Bankway only demanded the increased rent at a time subsequent to when they could have demanded it, essentially to obtain possession without the need to prove a relevant ground under the 1988 Act.[72] However, Arden LJ went further

> In my judgment, when the facts of this case are examined as a whole, it is clear, that, as the Judge found, clause 8(b)(iii) was merely a device. It was in reality a provision which would enable the landlord to obtain possession of the premises. As such, clause 8(b)(iii) masqueraded as a provision for an increase of rent: it was not in substance a provision for the payment of rent. It was introduced to enable the landlord to bring the assured tenancy to an end when it chose. In some cases the tenant might be expected to leave voluntarily. In other cases such as this, the landlord would have to make an application to the court but (subject to the outcome of this appeal) that would only be a formality since the rent was much higher than a tenant could be expected to pay. The landlord, therefore, did not have to give the tenants the last opportunity which they obtain in the usual way to pay the rent arrears at the door of the court to avoid an order for possession. The landlord may, as Miss Padley submits, have intended to demand rent but it had no genuine expectation that it would ever receive any rent under clause 8(b)(iii).[73]

She preferred to base her judgment on the basis that Bankway had effectively sought to contract out of the statutory protection, something which could not be done in the scheme of the 1988 Act. Pill LJ preferred to base his concurring judgment on the principle that the clause was inconsistent with the 1988 Act.[74] Bright concludes her comment on this case with the observation that: 'No longer will it be sufficient to ask if something is genuine, or allowed; instead the test

---

[71] That may have enabled them to take advantage of tax concessions at that time.

[72] See Susan Bright's critical commentary on these reasons, 'Avoiding Tenancy Legislation: Sham and Contracting Out Revisited' (2002) 61(1) *CLJ* 146, 165: 'Devious the clause may be, but it is hard to see how it is an unlawful contracting out of the legislation given that the legislation permits the landlord and tenant to agree the initial rent and any provisions for reviewing it'.

[73] At [55].

[74] At [68], which Bright also critiques at 166–67.

will be whether "in substance" it is allowed. This will be a much more difficult question to answer.'[75]

Debate 3

Rights and their amelioration

Most tenancy agreements will contain a list of obligations on one or both of the parties. This list usually relates to the core terms of the bargain – the rent to be payable and the term of the agreement – as well as peripheral terms. The great debates here are, first, over the extent to which it is proper for the law to interfere in bargains, and the second over the proper judicial approach. It has always been accepted that these obligations generally only apply to leases, and not licences, although the justification for that division seems rather unclear today.[76]

As regards the former, the debate was settled in the nineteenth century, perhaps paradoxically at the zenith of the free market movement, in favour of certain limited interventions justified on the ground of public health.[77] Many such interventions remain in place, largely unamended,[78] their justification now being to do with length of existence together with a more generalized recognition of an inequality in the bargaining power between landlord and tenant; one might say that such justifications lack empirical validity but the law is a blunt instrument.

As regards the proper judicial approach, it can certainly be argued that the interpretation given by judges to these obligations has been to narrow them at almost every turn, thus ameliorating the potential burden on landlords.[79] That is not to say that fairly trenchant criticisms of the law have not been made, but that judges have felt constrained often to take a narrow view.[80]

Certain terms are implied into certain agreements either by the common law or by statute. A principal such statutory implied term, in leases of less than seven years, is the duty on the landlord to keep the property and its services in repair.[81] It has been said that one local authority spent more in defending disrepair claims at one stage than it did in actually conducting repairs to its housing stock. Those days are likely to be over now.[82] In any event, the nature of the obligation is

---

[75] At 168.

[76] See Law Commission, *Renting Homes*, Law Com No 284 (Law Commission, 2003), paras 6.19–20.

[77] Cowan, n.17, pp. 9–11.

[78] See, for example, the now mostly useless statutory implied condition of habitability: Landlord and Tenant Act 1985, s. 8, and the discussion in *Quick v Taff-Ely BC* [1986] QB 809.

[79] This is the position taken in J. Reynolds, 'Statutory Covenants of Fitness and Repair: Social Legislation and the Judges' (1974) 37(3) *MLR* 377; cf. M. Robinson, ' "Social Legislation" and the Judges: A Note by Way of Rejoinder' (1976) 39(1) *MLR* 43.

[80] Most prominently, see *Quick v Taff-Ely BC* [1986] QB 809.

[81] Landlord and Tenant Act 1985, s. 11.

[82] The Pre-Action Protocol for Housing Disrepair Cases has effectively made most claims for breach of this covenant settle at a much earlier stage.

limited and only begins when the landlord has notice of the defect.[83] However, there are two other issues which should be considered: unfair terms in tenancy agreements, and tenancy deposits.

What seem to be potentially powerful rights for the tenant turn out to be rather limited. So, for example, the right to 'quiet enjoyment' means something rather less than this. In *Southwark LBC v Mills*,[84] the tenants in a block of flats were continually disturbed by their neighbours because of a lack of sound insulation – essentially, the tenants could hear everything going on in their neighbours' flats. As Lord Hoffmann put it, the flat is not quiet and the tenants are not enjoying it; yet the covenant simply meant that the tenant has a right to enjoy the flat free of substantial interference from their landlord or those claiming under the landlord.

UNFAIR TERMS

The Office for Fair Trading has regulatory oversight for the jurisdiction opening up through the Unfair Terms in Consumer Contracts Regulations 1999,[85] over contracts entered into between a 'seller or supplier' and a 'consumer'. These provisions have been held to apply to both private and public landlords as well as between a letting agent and non-business landlord.[86]

Where a term is not 'core' to the agreement, and has not been individually negotiated, it '... shall be regarded as unfair if, contrary to the requirement of good faith, it causes a significant imbalance in the parties' rights and obligations arising under the contract, to the detriment of the consumer'.[87] Core terms are those which are the essence of the contract: the price and the main subject matter of the contract, as these were regarded as more likely to have been negotiated between the parties.[88] The requirement of good faith is 'one of fair and open dealing', which might be expressed as transparency and not taking advantage of the consumer.[89] All terms, core or not, must be drafted in plain, intelligible language and, where there is doubt about their meaning, 'the interpretation most favourable to the consumer shall prevail'.[90]

The Office of Fair Trading (OFT) produces written guidance setting out certain terms which it regards as potentially unfair as well as how the regulations are interpreted by them.[91] This notes, for example, that fairness depends not only

---

[83] *O'Brien v Robinson* [1973] AC 912; for discussion and critique, see Reynolds, n.79. As regards the development of the regulatory oversight of local authorities to the current 'health and safety rating system', see R. Burridge & D. Ormandy, 'Health and Safety at Home: Private and Public Responsibility for Unsatisfactory Housing Conditions' (2007) 34(4) *Journal of Law and Society* 544.

[84] [2001] 1 AC 1.

[85] SI 1999/2083, implementing Council Directive 93/13/EEC.

[86] *R(Khatun) v Newham LBC* [2002] HLR 29; *Office of Fair Trading v Foxtons Ltd* [2009] EWHC 1681.

[87] Reg. 5.

[88] *Abbey National plc v Office of Fair Trading* [2009] EWCA Civ 116, at [52].

[89] *Director General of Fair Trading v First National Bank plc* [2002] 1 AC 481, at [17], Lord Bingham.

[90] Reg. 7; on the limitations of plain English, see R. Assy, 'Can the Law Speak Directly to Its Subjects? The Limitations of Plain Language' (2011) 38(3) *Journal of Law and Society* 376.

[91] Office of Fair Trading, *Guidance on Unfair Terms in Tenancy Agreements* (OFT, 2005).

on how a contractual term is intended to be used, but also how it could be used (which depends on its breadth).[92] In relation to rights of the landlord to re-enter the property on the tenant's default (forfeiture clauses), the OFT states that it does not object to the inclusion of such clauses provided that the landlord makes clear the circumstances under which the landlord is entitled to re-enter. In other words, a right of re-entry on its own is unlikely to be viewed as unfair; although such terms must be in plain language and cannot give the landlord greater powers to end the tenancy than they would have under the law.[93]

TENANCY DEPOSITS

The story of tenancy deposits is a story of the interaction between, on the one hand, the concern about over-regulation of the private rented sector being over-ridden by other concerns about landlord behaviour, perhaps due more to political considerations than knowledge, and, on the other hand, judicial concerns about over-regulation resulting in an extremely narrow view being taken, so as to render the law practically useless. It provides an excellent case study, then, of the different motivations in play between landlords and tenants, as well as law and policy.

The starting point is the campaign that was run for some time by the Citizens Advice Bureau about the inadequate protection given to tenancy deposits, which reflected a view among certain politicians about the need to rein in private landlords, and concerns over their management practices. Private landlord associations and organizations were on the defensive but seemed to accept the need for at least some regulation because it would improve the image of the landlord. Self-regulation was deemed unsuccessful, but the evaluation of that regime wondered whether there was a need for any further regulation at all. However, at a late stage in the debates leading to the Housing Act 2004, the then government introduced the new regime.

The current law is that all tenancy deposits paid by tenants to landlords under an assured shorthold tenancy must be protected with an authorized scheme from the time that they are received.[94] A deposit is defined as any money intended to be held by the landlord or otherwise as security for the performance of the tenant's obligations or the discharge of any of the tenant's liability arising under or in connection with the tenancy.[95] The 'initial requirements of an authorised scheme' must have been complied with by the landlord within 14 days of receipt of the deposit.[96] The landlord must provide certain information to the tenant about the scheme, initial requirements and the operation of these statutory provisions in a

---

[92] Para. 2.6.

[93] Paras 4.16–4.18.

[94] s. 213(1). The definition of a landlord includes 'a person or persons acting on [the landlord's] behalf in relation to the tenancy or tenancies'.

[95] s. 212(8).

[96] s.213(3)–(4).

prescribed form or to the same effect as such a form within 14 days of receipt of the deposit.[97] The parties cannot contract out of these provisions.

Failure to comply with the initial requirements of an authorized scheme, failure to provide the information in the correct format, or, in effect, being misinformed by the landlord that a scheme applies to the deposit, entitles the tenant or any person who pays the deposit on behalf of the tenant to apply to the county court for certain relief.[98] One element of that relief includes the severe penalty of the landlord paying the tenant three times the amount of the deposit;[99] there is also a restriction on the landlord's ability to obtain possession through a section 21 notice:

(1) If a tenancy deposit has been paid in connection with a shorthold tenancy, no section 21 notice may be given in relation to the tenancy at a time when –
   (a) the deposit is not being held in accordance with an authorised scheme, or
   (b) the initial requirements of such a scheme (see section 213(4)) have not been complied with in relation to the deposit.
(2) If section 213(6) [failure of landlord to provide information to the tenant] is not complied with in relation to a deposit given in connection with a shorthold tenancy, no section 21 notice may be given in relation to the tenancy until such time as section 213(6)(a) is complied with.[100]

After a period of considerable uncertainty as to the interpretation of the provisions, the Court of Appeal 'eviscerated'[101] the protection apparently guaranteed by those provisions. In , the Court of Appeal (Sedley LJ strongly dissenting) held that a landlord in default of protecting the deposit within the prescribed 14 days was not liable to pay the penalty if they protected the deposit at any time prior to the county court hearing.[102] The policy reason for the decision was as follows:

> Such interpretation appears to me to be not only firmly supported by what I would regard as the carefully chosen statutory language, it is also a properly precise, or strict, one to apply to legislation such as section 214 that is manifestly penal in intent. Moreover, it is an interpretation that is consistent with the purpose of the legislation. That purpose is to achieve the due protection of deposits paid by tenants, ideally within the 14-day period but, if not, then later. It cannot be its purpose to punish landlords who may for example, for innocent reasons, be just a day late in securing such protection.[103]

---

[97] s.213(5)–(6).
[98] s.214(1)–(2).
[99] s.214(4).
[100] s. 215.
[101] *Tiensia v Universal Estates, Honeysuckle Properties Ltd v Fletcher* [2011] HLR 10, at [51], Sedley LJ.
[102] [2011] HLR 10; for rich discussion, see <http://nearlylegal.co.uk/blog/2010/11/tenancy-deposit-protection-eviscerated/>
[103] At [40].

In *Gladehurst Properties Ltd v Hashemi*,[104] the Court of Appeal continued that process of evisceration by holding that the penalty could not apply after the tenancy had come to an end. Part of the Court's reasoning turned on the observation that the tenant has it in their hands to secure the enforcement of the rules by bringing a claim, just as with other covenants[105] (an argument with an air of unreality to it when one considers the strong possibility that, as a result, the tenant may well be faced with an eviction or, at a more base level, losing trust with the landlord). The Court also noted the anomalies which would be caused by the tenant's argument, but of course, the Court's construction itself creates anomalies, for it protects both the scrupulous landlord who returns the deposit (subject to any necessary deductions) and the unscrupulous landlord who does not (or makes unnecessary deductions).[106] If the scheme had any purpose, it was to resolve costly and unnecessary legal disputes between the parties, but the effect of *Gladehurst* is that they will return.[107]

The problems caused by these hastily drafted provisions were recognized by legislators. In the Localism Act 2011, an attempt has been made to ameliorate them through various technical amendments, and, in particular, a more reflexive penalty.[108]

Debate 4

Determining a tenancy

GENERAL PRINCIPLES

Residential occupancies generally have to be determined by court order.[109] There are exceptions, but the usual situation today is that either the tenant has the protection of the Housing Act 1988 or the Housing Act 1985, or the more limited protection conferred by the Protection from Eviction Act 1977. Although tenancies for a fixed term are, as a matter of property law, determined at the end of the fixed term by effluxion of time, if they fall within the protection of the Housing Acts, there is provision for them to roll on for further periods determined by the period for which rent is payable.[110]

Under the 1977 Act, the landlord must give the tenant or licensee a notice to quit a tenancy or a periodic licence which must be in writing, containing certain

---

[104] [2011] EWCA Civ 604; for excellent discussion, see <http://nearlylegal.co.uk/blog/2011/05/eviscerated-now-also-drawn-and-quartered/>

[105] At [38]–[39].

[106] At [40]–[42].

[107] Indeed, in *Gladehurst* itself, one issue was over the landlord's retention of an amount from the returned deposit, the amount of the retention being in dispute.

[108] Localism Act 2011, s. 184.

[109] As regards commercial occupancies, see S. Bright, *Landlord and Tenant Law in Context* (Hart, 2007) Part 7.

[110] Housing Act 1985, s. 86; Housing Act 1988, s. 5.

information, and give at least four weeks (or the contractual period, if longer) before it is to take effect.[111] After such a notice has been served, if the occupier continues lawfully residing in the premises, then they may only be evicted by due process of law, that is to say, a court order, a provision which amends the landlord's common law self-help remedy of ejectment.[112] These provisions do not, however, apply to 'excluded' tenancies and licences – where the occupier shares accommodation in certain circumstances with the landlord/licensor or a member of their family.[113]

In *Hammersmith and Fulham LBC v Monk*, the House of Lords held that one of two joint tenants could lawfully end the tenancy by giving the landlord a notice to quit under the common law.[114] This rule has been particularly valuable to social landlords in making provision to deal with alleged perpetrators of domestic violence. The leaving partner is able to determine the tenancy in its entirety, thus leaving the remaining occupier/s effectively as trespassers and, in theory at least,[115] the court must grant the landlord possession of the property. The reasoning of the House of Lords in *Monk* was based on the contractual nature of the tenancy agreement and by analogy with the principles of the law of contract.[116] Although *Monk* must now be regarded with some caution, due to human rights considerations (see Chapter 8), it remains a powerful tool at the hands of the landlord and a legitimate device, as well as demonstrating the power of the contractual nature of the lease as a reasoning device.

The general rule beyond this, however, is that the landlord must obtain a court order in accordance with the relevant provisions of the Housing Acts 1985 or 1988.[117] There are some exceptions to the landlords caught by these rules – including mutual co-operatives – who are governed by the common law principles as amended by the 1977 Act. The 1985 and 1988 Acts provide procedural and substantive protections to the occupiers. As regards the former, they require relevant notices to be served; as regards the latter, they limit the grounds on which the landlord is entitled to possession. Under the 1985 Act, all the grounds are discretionary – the landlord has to prove the ground *and* that it is reasonable to grant possession. Under the 1988 Act, some of the grounds are discretionary but there are also mandatory grounds. As we have noted, for an assured shorthold tenancy, the landlord can determine the tenancy by means of a notice, subject to a court order which, in theory at least, must be granted.[118]

---

[111] s. 5(1) & (1A).

[112] s. 3(1) & (2).

[113] ss. 5(1B) & 3(1) & (2).

[114] [1992] 1 AC 478.

[115] This rider refers to the discussion in Chapter 8 concerning the proportionality defence under Human Rights Act 1998, sch. 1, art. 8.

[116] [1992] 1 AC 478, 483–89, Lord Bridge.

[117] The former applies to those landlords which fulfil the landlord condition (s. 79), which are generally 'public'; the latter applies to private landlords, but including certain quasi-private landlords, like housing associations.

[118] 1988 Act, s. 21.

UNLAWFUL EVICTION AND HARASSMENT

Due process is a particularly powerful motif of this area of law. It offers a different and in some ways more humane vision of the balance between the rights of the parties than existed in the nineteenth century. Due process can involve a fairly simple rubber-stamping – as in the accelerated procedure which can be used to determine an assured shorthold tenancy – but the stamp is what is important. Anything less than the stamp will not do unless the occupier has abandoned the property or terminated their occupation. An eviction without due process runs the risk at least of being unlawful; actions short of an eviction, but with the intention of getting the occupier out, run the risk of being unlawful.[119] Potentially, such actions give rise to both criminal and civil liability.[120] That few are prosecuted, and fewer successfully so, is neither here nor there. The likelihood is that this type of conduct occurs more frequently than is seen in the courts but what was referred to above as the 'status of moveability' means that it is easier for occupiers to move on.[121]

Prosecution and regulation of the private rented sector is generally in the hands of the local authority. The police rarely get involved (and, when they do, have been known to assist the landlord in their unlawful acts out of ignorance of the law[122]) despite the evident denial of property rights inherent in the act/s. The local authority is caught facing both ways – on the one hand, it is responsible for the regulation of the private rented sector, but on the other it is also responsible for its promotion, particularly to assist low- and no-income households. Prosecution can act to counter that second motivation.[123] Another counter-motivation lies in the very obscurity inherent in the law and the possibility that, if pursuing a civil claim, the level of damages may not provide adequate recompense for the considerable time and emotional energy engaged in pursuing the claim.[124]

CONCLUSIONS

Superficially, the great debate in this chapter concerns the (thin) dividing line between property and personal rights, as exemplified by the contortions in the distinction between leases and licences, together with the pragmatic reliance on the contract or property element of the relationship when it suits. However, the purpose of this chapter has been to go beyond that formal law and highlight its contexts, for those contexts highlight other great debates about the role (or rule) of law in society. The concerns and interests of property law give way to everyday understandings about the relationship and taken-for-granted assumptions on

---

[119] Protection from Eviction Act 1977, s. 1.

[120] For discussion, see Cowan, n.7, ch. 12.

[121] See further D. Cowan, 'Harassment and Unlawful Eviction in the Private Rented Sector – A Study of Law (in-)Action' [2001] *Conveyancer and Property Lawyer* 249.

[122] See, for example, *Cowan v Chief Constable for Avon and Somerset Constabulary* [2002] HLR 44.

[123] D. Cowan & A. Marsh, 'There's Regulatory Crime and Then There's Landlord Crime: from "Rachmanites" to "Partners" in Meeting Housing Need' (2001) 64(6) *MLR* 831.

[124] See, for example, *King v Jackson* (1998) 30 HLR 539.

which the landlord and tenant relationship is based. Attention has been drawn to the tensions which exist in regulating renting; these tensions appear at the meta-level, in terms of ideological assumptions about landlordism. What has become clear, at the level of pragmatic politics, is that landlordism is very much here to stay and that landlords should be protected from over-regulation; the assumption is that over-regulation will stifle the development of private renting.[125]

Further Reading

S. Bright, 'Avoiding Tenancy Legislation: Sham and Contracting Out Revisited' (2002) *CLJ* 146.

D. Cowan, *Housing Law and Policy* (Cambridge University Press, 2011).

Law Commission, *Renting Homes: Status and Security*, Law Commission Consultation Paper No 162 (London: Law Commission, 2002).

J. Reynolds, 'Statutory Covenants of Fitness and Repair' (1974) 37(3) *MLR* 377.

P. Sparkes, 'Co-Tenants, Joint Tenants and Tenants in Common' (1989) 18(2) *AALR* 151.

---

[125] These arguments are further developed and contextualized in Cowan, n.7, ch. 3.

5

LAND REGISTRATION

INTRODUCTION

A central feature of modern English land law is the emphasis placed on registration of title (or, more accurately following the Land Registration Act 2002, title *by* registration) as the definitive authority on the validity and priority of competing interests in registered land. The development of a practice of land registration was one of the key aims of the 1925 legislation (see Chapter 3), although earlier iterations of the system of registered land dated back to the late 1800s. In 1857 the Royal Commission on Registration of Title proposed a system of registration based around a central registry in London with district offices. The Land Registration Act 1862 provided for the registration of freehold estates in land. The system of registration adopted in England had its origins in a system that had been piloted in South Australia by that colony's then Prime Minister, Sir Robert Torrens. That model became known as 'Torrens-style' registration and was subsequently adopted in many countries around the world. In this chapter, we address five great debates about land registration which broadly relate to (1) the relationship between mapping land and title; (2) the definitiveness of the register; (3) whether the bureaucratization of land is necessary and justified in the interests of efficiency and the shift to e-conveyancing; (4) the significance of rationality over material possession of land; and (5) the practical changes of the philosophical shift to title by registration.

Debate 1

How does the process of mapping territory affect conceptions of land ownership?

The development of land registration systems, designed to provide a public record of ownership and transactions in land, can be distinguished from the process of cadastral mapping, which is based on a detailed survey of territory for administrative purposes (usually planning or taxation), although there can be some overlap (for example, when the land registration system also functions as a cadastre).[1] The idea of cadastral mapping as an administrative tool dates back to the Romans, who drew up large-scale plans of the Empire to administer the allocation of land and facilitate the collection of taxes. Many subsequent cadastral mapping projects have linked property and topography with fiscal or juridical bureaucratic schemes.[2] The extent to which a map – even one based on a detailed survey of the territory – can adequately represent the social space to which it refers, and property rights in that space, is controversial; it is argued that 'property and cartography are quite different ways of knowing land: neither is a mirror of nature'.[3] Pottage explained that 'There is an essential distinction between the understandings which arise from the possession or use of land, and which support the attribution or recognition of property rights, and those which are presupposed by cartography'.[4] The map is only ever a representation of the land, and representations are always loaded with the meanings and values of the representor. Consequently, 'A pervasive theme in much contemporary commentary on cartography is that topography is never innocent. It serves a range of disguised interests.'[5]

The implications of this type of mapping exercise have attracted particular attention amongst post-modern and post-colonial geographers, who have emphasized the role of surveying and mapping of land as a key pillar in colonial policies and as one of the colonizer's tools for wielding power to dispossess indigenous populations.[6] There can be no doubt that the drawing of cadastral maps was an important step in enabling colonial powers to exercise control and exert administrative authority over territory. In imperialist terms, the cadastral map is viewed as a Western tool imposed on indigenous populations; lands that were deemed *terra nullius* were treated as empty of inhabitants with existing legal rights to the territory, and the process of cadastral mapping applied the colonizing state's property laws and conceptions of ownership to the mapped territory, so functioning as a tool to subject indigenous peoples to the laws of the colonizer. Thus, the colonizers often displaced (or uneasily co-existed with) existing customary conceptions of place, property and land ownership, under the moral justification of 'modernisation', or the claim of bringing order and civilization to bear over 'savagery'.[7] When Western imperialists mapped colonial territories, their cadastres tended

[1] E. Cooke, 'Land Cadastres/Registries in the Developed World' In S. Smith, M. Elsinga, L. Fox O'Mahony, S. Ong and S. Wachter (eds), *The International Encyclopaedia of Housing and Home* (Elsevier, 2011).

[2] A. Pottage, 'The Measure of Land' (1994) 57(3) *MLR* 361 at 374, fn 64.

[3] Ibid, 362.

[4] Ibid, 362–63.

[5] J. Harley, 'Deconstructing the Map' (1989) 26(1) *Cartographica* 1.

[6] K. Beamer and T. Ka'eo Duarte, 'Mapping the Hawaiian Kingdom: A Colonial Venture' (2006) 2 *Haw JL & Pol* 34; B. Braun, *The Intemperate Rainforest: Nature, Culture and Power on Canada's West Coast* (University of Minnesota Press, 2002); T. Mitchell, *Colonising Egypt* (Cambridge University Press, 1991); E. Stokes, 'Contesting Resources: Maori, Pakeha, and a Tenurial Revolution' in E. Pawson and T. Brooking (eds), *Environmental Histories of New Zealand* (Oxford University Press, 2002); C. Harris, 'How Did Colonialism Dispossess? Comments from An Edge of Empire' (2004) 94(1) *Annals of the Association of American Geographers* 165.

[7] Harris, n.6.

to reflect a particular, Western understanding of the world and of the meaning of place, which was often imposed notwithstanding its disjunctions with Native meanings, although it should be recognized that there was some variation in the extent to which surveys and maps produced in 'colonies' reflected, or were based upon, the original inhabitants' conceptions of the land and its boundaries.[8]

The ways in which colonial powers mapped indigenous land (with mapping a precursor to allocations of territory to incomers, and 'lands treated as empty slates that need to be rationally ordered for future land use purposes')[9] differed significantly from their mapping of their own land (when pre-existing use formed the basis of the map).[10] In either case, cadastral mapping had clear political and economic implications: it provided a technique for governing territory, usually for the purposes of exploiting its natural resources. While the colonial mapping enterprise differed significantly from mapping within England and Wales, both were driven by a combination of political (control) and economic (maximizing capital gain from the land) goals.

Attempts to embed registered land in England and Wales, dating back to 1862, swung between 'meticulous accuracy in defining the land, cost what it might in money and hostility between landowners'[11] and a combination of broadly defined boundaries combined with physical inspection of the land and discussions with persons in actual occupation to ascertain the extent of the property. This was the position adopted by the Land Registration Act 1925, which directed that the land be verbally described, and a plan included to *assist* identification of the property.[12] Under the scheme set up by the Land Registration Rules 1925, the Registry itself was authorized, using the Ordnance Survey maps as the basis for its plans, to produce accurate and co-ordinated maps where land was registered, while technological developments in recent decades have greatly enhanced the quality and accuracy of Ordnance Survey maps even in areas of unregistered land.

The science of mapping affected a shift from narrative topography – the 'topographical story' – which involved descriptions of land, with reference to local landmarks, or activities carried out on the land, which encapsulated the 'local sense of place and property',[13] to geometric topography. By this process, mapping translated memory and experience to geometry,[14] so that the 'cartographic ideal [became] a sort of "placeless" description, a tracing transferable between

---

[8] Beamer & Ka'eo Duarte, n.6, 35, arguing that colonial maps of the continental US were notable in their lack of regard for the indigenous peoples' conceptions of the land and its boundaries; see also E. Price, *Dividing the Land: Early American Beginnings of Our Private Property Mosaic* (University of Chicago Press, 1995) p. 11.

[9] Beamer & Ka'eo Duarte, n.6, 41.

[10] Ibid; citing J. Scott, *Seeing Like a State* (Yale University Press, 1998) p. 49.

[11] J. Stewart-Wallace, 'Land Registration in England in Relation to Mapping and Surveying' (1931) 17 *Conv* 45, at 48.

[12] Ibid, 49–50.

[13] Pottage (1994), n.2, 365.

[14] Ibid, 366.

localities',[15] to create a 'rational' or 'linear space'.[16] Territory was rationalized in the sense that the map followed principles of standardization, simplification and economy,[17] and through its promotion of, and reliance on, the science of mapping, registration 'made "land" a calculable and finite surface rather than a lived and remembered medium',[18] bringing into the public domain what was previously a private matter. Indeed, Pottage traces the bureaucratization of land to the mapping function of land registration:

> Registration extricated land from the network of relations and under-standings which formed the 'local knowledge' of different communities, relocated it on an abstract geometric map, and deciphered it according to a highly conventionalised topographic code. This process marked a trans-formation in the idea of land in law: property ceased to be a contractual construct and became a bureaucratic artefact.[19]

This shift had major implications for the development of conceptions of land ownership in England and Wales.

At first, registration of land in England and Wales was voluntary, but this was not terribly successful: not only was it not compulsory to register the ownership of the land, but once property was registered there was no compulsion to register any subsequent transactions, so that the person registered as owner of the property might not be the current owner. After 1862, reformers began to consider the prospect of compulsory registration, although they faced considerable opposition from the legal profession. It was therefore a triumph for land law reformers when the Land Registration Act 1925 introduced compulsory registration in England and Wales.[20] The key aims of the land registration system created in 1925 reso-nated with the general goals of the 1925 legislation, including easing, facilitating and speeding conveyancing, protecting the interests of purchasers and assuring the security of land transactions. The Land Registration Act 1925 formed the basis for the system of land ownership and transfer for over 75 years and still provides much of the structural underpinnings for the current system – by no means did the 2002 Act invent the wheel.

In 1998, a joint report of the Law Commission and the Land Registry had proposed an overhaul of the entire system of title registration. A further joint report, *Land Registration for the Twenty-First Century: A Conveyancing Revolution* was published in 2001, and the substantial changes proposed in this report were

---

[15] Ibid, 368.
[16] Ibid, 370.
[17] Ibid, 381.
[18] Ibid, 381.
[19] Ibid, 363.
[20] A. Offer, 'Lawyers and Land Law Revisited' (1994) 14(3) *OJLS* 269, arguing that the opposition of practi-tioners to the 1925 reforms were self-interested; and S. Anderson, *Lawyers and the Making of English Land Law, 1832–1940* (Clarendon Press, 1992) p. 227, arguing that these same practitioners were also keen to make a valuable contribution to the reform process.

implemented in the Land Registration Act 2002 (LRA 2002), which came into force on 13 October 2003.

Debate 2

Can (and should) the register be definitive of interests in land?

At its core, land law is composed of the rules that regulate competing interests, such as those of purchasers on the one hand, and owners or subsidiary interest-holders on the other. The role of any system of registration is underpinned by two key issues: when it is reasonable for the purchaser to be bound by prior subsidiary interests; and when it is reasonable to require that an interest in land be registered at the risk of defeasibility for non-registration. There are three types of registration system: (1) registration of deeds, where a copy of any deed affecting the property is kept in a central register (this system has not played a significant role in English land law); (2) registration of specific interests, for example, requiring that some or all equitable interests must be registered, as in the Land Charges Register for unregistered land in England and Wales; and (3) title registration, the most modern of the three types of system, and radically different from the other systems.

Under the English system of title registration, each title is registered with its own file which indicates the ownership of the property (a single plot of land may have more than one registered interest, for example a freehold and leasehold interest); most legal interests must be registered in order to have legal effect, and equitable rights must be protected by entry on the register. Registration is effectively a state guarantee of title to land; but interests protected by an entry in the register do not guarantee the existence of the right but merely ensure that, if the right exists, it will bind successors to the title. The system is underpinned by three core principles. The 'mirror principle' requires that the register reflect the position regarding the ownership of the land and the third party interests affecting it: the register should be a complete and accurate reflection of the state of the title to the land at any given time, so that it is possible to investigate title to land with the absolute minimum of additional enquiries and inspections. The 'curtain principle' requires that the register should be the sole and definitive source of information for purchasers, so that a purchaser does not need to go behind the 'curtain' to ascertain interests that will bind. Finally, the insurance principle refers to the state-backed guarantee that supports the information contained in the register, such that, even if the register is inaccurate, it is authoritative. If any loss is suffered as a result of reliance on an error in the register, compensation can be claimed from a state fund. The principal flaw in the application of these principles to registered land in England and Wales is the category of 'overriding interests' – interests that do not appear on the register, but are still binding on a purchaser.

The extent to which the land registry can be relied on as definitive of title constitutes one of the great debates of contemporary land law in England and Wales, and has triggered a series of further debates concerning the nature of land ownership and the extent to which the government (through the Land Registry) takes responsibility for protecting landowners' title once it is recognized through the register (see Chapter 6 on adverse possession). Aspects of this debate explored in this chapter include practical questions concerning the extent to which 'overriding interests' are permitted to constitute a 'crack' in the mirror principle, as well as more fundamental, philosophical questions about the nature of land ownership under the Land Registration Act 2002. The debate is positioned between the protection of the existing proprietary interests held by a range of claimants, and the facilitation of transactions by ensuring that purchasers are not bound by these interests unless they were on the register; between the protection of 'on the ground' interests and the transfer of clean title. Echoing the discussion of functions of land (for use and occupation, on the one hand, and its role in exchange, on the other) in Chapter 3, the Land Registration Act 2002 represented a crucial turning point in a related debate between the materiality of possession and the bureaucratization of title. Following the decisive steps taken towards the protection of purchasers, registered owners, and those interests which are *on* the register (as opposed to often less formal *off* register claims) in the Land Registration Act 2002, this chapter reflects on the implications of our commitment to perfecting the register for the philosophy of land law in England and Wales; the shift from land ownership rooted in possession; and an organic relationship between user and land to a bureaucratic system of title by registration which is increasingly removed from the land itself.

Debate 3

Is the bureaucratization of land necessary – and justified – in the interests of efficiency and e-conveyancing?

The business of title registration is performed by Her Majesty's Land Registry, a non-ministerial government department, with the Chief Land Registrar appointed by the Lord Chancellor. The administration of the system is organized around 24 District Land Registries which keep the register for land in their regions. With the largest property database in Europe, today's Land Registry underpins the economy of the United Kingdom by guaranteeing ownership of many billions of pounds worth of property. The economic function of the registry is reflected in the fact that (in normal economic conditions) approximately £1 million worth of property is processed every minute in England and Wales. In 1988, the information held by the Registry became open to the public, and the LRA 2002 allows any person to inspect and make copies of entries,[21] subject to some exclusions for sensitive information, and payment of a fee in certain cases. The register currently holds approximately 19.5 million registered titles, representing about 90 per cent of all titles in England and Wales (although considerably less of the land by

---

[21] LRA 2002, s. 66(1).

90

volume – approximately 70 per cent – with much of the unregistered land held by institutions, including the Crown).[22]

The land registry describes its current activities as registering title to land in England and Wales, and recording dealings (for example, sales and mortgages) with registered land. Its principal aims include 'maintaining and developing a stable, effective land registration system, guaranteeing title to registered estates and interests in land, enabling confident dealings in property and security of title by providing ready access to up-to-date and guaranteed land information, and matching the ever more ambitious performance targets set by the Lord Chancellor'.[23] The drive to ensure that the Land Registry is delivering value and efficiency influenced, in part, the move towards e-conveyancing for land transactions, which the LRA 2002 – described as a 'conveyancing revolution' – was intended to facilitate.

While earlier land registration provisions sought to ensure consistent approaches between unregistered and registered land, the LRA 2002 has moved away from that strategy, and is focused wholly on developing principles appropriate to registered land. A crucial feature (discussed below) is that it recognizes that the basis of title in unregistered land is *possession* while the basis of title in registered land is *registration*, and this philosophy is applied by tightening up the system to ensure that the register is as complete and accurate as possible. This was achieved by simplifying the system and by reducing the number of ways in which third-party interests can be recorded on the register. A further aspect to these reforms was that the 2002 Act paved the way for electronic conveyancing:

> The fundamental objective of the Bill is that, under the system of electronic dealing with land that it seeks to create, the register should be a complete and accurate reflection of the state of the title to the land at any given time, so that it is possible to investigate title to land online, with the absolute minimum of additional enquiries and inspections.[24]

When the 2002 Act was passed, it was intended that it would enable a shift to electronic conveyancing within three to five years. The development of the e-conveyancing project has been identified as an important aspect of the Land Registry's work to improve the quality of the service that it offers in facilitating land transactions – for example, by encouraging open access to chain information, and by providing a mechanism for all payments relating to transactions in a chain to be paid simultaneously and electronically, with automatic registration on completion.[25] It was hoped that this process would 'reduce the delay and anxiety which can be experienced in the house buying process'.[26]

---

22 M. Dixon, *Modern Land Law* (Routledge, 7th edn, 2010) p. 95, fn 1.

23 See Land Registry website <http://www.landregistry.gov.uk/>.

24 Land Registry and Law Commission, *Land Registration for the Twenty-First Century: A Conveyancing Revolution*, Law Com 271 (Law Commission, 2001) para. 1.5.

25 See Land Registry website <http://econsultations.e-conveyancing.gov.uk/consult.ti>.

26 Ibid.

Since electronic conveyancing requires that processes for the investigation of title are capable of being carried out online, it demands that the register is complete and accurate, with minimal need for additional enquiries and inspections. So, for example, one of the key changes introduced in the LRA 2002 in preparation for e-conveyancing was the abandonment of the requirement that a purchaser present a paper land certificate when applying for registration, in recognition of the philosophy that the register, not the land certificate, is now conclusive of title. It was intended that full electronic conveyancing would be introduced on a staged basis, allowing for a transitional period in which the electronic system would operate alongside the paper-based system until the paper-based system is gradually phased out. The process for achieving this was set out in Part 8 of the LRA 2002 and Schedule 5 (which addressed the practicalities of e-conveyancing). The first stage was to establish an electronic process for e-lodgments (fairly basic transactions such as changes of property address or property description), e-discharges (electronic discharges of registered charges) and e-charges (electronic registration of charges in respect of registered land), with e-conveyancing becoming the only method of transfer once the system is fully operational.[27] The Land Registry has been developing its e-conveyancing proposals since 2007 and during this time some of the secondary legislation required to give effect to the provisions contained in the Land Registration Act 2002 has been drafted,[28] although at present the full implementation of electronic, paperless conveyancing remains some way off.

The introduction of e-conveyancing raises several issues. For example, in relation to the formalities required for the creation and transfer of interests in land, the current law requires contracts relating to land to be in writing and creation or transfer of legal interests to be by deed. The move towards e-conveyancing requires amendments to these provisions so that electronic signatures are deemed to have the same effect as physical signatures, electronic documents are deemed to be deeds, and so on. The pilot scheme road-tested some aspects of electronic transactions, and some electronic entries connected with mortgages and certain types of e-services are now available. However, it is not yet clear whether the technology yet exists to support the goal of full e-conveyancing, or whether the system put in place will be limited to certain major transactions. Following its most recent consultation, the Land Registry concluded that, in light of difficulties reported by customers in the e-charges process, principally with e-signatures, and the concerns that this has prompted amongst stakeholders regarding the security of further e-conveyancing developments at present, the time is not yet right to offer e-transfers. Rather, the Land Registry has committed to addressing difficulties with e-charges and e-signatures first, and is putting the development of e-transfers on hold until the delivery systems for the receipt of electronic documents prepared in the traditional way have been fully automated.[29]

---

[27] LRA 2002, s. 91.

[28] The Land Registration (Electronic Conveyancing) Rules 2008 introduced the facility for e-charges.

[29] Land Registry, *Report on Responses to E-conveyancing Secondary Legislation Part 3* (2011), online at <http://www1.landregistry.gov.uk/upload/documents/econveyancing_cons.pdf>.

Debate 4

Has the Land Registration Act 2002 succeeded in establishing abstract rationality over material possession in English land law?

The movement towards e-conveyancing had a major influence on both the philosophy of land ownership and the technical changes set out in the LRA 2002. The key philosophical change set out in the Act concerned a shift from a concept of land ownership rooted in possession and an organic relationship between user and land, with title obtained through this process registered, to a bureaucratic system of title *by* registration. This bureaucratic system reflects our theme of *rationality* in land law, as discussed in Chapter 1. The philosophy of the LRA 2002 clearly favours the rational, objective and tangible values attributed to interests in land, while the proposition that a property may be socially, psychologically or emotionally meaningful is sidelined within this system. The LRA 2002 gave effect to a decisive shift in the frame of reference underpinning the ownership of land, with the concept of dwelling based on a material, possessive relationship with the land,[30] displaced by a new emphasis on the record – the register itself – as the basis of title. While the common law began from the factual situation, the LRA 2002 has largely eliminated considerations relating to the material use of land, in favour of the formal record entered on the register. This is a shift '... from possession to title, from empirically defined fact to state-defined entitlement, from property as a reflection of social actuality to property as a product of state-ordered or political fact. In short, instead of the citizen telling the state who owns land, the state will henceforth tell the citizen.'[31]

The impact of the LRA 2002 in (further) embedding the value of rationality in English land law was recognized by Gray and Gray, when they stated that:

> There has always been an instinctive bias in favour of transactional certainty in the land market and this perceived imperative has now acquired a heightened emphasis with the enactment of the Land Registration Act 2002. By various means this legislation infuses a new quality of rationality into dealings with land...The 2002 Act accordingly oversees an intensified system of almost universal recordation of property rights in the Land Register, thereby sharpening up the effects of dealings between strangers and reducing potential threats to any title taken by a transferee or mortgagee.[32]

The difference in approach can also be characterized as a movement away from an idea of the land which is the subject of the rights as place (that is, as a social setting

---

[30] The importance of 'possession' in the common law relating to land ownership reflected 'the organic element in the relationship between man and land': K. Gray and P. Symes, *Real Property and Real People* (Butterworths, 1981) pp. 48–49.

[31] K. Gray and S. Gray, 'The Rhetoric of Realty', in J. Getzler (ed.), *Rationalizing Property, Equity and Trusts: Essays in Honour of Edward Burn* (LexisNexis UK, 2003) p. 245.

[32] K. Gray and S. Gray, *Elements of Land Law* (Oxford University Press, 4th edn, 2005) [2.48].

in which the land – the space – provides the material, organic basis for life's core activities and so is invested with social meaning) to an abstract, rational representation of the land as space.[33] This philosophical conception of land ownership also further embeds the theme of alienability (see Chapter 1) by prioritizing the exchange value of the land (and the ease of the transaction itself) over interests in use, which are by their nature often created informally. The LRA 2002 moved the system of land registration in England and Wales decisively away from concerns about the 'natural' human interest in possession, instinctive recognition of the use value of the land, or impulses to protect the material attachment that results from long use, towards a rationally based, abstract, technical system.

The nature of the contrast between the traditional, common law-based notion of land ownership derived from possession in English law, and the abstract, bureaucratic system perfected in the LRA 2002 can be usefully demonstrated by reflecting on the values underpinning the common law approach. The traditional role of possession in concepts of land ownership appeared to be derived from an instinctive awareness that the value that an item of property represents to the possessor of that property is greater than the value that the property holds for a non-possessor, because of the material fact of possession. For example, Hume reasoned that the degree of harm caused to a possessor by losing that property would be greater than the harm suffered by depriving the non-possessor of the property, because:

> Men generally fix their affections more on what they are possess'd of than on what they never enjoyed … it would be greater cruelty to dispossess a man of anything than not to give it to him.[34]

This 'bias in favour of the factual situation'[35] was also reflected in Oliver Wendell Holmes' jurisprudential acknowledgment of the attachments that people form towards property through use:

> It is in the nature of a man's mind. A thing which you enjoyed or used as your own for a long time, whether property or opinion, takes root in your being and cannot be torn away without your resenting the act and trying to defend yourself, however you came by it. The law can ask no better justification than the deepest instincts of man.[36]

Notable English jurists Pollock and Maitland reasoned that: 'Possession as such deserves protection … He who possesses has by the mere fact of his possession more

---

[33] See A. Buttimer and D. Seamon (eds), *The Human Experience of Space and Place* (St. Martin's Press, 1980).

[34] D. Hume, *A Treatise of Human Nature* (Cambridge University Press, 1938, first published 1740), Book III, Part II, Sect. 1.

[35] A. Ehr-Soon Tay, 'Law, the Citizen and the State' in E. Kamenka, R. Brown, and A. E.-S. Tay, (eds) *Law and Society: The Crisis in Legal Ideas* (E Arnold, 1978), p. 11.

[36] O.W. Holmes, 'The Path of the Law' (1897) 10 *Harvard LR* 457, 477.

right in the thing than the non-possessor has.'[37] Indeed, this principle provided the basis for the pre-LRA 2002 doctrine of adverse possession.

The traditional English common law approach, in which rights in land derived from possession, can be contrasted with the registration-based approach of Roman law systems,[38] which provided that: '... a man's right to use and enjoy, to the exclusion of others, flowed from title, from a state-recognised acquisition or transfer of ownership ...'.[39] Alain Pottage has claimed that the move to registered land in 1925 had fundamental conceptual and political implications, which were 'glossed over' as merely easing conveyancing, when in fact it introduced a 'new grammar of property':[40]

> [R]egistration was not simply a different or better way of doing the job of conveyancing, but rather...brought with it a change in the understanding of what that job was; it transformed the basic conceptual and institutional resources which supported the process of conveyancing...it did not simplify existing processes of proof, rather it developed an entirely new understanding of what was being proved and transferred.[41]

The 2002 Act took a further step in transforming the fundamental basis of entitlement to land, from *possession* of land as a good root of title, to *registration* as the source of title.[42] For registered land, the 'basis of title...is not possession, but the register itself'.[43] As Fiona Burns explained:

> [I]n a title-by-registration system, possession is no longer the bedrock of land law. It is not necessary for a person to demonstrate some kind of physical nexus with the land in order to acquire seisin or other interests in the land. As possession declines as the normative principle, so the legitimacy of registration is amplified because the only way of dealing with the land is through alteration of the register.[44]

---

[37] F. Pollock and F. Maitland, *The History of the English Law before the Time of Edward I* (Cambridge University Press, 2nd edn, 1898) pp. 42–43. This phenomenon is recognized in the modern economic theory of the 'endowment effect': that is, that people place a higher sale price on what they already have than they would pay for the same thing if they did not own it – see C. Camerer, 'Individual Decision Making' in J. Kagel and A. Roth (eds), *The Handbook of Experimental Economics* (Princeton University Press, 1995) pp. 665–70, for an account of empirical studies of the endowment effect, and some possible psychological explanations for such effects; on the endowment effect as a status quo bias, see W. Samuelson and R. Zeckhauser, 'Status Quo Bias in Decision Making' (1988) 1 *Journal of Risk and Uncertainty* 7.

[38] Which continue to influence property ownership systems in continental Europe.

[39] Tay, n.35, p. 10.

[40] A. Pottage, 'The Originality of Registration' (1995) 15(3) *OJLS* 371, 377.

[41] Ibid, 372.

[42] The Law Commission has acknowledged that: '[a]t its most fundamental level, the basis of title to unregistered land is possession, whereas the basis of registered title is the fact of registration': Law Commission & HM Land Registry, *Land Registration for the Twenty-First Century: A Consultative Document*, Law Com No 254 (HMSO, 1998) [1.6].

[43] Ibid, [2.6].

[44] F. Burns, 'The Future of Prescriptive Easements in Australia and England' [2007] *Melbourne Univ LR* 3, 22.

Pottage demonstrated that, rather than changing the existing system of land transfer, the introduction of registration in the 1925 Act had 'constructed an entirely new foundation for property in land',[45] based not on deeds, contracts and conveyance but on the register, backed by insurance or indemnity. By removing most of the remaining vestiges of the possession-based system, the LRA 2002 has elevated the rational, measurable, objective, financial exchange interest in land ownership as recorded on the register, over the more subjective, emotional and potentially unquantifiable interests associated with material possession and use. This trope had already gained ascendency in the 1925 legislation, and the LRA 2002 simply further embedded the capital land owner's interest in the exchange value of land. Pottage underlined the substitution of the social basis for land ownership with a bureaucratic system: 'Property was no longer grounded in a practice of social mnemonics – the rich medium of practical social memory – but in administrative practice'.[46] The result is that the law and practices governing ownership of land are distanced from the thing – the land – itself, and from the human experiences of the people who use the land.

Debate 5

What practical changes were triggered by this philosophical shift?

The 2002 Act sought to pave the way for electronic conveyancing by making the register more complete in a range of specific ways: it reduced the categories of overriding interests (interests that can bind a purchase without entry on the register); it encouraged the entry of overriding interests onto the register; it extended the function of registration to more interests (for example, expanding the category of registrable leases); and it limited the cautions that could be made against first registration. The Act also sought to modernize the process of registration through more logical approaches to drafting and the use of modern language, by rationalizing the protection of third-party interests, reforming the law relating to adverse possession, eliminating land certificates and charge certificates, and providing for the independent adjudication of disputes. Specific strategies to reduce the risk posed by third-party interests in land included the prohibition of new cautions against dealings with land; and the category of interests previously known as inhibitions was subsumed into restrictions, so reducing the categories of third-party interests for which a purchaser needs to be alert to two: notices and restrictions. A clearer demarcation was made between these two categories and, to allow for its broader functions, notices can now be either agreed or unilateral. Finally, the troublesome 'beneficial interest behind a trust of land' – the interest

---

[45] Pottage, n.40, 386.
[46] Ibid; see also Pottage, n.2.

that a co-owner may acquire in (usually family) property – can only be protected by way of restriction.

REGISTRABLE INTERESTS AND DISPOSITIONS

In unregistered land, an interest is created or a transfer takes place when the sale is completed and the deed of conveyance signed; when land is registered, the interest is not created or transfer is not completed until the transfer form has been registered and the name of the purchaser entered into the register.[47] One distinctive feature of transactions in registered land (compared to unregistered land transactions) is that the legal interest does not pass to the purchaser on exchange of contracts or completion, but vests only on registration.[48] Only certain categories of legal estates and interests can be registered, and these registrable interests have their own files in the Land Registry. The list of registrable interests has been expanded by the LRA 2002,[49] so that the list now includes the fee simple absolute in possession, leasehold estates in possession for longer than seven years (whether the landlord's title is registered or not), future leases (leases which commence later than three months from the date of creation) and discontinuous leases (e.g. a lease of a property for three months every year), rentcharges, legal franchises forever or for a fixed term later than seven years and legal *profits à prendre* in gross (not attached to the land) forever or for a fixed term of greater than seven years (for example, a right to hunt).

Registrable dispositions – transactions in relation to land that must be completed by registration – tend to relate to legal (rather than equitable) interests and are recorded against an existing registered title. A registrable disposition does not operate at law until it is registered,[50] and such dispositions include transfers of registered land; a grant from registered land of a lease of more than seven years; a lease that takes effect in possession after three months; a lease where the term is discontinuous; or a grant of a legal charge over registered land and certain easements and profits. Only relatively short leases (for less than seven years) do not need to be registered to take effect.[51] This can be contrasted with the pre-2002 position, when the bar for a short lease that did not require registration (but could be an overriding interest) was set at 21 years.[52] Obviously, the more expansive the category of registrable interests and dispositions, the more information is provided to the prospective purchaser on the face of the register, and the less additional inquiry is required to ensure that the purchaser is fully aware of what they are going to get with the title.

In addition to these major aspects of title, registered land can also be affected by burdens and incumbrances (previously known as minor interests), which are

---

[47] LRA 2002, s. 27.
[48] LRA 2002, s. 58.
[49] ss. 2–8.
[50] At best, it can only take effect in equity: LRA 2002, s. 27(1).
[51] LRA 2002, s. 29(4).
[52] LRA 1925, s. 70(1)(k).

not registrable in their own right but (usually)[53] must be entered on the register against the main title to bind a purchaser; and by overriding interests, a category of interest that can bind a purchaser even though they are not registered. The 2002 Act has increased the categories of burden or incumbrance that can be registered by restriction or by notice, again with a view to moving towards a more perfect register in which all interests affecting the land are evident on the face of the file. These categories are residual, in the sense that if the interest in question is not substantively registrable, and is not an overriding interest, it must be protected by registration against the substantive title. Against this objective, overriding interests – which operate outside the register – have been described as constituting a crack in the mirror principle, and regarded as a continuing source of tension within the system of title registration.

OVERRIDING INTERESTS

While the conceptual shift from unregistered to registered land has been comprehensive, some commentators might argue that so long as the category of overriding interests continues to exist, the transformation of land law will not be absolute. Yet, beyond the bureaucratic aims of title registration, the continued existence of the category of overriding interests also invokes another important debate concerning the protection of certain categories of vulnerable interests (for example, interests created informally) in their proprietary form; that is, against the land itself (in effect, against the purchaser), rather than as a claim for damages against the vendor of the land. In recent years, this debate has, in certain sub-categories of interest, become oriented around the (purchaser-facing) question of the discoverability of the interest: has the purchaser done all she could reasonably be expected to do to identify and overcome any claims that might subsequently be made against the land? The great debate surrounding overriding interests, before and after the LRA 2002, has been about where that line of reasonableness in relation to the inquiries or inspections that a purchaser of registered land should be expected to carry out should be drawn. What makes an interest discoverable? And is it fair for purchasers to be bound by interests that are not discoverable? The terms in which the discoverability agenda has been formulated are themselves informed by an agenda that – despite the continued existence of the category – is focused on the purchaser's perspective rather than the interest holders (we do not ask when it is reasonable for a subsidiary interest holder to lose their proprietary interest in the land).

From a purist perspective, the activities of inspection and notice to identify interests affecting the land are part of the old system of unregistered land, and have no place in a modern bureaucratic system to title registration. Indeed, while

---

[53] Following the 2002 Act, some overriding interests are also registrable (although they may still be overriding without registration), to encourage as much information concerning the title onto the register as possible.

the LRA 1925 set out an extensive list of overriding interests,[54] one of the main aims of the LRA 2002 was to make the register as comprehensive as possible and to minimize the number of interests that are capable of binding without appearing on the register. This has been achieved by retaining the concept of overriding interests but limiting the category to those interests which are proprietary in nature and where it is considered unreasonable, unrealistic or uneconomical to expect the right to be registered. Thus, many interests that were overriding under the LRA 1925 are no longer overriding and now have specific registration requirements (as burdens or incumbrances, see below). Many of the interests that retain their overriding status have been more clearly drafted, so as to limit their application and to avoid uncertainties in their operation, while a general principle has been applied that rights that are expressly created should in principle be subject to registration. For example, informally created legal easements and profits[55] are potentially overriding, but only bind the purchaser in fact if (a) the purchaser had actual knowledge or constructive knowledge (i.e. obvious on a reasonably careful inspection) of the existence of the easement, or (b) the easement has been exercised within the last year. This approach demonstrates the incorporation of the discoverability requirement with respect to even those interests that are informally created (and with reference to which the argument that the interest-holder could reasonably be expected to take positive steps to protect their interests is significantly weaker), reflecting the dominance of the purchaser perspective (and the commitment to formality) over the interest-holder perspective (and recognition of the realities of informality in certain types of relationship) in the LRA 2002, at least in relation to easements that have not been recently exercised

Leases granted for a term not exceeding seven years from the date of grant of lease are overriding,[56] unless the tenant does not take possession until three months after the grant of the lease (these reversionary leases or future leases are more difficult for a purchaser to discover); or if the lease is discontinuous (for example, a lease of a property for a month a year, over three years – again, difficult to discover); and also excluding the grant of certain rights under the Housing Act 1985. The distinction between legal interests (which attract a higher level of protection within the registration system) and equitable interests (more readily defeated unless registered) is also maintained in the case of lease, as equitable leases are not overriding unless the tenant is in actual occupation (so making the interest more discoverable).

Most equitable interests or minor interests will bind purchasers if they are protected by entry on the register. If not so protected, they may still bind

---

[54] LRA 1925, s. 70.

[55] Easements created under LPA 1925, s. 62, and easements that are implied under the rule in *Wheeldon v Burrows* (1879) 12 Ch D 31, the doctrine of necessity or common intention: LRA 2002, sch. 3, para. 3; see Chapter 7. Legal easements that are created expressly must be registered as a disposition. Equitable easements must be protected as a minor interest.

[56] LRA 2002, sch. 3, para. 1.

purchasers if the beneficiary is in actual occupation of the property. The interests of persons in actual occupation attract special protection under Schedule 3, paragraph 2 of the 2002 Act. Interests in actual occupation were originally deemed overriding under section 70(1)(g) of the LRA 1925, which covered 'the rights of every person in actual occupation of the land or in receipt of rents and profits thereof, save where inquiry is made of such a person and the rights are not' disclosed'. The purpose of this section was to protect the rights of those persons actually living in the property, who might risk losing their interests 'in the welter of registration'.[57] This concept was carried forward into the LRA 2002 through Schedule 3, paragraph 2, which incorporated two components from section 70(1) (g) into the modified version in the LRA 2002 – the existence of a right, and the holder of the right being in actual occupation of the land – but which excluded from the category 'an interest – (i) which belonged to a person whose occupation would not have been obvious on a reasonably careful inspection of the land at the time of the disposition, and (ii) of which the person to whom the disposition is made does not have actual knowledge at that time'.[58]

There must be an interest that is capable being overriding (carried across the transaction). If the claimant has no interest in the land, there is nothing to override the transaction.[59] The person claiming that the interest is overriding must be in actual occupation of the land at the date of disposition. That occupation must have been obvious to the purchaser on a reasonably careful inspection of the land at the time of the disposition, and the purchaser did not have actual knowledge of the interest. This is a new requirement to address concerns that, under the LRA 1925, purchasers were being held to interests that they could not have been expected to discover. Yet, the uncertainties that proved controversial under LRA 1925 section 70(1)(g) have not been fully resolved by Schedule 3, paragraph 2 of the LRA 2002. Indeed, in order to establish that an interest holder was in actual occupation, guidance provided in cases decided under section 70(1)(g) will remain relevant. For example in determining – as a question of fact – whether someone is in actual occupation, the court will consider the normal usage of the property.[60] Absence from the property for a short period of time does not preclude a person from being considered to be in actual occupation;[61] and actual occupation does not have to be exclusive or continuous, although – illustrating the shift towards purchaser protections – under the reformulated provision in the LRA 2002, occupation would now have to be discoverable notwithstanding the occupier's absence from the property. Pre-2002 case law also established that the nature of

---

[57] *Strand Securities Ltd v Caswell* [1965] Ch 958, at 979, Lord Denning.
[58] LRA 2002, sch 3. para. 2(c).
[59] *National Provincial Bank Ltd v Ainsworth* [1965] AC 1175; cf. *Williams and Glyn's Bank v Boland* [1981] AC 487, in which Mrs Boland's equitable interest under a trust, combined with actual occupation, was an overriding interest (and therefore binding on the bank).
[60] See, for example, *Kling v Keston Properties Ltd* (1985) 49 P & CR 212 (using a garage to park cars did not require that there be a car there constantly); and *Malory Enterprises v Cheshire Homes* [2002] 3 WLR 1 (use of property for storage requires keeping it locked and fenced).
[61] *Chhokar v Chhokar* [1984] FLR 313 (absence in hospital while having a baby).

the property may be relevant to the application of the actual occupation test;[62] that preparatory acts prior to fully moving in will generally not be considered sufficient to give rise to actual occupation;[63] and that a claimant cannot generally claim actual occupation through the occupation of another.[64]

[The continuity between the pre-2002 case law and the 2002 Act demonstrates the convergence of judicial and legislative policy in tilting the debate concerning when the interests of persons in actual occupation are binding in favour of purchasers.] Even the new discoverability requirement was pre-empted by the interpretation of actual occupation in cases such as *Abbey National Building Society v Cann*[65] and *Malory Enterprises Ltd v Cheshire Homes Ltd*.[66] While the LRA 2002 has clearly embedded the purchaser-protecting discoverability requirement into its formulation to carry the interests of persons in actual occupation across the transaction, the issues underlying the earlier debate remain extant.[67] This provision strikes a balance between the informally created interests of claimants who cannot reasonably be expected to protect themselves (thus their inclusion in the retrenched category of overriding interests), and the protection of purchasers who have taken reasonable steps to discover such interests. Nevertheless, as Jackson has observed, the policy that land should be freely transferable is deeply engrained in English property law,[68] so much so that it sometimes becomes what Harpum described as an 'unspoken premise',[69] fading into the background of biases with which we perceive land law.

While the discoverability criterion would appear adequate to protect any purchaser who has taken reasonable steps, any remaining vulnerability of purchasers to the interests of a beneficiary under a trust can be eliminated through the principle of overreaching, where the purchaser pays the purchase money to two or more trustees. According to the interpretation applied by the courts in *Williams & Glyn's Bank Ltd v Boland*,[70] the doctrine of overreaching applies in registered land, so that it is only if the claimant's interest is not overreached that it may be overriding and so bind the purchaser through the actual occupation provision.

---

[62] *Lloyd's Bank plc v Rosset* [1989] 3 All ER 915 (where the property was semi-derelict and unfit for occupation, the presence of builders was sufficient).

[63] *Abbey National Building Society v Cann* [1991] 1 AC 56 (furniture and laying of carpets not actual occupation).

[64] *Strand Securities Ltd v Caswell* [1965] Ch 958 (step-father trying to claim actual occupation through step-daughter as his agent; *Hypo-Mortgage Services Ltd v Robinson* [1997] 2 FLR 71 (parents cannot claim through their children).

[65] [1991] 1 AC 56.

[66] [2002] Ch 216. See also *Hodgson v Marks* [1971] Ch 892; *Lloyd's Bank plc v Rosset* [1989] Ch 350; *Ferrishurst v Wallcite Ltd* [1999] Ch 355. See also P. Sparkes, 'The Discoverability of Occupiers of Registered Land' [1989] *Conv* 342; C. Harpum, 'Overreaching, Trustees' Powers and the Reform of the 1925 Legislation' [1990] *CLJ* 277; J. Stevens, 'Is Justice a Priority in Priorities? Law Reform and the Re-Introduction of Morality to Registered Conveyancing' in F. Meisel and P. Cook (eds), *Property and Protection: Essays in Honour of Brian Harvey* (Hart Publishing, 2000).

[67] N. Jackson, 'Title by Registration and Concealed Overriding Interests: The Cause and Effect of Antipathy to Documentary Proof' (2003) 119 *LQR* 660.

[68] Ibid, 662.

[69] C. Harpum, 'Property in An Electronic Age' in E. Cooke (ed.), *Modern Studies in Property Law* (Hart Publishing, 2001) p. 4.

[70] [1981] AC 487.

Conversely, where the claimant's interest has been overreached, there can be no question of it overriding the transaction, even if the beneficiary is in actual occupation.[71] The availability of overreaching has significant implications for the protection of the occupier's interest in property *as a home*. Where occupiers' interests are subject to overreaching, the interest is converted from ownership of the home to a claim against the capital realized on sale, thus undermining the idea that home holds any value beyond its capital value.[72]

The application of the English overreaching provision has also been criticized on the basis that it was not intended to operate on registered land,[73] which has its own overreaching machinery in as much as all interests that are not registered and are not overriding are overreached on any sale[74] (note, however, that a beneficiary under a trust can enter a restriction on the register to prevent the purchase money being paid to less than two trustees). Jackson argued that '... the *Boland* interpretation of the overriding/overreaching provisions raises more problems and inconsistencies than it answers',[75] and that a proper interpretation of the overreaching provisions in the Land Registration Act 1925 would have led to the conclusion that '*but for* the occupation of the beneficiary, the interest in *Boland* would have been overreached by the sole trustee'.[76] Since the equitable interests in these cases were, at the relevant time, not 'interests in land' but 'purely personal rights against the trustee(s)',[77] they were not capable of affecting the legal estate. Jackson reasoned that 'As any disposition of registered land will overreach the beneficial interests under a trust, the inescapable construction of the Land Registration Act 1925 is that trust interests are incapable of being overriding',[78] although she did allow for the possibility that interests in actual occupation be excepted, with 'the idea...that overreaching would be displaced where the beneficiary was in occupation, so that the interests would not be transformed into a personal right at all'.[79] By this reasoning, Jackson argued that a correct interpretation of the English provisions would regard actual occupation as preventing overreaching: 'in effect, the opposite of the ratio in *Boland* and *Flegg*'.[80] While this interpretation was recently adopted by the Northern Ireland Law Commission in its recommendations for land law reform,[81]

---

[71] *City of London Building Society v Flegg* [1988] AC 54 (the beneficial interest of the trustees' parents was overreached by payment to two trustees. As the interest was overreached, there was no 'interest in land' that could become overriding by virtue of actual occupation.)

[72] For a discussion of the range of values which home represents to occupiers, see L. Fox, *Conceptualising Home: Theories, Laws and Policies* (Hart Publishing, 2006).

[73] See N. Jackson, 'Overreaching in Registered Land Law' (2006) 69(2) *MLR* 214.

[74] Jackson argued that the category of overriding interests was not intended to include beneficial interests under a trust, which were relatively uncommon in 1925.

[75] Ibid, 237.

[76] Ibid, at 238. Emphasis in original.

[77] Ibid.

[78] Ibid, at 238–39.

[79] Ibid, 240.

[80] Ibid.

[81] Northern Ireland Law Commission, *Report: Land Law* (NILC 8) (Belfast: TSO, 2010); see L. Fox O'Mahony, 'Something Old, Something New, Something Borrowed: The Reform of Northern Ireland Land Law' [2011] *Conv* 356.

the interaction of overriding interests and the doctrine of overreaching remains subject to debate within English land law.

CONCLUSIONS

In Chapter 1 we considered a series of central themes which we have identified as significant in contemporary property law debates. Several of these themes are represented in the shift from a possession basis for land ownership (pre-registration) to the bureaucratic characteristics of registered land, as perfected in the LRA 2002. The goals of land registration are clearly aligned with the drive towards alienability in the 1925 legislation, which was reinforced in the 2002 Act; the orientation of land registration is rationalist, particularly as this has been understood within the economic model of rationality, valuing the security of long-term expectations; the reliability of investment strategies; the rationality of decision-making about future land use; stable forward planning; the need to protect titles taken by purchasers and creditors; the importance of ensuring that the substantial wealth tied up in land should not be rendered economically sterile; and the objective of facilitating property transactions as smoothly and effectively as possible. Finally, the development of land registration reflects a conception of property law as concerned not with place but with space: it closes out the idea of property as a way of 'being in the world', of land as the physical, organic basis for human activity, in favour of a vision of property as a commodified asset to be traded as efficiently as possible in pursuit of capital gain. Pottage claimed that 'Registration sought entirely to remove property from its natural habitat, from the realm of practical presuppositions and expectations which underpin the attribution of formal property rights'.[82] Both property in land, and the topography through which the physical manifestation of the land was represented, were reduced to entries on the register.[83] Studies of bureaucratic organizations reveal the aptness of the perfected model of land registration in pursuing these goals. Bureaucratic organizations are defined by rule-bound procedures; they respond to written rather than verbal discourse; their procedures are enacted by experts using specialized and technical languages of discourse; and their aims are to achieve speed, precision, clarity, and objectivity in carrying out their functions.[84] The rise in bureaucratic values in land law is instrumental in closing out concerns for human behaviour or emotions. As Weber argued, bureaucracy:

> ... develops the more perfectly the more the bureaucracy is 'dehumanized', the more completely it succeeds in eliminating from official business love,

---

[82] Pottage, n.2, 361–62.

[83] Ibid, 362.

[84] K. Dovey, 'Home and Homelessness' in I. Altman and C. Werner (eds), *Home Environments* (Plenum Press, 1985) p. 55.

hatred, and all purely personal, irrational, and emotional elements which escape calculation.[85]

As the system of title registration as a means of regulating dealings affecting land becomes increasingly procedural, it embeds the reduction of *home* to *house*, of *place* to *space*, of experiential meaning to tangible, fungible, commoditized value.

It can be argued that this development is a necessary feature of a modern, commercialized system of land law, in which both commercial property transactions and the expanded owner-occupied sector depend on a system which prioritizes speed, security and ease and affordability of conveyancing. Those interests trump the protection of informal interests or sensitivity to the emotional attachments that users hold for their land. In the US, for example, where registration of title has not taken hold in a mainstream way,[86] the insurance function performed by the Land Registry in England and Wales has taken the form of private title insurance: a form of indemnity insurance against financial loss from defects in the title to real property taken out at the consumer's (purchaser's) or lender's expense to mitigate the relative inadequacy of the US title system.[87] While it is possible to take out title insurance in England and Wales to protect against losses in particularly complex or high-risk transactions, where there is an evident defect in title, it is not routinely used in normal residential or commercial transactions. Registration of title has virtually eliminated this expensive adjunct to secure transactions, by deflecting the insurance function onto the state through the Land Registry[88] and introducing a measure of certainty to supplement the simplification strategy of the 1925 legislation.[89]

While there is undoubtedly merit in the arguments in favour of registration of title *per se*, what is less convincingly established is the necessity for the extent to which the LRA 2002 has eroded the status of informal interests. For example, Dixon suggested that he was: '(possibly in a minority of one) [in that he] regards the reform of the process of adverse possession by the 2002 Act as an unnecessary and economically unjustified "bolt on" to the reform of registered land'.[90] While there can be little doubt that many of the reforms set out in the 2002 Act are instrumental in enhancing the maturity of the English system of land ownership, this move towards greater rationality also gives effect to a particular political ideology and approach to ownership. Gray and Gray have argued that:

> …the ultimate achievement of the Land Registration Act 2002 is its ruthless maximisation of rational legal order, an aim which is symbolised by

---

[85] M. Weber, 'Essay on Bureaucracy' in F. Rourke (ed.), *Bureaucratic Power in National Politics* (Little, Brown & Co, 1978) p.90.

[86] Only a very few, small US jurisdictions have versions of title registration.

[87] B. Burke, *Law of Title Insurance* (Aspen Publishers, 3rd edn, 2000).

[88] This insurance function is also shared by (and in most unregistered land transactions, assumed by) solicitors' professional indemnity insurance.

[89] Pottage, n.40, 390.

[90] M. Dixon, 'Adverse Possession and Human Rights' [2005] *Conv* 345, 351.

> the statutory vision of an electronic register of virtually indefeasible titles, transactable by automated dealings and guaranteed by the state. Under this tightly organised regime, estate ownership, as constituted by the register record, becomes a heavily protected phenomenon, leaving little room for the operation 'off the record' of some ancient and pragmatic principle of long possession.[91]

This bureaucratic system arguably favours those who are well-informed as to how to protect their rights, over the right-holder who has acquired a right informally. The practical effect of the philosophical commitments underpinning the LRA 2002 have involved a fairly relentless tide in favour of protecting legal title holders and purchasers (the capital interest or 'monied might' of property relationships) against informal claims such as those brought by squatters or the off-title interests of persons in occupation of the land.

To the extent that such informal interests might have been accepted as carrying some claim to protection, the philosophy of the LRA 2002 overrode such claims on the basis that the reforms set out in the Act were necessary to develop the register in preparation for the commercial behemoth of e-conveyancing. It was perhaps surprising that, following the very slow development of registered land in England and Wales throughout the twentieth century, the LRA 2002 has, in its absolute commitment to perfecting the register, leap-frogged the English system beyond even the mature Torrens jurisdictions of some Australian states.[92] Burns has suggested that this can be explained by the origins of the Australian Torrens systems in the nineteenth-century goal of implementing 'a system for common land transactions which was cheap and simple', but which could accommodate 'long-established de facto enjoyment...in some way within the system'.[93] The LRA 2002 had the distinct objective of preparing for e-conveyancing, making the driver for a hard-edged system much more powerful. As we wait to discover whether, and to what extent, the e-conveyancing project will be deemed a success, it remains to be seen whether this justificatory for the reforms in the LRA 2002 will prove to be robust.

Further Reading

B. Boguzs, 'Defining the Scope of Actual Occupation Under the LRA 2002: Some Recent Judicial Clarification' (2011) *Conv* 268.

M. Dixon, 'The Reform of Property Law and the Land Registration Act 2002: A Risk Assessment', (2003) *Conv* 136.

C. Harpum, 'Property in an Electronic Age', in E. Cooke (ed.), *Modern Studies in Property Law* (Hart Publishing, 2007).

---

[91] Gray & Gray, n.32, 364.

[92] Which continue to allow title based on possession without registration: Victoria and Western Australia.

[93] F. Burns, 'The Future of Prescriptive Easements in Australia and England' [2007] *Melbourne Univ LR* 3, 29.

N. Jackson, 'Title by Registration and Concealed Overriding Interests: The Cause and Effect of Antipathy to Documentary Proof' (2003) 119 *LQR* 660.

A. Nair, 'Morality and the Mirror: the Normative Limits of the Principles of Land Registration' In S. Bright (ed.), *Modern Studies in Property Law, vol 6* (Hart Publishing, 2011).

6

UNLAWFUL OCCUPATION OF LAND: SQUATTING AND ADVERSE POSSESSION

INTRODUCTION

The philosophy and policies of the Land Registration Act 2002 – considered in the previous chapter – are sharpened by the issues surrounding the unlawful *use* of land by 'squatters'. Squatting can be described as the unauthorized occupation of land belonging to another, and 'a squatter … [as] one who, without colour of right, enters on an unoccupied house or land, intending to stay there as long as he can'.[1] When such unlawful occupation extended over a sufficiently long period of time (in England and Wales, 12 years),[2] the traditional doctrine of adverse possession enabled such an occupier – through a combination of the limitation principle (which extinguished the displaced owner's right to bring an action to recover the land after 12 years)[3] and the doctrine of relativity of title (by which law protects the relatively stronger claim in any bilateral contest) – to acquire a status of irremovability when it came to defending their occupation of the land. Furthermore, in unregistered land – where possession provides the root of title – the squatter was the holder of a new common law estate in the land derived from her own possession; while in registered land – prior to the LRA 2002 – the squatter acquired *beneficial* ownership of the property automatically, under a statutory trust, and completion of the legal title to the land (by closing the registered proprietor's title and opening a new title held by the squatter)[4] was simply a matter of making an application to the Land Registry. Following the LRA 2002 the squatter of registered land obtains a freehold title by virtue of adverse possession but this title is extinguished if the squatter succeeds in an application to be registered under the legislation as proprietor of an estate in land.[5]

---

[1] *McPhail v Persons Unknown* [1973] Ch 447, 456B.

[2] Where land is unregistered, and prior to the Land Registration Act 2002 for registered land.

[3] Limitation Act 1980, s. 15.

[4] *Spectrum Investment v Holmes* [1981] 1 WLR 221; *Central London Commercial Estates Ltd v Kato Kagaku Ltd* [1998] 4 All ER 948.

[5] LRA 2002, sch. 9, para. 1.

However, in a move that exemplifies the approach of the LRA 2002, Schedule 6 effectively limits the circumstances in which a squatter can claim title to registered land to cases in which the squatter has an estoppel in his or her favour; where the squatter has some other entitlement to be registered (e.g. an estate contract, inheritance); where the dispute concerns a mistake in good faith concerning a boundary;[6] or where the registered proprietor makes no objection to squatter's claim.[7] Yet, while the reform of adverse possession in the 2002 Act was presented (and largely accepted)[8] as rooted in strategies linked to registration, it also implemented a specific moral agenda against the unlawful occupation of land.[9] This anti-squatting agenda is also evident in the Coalition Government's recent consultation on the criminalization of squatting.[10]

Both the legal response to the phenomenon of squatting as a social fact, and property law's doctrine of adverse possession, invoke debates concerning the appropriate balance between the rights of a land owner (particularly when that land owner does not make use of their land)[11] and the interests of the squatter (who is making use of the land, usually – in the case of urban squatting in particular – for occupation as a home). To suggest that such a balance can be struck according to a morally neutral, rights-based approach does little justice to the reality of the contest at stake here. Historically, the place of adverse possession within the framework of property law was supported by a range of justifications, including: the avoidance of stale claims; preventing hardship to a squatter who has been in occupation for a long time; promoting effective land use; and resolving conveyancing problems. The combined effect of the LRA 2002 and calls for the criminalization of the activity of squatting have progressively eroded these justifications, so that what is left is a contest between a land owner – whose proprietary claim is undergirded by a deeply embedded political and economic agenda in support of (formal) property rights – and a squatter – whose act of squatting seems now to be viewed as immoral and (tantamount to) a criminal act. This chapter considers these developments against the backdrop of the ideas developed in this book, including: the elevation of formal title over material, physical occupation in conceptions of land ownership; the selective application of norms of responsibility to property law's neoliberal subjects; the elevation of individual interests over community considerations in private property disputes; and the pursuit of economic security over social need in laws and policies concerning the ownership and regulation of land.

---

[6] LRA 2002, sch. 6, para. 5.

[7] LRA 2002, sch. 6, paras 2–3.

[8] For contrasting views, see M. Dixon, 'Adverse Possession and Human Rights' [2005] *Conv* 345; M. Dixon, 'Adverse Possession in Three Jurisdictions' [2006] *Conv* 179; N. Cobb and L. Fox, 'Living Outside the System? The (Im)Morality of Urban Squatting' (2007) 27(2) *Legal Studies* 236.

[9] Cobb & Fox, n.8.

[10] Ministry of Justice, *Options for Dealing with Squatting* (Home Office, 2011).

[11] The remoteness of such a land owner from the material reality of the land itself is reflected in the moniker sometimes used in this context of 'paper-title holder'.

We discuss three great debates in this chapter. We begin with a discussion of whether squatting should be criminalized. We then move on to discuss the balance between private rights and public obligations, drawing attention to the ethic of stewardship. Finally, we discuss squatters' acquisition of title to land.

Debate 1

Should squatting be criminalized?

When demobilized soldiers returned to London following the Second World War to find their homes destroyed by the Blitz, up to 40,000 took up occupation with their families in empty homes, hospitals and military camps. To modern eyes, the response of the media to this, the first organized post-war urban squatting movement – and the systematic trespass to land it entailed – seems unusually accommodating; perhaps most intriguingly, the *Daily Mail* 'laud[ed] what it saw as "the robust common sense of ordinary men and women"'.[12] However, by the late 1960s and early 1970s, at a time when another housing crisis was attracting a new generation of urban squatters, the response of the media to the phenomenon had radically changed, as an editorial from the *Daily Telegraph* in July 1975 demonstrates:

> Of the many strange and frightening features of contemporary British life, none carries a more obvious and direct threat to society's survival than the growing phenomenon of squatting. Innumerable houses up and down the country are now in illegal occupation by organized gangs of thugs, layabouts and revolutionary fanatics. Costly and irrecoverable damage is continually being done to private property from sheer malice…In reality the motive for most of this squatting is either political – a settled purpose of subverting public order – or simple greed and aggression.[13]

Previously, a consensus of sorts had settled in England and Wales, by which trespass to land was accepted to be a civil matter, with possession orders, injunctions and damages the appropriate tools to address unauthorized occupation. Yet, in addition to the steps that have been taken to speed up and strengthen the process by which owners or legal occupiers secure and enforce possession,[14] an increasing momentum has emerged on the part of the state and in public opinion favouring the ethics and efficacy of criminal sanction to address the 'problem' of squatting.

---

[12] M. Whitaker, 'People Power', *Roof*, 2 January 2007 <http://www.roofmag.org.uk/>, last accessed 31 October 2011.

[13] M. Brake and C. Hale, *Public Order and Private Lives: the Politics of Law and Order: A Critique of Conservative Criminology* (Routledge, 1991) p. 43.

[14] See Civil Procedure Rules 1998, Rule 55.8, which permits both a summary eviction procedure for trespassers, and, in Part III, a system of Interim Possession Orders, backed by criminal sanctions for breach: CJPOA 1994, s. 76.

In 1974, the Law Commission had been instructed by government 'to consider in what circumstances entering and remaining on property should constitute a criminal offence'.[15] The legislation which was enacted – the Criminal Law Act 1977 – reworked the structure of criminal liability around trespass in buildings, with an explicit focus on squatting. Two new offences set out in the 1977 Act continue to govern criminal liability in respect of squatting, subject to limited but significant amendments introduced in 1994.[16] Section 6 created the offence of using or threatening violence to gain entry to property in occupation by someone opposed to that entry.[17] Although its main purpose was to prevent breaches of the peace, rather than shoring up property rights,[18] the protection of *anyone* in occupation of property at the time of entry extended the ambit of the criminal offence in principle not only to someone who entered into property against the wishes of the owner or legal occupier, but also to owners and legal occupiers if they took steps to retrieve property from squatters using violence or the threat of violence. Yet, section 6 is subject to two important exceptions, which reveal the influence of increasing concern with the practice of squatting on the development of the legislation. The offence does not apply to owners or legal occupiers who use or threaten violence if they are 'displaced residential occupiers', or those who were using the premises as a home at the time it was occupied by squatters. Nor does it extend to 'protected intending occupiers' or those who, while not in occupation at the time property was squatted, have an immediate need to use the premises as a home.[19]

The power of self-help against squatters who occupy property required as a home is supported by the additional criminal offence of adverse occupation of residential premises, contained in section 7 of the 1977 Act. That prohibits 'failing to leave' property which is entered as a trespasser, when asked to do so by either a displaced residential occupier[20] or a protected intending occupier.[21] The offence affects only those squatters who occupy property needed immediately as a home, and only after they resist requests to leave the property by those so needing it. Nevertheless, the 1977 Act demonstrates an acceptance that, in certain limited circumstances, the imposition of criminal liability is a suitable response to occupation of buildings by squatters. In parallel to the power of self-help for owners

---

[15] Law Commission Working Paper No 54, *Criminal Law: Offences of Entering and Remaining on Property* (TSO, 1974); Law Commission Report 76, *Criminal Law: Report on Conspiracy and Criminal Law Reform* (TSO, 1974).

[16] Criminal Justice and Public Order Act 1994; Home Office, *Squatting: A Consultation Paper* (1991).

[17] This offence replaced the Forcible Entry Acts, medieval statutes which had previously formed the basis for 'squatter's rights' prior to the enactment of the Criminal Law Act 1977.

[18] Law Commission Report, n.15, para. 2.49.

[19] The Law Commission proposed that owners or legal occupiers should not be granted a power of self-help against occupiers as protected intending occupiers, but only if they were displaced residential occupiers. The 1977 Act implemented the Commission's recommendation. However, the Major government extended the protection of self-help to protected intending occupiers in 1994.

[20] CLA 1977, s. 7(3).

[21] Section 12A of the CLA 1977, as amended by Criminal Justice and Public Order Act 1994. The Law Commission opposed the extension of this offence to protected intending occupiers, but the 1977 Act included them.

and legal occupiers recreated by section 6, the offence under section 7 strengthens the protection for owners and legal occupiers who require immediate use of property occupied by squatters as a home.

For several decades, the 1977 Act appeared to provide a relatively resilient settlement on the role of criminal law in addressing squatting. Amended only once, in 1994, it ushered in a seemingly stable system of limited criminal liability for certain forms of squatting as well as bolstering the powers of owners and legal occupiers to self-help when seeking to recover property from squatters. However, in 2011, this settlement came under scrutiny once again. Since the formation of the Coalition Government in May 2010, the reporting of squatting has taken on a renewed significance. This followed, predictably, a raft of stories about squatters in the media, and seems to have been shaped by previous Conservative policy in the area.[22] In March 2011, the Department of Communities and Local Government and the Ministry of Justice issued joint guidelines explaining the legal measures available to deal with squatters in buildings.[23]

They also announced that the government was conducting a review to consider the need for a new criminal offence of squatting in buildings. A consultation paper followed in June 2011, which put forward several proposals to address 'the distress and misery that squatters can cause'.[24] The explicit agenda of these proposals, which were concerned solely with the role of criminal law in responding to squatting,[25] was to afford the protection of the criminal law not only to those owners and legal occupiers who require immediate use as a home of property occupied by squatters (the settlement under the 1977 Act) but *all owners and legal occupiers*. The consultation paper proposed two alternative approaches. On one hand, the paper suggested the option of strengthening the protections afforded against squatters by sections 6 and 7 of the 1977 Act. The paper put forward the possibility of repealing section 6 altogether, or else exempting all owners and legal occupiers of property from its ambit, expanding the powers of self-help available to retrieve property from squatters. It also proposed to extend the 'failing to leave' offence under section 7 to empower any and all owners and legal occupiers to order squatters to leave their property, with criminal liability attaching to the failure to take reasonable steps to comply with the order.

Alternatively, the consultation paper set out a more wide-ranging and radical approach to the criminalization of squatting. It suggested the creation of a new offence of 'entering and occupying premises as a trespasser'.[26] This option would

---

[22] Before the coalition, the Conservatives in opposition had previously announced plans to introduce an offence of 'intentional trespass'. Its concern was the need for strengthening even further the criminal sanctions to deter Gypsies, travellers and squatters (and others) from occupying both open land and buildings: R. Prince, 'Conservatives to Unveil Plans to Stop Illegal Gypsy Encampments' *Daily Telegraph*, 12 February 2010.

[23] M. Hickman, 'Clarke Cracks Down on Wave of Squatters' *Independent*, 19 March 2011.

[24] Ministry of Justice, n.10, Foreword.

[25] In July 2011, the Legal Aid, Sentencing and Punishment of Offenders Bill proposed to remove access to legal aid for squatter trespassers: see clause 8, and sch. 1, para. 27.

[26] Ministry of Justice, n.10, para. 21.

significantly extend criminal liability for squatting: as with the government's proposed expansion of the 'failure to leave' offence under section 7 of the Act, the new offence would apply to all types of premises, even if they were not required by the owner or legal occupier for immediate use as a home.[27] However, the proposed offence also departed significantly from the approach adopted under section 7 by imposing liability (and empowering police to effect arrest) as soon as a squatter enters and occupies, rather than at the (later) point at which he or she fails to leave when asked to do so by the owner or legal occupier. The offence would therefore impose liability (and permit enforcement) even where the owner or legal occupier cannot be identified or located. It is this path which has been taken by the Coalition Government in the Legal Aid, Sentencing and Punishment of Offenders Bill, while limiting the offence to residential property only.[28]

The move to criminalization has been shaped by wider constructions of squatting and the squatter within popular discourse.[29] The validity of criminal law depends on conceptions of individual wrongdoing and blame, and media representations of squatting are replete with stories that present squatting as no more than a lifestyle choice, and construct squatters as irresponsible, feckless and the source of crime and anti-social behaviour.[30] There is, however, a counterpoint to this rhetoric of moral indignation and culpability.[31] Research has shown that for many squatting is not a lifestyle choice but a necessity brought about by the lack of decent and affordable housing, particularly in areas such as London with high demand and limited supplies of low-cost privately rented homes as well as social housing.[32] These squatters have been described as part of the 'hidden homeless', and it has been noted that squatting attracts some of the most vulnerable, with often the greatest housing need as well as ancillary needs (mental illness, drug or alcohol dependency, recent release from prison) which can make it especially difficult for them to access mainstream housing support.[33]

Recognizing the role of housing need and homelessness in decisions to squat adds a new layer of complexity to the debates around the criminalization of squatters. Several questions might usefully be asked about the urge to criminalize in light of this alternative conception of the squatter's motivation. Is the use of criminal law an inappropriately severe response to what is sometimes a response grounded in necessity rather than mere choice or lifestyle? Is it acceptable to label and stigmatize as criminals those who are some of the most vulnerable in society? And does the individualized conception of the problem of squatting draw our

---

[27] Although the government asked consultees if some types of building (including long-term empty buildings) should be excluded from the ambit of any new criminal offence: Ministry of Justice, n.10 p. 9.

[28] Ministry of Justice, n.10.

[29] It is a recurring criticism of the measures adopted by the state to address squatting that they are often introduced in the absence of reliable data about the nature and extent of the practice: see House of Commons Research Paper, *Squatting* (House of Commons, 1991).

[30] Cobb and Fox, n.8.

[31] Ibid.

[32] Crisis, *Life on the Margins: The Experiences of Homeless People Living in Squats* (Crisis, 2004).

[33] Crisis, *The Hidden Truth about Homelessness* (Crisis, 2011).

attention away from (and allow the state to ignore its own responsibilities for) the structural problems with the current housing market which have created the conditions that have encouraged squatting to take root? Typically, when the state wishes to extend the reach of the criminal law to squatters, such arguments are given short shrift, as the Coalition's consultation paper clearly illustrates:

> [T]he Government does not accept the claim that is sometimes made that squatting is a reasonable recourse of the homeless resulting from social deprivation. There are avenues open to those who are genuinely destitute and who need shelter which do not involve occupying somebody else's property without authority. No matter how compelling or difficult the squatter's own circumstances, it is wrong that legitimate occupants should be deprived of the use of their property.[34]

Whether the mere existence of a bureaucratic system of housing allocation is sufficient to justify criminalizing those who squat due to housing need and homelessness remains contentious without closer examination of the performance of the system in practice, and the reasons why some squatters may struggle to engage with that system.

Is there more mileage in the claim that, regardless of the squatter's circumstances, the criminal law is an appropriate vehicle by which to protect the owner or legal occupier against 'deprivation of the use of property'? At first glance, this is a much more powerful argument in support of criminalization, drawing attention away from a squatter's motivation and instead towards the harm caused by his or her occupation of property contrary to the rights and entitlements of another. Irrespective of the *reasons* for squatting, it might be argued, the *impact* of squatting on owners or legal occupiers justifies a more punitive response. The consultation paper develops this line of argument further:

> [m]ost people would agree that the act of occupying somebody else's property without permission is wrong, *particularly when the occupation causes the property owner to become homeless or impacts negatively on the owner's business.*[35]

This concern – that owners will be deprived of the use value of their properties, whether residential or commercial – is a well-established trope in contemporary debates around squatting and its control.

One popular representation responding to the deprivation of use value by squatting is what Vincent-Jones has described as the 'moral panic' surrounding 'the stereotype of the invasive squatter', assaulting the homes or businesses of those who temporarily leave occupied premises unattended.[36] However, though

---

[34] Ministry of Justice, n.10, p. 1. See also Home Office, *Squatting* (Home Office, 1991).

[35] Ministry of Justice, n.10, para. 19 (emphasis added).

[36] P. Vincent-Jones, 'Private Property and Public Order: the Hippy Convoy and Criminal Trespass' (1986) 13(3) *Journal of Law and Society* 343, 351.

scenarios of this type may sometimes occur,[37] the vast majority of squatters occupy long-term empty properties, or those planned for future occupation, left empty deliberately to maximize their future resale value,[38] or, in some cases, 'lost' by their owners. Indeed, 'spikes' in the prevalence of squatting depend as much on the availability of empty properties as the absence of affordable and decent housing. It is therefore unlikely that owners or legal occupiers will be deprived of the immediate use value of premises of which they were previously in occupation; although, so long as squatted long- term empty properties are not 'lost' in the sense that the owner is unaware of their ownership,[39] the owners, or those to whom they later grant rights of occupation, may in the future have an immediate need to use those premises.

The Coalition Government's stated concern with protecting owners and legal occupiers made homeless by squatters belies the fact that the government's purported concern with the deprivations caused to owners or legal occupiers who need property as a home are dealt with more than adequately by the law as it stands. Where the criminal law may fall short is in those circumstances in which squatted premises are required for immediate *commercial* use, either because the owner or legal occupier has been displaced by the squatters, or has an immediate future need for the property for business purposes. That type of property, however, will not be affected by the Coalition's proposed change to the law, which – following consultation – will now extend to residential property alone. This restriction was motivated primarily by the government's concern that an offence applying to commercial property would curtail the right to peaceful protest, such as university sit-ins and occupations of business premises in support of industrial action.[40]

Whatever one's view on the justifiability of criminal liability for squatters who deprive owners or legal occupiers of the immediate use value of their premises, it is clear that the government's purported concern with the deprivation of use value is not reflected in the scope and scale of the new offence that it has proposed. Notably, the offence of squatting in residential premises is not restricted in practice to premises required for immediate use. Instead, the offence will empower the police to take action against squatters whether or not the owner or legal occupier requires the property for any future purpose at all. In short, even though the harm of squatting might be presented as deprivation of use value, the proposed offence could be used to protect nothing more than bare proprietary interests. This represents a significant leap from the settlement created by the Law Commission

---

[37] For an (deliberately provocative) illustration, see R. Kisiel, 'Knife-Wielding Lithuanian Squatters Who Move in when Residents Go Out' *Daily Mail*, 24 September 2010.

[38] For an indication of the interest of squatters in these properties, consider the successful Freedom of Information request submitted by the Advisory Service for Squatters, requiring Camden Council to release information about void residential properties owned by the council and private organizations in the area: *Voyias v Information Commissioner & London Borough of Camden* [2011] EA/2011/0007, 2 September 2011.

[39] As was sometimes the case in relation to local authority properties in the 1980s; see Cobb and Fox, n.8.

[40] Ministry of Justice, n.10, pp. 37–38.

and the legislators of the Criminal Law Act 1977, all of whom saw the need for immediate use for property, whether as a displaced or intending occupier, as the *sine qua non* of criminal liability.

Autobiographical note

Neil and Dave on the (legal) politics of squatting

Neil writes:

I was compelled by frustration to respond to the government's consultation on the new offence of squatting in buildings. The demonization of squatters in recent years, especially by the media, has always jarred with my own experience of squats. The few I came across as a student in Bristol were long-term empty properties that, in the hands of their new occupiers, were tended well and used creatively. For poorer students they were godsends. I can only imagine the housing pressures now faced by many students at university today in the wake of the increase in fees.

What also leaves me cold is the crude attempt to respond to the complexities of the deepening housing crisis by punishing the most marginalized, and diverting policing resources to protect the interests of wealthy absent property owners, who remain primarily responsible for the serious problem of long-term empty homes. It is no surprise that the state's response to squatting remains such a potent political fault line, when it divides right from left so successfully.

But it's my experience of the consultation process that makes me particularly angry. Out of 2,217 responses to the consultation 2,126 were received from members of the public concerned about the impact of criminalizing squatting. Only 25 responses were from members of the public concerned about the harm squatting can cause. As such, the government's conclusion that it was right to press ahead with the new offence 'given the level of public concern about this issue' raises questions about its commitment to evidence-led policy-making. It took just three weeks for the Ministry of Justice to publish its response to the consultation, just in time for the new offence to be added to the Legal Aid Bill as a last- minute amendment, with minimal debate, before it left the Commons for the Lords. Which indicates that the government's mind was made up long before the consultation began, and in turn leaves one wondering what the point of the process was.

Dave writes:

Before and after the consultation document to which Neil responded, I was one of many who became concerned by the Coalition Government's representation of the current law. The question should have been whether the then current law was sufficient and whether it was enforced appropriately. The answer to the former question was probably that it could have been 'tweaked'; the answer to the latter was that it appeared to be poorly understood by the police and not enforced. All of the media-produced examples of the terrible effects squatting had on the owners of the properties were not the 'fault' of the law *per se* (in fact, they could have been dealt with relatively quickly through a combination of police enforcement and interim possession orders) but its inadequate understanding and enforcement. 'Nearly Legal', who authors a brilliant and highly recommended housing and property law blog, organized over 160 housing and property lawyers (there were 169 personal signatories and one organization – Housing Law Practitioners Association) to sign a letter which stated our (I was a signatory) concerns about '... such repeated inaccurate reporting of this issue [which] has created fear for homeowners, confusion for the police and ill informed debate among both the public and politicians on reforming the law'. The letter went on to clarify the precise extent of the then law (http://www.guardian.co.uk/society/2011/sep/25/squatting-law-media-politicians). Mike Weatherley MP, a Conservative MP in favour of criminalizing squatting, sent a letter to the *Guardian* in response (http://www.guardian.co.uk/society/2011/sep/29/lawyers-interest-in-squatting-law). In it he wrote 'The self-proclaimed experts who signed the letter, sheep-like, have a huge vested interest when it comes to fees after all'; and, with a final flourish, he added:

'The police will not assist with an eviction in most cases without the backing of a magistrate's order. This takes sometimes a few hours, sometimes it's the next day. In the meantime, the unlawful occupiers will have been damaging your home, using your electricity, drinking your wine and sleeping in your beds. The police should be able to act immediately. Squatters need the threat of a criminal conviction to stop them. If any of those who signed the letter doubt this, then let me throw down the gauntlet – vacate your house for a few days and advertise its emptiness on the appropriate squatter sites. We will see how quickly you can get them out and just how distressed you are at the lack of justice. Maybe then you will think twice before defending squatters. It's no wonder that the public have lost faith in our legal system'.

Nearly Legal contained two blog entries in response to that letter. The first was by David Smith, an eminent, knowledgeable contributor, who wrote in careful, measured tones a brilliant response (http://nearlylegal.co.uk/blog/2011/09/squatting-a-reply-to-mike-weatherley-mp/). Quite different in tone, although equally brilliant, was the response from a person called 'the Chief', who savagely and wittily countered Mr Weatherley's arguments (http://nearlylegal.co.uk/blog/2011/09/pass-me-down-the-wine/). But, while those responses gave me fresh heart, the government continued with its reforming zeal. It is appropriate, as he organized and wrote the original multi-signatory letter, to leave the last word on this subject to Nearly Legal himself who, in a blog entry entitled 'Forward to the 18th Century', wrote:

The consultation response, which is supposed to justify this amendment, is a confused affair, right from Crispin Blunt's foreword, where after noting that it is already an offence to continue to occupy someone's home, he promotes the amendment in these terms 'But the offence will provide greater protection in circumstances where the harm caused is the greatest – squatting in someone's home. This behaviour is unacceptable and must be stopped'. Mr Blunt should perhaps have read the response first. In particular the parts pointing out that failure to enforce existing powers by the police was a problem reported in landlords/property owners responses, see Q.19. In addition delays in court timetables and in bailiffs' appointments were raised by these respondents. This is, of course, a funding issue that is only going to get worse.

The Metropolitan Police, on behalf of ACPO [Association of Chief Police Officers], opposed any change to the current law, while admitting that, well, maybe a bit of training on CLA 1977 wouldn't go amiss for officers.

The equality impact assessment accompanying the consultation response also concedes that, even after this whole exercise, the MoJ have no real idea about the scale of the problem, or how far it is a problem. They estimate between '200 to 2100 criminal squatting cases in residential property' per annum. That is a broad range, equating to 'dunno'.

The equality impact assessment notes that, on the basis of the reports prepared for Crisis and others, the proposal would impact disproportionately on the young and the disabled. But, well, tough. (http://nearlylegal. co.uk/blog/2011/10/forward-to-the-18th-century/)

Plus ça change.

Debate 2

Private rights versus public responsibilities: land owners and the ethic of stewardship

The government's proposals to criminalize squatting, even in situations in which there is no deprivation of immediate use value of property, suggest it is concerned less with the deprivation of use value and more with protecting the rights of property owners. Thus, the present rhetoric of criminalization implies that squatting is intrinsically problematic simply because it constitutes an infringement of proprietary rights, regardless of the material effect of unauthorized occupation on owners or legal occupiers (whether loss of immediate use as a home, as commercial premises, or otherwise). The overall effect is the moralization of the squatter and squatting, while the use (or not) made by the owner or legal occupier of property is deemed morally irrelevant to the scope of criminal liability. This can be contrasted with the position under the 1977 Act, which placed an implicit moral value on the deprivation of an owner or legal occupier's use of premises as a home. In this way, contemporary debates regarding the criminalization of squatting also help to draw our attention conveniently away from the responsibility which might be apportioned to property owners (and the state) for allowing property to be used in ways which create the conditions in which squatting thrives.

Understanding squatting as (at least to some extent) a symptom of housing need and homelessness highlights the causal role played not only by an inadequate supply of decent and affordable housing, but also by the availability of long-term empty properties, which remain the most attractive option for squatters seeking stable residential accommodation. Empty properties of this kind have been identified as a problem not only because they encourage squatting, but because bringing empty homes into residential use potentially helps meet demand for residential accommodation.[41] There is at least some passing recognition of the role played by empty properties in encouraging squatting, and the shared responsibility of the state and owners in failing to tackle this problem, in the Coalition consultation, where a review of what steps might be taken to bring more empty properties into residential use was also announced.[42]

That the government has pressed ahead first with proposals to criminalize squatters suggests, though, that squatters are more easily subject to blame than owners of empty properties or the state. Nevertheless, focusing for the moment on the responsibilities that might be understood to fall on the owner of empty property to bring those premises back into use, to what extent can squatting be constructed as a problem which implicates not only the moral failure of the squatter (if at all) but also the moral failure of the owner of squatted property to satisfy the ethics of effective stewardship of land? And how might this affect how we think about the appropriate response of the state (and so law) to the phenomenon of squatting?

The ethical argument that land ownership imposes a duty of effective stewardship is based on the public interest in effective land use[43] and the view that '[t]he quest to protect the privileges of private property against all intruders regardless of the price or need … is an unholy one'.[44] The stewardship perspective posits that private landowners are the bearers not only of rights in respect of land, but are also subject to a corresponding duty or responsibility to ensure that the limited and vital resource of land is managed fairly on behalf of the community as a whole.

---

[41] See, for example, Office of the Deputy Prime Minister, *Empty Homes: Temporary Management, Lasting Solutions: A Consultation Paper* (TSO, 2003); Office of the Deputy Prime Minister, *Empty Property: Unlocking the Potential – A Case for Action* (TSO, 2003).

[42] Ministry of Justice, n.10, Foreword.

[43] See, for example, J. Karp, 'A Private Property Duty of Stewardship: Changing Our Land Ethic' (1993) 23(3) *Environmental Law* 737; L. Caldwell and K. Shrader-Frechette, *Policy for Land: Law and Ethics* (Rowman & Littlefield, 1993) ch. 7.

[44] Karp, n.43.

Yet, this perspective does not sit easily within the traditional common law framework of property law. The common law typically conceived of property interests as vested in individuals (or groups of individuals), rather than the interests of the community or the public interest.

While the idea that landowners have a responsibility to 'steward' their land effectively has been displaced by a moral agenda against both the activity of squatting and the loss of title through adverse possession, this reflects a particular set of political priorities (underpinned by economic rationality) that has only emerged and achieved dominance in England and Wales in recent decades. Yet, in other contexts – whether in other jurisdictions, other disciplines, or even simply outside the realm of real property within English law – the philosophy of stewardship has continued to attract support (in some cases, increasingly) on the basis that it provides a defensible basis on which to develop strategies for the allocation or protection of scarce resources. For example, Gray identified what he described as a form of 'equitable property' in 'the quality and conservation of the natural environment'.[45] He argued that this formed the basis of a new type of property claim – not concerned with merely empowering exclusion but with empowering reasonable shared access to valued resources for all citizens. Gray emphasized the prominence of *responsibility* – rather than merely rights – in this conception of property; a responsibility that is rooted in 'an overriding duty to "look after [sic] country"'.[46] Indeed, Gray claimed that there had been a marked resurgence of civic reciprocity as a key concept in property law discourse,[47] at least in relation to significant public issues, for example, relating to the environmental quality of life we enjoy, invariably in common with our fellow citizens.

This concept of responsibility can be discerned in a range of property contexts, particularly in the contexts of planning law or environmental protection: for example, the categories of 'listed buildings'[48] and 'ancient monuments' identify specific properties which have been designated as part of the built historic environment, so that their preservation is deemed to be in the public interest. They cannot be altered, extended or demolished without express permission from the local planning authority.[49] The concept of stewardship has also emerged in the context of indigenous rights to land, and rights to natural resources based on patterns of use and occupancy[50] have been a central part of the indigenous

---

[45] K. Gray, 'Equitable Property' (1994) 47 *Current Legal Problems* 137, 188.

[46] Ibid, 189.

[47] See also K. Gray and S. Gray, 'The Rhetoric of Realty' in J. Getzler (ed.), *Rationalizing Property, Equity and Trusts: Essays in Honour of Edward Burn* (LexisNexis Butterworth, 2003) pp. 265–78.

[48] Structures which have been placed on the Statutory List of Buildings of Special Architectural or Historic Interest.

[49] See, for example, the Town and Country Planning Act 1947.

[50] See, for example, provisions of the American Declaration on the Rights and Duties of Man and the American Convention on Human Rights that affirm rights of indigenous peoples to lands and natural resources on the basis of traditional patterns of use and occupancy. McEvoy discusses the clash between common law conceptions of private property and indigenous practices of land holding: A. McEvoy, 'Markets and Ethics in US Property Law' in H. Jacobs (ed.), *Who Owns America? Social Conflict over Property Rights* (University of Wisconsin Press, 1998).

peoples' rights movements in the Americas, Australia, New Zealand and other parts of the world.[51] The indigenous rights movements emphasize the centrality of traditional land use to the cultural survival and physical well-being of indigenous communities, as well as the beliefs of many indigenous peoples that they bear a collective responsibility to steward the land. For example, in *Begay v Keedah*,[52] the Navajo Supreme Court described the differences between the Navajo concept of land ownership and land tenure under the English common law:

> Traditional Navajo land tenure is not the same as English common law tenure...Navajos have always occupied land in family units, using the land for subsistence. Families and subsistence residential units (as they are sometimes called) hold land in a form of communal ownership.

Land and its resources are not viewed as primarily economic assets for exchange, but as a resource for use which imparts a sacred trust:

> Our lands are a sacred gift. The land is provided for the continued use, benefit and enjoyment of our people, and it is our ultimate obligation to the Great Spirit to care for and protect it.[53]

The concept of indigenous sovereignty thus includes the right *and responsibility* of indigenous nations to care for and protect traditional lands and resources.

This concept of responsibility for land as a valuable resource is also inherent to the Islamic conception of property rights, which '...conceives of land as a sacred trust',[54] supporting a duty of stewardship on the basis that '[p]roperty and land vest in God, but are temporarily enjoyed by men and women through responsibility or trust...conditional on the requirement that property not be used wastefully ...'.[55] This perspective is also supported by the concept of property rights in Islamic economics, which 'has implications far beyond the material domain as it lays stress on responsibility, poverty alleviation and redistribution',[56] and seeks to work from 'a holistic, authentic, moral, ethical and legal land rights code'.[57] The relevance of this approach to squatters and unsupervised land is most clearly illustrated by the Islamic concept of *mewat* or 'dead land', which allows individuals to claim for their own use land that is empty and uncultivated or undeveloped.[58]

---

[51] S. Anaya and R. Williams Jr, 'The Protection of Indigenous Peoples' Rights Over Lands and Natural Resources Under the Inter-American Human Rights System' (2001) 14(1) *Harvard Human Rights Journal* 33.

[52] 19 *Indian L Rep* 6021, 6022 (Navajo 1991).

[53] Union of British Colombia Indian Chiefs, *Aboriginal Title and Rights Position Paper* (1978).

[54] UN-HABITAT, Islam, Land & Property Research Series, Paper 1: Islamic Land Theories and Their Application (UN-HABITAT, 2005) p. 8.

[55] Ibid, 10.

[56] Ibid, 14.

[57] Ibid.

[58] See S. Sait and H. Lim, *Land, Law & Islam: Property & Human Rights in the Muslim World* (Zed, 2006) p. 61.

The concept of an ethic of care has been a significant theme in recent scholar-ship across the social sciences, notably in feminist theory,[59] and has been applied to a range of contemporary moral dilemmas, including the role of the dispassion-ate workings of market institutions, 'infused with an individualised competitive imperative',[60] compared to the responsibilities of the state in respect of social justice and inequality in housing. Where the ethic of rights and justice values individualized, commoditized rights to exclusion and control, an ethic of care and responsibility values interpersonal, intergenerational community interests. Yet, while the ethic of care invokes moral responsibilities, in the legal domain it is usually trumped by the rights-and-entitlements discourse of ownership. For example, even in the context of cultural property, where the concepts of stew-ardship and the ethic of care are clearly present, they take second place to the discourse of property rights.[61] It is only where specific public law protections are layered on top of the common law – for example, in relation to planning or environmental law, or land explicitly designated as commons land[62] – that the community interest in stewardship and the values of access and use (rather than exclusion and exchange) can play a role in the mediation of property claims.[63] Even in the context of commons land and public rights of access to the country-side, it has been argued that public rights created by legislation are 'subverted by vested interests and the ideological power of private property'.[64]

Yet, as with so many of the debates we consider in this book, this is not an inevitable feature of property law: the roots of a concept of stewardship within the English common law doctrines governing property were very much present in feudal structures and pre-1925.[65] Rather, it is the ideological framework of property law since 1925, and even more so since the LRA 2002, that is averse to restrictions on, or threats to the security of, formal land ownership rights. Indeed, the idea of communal or collective land rights has been so divorced from conventional models of ownership that it is constructed as a form of resistance to the political

---

[59] See for example, C. Gilligan, *In a Different Voice* (Harvard University Press, 1982), identifying a gendered distinction between 'masculine' (associated with an 'ethic of rights and justice') and 'feminine' (associ-ated with an 'ethic of care and responsibility') moralities.

[60] S. Smith, 'States, Markets and An Ethic of Care' (2005) 24(1) *Political Geography* 1.

[61] See, for example, J. Sax, *Playing Darts with a Rembrandt: Public and Private Rights in Cultural Treasures* (University of Michigan Press, 1999), discussing the rights of the private owner of a work of art to destroy his property.

[62] See the Commons Act 2006, which allowed for the registration of common land or town or village greens. The concept underlying commons land is that it belongs to no-one and everyone; it can be used by all but appropriated by none.

[63] In the US, Alexander has challenged the idea that exclusion is the core of property, arguing instead that there is a competing tradition within property law which recognizes the communitarian nature of property ownership: see, for example, G. Alexander, 'Takings and the Post-Modern Dialectic of Property' (1992) 9 *Const Comment* 259. More recently, Alexander has identified this civic vision of property as the 'social-obligation' norm: see, for example, G. Alexander, 'The Social-Obligation Norm in American Property Law' (2009) 94 *Cornell L Rev* 745.

[64] J. Mitchell, 'What Public Presence? Access, Commons and Property Rights' (2008) 17(3) *Social and Legal Studies* 351, 352.

[65] For example, the strict settlement, which explicitly preserved interests in land for future generations.

ideology of private property.[66] For example, the criminalization of squatting has re-cast the debate concerning homeless squatters in empty properties so that the utilitarian argument that the land owner (who is neither using the property nor adequately fulfilling the duty of stewardship over their land) in fact has a morally weaker claim to that property compared to a squatter (who is making effective use of the property, and who is in desperate and pressing need of shelter) is excluded from the dominant discourse oriented around the idea that the squatter *is* the social problem.

The extent to which English law allows for the possibility of resistance to private ownership as exclusion, including by those who are marginalized under current property arrangements, has also been dramatically curtailed by the reform of adverse possession in the LRA 2002. As the discussion in the next section will demonstrate, this has fundamentally altered the matrix of rights and duties attendant on land ownership in England and Wales. In the great debate between the private, individualized, capitalized interests of the land owner and the public, community, socialized interests of the land user,[67] the LRA 2002 provides one example of the more generally acknowledged pre-eminence afforded to private interests in land.

Debate 3

Owners versus squatters :adverse possession and the acquisition of title to land

The LRA 2002 adopted a strong policy position against adverse possession, effectively limiting the circumstances in which a squatter could claim title to registered land to either the three narrow 'special cases' exemptions, which were designed more to enhance the technocratic system than to facilitate a social and/or political objective; or to those (very unlikely) circumstances in which the registered proprietor makes no objection to the squatter's claim once notified. The erosion of traditional principles of adverse possession by the LRA 2002, together with the decision of the Grand Chamber of the European Court of Human Rights in *Pye v The United Kingdom*[68] have embedded a new legal order for the regulation of title by adverse possession, underpinned by a set of taken-for-granted moral perspectives which reflect a wholly negative view of the activity of squatting.[69] These changes have taken place in parallel to a discourse of moral outrage towards squatters *per se*. From that perspective, it is unsurprising that English law has

---

[66] J. Holder and T. Flessas, 'Emerging Commons' (2008) 17(3) *Social and Legal Studies* 299.

[67] Although an individual person in adverse possession (the 'squatter') is not 'the public' as such, in cases involving homeless squatters, the individual is representative of a social responsibility on the part of the community as a whole to respond to the needs of marginalized and vulnerable populations.

[68] *Application no. 44302/02*; available online at <http://cmiskp.echr.coe.int/tkp197/view.asp?action=html&documentId=822955&portal=hbkm&source=externalbydocnumber&table=F69A27FD8FB86142BF01C1166DEA398649> (last accessed15 November 2011).

[69] See Cobb and Fox, n.8.

rejected the doctrine which allowed trespassers to land to secure a title interest against the registered proprietor.[70] The erosion of adverse possession in England and Wales was presented by the Law Commission and Land Registry as a necessary adjunct to the ever-tighter principles of registration implemented in the 2002 Act; although this perspective has been questioned by some scholars,[71] and is arguably at odds with the continued existence of traditional principles of adverse possession in many mature Torrens-style land registration systems.[72]

The erosion of the traditional doctrine of adverse possession in the LRA 2002 is certainly consistent with the principles of title registration advanced in that Act. However, there was clearly another agenda at work here, which went beyond the technicalities of land registration to the values that underpin the English system of land ownership and property rights. This agenda, which has also been advanced through judicial dicta, reflects the ethic of justice and rights discussed in the previous section. For example, Lord Bingham described the operation of the pre-2002 principles of adverse possession as 'apparently unjust',[73] while Neuberger J claimed that it was: '…hard to see what principle of justice entitles the trespasser to acquire the land for nothing from the owner simply because he has been permitted to remain there for 12 years'; such a conclusion '…does not accord with justice, and cannot be justified by practical considerations, [is] draconian to the owner and a windfall for the squatter'.[74] Indeed, the House of Lords explicitly identified an anti-stewardship ethic when expressing regret that the pre-2002 principles required that it find in favour of the squatter. In Lord Hope's opinion, the unfairness of the traditional doctrine of adverse possession was not 'the absence of compensation, although that is an important factor, but…the lack of safeguards against oversight or inadvertence on the part of the registered proprietor'.[75]

While the human rights dimension of the English adverse possession debate was forestalled by the extended litigation in *Pye v Graham*,[76] and subsequently, in the European Court of Human Rights in *Pye v UK*[77] – decisions which themselves were shaped by England's domestic property politics[78] – these very decisions have re-invigorated the debate between possession and registration, and their respective

---

[70] Ibid, fn 4.

[71] Dixon described 'the reform of the process of adverse possession by the 2002 Act as an unnecessary and economically unjustified "bolt on" to the reform of registered land': Dixon (2005), n.8, 351.

[72] See *Adverse Possession*, a Report by the British Institution of International and Comparative Law for Her Majesty's Court Service (September 2006), which outlines the key principles of adverse possession across a range of ECHR and common law jurisdictions.

[73] *JA Pye (Oxford) Ltd v Graham* [2003] 1 AC 419, [2], *per* Lord Bingham.

[74] *JA Pye (Oxford) Ltd v Graham* [2000] Ch 676, 709–10.

[75] *Pye*, HL, n.X, [73].

[76] Ibid.

[77] *JA Pye (Oxford) Ltd v United Kingdom* (2006) 43 EHRR 3 (Chamber judgment); *Case of J.A. Pye (Oxford) Ltd and JA Pye (Oxford) Land Ltd v The United Kingdom* (Application no. 44302/02), (Grand Chamber judgment).

[78] L. Fox O'Mahony and N. Cobb, 'Taxonomies of Squatting: Unlawful Occupation in a New Legal Order' (2008) 71(6) *MLR* 878.

underlying values of social use and economic efficiency, in other jurisdictions.[79] These values, in turn, come back to what we think it means to own land, and what weight we attach to the possession or use of the land. The curtailment of adverse possession clearly demonstrates a preference for rights of exclusion over rights of access in our conception of property ownership, for the abstract rights of title over what is in fact occurring on the land.

The political nature of the LRA 2002, and the importance of perspective, was illustrated in interesting ways by the approach to adverse possession taken by the Northern Ireland Law Commission in its recent report on Land Law.[80] While the Commission made extensive reference to the approach adopted by its English counterpart, its search for local solutions led to a rejection of the decisive policy departure taken by the English law in the LRA 2002. The Northern Ireland analysis explicitly recognized that the question of reform in this area required a careful consideration of the values and ethics that underpin the doctrine as well as its practical effects. Perhaps most significantly in comparison with the English experience, the political and moral agenda against squatting has not been a prominent feature in the Northern Ireland context. The result was that, when balancing the interests at stake, it was possible to talk in terms of the traditional justifications for the doctrine.[81] While the Commission's analysis of these traditional bases for the squatter's claim were not deemed sufficiently decisive to resolve the debate, the complexities of the social and economic issues that lie behind the law of adverse possession were clearly acknowledged.

While the English approach to adverse possession was heavily influenced by the context of land registration, it was also clearly shaped by the political and moral agenda against trespass to land and squatting (now designated land theft). Indeed, the Northern Ireland Law Commission explicitly stated that it did not wish to adopt an ethical stance on adverse possession,[82] and rejected the moral agenda (referred to as the ethical element) introduced by the LRA 2002 through the good faith requirement attached to the exception for boundary mistakes.[83] The Commission also expressed 'considerable reservations' about the ethical implications of the shift in balance between landowner and squatter in the LRA

---

[79] For example, Griggs has defined the debate underlying contemporary adverse possession discourse in Australia as between the 'economic imperatives' of the Torrens system and the traditional importance of possession to land ownership: L. Griggs, 'Possession, Indefeasibility and Human Rights' (2008) 8(2) *Queensland University of Technology Law and Justice Journal* 286.

[80] Northern Ireland Law Commission, *Report: Land Law*, NILC 8 (Belfast: TSO, 2010); the report followed a detailed discussion of adverse possession in Northern Ireland Law Commission, *Supplementary Consultation Paper, Land Law*, NILC No 3 (Northern Ireland Law Commission, 2010).

[81] For example, the avoidance of stale claims, or owners sleeping on their rights, the hardship arguments on the side of both the squatter and the land owner, the claim that adverse possession in fact promotes effective land use, and the ethical argument that land ownership imposes a moral duty of effective stewardship on the owner, to look beyond their own selfish interests to ensure that this limited and vital commodity is managed fairly on behalf of the community as a whole

[82] '... partly because it would require the courts to consider the motives, intentions and beliefs of the parties. It would be likely to make the law much more complicated and thereby run counter to the Commission's primary aim of simplicity, clarity and certainty': Supplementary Paper, para. 2.42.

[83] LRA 2002, sch. 6, para. 5(4)(c).

2002, which 'greatly increases the protection of the owner from a failure to keep an eye on the property'.[84] It is, of course, arguable that one cannot avoid moral judgments in this context, as they are implicit (one way or the other) to both an acceptance of the justifications for the doctrine, and also the rejection of those justifications (as has occurred in England and Wales in respect of registered land).

CONCLUSION

Both the agenda for criminalization of squatting and the erosion of the traditional doctrine of adverse possession in the LRA 2002 are clearly embedded within a broader commitment to the protection of property/capital ownership interests, the commodification of real property, and the pursuit of economic security for those who hold formal rights in land. This agenda is neoliberal in the sense that it protects and prioritizes the market; but paradoxically it also reveals a tension within the neoliberal agenda. While neoliberalism is associated with ideas of self-responsibility and self-provision, the criminalization of squatting would bring what has historically been a civil law dispute for the recovery of land between two private individuals – with the land owner held responsible for protecting her own interests by discovering and acting to remove the squatter – into the realm of public protection, so empowering the police – without any intervening judicial process to adjudicate the parties' respective claims – to enforce the land owner's paper title.

This potential use of the criminal law to protect land owners who have failed to discharge their duty of stewardship inverts the neoliberal ideas of individual self-responsibility and non-intervention in private law. Similarly, the LRA 2002 rejects both the self-help activity of squatting by homeless populations (a practice widely recognized in many other jurisdictions) and the proposition that land owners are responsible for stewarding their own land. Rather, property law – through the agency of the Land Registry – has stepped into what was once regarded as a private dispute to safeguard the proprietary rights and entitlements of land owners who, it must be assumed, can no longer be held responsible (on pain of losing their investment in the land) for discovering and taking steps to remove unlawful occupiers within the traditional 12-year window. Indeed, it is arguable that both developments support the argument that the concept of individual responsibility underpinning neoliberal policies is geared towards – and sometimes conveniently forgotten to facilitate – the interests of a particular type of status- and capital-owning individual.

Further Reading

N. Cobb and L. Fox, 'Living Outside the System? The (Im)Morality of Urban Squatting' (2007) 27(2) *Legal Studies* 236.

L. Fox O'Mahony and N. Cobb, 'Taxonomies of Squatting: Unlawful Occupation in a New Legal Order' (2008) 71(6) *MLR* 878.

---

[84] Supplementary Paper, para. 2.50.

K. Reeve with E. Batty, *The Hidden Truth about Homelessness: Experiences of Single Homelessness in England* (Crisis, 2011), http://www.crisis.org.uk/data/files/publications/HiddenTruthAboutHomelessness_web.pdf

P. Vincent-Jones, 'Private Property and Public Order: The Hippy Convoy and Criminal Trespass' (1986) 13(3) *Journal of Law and Society* 343.

7

THIRD-PARTY INTERESTS IN THE USE AND CONTROL OF LAND

INTRODUCTION

This chapter focuses on two categories of burden on land: easements (obligations that benefit and burden two separate pieces of land) and restrictive freehold (and, more recently, commonhold) covenants (promises restricting the use of freehold land). It proposes that these private law obligations cannot be fully understood without also considering the broader context of public law obligations that relate to the use of land. Consequently, this chapter explores the nature and development of easements and restrictive covenants in the context of the social, economic and political arguments for permitting third parties to control use of land by private owners, as well as the control and regulation of land use as a public function. The chapter also considers the historical context in which the legal framework for the regulation of third-party interests in the use of land has evolved. While easements have been recognized since time immemorial (originally in response to agricultural needs), restrictive freehold covenants are a relatively modern invention, triggered by a specific social need. The restrictive freehold covenant was first recognized in English courts at the height of the Second Industrial Revolution, in the landmark case of *Tulk v Moxhay*.[1] The industrial revolutions had a huge impact on urbanization of England, which in turn raised major issues for land control. Increased population density and the proliferation of land uses required 'effective techniques to control the manner in which land was used so as to avoid one landowner's interfering with the interests of his neighbour'.[2] The impact of these changes in land use patterns, as well as more recent demands for the commercialization and commodification of interests in land, alongside the growing emphasis on registration and discoverability as the requirements for enforceability, have put in play a series of debates which are explored in this chapter.

Each of these debates is linked to the tension between the private property owner's right to exclude all others from his land and the general public interest

---

[1] (1848) 2 Ph 774; (1848) 47 ER 1345.

[2] P. McCarthy, 'The Enforcement of Restrictive Covenants in France and Belgium: Judicial Discretion and Urban Planning' (1973) 73(1) *Colum L Rev* 1.

in the use of land as a valuable resource. This tension can be seen in the over-laps between strategies developed by private law and (latterly in the UK) public law to enable the control of a private owner's use of their land, as well as in the principles by which conflicts of interest between land owner and neighbours are resolved. While Gray and Gray identified land transactions between strangers as characterized by meta-norms of heightened rationality[3] (according to which the land is valued, perhaps even exclusively, according to its exchange value),[4] in cases involving neighbouring land owners they argued that the legal framework is shaped by a norm of reasonableness. The distinctive feature of the relation-ship between neighbours was identified as different from that between strangers. The parties have entered into voluntarily assumed relationships of 'medium-term proximity', giving them an extended timescale against which they will need to co-operate: 'with the result that neighbours tend to enjoy a longer line of social credit than is possible in random commercial interactions between strangers'.[5] Gray and Gray described these relationships as having 'an on-going, interactive and quasi-public quality', within a community domain shaped by shared and mutual interests, 'temper[ing] the aggressive pursuit of individual self-interest' which has come to be associated with land purchases and mortgage transactions, for example.

This led them to conclude that in relation to third-party burdens on land the dominant modes for thinking about rights and interests 'within the forum of the neighbourhood' are provided by the use value of the land, rather than its exchange value (see Chapter 3); the reasonableness of actions rather than economic ration-ality; social co-operation rather than self-interest; and duties and responsibil-ities rather than simply rights.[6] This 'neighbourhood' principle is manifest in a number of ways that create burdens on the private owner's absolute dominion over her land. While the common law (and latterly equity also) contributed the easement and the *profit à prendre*, and the Court of Chancery conjured up the restrictive freehold covenant, Parliament has also frequently intervened to recog-nize specific policy-driven burdens on private ownership – for example, through the Countryside and Rights of Way Act 2000, which limited private ownership over open countryside by creating public rights of way (a right to roam) with a view to giving people greater freedom to explore and to enjoy the health benefits of fresh air and exercise. There is also a relationship between the emergence and application of private rights controlling the use of land (initially through lease-hold covenants, and from 1848 through restrictive freehold covenants) and the development of public planning law.

In this chapter, we frame these questions in terms of four great debates. First, we consider whether positive covenants should be enforceable against successors

---

[3] See K. Gray and S. Gray, 'The Rhetoric of Realty' in J. Getzler (ed.), *Rationalising Property, Equity and Trusts: Essays in Honour of Edward Burn* (LexisNexis UK, 2003) esp. pp. 253–65.
[4] Gray & Gray, n.3, p. 241.
[5] Ibid, p. 242.
[6] Ibid, p. 256.

in title; second, we consider whether controls are better accomplished through private or public law; third, we ask about the impacts of the legal frameworks enabling governance of use rights; and finally, whether property law should control the permissible content of easements and freehold covenants.

Debate 1

Should positive freehold covenants be enforceable against successors in title?

Prior to the decision in *Tulk v Moxhay*,[7] promises relating to the use of land were mere contracts, personal obligations which were not generally assignable to third parties. At common law, while the benefit of the full range of freehold covenants could be enforced by a successor in title so long as the requirements set out in *Smith & Snipes Hall Farm v River Douglas Catchment Board*[8] were satisfied, the burden of freehold covenants could not (directly) pass to a successor in title.[9] It was the reluctance of common law courts to accept that the burden of covenants might run – in light of the implications this would have in allowing private property ownership of freehold land to be burdened by promises made by another – which led to equitable intervention in 1848.[10] The decision to allow a restrictive freehold covenant to bind successors in title in equity coincided with the urban growth in development, as well as the emergence of concerns about the quality of amenities for residential occupiers. Urbanization increased the demand for private living space, and growing crime rates heightened concerns about security, privacy and exclusivity.[11] A demand emerged for a technique to enable the type of control over use of freehold land as had been enjoyed through the more readily enforceable leasehold covenant.

The emergence of the restrictive covenant as an instrument recognized as property also responded to the *laissez-faire* policies of the time, as they could be justified by their roots in the voluntary agreement of the parties. Yet, while the popular story suggests that – under careful judicial development – these private agreements became useful tools to control the use of land,[12] the current status of Leicester Square (the location of the dispute in *Tulk*) resulted not from the freehold covenant applied to it, but from the subsequent public governance of land

---

[7] (1848) 2 Ph 774; (1848) 47 ER 1345.

[8] [1949] 2 KB 500.

[9] 'English common law dogmatically insists that only the benefit, and not the burden, of a freehold covenant may run with the land': K. Gray and S. Gray, *Elements of Land Law* (Oxford University Press, 5th edn, 2009), para. 3.3.24.

[10] That having been said, the reasoning in *Tulk* was circular – the right was binding because the stranger had notice of it. It was only subsequent authorities which rationalized and narrowed the jurisdiction – see, in particular, *Haywood v Brunswick Permanent Benefit BS* (1881) 8 QBD 403.

[11] S. Blandy, 'Gated Communities in England: Historical Perspectives and Current Developments' (2006) 66(1) *Geojournal* 15, 18.

[12] McCarthy, n.2, 2.

use. In fact, the restrictive covenant regime offered limited scope to maintain a high-functioning open space arrangement on the square, and thirty years after the decision the land was philanthropically donated to the local government authority, to be used as a public square.[13] It is therefore the power of the public authority, not the private covenant, which is responsible for today's Leicester Square.

The judicial resistance to positive covenants having similar effects is related to concerns about the doctrine of privity of contract. We can enable certain limited covenants, which comply with the relevant conditions (restrictive in nature, intended to bind third parties, protected as necessary on the register), to have durable effect, but to go beyond that would affect the hallowed doctrine of privity. This is what seems to lie behind Lord Templeman's insistence in *Rhone v Stephens*, which he expressed in circular reasoning as follows: 'Enforcement of a positive covenant lies in contract; a positive covenant compels an owner to exercise his rights. Enforcement of a negative covenant lies in property; a negative covenant deprives the owner of a right over property.'[14] By that stage, as Lord Templeman remarked, it was too late to overturn a rule of such elementary principle which had guided behaviour since its inception.[15] In fact, the original basis for the rule, as suggested by Cotton LJ in *Austerberry v Oldham Corporation*, was that '... a court of equity does not and ought not to enforce a covenant binding only in equity in such a way as to require the successors of the covenantor himself, they having entered into no covenant, to expend sums of money in accordance with what the original covenantor bound himself to do'.[16]

There is some basis for suggesting that the rule is not as strict as it might have been thought to be. There are ways to circumvent its strict application, most particularly through the doctrine of mutual benefit and burden.[17] However, one result of the decision in *Rhone* is that route has been narrowed considerably.[18]

Debate 2

Should controls on land use be achieved through public law or private law?

The law governing burdens on land can be positioned within a broader set of laws and policies concerned with the regulation of land use. We typically tend to think of controls over land use as being primarily public, administered (in the public interest) through planning law and environmental law. Yet private law (in the form of property law's easement and restrictive covenant, and tort's doctrine

---

[13] J. Smith, '*Tulk v Moxhay*: The Fight to Develop Leicester Square' in G. Korngold and A. Morriss (eds) *Property Stories* (Foundation Press, 2nd edn, 2009).
[14] [1994] 2 AC 310, 318.
[15] At 321.
[16] (1885) 29 CH D 750, 774.
[17] See, particularly, *Halsall v Brizell* [1957] Ch 169.
[18] *Thamesmead Town Ltd v Allotey* (1998) 30 HLR 1052.

of nuisance[19]) has also played its part in both the historical development of land use policies and in the matrix of controls that regulate the uses that contemporary private land owners can make of their land.

The idea that law places limits on the use of privately held land by an absolute owner raises important debates relating to popular conceptions of private ownership, on the one hand, and community ethics concerning land as a valued resource, on the other. Just how private is – or should be – ownership of land? Popular ethics concerning land use shift in response to political ideologies and socio-economic conditions: for example, the dramatic growth in owner-occupation in the twentieth century popularized the view that 'an Englishman's home is his castle'; but this came under challenge when Madonna (largely successfully) opposed the claim that the 'right to roam' in the Countryside and Rights of Way Act 2000 created public rights to enter onto her English country estate.[20] The issue of third-party rights to control the use of privately owned land usually invokes quality of life and environmental considerations, whether on the part of the community at large (the so-called public interest), or one or more private individuals who own or occupy proximate land. While this chapter primarily explores the principles that have informed the development of these private rights to control land use, both public and private actions concerning land use are (explicitly or, in the case of private claims, sometimes implicitly) potentially informed by a broad range of ethical, aesthetic, ecological and socio-economic values concerning land use.[21]

Although questions concerning the permissible limits within which private land owners may exploit their land are now mostly addressed through planning law and environmental law, both of these branches of law are of relatively recent vintage in England and Wales. Indeed, historically, it was private property law which played the primary role in regulating how occupiers of land shared space as neighbours. The English planning system did not reach maturity until 1947, when local authorities were empowered to grant or refuse permission for development on land.[22] Indeed, the modern planning regime evolved from the control of building under the Public Health Acts, which in turn had emerged from the private exercise of building controls through property law.[23] One has only to consider

---

[19] See J. Penner, 'Nuisance and the Character of the Neighbourhood' (1993) 5(1) *Journal of Environmental Law* 1, for discussion of how the concern with the 'character of the neighbourhood' cuts across the tort of nuisance and property law doctrines.

[20] The planning hearing determined that only two out of 17 parcels of land initially identified by the Countryside Agency would be deemed 'open countryside' and so accessible to the public – see <http://www.independent.co.uk/environment/madonna-wins-battle-over-right-to-roam-732731.html>.

[21] See L. Caldwell and K. Shrader-Frechette, *Policy for Land: Law and Ethics* (Rowman & Littlefield Publishers Inc., 1993).

[22] Town and Country Planning Act 1947; although the fundamentals of a planning system that involved plan making or zoning was put in place by the Housing, Town Planning, etc. Act 1909, and developed in the Housing and Town Planning Act 1919 as well as the Town and Country Planning Act 1932.

[23] P. Booth, 'From Regulation to Discretion: The Evolution of Development Control in the British Planning System, 1909–1947' (1999) 14(3) *Planning Perspectives* 277. Booth specifically points to building leases as a source of private control, although restrictive freehold covenants also performed this function.

the facts of the landmark restrictive covenants case, *Tulk v Moxhay*,[24] in which an agreement between private freeholders to keep an area of square garden and pleasure ground in Leicester Square, London 'in an open state, uncovered with any buildings, in neat and ornamental order' was enforced to prevent building on the open space that is now a central landmark in London's West End.[25]

The decision of the Chancery Court that the burden of freehold covenants should be enforceable in equity was timely, and pre-empted the socio-economic shift in emphasis from leasehold to freehold ownership.[26] In the early phase of the Industrial Revolution, from the late eighteenth century, the existence of enforceable leasehold covenants had:

> prove[n] to be enormously effective in both releasing land for urban development and in controlling the form of that development. Such restrictive covenants could apply both to the form and construction of the buildings and to the use to which they were put. Covenants regularly excluded commercial uses in residential areas or prevented the opening of pubs or taverns...Public control, by contrast, was rudimentary.[27]

The private leasehold system regulated matters relating to the amenity value of the property, the character of the neighbourhood for other property owners, and the function of these private rights in enabling control over land use. By the early twentieth century, however – and even with the added facility to enforce restrictive covenants against freehold owners – the limitations of this private system to achieve what was increasingly recognized as a public interest became clear. For one thing, it depended on private owners taking the initiative to insert appropriate covenants into their transactions. The extent to which private owners conceived of their role as including such a responsibility was attenuated by the early twentieth century, so that 'while in the past landowners had acted in enlightened self-interest "to promote the amenities of the neighbourhood", newer types of land owner just dealt with land as a commodity'.[28] The private system was also limited as it simply addressed issues such as 'amenity' or the 'character of the neighbourhood' in the interests of the property owner rather than the non-owner. Thus, Booth noted that: 'The system worked well where economic advantage was to be gained by targeting a well-to-do clientele who would expect their amenities to be protected, but landlords did not care to take special measures in areas destined for the working classes, where standards of building might well be much lower'.[29]

---

[24] (1848) 2 Ph 774; (1848) 47 ER 1345.

[25] It is to be noted, of course, that the covenant was, at least in part, positive in nature, in requiring the 'neat and ornamental order'.

[26] Right up until the First World War, most people, regardless of income, rented their homes from private landlords; see M. Ball, *Housing Policy and Economic Power: The Political Economy of Owner Occupation* (Methuen, 1983).

[27] Booth, n.23, 281.

[28] Ibid, 282.

[29] Ibid, 282.

A further distinction can be drawn, within the categories of private control, between the tortious claim in nuisance, and the proprietary or quasi-proprietary rights conferred by easements and restrictive covenants. If the tort of nuisance is an 'unlawful interference with a person's use or enjoyment of land, or some right over, or in connection with it',[30] then the existence of a (quasi-) proprietary burden on land creates the lawful basis for an interference with the land owner's use or enjoyment of her own land. In both cases, the claim is private in the sense that it arises between two private parties, each of whom has an interest in a parcel of neighbouring land. Penner has explained the existence of these types of obligation between neighbours on the basis that: 'Land is not the sort of property over which dominion can be exercised in disregard of the fact that land is situated in a particular place, and thus is by nature bound to the property of others'.[31] It has been argued that nuisance law can be regarded as part of the law of servitudes,[32] as it deals with how one land occupier's use of land may interfere with that of another, neighbouring, land owner. Indeed, in US law schools, courses on land use generally cover both public regulation of growth and development controls on land and private land use arrangements,[33] which may both reinforce public regulation, and achieve forms and levels of control that public actions cannot.

Debate 3

What are the impacts of legal frameworks enabling private governance of use rights in land?

The rule that positive covenants do not run with the land has been hugely inconvenient to certain developments. There have been reported difficulties where apartments for which the enforceability of common obligations (for example, to maintain common areas of the building) were held on freehold rather than leasehold title. Such properties can now be held on 'commonhold', by virtue of the Commonhold and Leasehold Reform Act 2002 – a new type of freehold title which allows for the enforcement of community obligations through a commonhold association where the nature of the property is truly interdependent, and includes the sharing of common parts. The commonhold association acts as a micro-government, making decisions for the members.[34] Indeed, it is this type of private governance – rather than a physical obstruction, a gate – that has been identified as the defining feature of the gated community.[35]

---

[30] W. Rogers, *Winfield and Jolowicz on Tort* (Sweet & Maxwell, 13th edn, 1989) p. 378.

[31] Penner, n.19, 5.

[32] A.W.B. Simpson, *An Introduction to the History of Land Law* (Oxford University Press, 1961) pp. 245–46.

[33] See, for example, course texts such as R. Ellickson and V. Been, *Land Use Controls: Cases and Materials* (Aspen Law and Business, 3rd edn, 2005).

[34] C. Webster and R. Le Goix, 'Planning by Commonhold' (2005) 25(4) *Economic Affairs* 19.

[35] Ibid.

Commonhold is thus regarded as opening up new opportunities for privately managed local planning and neighbourhood management schemes in England and Wales. Beyond the basics of maintaining communal areas in a block of flats, commonhold allows the possibility of freehold ownership of land, combined with the provision of a 'bespoke package of paid-for neighbourhood facilities and services [making] it possible for middle- and higher-income people to move back into the city. The amenities bundled into the schemes by developers include secure access, uncongested parking and good quality, uncongested on-site facilities'.[36] This can be viewed as the ultimate privatization of housing: what would previously have been viewed as public neighbourhood amenities are re-created as private goods exclusive to the commonhold owners within the development,[37] so enabling the residents of such a community to opt out of the public system.[38] While this type of scheme involves the exercise of private law rights to control the use of land, it can be regarded as an opt-in scheme, to the extent that buyers of properties within commonhold developments should typically receive very clear information about the nature of the rights and responsibilities (usually financial) to which they will be subject; and the commonhold association itself functions as a kind of representative democracy within this micro-state.

Lee and Webster have described the worldwide growth in gated communities as a 'general enclosure of the urban commons',[39] with potential implications for the availability of amenities and neighbourhood goods on a social (rather than private) basis. This raises a new set of policy issues: while there are clearly benefits for those who buy in to this type of property ownership, there are also potentially negative spill-over effects for those who are outside, particularly if the concentration of wealth within the private community has an adverse impact on the viability of amenities in the public neighbourhood. Other risks of privately controlled neighbourhoods include spatial-social segregation and homogenization of neighbourhoods; and political fragmentation, which disrupts the processes of redistributive taxation.[40] While there is little evidence as yet to indicate that the advent of commonhold has resulted in a significant upsurge in gated communities in England and Wales, developers and local authorities have predicted significant growth in the market in the coming decades.[41]

These gated communities are communities of exclusivity, in the sense that residents lead separated or segregated lives, although this does not always mean luxury or elite lifestyles: it can also be used to describe the refugee camp, or the ghetto.[42] As this implies, not all instances of gated living are chosen by the

---

[36] Ibid, 20.

[37] For discussion of the tradition of private amenities associated with affluent housing in England, see Blandy, n.11.

[38] G. Alexander, 'The Publicness of Private Land Use Controls' (1999) 3(2) *Edinburgh L Rev* 176, 181.

[39] S. Lee and C. Webster, 'Enclosure of the Urban Commons' (2006) 66(1) *GeoJournal* 27.

[40] Webster & Le Goix, n.34, 21–22.

[41] R. Atkinson, S. Blandy, J. Flint and D. Lister, 'Gated Cities of Today: Barricaded Residential Developments in England', Glasgow University Centre for Neighbourhood Research Paper 21, (2004).

[42] S. Brunn, 'Gated Minds and Gated Lives as Worlds of Exclusion and Fear' (2006) 66(1) *GeoJournal* 5.

residents: the decision to separate a sub-population may be made by the residents themselves or by the wider community; although those gated communities which are not chosen by the residents through the exercise of private property rights are less likely to be governed by formal (as opposed to informal) rules set out in legally binding covenants. What they have in common, however, is that as spaces and places they represent worlds of exclusion rather than worlds of inclusion. In the case of intentional communities governed by private rules, they employ a concept of property as a tool of exclusion rather than access, to enable them to live lives that are not fully integrated in their society. To the extent that private property law allows these limitations on the spatial rights of the community, as well as empowering residents to create domains of self-governance, it enables us to think about our communities in ways that are territorially bounded.

The phenomenon of privatized space can be contrasted with the urban commons movement, which debates the possibilities for recognizing shared public interests in urban space through alternative property rights models.[43] The idea of the urban commons is based on the historic English rural commons, where designated rural space was treated as subject to common ownership rights (i.e. belonging to everyone and no one). From the sixteenth century onwards,[44] these rural commons were enclosed or brought under private ownership (with a specific emphasis on the property right to extract economic benefit from the land), in a process triggered by what has been labelled 'the tragedy of the commons'.[45] As rights to land become increasingly valuable, so the argument goes, each person with access to the land seeks to maximize their gain from it (for example, by over-grazing their herd). This then supports a movement towards privatization (the enclosure of the commons) to restrain competition and protect the resource against depletion by overuse. It has been argued that this rationale can also be applied to contemporary urban resources or public goods (for example, parks and gardens, leisure facilities, playgrounds), whose overuse by the public tends to deplete the value of these resources. The tendency towards enclosure (or privatization) of land that serves as a public or civic good has been described as an 'inescapable consequence of economic progress',[46] so that the continued existence of a community's public goods thus depends on the existence of a legal mechanism to protect the community's property interest over the shared goods.

In the case of the rural enclosures of the eighteenth and nineteenth centuries, it was the land owners who were in political power. They were in an ideal position to push through Parliament legislation which protected their economic and trade

---

[43] As evidenced, for example, in the Commons Act 2006; see also Lee and Webster, n.39.

[44] When the value of agricultural land increased dramatically with the rising commercial demand for wool and cloth.

[45] G. Hardin, 'The Tragedy of the Commons'(1968) 162 *Science* 1243; and see further the Special Issue of *Social and Legal Studies* (2008) 17(3), dedicated to this issue.

[46] Lee & Webster, n.39, 29; see also C. Webster, 'Property Rights and the Public Realm: Gates, Green Belts and Gemeinschaft' (2002) 29 *Environment and Planning B* 397; C. Webster, 'The Nature of the Neighbourhood' (2003) 40 *Urban Studies* 2591; C. Webster & L. Lai, *Property Rights, Planning and Markets: Managing Spontaneous Cities* (Edward Elgar, 2003).

interests in the use of the land for certain agricultural activities.[47] While 'the social costs associated with the adversely affected welfare of the landless, although significant, were not born [sic] by most landowners, who tended to ignore them in the face of such substantial economic opportunity'.[48] The rural enclosures marked a decisive shift in English property rights, through which centuries of common ownership evaporated into a new culture of private ownership, justified by reference to the value of the land for trade and commerce. In the case of urban enclosure, Lee and Webster have argued that 'exclusion is an unavoidable and inevitable accompanying component to urban and economic development. Boundaries are necessary to delineate property rights amongst competing demands for land and all manner of scarce resources'.[49] This is, in effect, the fundamental principle of the institution of private property, so it is hardly surprising that it has played a major role in the development of property law's arrangements for governing access to, and exclusion from, land.

English property legislation in the last decade or two has balanced the debates between access to land as urban or rural commons (for example, through the Commons Act 2006, or the protection of the right to roam in the Countryside and Rights of Way Act 2000) and exclusion through the facility to create privately governed commonhold communities (Commonhold and Leasehold Reform Act 2002). Findings to date suggest that large-scale gated communities in England and Wales remain relatively scarce.[50] Now that the legal structures are in place to support the development of urban enclosure, their development is likely to be determined by user demand and the dynamics of the market, rather than by public policy.

Autobiographical note

Public rights of way and private *profits à prendre*

Every evening, unless it's raining, we take a family walk along the river beside our house, up through the orchard and around by the farm. Our 21-month-old son looks forward to – and starts to talk about – this walk from the moment we leave the nursery. We talk about the fish and the ducks in the river, the cows and the rabbits in the field, and the barn where the cows will go to bed at night. We climb over stiles, look at the yellow flowers and learn not to touch the nettles. The land across which we walk is private property: there are signs along the riverside indicating that it is private land, and that (the profit of) fishing in the river is restricted to members of Durham Anglers Club. But the paths we follow are ancient public rights of way. These days, the farm land is the edge

---

[47] Lee & Webster, n.39, 31.
[48] Ibid.
[49] Ibid, 32.
[50] Atkinson, Blandy, Flint and Lister, n.41.

of a conservation area, and the paths don't really 'go' anywhere, in the modern directive sense. But along the way we walk under the arch of an old gate house, built in 1112, which (situated out on the edge of the city) was at one time the fever hospital; and past the ruins of what our local history books tell us was once a medieval pub. The landscape bears the remnants of the various uses which the land has had over centuries, and provides welcome amenities of fresh air, exercise and nature trail. Before we moved here, I didn't really appreciate the value of public rights of way other than for access to a destination. In fact, as an ancient city, Durham is full of vennels and alleyways that have long been used as short-cuts to access parts of the city, as well as long-used pathways across the more rural outskirts of the city. But it is the amenity value of these public footpaths – rather than their access function – that has turned out to have real value. Of course, while this amenity is free at the point of use, it forms part and parcel of the market value of neighbouring property, so that access to such spaces may not be random but can become a selling point for middle-class family homes in desirable locations.

THE CATEGORIES OF EASEMENT AND RESTRICTIVE FREEHOLD COVENANT

The development of statutory schemes such as the commonhold interest was a direct response to the limited scope and reach of the common law principles of easements and restrictive freehold covenants.[51] For one thing, there are carefully guarded restrictions on the permitted content of both types of servitude, in recognition of the burden which the existence of proprietary third-party interests imposes on private ownership of land. Secondly, there are strict rules concerning the circumstances in which such obligations are created, and the requirements that must be followed if they are to bind third parties and successors in title. In both cases, the Land Registration Act (LRA) 2002 has attempted to tighten up the registration requirement as a condition of enforceability for burdens on land, with discoverability emerging as the watchword to ensure priority against purchasers. The formalities surrounding the creation of these rights, their limited scope, and the strict rules governing their enforceability reflect the perception within English land law that third-party rights in the form of such servitudes represent a major incursion on the freedom of the private property owner,[52] and so should not readily be acceded to without clear justification.

---

[51] See D. Clarke, 'Occupying "Cheek by Jowl": Property Issues Arising from Communal Living' in S. Bright and J. Dewar (eds) *Land Law: Themes and Perspectives* (Oxford University Press, 1998).

[52] Which, once recognized and registered, are not readily extinguished.

Each category of burden has – both separately and concurrently – attracted the attention of the Law Commission on several occasions over the last few decades.[53] A number of reform attempts have been made in relation to both easements (often with an emphasis on easements created by prescription) and freehold covenants (mostly in relation to positive covenants) but with only limited results to date. In 1971, the Law Commission published a working paper on *Transfer of Land: Appurtenant Rights*[54] which proposed a statutory scheme to regulate both forms of interest, but remained unimplemented and was subsequently deemed too ambitious.[55] The 1984 report was confined to covenants, and set out proposals for a new land obligation, which would enable both positive and negative obligations, once registered, to be enforceable as an interest in land. The 1991 report, *Transfer of Land: Obsolete Restrictive Covenants*,[56] recommended that covenants automatically expire after 80 years, subject to a right of appeal by the owner of the right, and the consultation paper preceding the Land Registration Act 2002 identified a range of concerns relating to easements, including the inappropriateness of lost modern grant in relation to registered title; the problem of three methods of prescription (suggesting that common law prescription and lost modern grant should be abolished, leaving only statutory prescription, although not in its existing form).[57] These provisional recommendations were abandoned in the Final Report on Land Registration.[58]

In the 2002 edition of *Gale on Easements*, the author noted that: 'The Law Commission has ducked the law of easements more than once. We understand that it may now be girding its loins for the task of cleansing this particular Augean stable.'[59] Following the enactment of the LRA 2002, a new reform initiative focused on land obligations (easements, *profits à prendre* and freehold covenants) was launched, with a final report published in 2011.[60] The recommendations set out in this report and discussed below are wide-ranging, with identified goals of simplification, fairness and efficiency.[61]

---

[53] Indeed, on the eve of the creation of the Law Commission, its predecessor, the Law Reform Committee, published its 14th Report on *Acquisition of Easements and Profits by Prescription* (Cmnd 3100); Law Commission publications concerning burdens on land have included Law Commission, *Transfer of Land: Appurtenant Rights*, Law Commission Working Paper No 36 (HMSO, 1971); Law Commission, *Transfer of Land: The Law of Positive and Restrictive Covenants*, Law Commission Report No 127 (HMSO, 1984); Law Commission, *Making Land Work: Easements, Covenants and Profits à Prendre*, Law Commission Report No 327 (TSO, 2011).
[54] Law Commission Working Paper No 36 (HMSO, 1971).
[55] Law Commission (1984), n.53, para. 1.6.
[56] Law Com No 201.
[57] Law Com No 254.
[58] Law Com No 271, para. 1.19.
[59] J. Gaunt and P. Morgan, *Gale on Easements* (Sweet & Maxwell, 17th edn, 2002) p. vi.
[60] Law Commission, *Making Land Work: Easements, Covenants and Profits à Prendre*, Law Com No 327, HC 1067 (TSO, 2011).
[61] Ibid, para. 1.26.

Debate 4

Should property law control the permissible content of easements and freehold covenants?

The category of easements as recognized in English law has developed gradually through judicial reasoning. There is no definition or closed list (as there is in some other jurisdictions), although there are guidelines concerning the nature of an easement. For a claim to come within the category of easements, the following elements are required:[62] (1) a dominant and servient tenement;[63] (2) that the easement accommodate the dominant tenement;[64] (3) that the dominant and servient tenements are owned or occupied by different people; and (4) that the right is capable of forming the subject matter of a grant. This final requirement has its origins in the fallacy that all easements were originally granted, and demands that the easement is (a) sufficiently certain; and (b) within the general nature of rights recognized as easements.

The courts have exercised caution in extending this category of rights, in light of the substantial nature of the burden that an easement may entail. For example, while easements may be either *permissive* (allowing the dominant land owner to carry out some activity on the servient land, for example, a right of way, the right to park a car on neighbouring land, rights to lay gas mains or electric cables and the right to go on the land to inspect and maintain them); or restrictive (a right to restrain activity on the servient land, and so exercise a degree of control over how the servient owner uses their own land), they should not be personal. There is also a reluctance to recognize easements that impose a positive obligation (i.e. one which incurs expenditure) on the servient land.[65] The category of restrictive easements is limited to: (1) the right to light – that is, that the light flowing to a window shall not be unreasonably obstructed;[66] (2) the right to the free flow of air through a defined aperture (e.g. a ventilation shaft);[67] (3) the right to support of buildings – that is, a right to restrain any use of the servient land or build-

---

[62] *Re Ellenborough Park* [1956] Ch 131.

[63] In *London & Blenheim Estates* v *Ladbroke Retail Park* [1994] 1 WLR 31, it was held that there could be no easement of parking cars on a piece of land, because at the time the easement was allegedly created, there was no dominant and servient tenement.

[64] The easement must benefit the land, not confer a personal benefit on the holder of the land: for example, in *Hill* v *Tupper* (1863) 2 H & C 121, an alleged right over land adjoining a canal, which was enjoyed in conjunction with the right to hire out pleasure boats on the canal was held not to be an easement, since the right to hire out boats was more important than the easement, so that the personal benefit associated with the claim outweighed the benefit to the land. While they need not be contiguous, the dominant and servient tenements must also be of sufficient proximity to each other for the benefit to be real: in *Bailey* v *Stephens* (1862) 12 CB(NS) 91 the court held that land in Northumberland could not benefit land in Kent.

[65] An exception is the 'spurious' easement of fencing: *Crowe v Wood* [1971] 1 QB 77.

[66] The right to light has long been recognized as a special category of easement and is specially protected by statute; see Prescription Act 1832, Right to Light Act 1959.

[67] Although there is no right to an uninterrupted flow of air for chimneys, which was deemed to be too broad: *Bryant v Lefever* (1879) 4 CPD 172.

ings on the servient land that will interfere with the support afforded by them to adjoining buildings on the dominant land;[68] (4) a right to continued flow of water through an artificial watercourse; and (5) the right to use space for storage.[69] Rights which have *not* been recognized as easements include the right to a view[70] and easements of privacy,[71] and there is no easement to uninterrupted receipt of a television signal.[72] Rights which involve expenditure cannot generally be regarded as easements, because the duty of a servient owner is negative (that is, not to interfere with the dominant owner's enjoyment) rather than positive, although (perhaps demonstrating the pragmatic development of the category of easements to meet needs to control land use) an exception to this principle is the easement of fencing to keep in livestock, recognized in *Crow v Wood*.[73] Finally, rights which involve exclusive or joint user are also unlikely to be regarded as easements.[74]

The most significant restriction on the permissible content of freehold covenants at common law is that they must be negative in nature. While the parties to the original covenant may make positive promises towards one another, which are normally enforceable in *contract*, successors in title of the original parties to the agreement are only bound by the covenant if the principles of property law which have grown up around freehold covenants are satisfied. At common law, the benefit of a freehold covenant could pass to a successor in title, but not the burden,[75] and it was only with the decision in *Tulk v Moxhay* in 1848,[76] as subsequently interpreted, that it became possible for the burden of restrictive covenants to pass to successors in title.

The Law Commission's 2011 proposals would relax the permissible content of both easements and freehold covenants. Specific proposals included a more relaxed approach to easements conferring rights to extensive or exclusive use,[77] and a scheme through which both positive and negative covenants would become

---

[68] *Dalton v Angus* (1881) 6 App Cas 740; note that this right is distinct from the natural right to support of land; it is not automatic and must be acquired as an easement. If such an easement is acquired (for example, by prescription), then the servient tenement owner cannot demolish buildings on his or her land that provide support for buildings on the dominant land. There is no easement of protection by one building of another from weather: *Phillips v Pears* [1965] 1 QB 76.

[69] *Wright v Macadam* [1949] 2 KB 744.

[70] Deemed too broad: *Aldred's Case* (1610) 9 Co Rep 57b.

[71] *Browne v Flower* [1911] 1 Ch 219.

[72] *Hunter v Canary Wharf Ltd* [1997] AC 655.

[73] [1971] 1 QB 77.

[74] In *Copeland v Greenhalf* [1952] Ch 488 the right to park lorries on land was taking up most of the land, and the court held that joint or exclusive possession cannot be regarded as an easement. This is, however, a question of degree: see *London & Blenheim Estates v Ladbroke Retail Parks Ltd* [1992] 1 WLR 1278; *Bachelor v Marlow* (2001) 32 P&CR 36; *Hair v Gillman* (2000) 80 P&CR 108. Indeed, the House of Lords in *Moncrieff v Jamieson* [2007] 1 WLR 2620 seemed less than convinced by this bar.

[75] There were methods by which this rule could be circumvented. The doctrine of mutual benefit and burden was discussed above. Other methods include where property was transferred by lease instead of conveying fee simple; or where successors in title were enabled to sue directly on the contract, for example, through the Contracts (Rights of Third Parties) Act 1999.

[76] (1848) 2 Ph 774; (1848) 47 ER 1345.

[77] Law Commission, *Making Land Work: Easements, Covenants and Profits à Prendre*, Law Com No 327, HC 1067 (TSO, 2011), para. 3.209.

land obligations. The latter extends the scope for the creation of covenants that are enforceable as interests in land from commonhold properties to all land.[78] Although the Commission acknowledged the arguments against allowing positive burdens to run (for example, in restricting or constraining choice), and noted that the economic case for enforceable positive covenants had not specifically been made,[79] it concluded that since it is already possible to achieve enforceable positive covenants by roundabout means (for example, indemnity contracts), 'the market has made its own case'.[80] These developments would allow considerably greater incursion on the freedoms of the freehold owner. As the next section will show, this approach is justified by the Commission's emphasis on registration and information as the guardians of fairness in this context.[81]

Debate 5

When should easements and covenants bind third party purchasers?

The rules concerning the creation – and to some extent the enforcement – of easements and freehold covenants invoke a debate between what Epstein described as 'a theme persistent in all legal discourse: the tension between private volition and social control'.[82] In the context of burdens of land, this debate has been expressed as one between a 'strict contractarian ethic' (the argument that law should defer to the intentions of the parties, to avoid limiting freedom of action) on the one hand,[83] and the argument that property law should include concessions to a 'regulatory or interventionist ideology'.[84] Alexander has noted that in a private property regime that emphasizes the freedom of the private owner there is a 'strong presumption' in favour of private volition, so that purchasers are only bound by those burdens which they have chosen, either by direct consent or where the burden was listed on the register and so was clearly identified as part of the bargain when the land was acquired.

> The notion of a land-use obligation binding persons who did not make the promise presents something of an anomaly in the liberal conception of property. Indeed, the term 'servitude' embarrasses a property regime committed to the autonomy of private owners.[85]

---

[78] Ibid, para. 5.30.
[79] Ibid, para. 5.35.
[80] Ibid, para. 5.36.
[81] Ibid, para. 5.59–5.62.
[82] See, for example, R. Epstein, 'Notice and Freedom of Contract in the Law of Servitudes' (1982) 55 *S Cal L Rev* 1353.
[83] Ibid.
[84] G. Alexander, 'Freedom, Coercion, and the Law of Servitudes' (1987) 73 *Cornell L Rev* 883. Alexander argues that the distinctions within this dichotomy are in fact blurred, to the extent that 'choiceless' is often experienced by parties within nominally consensual land transactions.
[85] Ibid, 889.

The rationale which has been created to justify the possibility of burdens that bind successors in title is rooted in the purchaser's knowledge of the burden – or, at least, the discoverability of the obligation when the land is transferred. Table 7.1 demonstrates how the LRA 2002 has embedded the twin requirements of registration and discoverability in the rules governing both legal and equitable easements. Where land is unregistered, the old distinction between legal and equitable easements continued to determine whether they bind the world without registration (legal easements) or require registration as a land charge (equitable easements).

Similarly, in the case of restrictive freehold covenants (and alongside the other requirements for the burden to run in equity), it is necessary that the covenant was registered either as a Class D(ii) land charge,[86] or, in the case of registered land, protecting it by the entry of a notice against the title of the servient land.[87] The emphasis on registration in respect of both types of burden on land[88] is consistent with the bureaucratic nature of title registration after the LRA 2002, while the introduction of discoverability requirements in respect of informally created and equitable easements underlines the (commercially justified) bias towards prioritizing the protection of purchasers over those of subsidiary interest holders. It purports to give effect to the choices of the purchaser, as the decision to go ahead with the purchase of land subject to a registered or discoverable obligation is deemed to be tantamount to consent to be subject to the obligation. Reliance on registration and discoverability as the guardians of fairness when creating, or enforcing, third-party rights in land is also evident in the Law Commission's most recent Report. The reform initiative was embedded in recognition of the role of easements and covenants in enabling the effective use of land,[89] but subject to the principle that such obligations be registered if they are to bind third parties. This rationale for a strategy that justifies reliance on registration and discoverability for the protection of private property interests in land (as proxies for the purchaser's free choice in undertaking the burden) was challenged by Alexander. He argued that the use of the (false) dichotomy between free choice (as the guiding tenet of private law) and collective coercion (where public intervention is justified) serves to privilege private law regulation (designated as choice) over public regulation (deemed choicelessness) as a means of governing land use.[90] While this issue has been extensively debated in the US literature, it remains to be seen whether the Law Commission's report will prompt any home-grown challenges to what has become a deeply embedded belief in the philosophy of permitting increasing scope for private regulation of land use so long as the controls are registered and/ or discoverable.

---

[86] Land Charges Act 1972, s.2(5).

[87] LRA 2002.

[88] Although the method of registration varies, with expressly created legal easements substantively registrable as interests in land, and equitable easements and restrictive covenants registrable though a notice on the register.

[89] Law Commission, *Making Land Work: Easements, Covenants and Profits à Prendre*, Law Com No 327, HC 1067 (The Stationery Office, 2011), para. 1.4.

[90] Alexander, n.38.

Table 7.1   Easements and transmissibility to third parties: a short guide

When are third parties bound by the easement?	**UNREGISTERED LAND**
LEGAL EASEMENTS	Legal proprietary interests in unregistered land **bind all the world**
EQUITABLE EASEMENTS	Equitable easements in unregistered land are interests capable of registration as a land charge if they were created on or after 1 January 1926, and so must be registered in accordance with the Land Charges Act 1972 if they are to bind third parties (LCA 1972, s2(2)).
When are third parties bound by the easement?	**REGISTERED LAND (easements created before 13 October 2003)**
LEGAL EASEMENTS	Legal easements created before 13 October 2003 are *overriding interests* and so they bind the purchaser of registered land without need for registration (LRA 1925, s70(1)(a)).
EQUITABLE EASEMENTS	Equitable easements created before 13 October 2003 are *overriding interests* so long as the easement is exercised openly (*Celsteel Ltd v Alton House Holdings Ltd* [1985]1 WLR 204).
When are third parties bound by the easement?	**REGISTERED LAND (easements created from 13 October 2003)**
LEGAL EASEMENTS	**Some** legal easements remain overriding – depending on how they were created; others must be registered to bind third parties.
	Expressly created easements (grant or reservation) *must be registered;* they are *not* overriding interests (LRA 2002, s.27(2)(d) & (e))
	Informally created easements *may be overriding interests*; that is, easements arising by ▶ Section 62, LPA 1925 – (LRA 2002, s.27(7)) ▶ Implied easements (necessity, common intention, *Wheeldon v Burrows* (1879) 12 Ch D 31) – (LRA 2002, sch. 3). However note that for informally created legal easements to be overriding interests you must *also* show that the easement was within the knowledge or notice (obvious on reasonably careful inspection) of the purchaser, or that it has been exercised in the last year (LRA 2002, sch. 3, para. 3).
EQUITABLE EASEMENTS	*Never overriding;* must be registered as a burden on the registered title.

CONCLUSIONS

While both the easement and the restrictive covenant perform important functions in English land law, each operates under strict conditions, designed to limit the nature and extent of the burdens imposed through private law on the owners of land. Yet, however one strikes the balance between private ordering and intervention, public law and private property law in relation to third party interests in land, it is important to be aware that what, on the surface, are often presented as settled doctrinal rules with no political or policy agenda in fact conceal value-laden choices concerning access to, and exclusion from, the limited resource of land.

Further Reading

S. Blandy, 'Gated Communities in England: Historical Perspectives and Current Developments' (2006) 66(1) *Geojournal* 15.

A. Bottomley, 'A Trip to the Mall: Revisiting the Public/Private Divide' in H. Lim and A. Bottomley (eds), *Feminist Perspectives on Land Law* (Routledge-Glasshouse, 2007).

R. Epstein, 'Notice and Freedom of Contract in the Law of Servitudes' (1982) 55(4) *S Cal L Rev* 1353.

S. Lee and C. Webster, 'Enclosure of the Urban Commons' (2006) 66(1) *Geojournal* 27.

8

HUMAN RIGHTS AND PROPERTY LAW

INTRODUCTION

Previous chapters in this book have briefly mentioned human rights – in relation to the mortgagee's right to possession, the doctrine of overreaching, and the landlord's right to possession of the occupied property. This chapter faces the issue head on. The great debate which raged during the Noughties, and partly resolved as that decade ended, was the extent to which property rights and human rights intersect and interact. Although this chapter could range widely, its focus is on two elements: mandatory rights to possession (Debate 1); and peaceful enjoyment of possessions (Debate 2). The former concerns Article 8 of the European Convention on Human Rights (given effect in Schedule 1, Human Rights Act 1998 (HRA)); the latter concerns Article 1, First Protocol, ECHR (1998 Act, sch. 1 (A1P1)). As regards the former, the issues are now well-advanced and clear, involving the balancing of cherished assumptions about absolute rights to property with 'home' rights. As regards the latter, our sense is that the issues have been less well-advanced, and we provide two examples: adverse possession and shared ownership. As regards the former, this has now been resolved; as regards the latter, interesting problems arise which may well define the debate further. There may well be overlaps in certain cases, regarding certain issues.[1]

Debate 1

Mandatory rights to possession

It is of the essence of superior property rights that the holder of those rights has better title to the property than the occupier. Unless otherwise protected, the holder of the superior property right is entitled to possession of the property as a matter of right against a range of interposers. Interposers is not a particularly

---

[1] For example, in the case of shared ownership, where possession is sought by the landlord on a mandatory ground, as to which, see D. Cowan, 'A Ticking Time Bomb' (2011) 161(7467) *New Law Journal* 729.

helpful word, it is accepted, but it carries with it a certain meaning. The interposer is the household which occupies the property. They may do so with rights to do so – for example, a tenant is an interposer between the landlord and the property. Alternatively, they may do so without rights to do so, for example, a trespasser is an interposer between the person with superior rights and the property. Where the court has a *discretion* whether to grant possession against the interposer, properly no human rights issue arises.[2] It is where the court has no discretion – it *must* make the possession order – that the real rights-based issues arise.

There has been considerable litigation on this point, and that litigation is by no means over. In this part, we begin with a brief analysis of Article 8. We then show how the pre-eminence given to property rights has withered under consistent battering from the European Court of Human Rights (ECtHR), leading to the acceptance by the UK Supreme Court that it must follow the approach taken by the ECtHR in perhaps the most significant case of our generation: *Manchester City Council v Pinnock*.[3] Finally, we isolate certain potential lines of future argument, where either the dividing lines are currently unclear or fresh issues arise.

THE ISSUE STATED

Article 8 provides:

> Right to respect for private and family life
>
> 1 Everyone has the right to respect for his private and family life, his home and his correspondence.
> 2 There shall be no interference by a public authority with the exercise of this right except such as is in accordance with the law and is necessary in a democratic society in the interests of national security, public safety or the economic well-being of the country, for the prevention of disorder or crime, for the protection of health or morals, or for the protection of the rights and freedoms of others.

Article 8 does not guarantee a home for each household or at all. It merely provides that we all have a 'right to respect' for our home (thus assuming that we already have one and, if we don't, then tough). In itself, that right to respect appears rather limited. Secondly, paragraph 2 clearly qualifies this right to respect. It is now trite to say that whether something is 'necessary' or not is a question of proportionality, a balance between the rights of the parties and the state. In essence, the question before the courts has been whether mandatory possession proceedings enable the judge to conduct that assessment; put another way, it is

---

[2] One can see this best in those cases which have sought to challenge the jurisdiction of the court under Trust of Land Act 1996, s. 14 and Insolvency Act 1986 (as amended), s. 335A through the use of human rights-based arguments: *Barca v Mears* [2004] EWHC 2170 (Ch); *Nicholls v Lan* [2006] EWHC 1255 (Ch).

[3] [2010] 3 WLR 1441, described as follows: '... there is now a new giant on the scene, one judgment to rule them all and in its 9 strong constitution bind them', <http://nearlylegal.co.uk/blog/2010/11/brave-new-world-or-same-old-story/>

whether the property rights to possession are so significant that any assessment of the proportionality of the act is entirely irrelevant. Let us leave to one side, for now, the question about whether these rights are generally applicable between private and/or public actors – this is a significant question in its own right which will bother the Supreme Court again sooner or later.

There are two other preliminary matters. First, there is the way in which the court must approach the question when a principle or statutory provision of English law is out of step – incompatible – with the HRA. The court has one of two options: it can either 'read down' the provision, so as to make it compatible, or it can make a declaration of incompatibility, which is for Parliament (not the court) to resolve.[4] Second, there is the precedent value of ECtHR decisions. UK courts must 'take into account' any 'judgment, decision, declaration or advisory opinion' of the ECtHR.[5] They need not slavishly follow the ECtHR. This has led to the UK courts entering into what they have described as 'valuable dialogue' with the ECtHR in certain areas 'where [the Supreme Court] has concerns as to whether a decision of the Strasbourg Court sufficiently appreciates or accommodates particular aspects of our domestic process'.[6]

THE 'HOME'

The precondition for Article 8's operation in this context is that the property must be the household's 'home'. The notion of 'home' has been discussed elsewhere in this book, but there is one thing that is absolutely clear: 'home' is independent of, and not dependent on, any rights which the occupying household may or may not have in relation to the property. In *Qazi v Harrow LBC*, Lord Scott seemed to suggest the contrary when he argued that

> Each home had been established on the basis of a proprietary interest in the premises obtained under the contractual tenancy granted by the landlord. How could the termination of that tenancy in a manner consistent with its contractual and proprietary incidents be held to constitute a lack of respect for the home that had been thus established? The home was always subject to those contractual and proprietary incidents. The contrary view seems to me to treat a 'home' as something ethereal, floating in the air, unconnected to bricks and mortar and land.[7]

This narrow view of 'home' is certainly not consonant with the approach taken by the ECtHR, nor with the jurisprudence in the UK.[8] It was arguably also inconsistent with the views of the majority in *Qazi*. The understanding of 'home' is, it seems, 'ethereal, floating in the air', for it seems to connote some sort of psycho-

---

[4] 1998 Act, ss. 3 and 4.
[5] 1998 Act, s. 2(1).
[6] *R v Horncastle* [2009] UKSC 14, [11].
[7] [2004] 1 AC 983, [145].
[8] See the critique by T. Allen, *Property and the Human Rights Act 1998* (Hart, 2005) p. 230.

social attachment to place. As the ECtHR has put it, home connotes '... the existence of sufficient and continuous links with a specific place'.[9] This first denial of the significance of the interposer's property rights is significant because it simply unpicks the assumptions of property law – the contractual and proprietary incidents, which so engaged Lord Scott – in favour of a much broader, contextual approach to home. As Lord Hope put it, in *Hounslow LBC v Powell*, 'This issue is likely to be of concern only in cases where an order for possession is sought against a defendant who has only recently moved into accommodation on a temporary or precarious basis.'[10]

QAZI: THE ZENITH OF THE PROPERTY RIGHTS THESIS

It is fair to say that *Qazi v Harrow LBC*[11] offers the zenith of the supremacy of property rights over the interposer's human rights. Mr Qazi and his then wife occupied a property with their daughter. The then Mrs Qazi left the property and served a notice to quit, which determined the tenancy. Mr Qazi was refused a sole tenancy of the property but subsequently re-married and his new wife joined him in the property, after which they had two further children. Harrow claimed possession of the property which Mr Qazi defended on the basis of his rights under Article 8. Now, the way the case progressed (in retrospect) was not ideal because there was no attack on the mechanism used by the first Mrs Qazi to determine the tenancy.[12] The question for the House of Lords was, in essence, whether Mr Qazi's Article 8 rights overrode Harrow's right to possession. The House of Lords, by a majority, said that they did not. The process of reasoning which informed the majority judgments prized property rights above all else. This comes across most clearly in the opinion of Lord Scott, who begins his discussion of this issue with the observation that 'The intention of these instruments was to enshrine fundamental rights and freedoms. It was not the intention to engage in social engineering in the housing field.'[13] He went on:

> If, on the other hand, the tenant has no right to remain in possession as against the landlord he cannot claim such right under article 8. To hold otherwise, to hold that article 8 can vest property rights in the tenant and diminish the landlord's contractual and property rights, would be to attribute to article 8 an effect that it was never intended to have. Article

---

[9] *Paulic v Croatia* (App no 3572/06), 22 October 2009, at [33].

[10] [2011] 2 WLR 287, [33], citing *Leeds CC v Price* [2006] AC 465 in which the interposing occupiers had been on the land for two days.

[11] [2004] 1 AC 983.

[12] See, for example, para. [60], Lord Hope, 'It is to be noted that the respondent does not contend that there has been an interference with his right to respect for his private and family life or his correspondence. The argument is directed entirely to his right to respect for his home.' The mechanism was the rule in *Hammersmith LBC v Monk* [1992] 1 AC 478, which was subsequently found by the ECtHR not to provide the requisite procedural protection to the remaining occupier/s in *McCann v UK* (2008) 47 EHRR 40.

[13] At [123].

8 was intended to deal with the arbitrary intrusion by state or public authorities into a citizen's home life. It was not intended to operate as an amendment or improvement of whatever social housing legislation the signatory state had chosen to enact. There is nothing in Strasbourg case law to suggest the contrary.[14]

And further:

> If Mr Qazi has no contractual or proprietary right under the ordinary law to resist the council's claim for possession, and it is accepted he has not, the acceptance by the court of a defence based on article 8 would give him a possessory right over [the property] that he would not otherwise have. It would deprive the council of its right under the ordinary law to immediate possession. It would constitute an amendment of the domestic social housing legislation. It would give article 8 an effect it was never intended to have and which it has never been given by the Strasbourg tribunals responsible for implementing the Convention.[15]

In the course of an outspoken, forthright attack on the decision of the majority, Lord Steyn noted that 'The basic fallacy in the approach is that it allows domestic notions of title, legal and equitable rights, and interests, to colour the interpretation of article 8(1). The decision of today does not fit into the new landscape created by the Human Rights Act 1998.'[16] This analysis was both prescient and, in retrospect, spot on. The approach taken by the majority in *Qazi* was soon superseded by an attempt to mediate, perhaps pragmatically, between the approach taken by the ECtHR and public law principles. The key point, however, is that the property rights thesis was forced to give way to a more Europeanized version through which the interposer could challenge the decisions of the public authority.

THE GATEWAYS

It soon became clear that *Qazi v Harrow LBC*[17] was by no means the last word on the matter as the House of Lords had hoped. A succession of cases sought to engage Article 8 rights in a rather more sophisticated way, arguing that the basis for the decision to claim possession and the means by which possession could be obtained in English law was impeachable by reference to Article 8. In *Kay v Lambeth LBC*,[18] the House of Lords returned to the issue in the context of occupiers having no more than a personal right of occupation. *Kay* is the successor to *Bruton*, considered in Chapter 4. London and Quadrant, after the adverse judgment in that matter, surrendered its interest in the property to Lambeth, a

---

[14] At [125].
[15] At [151].
[16] At [27].
[17] [2004] 1 AC 983.
[18] [2006] 2 AC 465.

surrender which effectively undercut Mr Bruton's successful claim rendering him and the other residents no more than unauthorized occupiers of the property. In defence to the council's claim for possession, Mr Kay, another occupier, raised his Article 8 right. Before the House of Lords, *Kay* was joined with *Leeds CC v Price*, a claim for possession against travellers who were the unauthorized occupiers of a site for two days by the time of the council's claim. Again, they raised an Article 8 defence to the claim and both were unsuccessful but the decision was again on a knife-edge (4–3).

In what has come to be seen as the ratio of the decision, Lord Hope identified two gateways which occupiers would have to open in order successfully to challenge the council's decision. The first, 'gateway (a)', could be opened if the occupier was able to show that there was a seriously arguable case that the law enabling the court to make the possession order was incompatible with Article 8. If so, the county court judge hearing the possession claim had two options – either to read the provision in accordance with Article 8 (in so far as it was able to do so) or remit the matter to the High Court for a determination of the compatibility issue. The scope of gateway (a) was always regarded as narrow out of deference to Parliamentary intention and the 'margin of appreciation' given by the ECtHR to member states. As Lord Bingham, in the minority in *Kay* but summarizing also the opinion of all members of the House of Lords, put it, 'Our housing legislation strikes a balance between the competing claims to which scarcity gives rise, taking account, no doubt imperfectly but as well as may be, of the human, social and economic considerations involved. And it is, of course, to housing authorities such as the respondents that Parliament has entrusted the power of managing and allocating the local authority housing stock and the pitches on local authority gipsy sites.'[19]

The second gateway, gateway (b), simply re-envisioned the common law principles that an occupier can raise, by way of defence to a claim for possession matters, of public law '... to challenge the decision of a public authority to recover possession as an improper exercise of its powers at common law on the ground that it was a decision that no reasonable person would consider justifiable'.[20] Again, the threshold was that such a defence must be 'seriously arguable'.

The acceptance that the interposer could raise such a defence led to further refinement by the House of Lords in *Birmingham CC v Doherty*.[21] This case again involved the local authority seeking possession against travellers. The travellers occupied two local authority pitches under licences, which Birmingham determined by the service of notice terminating the licences. Birmingham wanted to redevelop the site so that it could be used for 'genuine' travellers as temporary accommodation. The Doherty extended family had occupied the site for 17 years. There was no allegation of misconduct against them and no allegation of breach

---

[19] *Kay*, at [33]; see also Lord Hope at [108], Lord Scott at [169], and Baroness Hale at [190], and see also *Blecic v Croatia* (2004) 41 EHRR 185.

[20] At [110], Lord Hope, referring to *Wandsworth LBC v Winder* [1985] AC 461.

[21] [2009] 1 AC 367.

of the licence agreement. The basis of the claim for possession was, simply, the council's right to determine the proper use of the site. The House of Lords held against the council in the sense that they remitted the matter back to the county court for consideration of the matter in light of the statement of principle by the House so that the county court was forced to re-visit the gateway (b) defence (indeed, *Doherty* is one of the few successful gateway (b) defences).[22]

Lord Hope gave the leading judgment, in which he said:

> I think that in this situation it would be unduly formalistic to confine the review strictly to traditional Wednesbury grounds. The considerations that can be brought into account in this case are wider. An examination of the question whether the respondent's decision was reasonable, having regard to the aim which it was pursuing and to the length of time that the appellant and his family have resided on the site, would be appropriate. But the requisite scrutiny would not involve the judge substituting his own opinion for that of the local authority. In my opinion the test of reasonableness should be, as I said in para 110 of Kay, whether the decision to recover possession was one which no reasonable person would consider justifiable. The further point to which Lord Brown referred will have a part to play in that assessment.[23]

Lord Brown had referred in *Kay* to the possibility that a *Wednesbury* unreasonableness argument could have been mounted successfully in *Connors v UK* (which concerned a gypsy family which was served a notice to quit on the basis of unsubstantiated allegations of nuisance and which did not have an opportunity to rebut those allegations):

> ...having regard to the great length of time (most of the preceding 16 years) that that gipsy family had resided on the site, it was unreasonable, indeed grossly unfair, for the local authority to claim possession merely on the basis of a determined licence without the need to make good any underlying reason for taking such precipitate action.[24]

Lord Hope's approach in *Doherty* was taken as 'narrow[ing] (without closing) the gap between HRA grounds and traditional judicial review grounds'.[25]

This dramatic set of developments in *Kay* and *Doherty* was entirely due to the incoming tide of judgments post-*Qazi* from the ECtHR, which indicated that the property rights thesis of *Qazi* was questionable (even though an application to the ECtHR in *Qazi* itself was deemed inadmissible). In a series of judgments, beginning with *Connors v UK*,[26] the ECtHR clearly expressed a radically different

---

[22] Along with *McGlynn v Welwyn Hatfield DC* [2009] EWCA Civ 285 and *Croydon LBC v Barber* [2010] HLR 26.
[23] At [55].
[24] At [210].
[25] At [116], Lord Walker.
[26] (2004) 40 EHRR 189.

interpretation of Article 8 from the House of Lords in *Qazi*. This interpretation appropriated to Article 8 both substantive and procedural protection, '... namely the requirement to establish proper justification for the serious interference with his rights and consequently cannot be regarded as justified by a "pressing social need" or proportionate to the legitimate aim being pursued'.[27] *Connors* gave rise to a substantial body of case law developed by the ECtHR under which standard paragraphs would be repeated again and again, as if to emphasize the lack of uniformity of UK law with Article 8:

> The loss of one's home is a most extreme form of interference with the right to respect for the home. Any person at risk of an interference of this magnitude should in principle be able to have the proportionality of the measure determined by an independent tribunal in the light of the relevant principles under Art.8 of the Convention, notwithstanding that, under domestic law, his right of occupation has come to an end.[28]

The ECtHR was clearly identifying the requirement for procedural protection in court proceedings for possession of the interposer's 'home'. That procedural protection was the requirement on the judge to consider the proportionality of the eviction. *Connors* preceded *Kay*, and the House of Lords in *Kay* believed that it had achieved a sufficient balance between the gateways and Article 8, as interpreted in *Connors*, to enable English law to be compatible with the approach taken by the ECtHR. In this context, Lord Brown's comment about the length of residence as a factor going to the gateway (b) challenge was significant.

In *McCann v UK*,[29] though, the ECtHR seemed to indicate that the gateways were insufficient (Mr McCann had sought judicial review of the council's decision to proceed with the eviction but had not been given leave to make the claim by the High Court). *McCann* was a direct challenge to the rule in *Hammersmith and Fulham LBC v Monk* that one joint tenant can determine the entire tenancy, including the other joint tenant/s interest, by serving a notice to quit on the landlord. Mrs McCann, who had been allegedly the subject of domestic violence, had served that notice at the request of the council. The ECtHR noted that

> Had the local authority sought to evict the applicant in accordance with this statutory scheme, it would have been open to the applicant to ask the court to examine, for example, whether his wife had really left the family home because of domestic violence and whether in his personal circumstances, including his need to provide accommodation for his children during overnight visits several times a week, it was reasonable to grant the possession order.[30]

---

[27] See *Connors* at [95].
[28] *McCann v UK*, at [50].
[29] (2008) 47 EHRR 40.
[30] *McCann v UK*, at [51].

The point was that Mr McCann had never had the opportunity to dispute his wife's allegations and, indeed, never had the opportunity to have the court consider the proportionality of his eviction.[31] The court also noted that 'Judicial review procedure is not well-adapted for the resolution of sensitive factual questions which are better left to the County Court responsible for ordering possession'.[32]

The ECtHR judgment in *McCann* was given after the hearing of the argument in *Doherty* but before judgment. The House of Lords were faced, therefore, with a judgment which was a direct challenge even to the jurisdiction opened up in *Kay*. Worse, the ECtHR in *McCann* appeared to justify the reasoning of the minority in *Kay*, arguing that there would be no 'serious consequences' for the system of seeking possession as it would only be in 'very exceptional cases that an applicant would succeed in raising an arguable case which would require a court to examine the issue'.[33] The House of Lords in *Doherty* proceeded to seek to dismantle the reasoning in *McCann*, directly questioning its authority, practicality and legitimacy, with Lord Scott in particular deprecating the position adopted by the ECtHR in that case.[34] In more measured terms, Lord Hope expressed the view that the 'highly exceptional' test '... suffers from a fundamental defect which renders it almost useless in the domestic context. It lacks any firm objective criterion by which a judgment can be made as to which cases will achieve this standard and which will not'.[35]

Why did the House of Lords in *Doherty* stick to the *Kay* gateways, albeit slightly refined? Cowan et al. have identified two core propositions underpinning the approach taken, which explain the rigid adherence to the gateways at that time:

> The gateway metaphor is powerfully deployed in these cases to suggest a way in to challenge judicial decisions, but it is firmly slammed shut in most cases either as a matter of law or, just as significantly (because such case management is usually silenced, conducted underground in mysterious proceedings, often conducted by telephone, extremely rarely subject to appeal because based on absolute discretion of the District Judge, and thus rarely the subject of academic engagement), procedurally. Those internal logics appear to be two, interrelated objectives.
>
> First, and most significantly, there is protection of the integrity of the process. Time and again in the cases, we are told that most gateway (b) claims can, and should, be disposed of summarily, presumably as part of the list. Even Lord Bingham, who was in the minority in *Kay*, was clear that this was '... an important aspect of these appeals, and one that has caused the House much concern' but was a concern which could be assuaged by the

[31] At [53].

[32] At [53].

[33] At [54].

[34] At [82]–[87], describing the reasoning as 'quite astonishing' and arguing that any domestic judge would be bound to take the proportionality of the decision into account (at [86] and [87] respectively), a position which in itself seemed counter-intuitive if possession is mandatory.

[35] At [20].

high standard (which all Counsel who appeared accepted) to be applied.[36] In *Stokes [v Brent LBC]*,[37] protection of the integrity of the possession process, and particularly distinguishing it from public law claims, created a procedural distinction which appears hard to justify (principle g above). Protecting the process must be managed against the contrary proposition of allowing occupiers to give full vent to their challenges as a result of the procedural and legal checks at this stage.

Second, it follows from that first point certainly as an outcome but, we suggest, also as part of the internal logic of public law itself, that considerable latitude is to be given to social housing providers in their possession claims. Part of the rationality behind that principle is deference to the nature of mandatory possession proceedings, as developed by the courts and appears in statutory provisions. However, it is also, at least, implicit in the higher standard required (as indeed it is in the permission stage for judicial review). This suggests an empirical conclusion, which may not be warranted, that social housing providers make rational, lawful decisions which comply with their policies and procedures. Curtailing the defences of occupiers only makes sense when this internal logic of the process is applied.[38]

So, the tension was as much over the practical effect of accepting the ECtHR's adherence to requiring the proportionality of the eviction to be decided as on the basic doctrine.

The House of Lords' position in *Doherty* became untenable after further decisions of the ECtHR.[39] Those decisions reiterated and restated *Connors* so that, as one blog entry put it:

In Pulp Fiction, John Travolta's character explains to Samuel L Jackson's that it is the 'little differences' in Europe that make it interesting – they do things differently there. Because France has the metric system, the burger joint calls a 'quarter pounder' burger a 'Royale with cheese'. *Zehentner v Austria*, a judgement of the First Section of the European Court of Human Rights, demonstrates yet again that the ECHR has a different approach to mandatory rights to possession than the House of Lords has expressed in the trilogy of cases (*Buckley, Connors, McCann* and *Cosic* against *Qazi, Kay, Doherty*). It surely cannot be much longer before the Supreme Court is required to revisit this issue. Should the Supreme Court now be dealing with Royales with (or without) cheese or remain wedded to their quarter pounders?[40]

---

[36] At [27] and [39] esp. point (4).

[37] [2009] EWHC 1426 (QB); and [2010] EWCA Civ 626.

[38] D. Cowan, C. Hunter & H. Pawson, 'Jurisdiction and Scale: Mandatory Possession Proceedings, Social Housing, and Human Rights' (2012) 39(2) *Journal of Law and Society* 269, 280–81.

[39] See *Ćosić v Croatia* (App no 28261/06); *Zehentner v Austria* (App no 20082/02); *Paulić v Croatia* (App no 3572/06); *Kryvitska and Kryvitskyy v Ukraine* (App no 30856/03).

[40] <http://nearlylegal.co.uk/blog/2009/10/14-pounder-or-royale-with-cheese-zehentner-v-austria/>

Mr Kay's case, when before the ECtHR, fell for the same reasons as all the others, the court noting that his case had failed before the House of Lords because '... it was not possible at that time to challenge the decision of a local authority to seek a possession order on the basis of the alleged disproportionality of that decision in light of personal circumstances'.[41]

'ONE RING TO RULE THEM ALL ...'[42]

In the canon of property law, there are some crucial cases which require digesting but none more crucial than *Manchester City Council v Pinnock* and its successor *Hounslow LBC v Powell*.[43] In these cases, the Supreme Court introduced and refined (to a certain extent) the proportionality defence to mandatory possession proceedings. The defence must be raised by the interposer and it must be 'seriously arguable'.[44] While recognizing that the court is not bound to follow every decision of the ECtHR, the Supreme Court in *Pinnock* said:

> Where...there is a clear and constant line of decisions whose effect is not inconsistent with some fundamental substantive or procedural aspect of our law, and whose reasoning does not appear to overlook or misunderstand some argument or point or principle, we consider that it would be wrong for this court not to follow the line.[45]

That point had now been reached in the ECtHR jurisprudence on Article 8 and possession. Thus the Supreme Court adopted the minority reasoning in *Kay* that:

> ...where a court is asked to make an order for possession of a person's home at the suit of a local authority the court must have the power to assess the proportionality of making the order, and, in making that assessment, to resolve any relevant dispute of fact.[46]

Difficult questions remain,[47] but the property law thesis in *Qazi v Harrow LBC*[48] has been re-balanced without being comprehensively defeated. In essence, the question for the court in any claim to possession brought (at least) based on absolute right – that is, a mandatory claim – the judge must consider the proportionality of the eviction if that question is raised by the occupier/s. The re-balancing of the property law thesis was, pragmatically, to regard it as not just one factor to be

---

[41] *Kay v United Kingdom* (37341.06) [2011] HLR 2, [74].

[42] As *Pinnock* was introduced: <http://nearlylegal.co.uk/blog/2010/11/brave-new-world-or-same-old-story/>

[43] Respectively: [2010] 3 WLR 1441; [2011] 2 WLR 287.

[44] See, for example, *Powell*, at [33], Lord Hope; note Lord Phillips' observation in *Powell*, at [92], as regards the introductory tenancy regime, that it would only be in 'very highly exceptional cases' that such a challenge could be mounted.

[45] *Pinnock*, at [48].

[46] *Pinnock*, at [49].

[47] See D. Cowan & C. Hunter, ' "Yeah but, no but": *Pinnock* and *Powell* in the Supreme Court', (2012) 75(1) *MLR* 78.

[48] [2004] 1 AC 983.

taken into consideration but a highly significant element of the balance implied by the proportionality jurisdiction in combination with the broader public law obligations of the landlord:

> Where a person has no right in domestic law to remain in occupation of his home, the proportionality of making an order for possession at the suit of the local authority will be supported not merely by the fact that it would serve to vindicate the authority's ownership rights. It will also, at least normally, be supported by the fact that it would enable the authority to comply with its duties in relation to the distribution and management of its housing stock, including, for example, the fair allocation of its housing, the redevelopment of the site, the refurbishing of sub-standard accommodation, the need to move people who are in accommodation that now exceeds their needs, and the need to move vulnerable people into sheltered or warden-assisted housing. Furthermore, in many cases (such as this appeal) other cogent reasons, such as the need to remove a source of nuisance to neighbours, may support the proportionality of dispossessing the occupiers.[49]

Further:

> Unencumbered property rights, even where they are enjoyed by a public body such as a local authority, are of real weight when it comes to proportionality. So, too, is the right – indeed the obligation – of a local authority to decide who should occupy its residential property.[50]

It must now be accepted that an absolute right to possession is, simply, insufficient on its own to meet the proportionality jurisdiction successfully; it is that right in combination with the other rights and obligations of the 'social' landlord which does the job.

All of that is clear now. What is unclear, however, is what a successful proportionality challenge might look like and, equally, whether such a successful challenge would not also be successful within gateway (b). In *Pinnock*, the Supreme Court, rather whimsically, said that they were happy to leave the parameters of the proportionality challenge to the good sense and experience of the county court judge.[51] Certain factors clearly require balancing, including any specific use which the landlord wishes for the property,[52] the personal circumstances and vulnerability of the interposer,[53] and the statutory basis under which the interposer occupies, or has occupied, the property.[54]

---

49 *Pinnock*, at [52]; see also *Powell*, at [37], Lord Hope, and [88], Lord Phillips.
50 *Pinnock*, at [54].
51 *Pinnock*, at [57].
52 *Pinnock*, at [53], although such use must be expressly claimed and proved.
53 See, in particular, *Pinnock*, at [64].
54 This was particularly emphasized in both *Pinnock* and *Powell* because, where that regime provides substantive and/or procedural protections, such as a right for the interposer to request that the claimant reviews their decision, it may require greater scrutiny.

Autobiographical note

In another life ...

In 2006, I took the step of joining the Bar, doing my pupillage and beginning an occasional career. There is an intersection between my academic and practising interests. I work in housing and property, and argue the toss. I find it interesting intellectually as an exercise but also because of what it does to my understandings as a socio-legal academic. I have argued a few cases now around proportionality, mostly on the papers and once or twice in full-pitched battle in county courts, and argued a few cases based on the gateway (b) defence.

My own experience is that the kind of 'summary jurisdiction' that the Supreme Court was suggesting in both *Pinnock* and *Powell* rarely works in that way – the court cannot hear detailed argument at the first, five-minute, hearing, and will adjourn it to a lengthier hearing. Practically, then, the kinds of concerns raised by the higher courts about the effects of gateway (b) and proportionality defences, which led to the high threshold required for the occupier to show, are playing out, possibly unevenly, across courts in England and Wales. My barrister friends tell me that the Court of Appeal has a stack of cases which they're going to hear later this year (2012), which will lead to many of the uncertainties being dealt with; but, in the interregnum, my sense is that we're all playing it a little 'by ear'. These are exciting times to be a student, academic, and practitioner!

For property lawyers, the key concern must be the reach of this new jurisdiction. It clearly affects all landlords that are exercising 'functions of a public nature' as opposed to 'where the nature of the act is private'.[55] The Court of Appeal has said, broadly, that the management of housing, including eviction, is a function of a public nature,[56] but this does not quite answer the more general question as to whether the identity of the landlord matters and, indeed, whether the jurisdiction extends beyond that to others, such as lenders and receivers exercising rights to possession and/or sale.[57] Traditionally, one applies a factor-based approach to this question as exemplified by the House of Lords decision in *YL v Birmingham City*

---

[55] s. 6(3)(b) and (5) respectively.
[56] *Weaver v London and Quadrant HT* [2009] HLR 40; see also *Eastland Homes Partnerships Ltd v Whyte* [2010] EWHC 695 (QB) and *R(McIntyre) v Gentoo Group Ltd* [2010] EWHC 5 (Admin).
[57] See *Ropaigealach v Barclays Bank* [2000] QB 263 and *Horsham Properties v Clark & Beech* [2008] EWHC 2327 (Ch); even where the provisions of the Mortgage Repossessions (Protection of Tenants etc) Act 2010 give limited protection to the unauthorized tenant. *Horsham* proceeded on A1P1, discussed below, and so the Article 8 argument (which was said to fail if the argument on A1P1 failed) was not put to the court, but, at [49], Briggs J relied on *Qazi* in relation to the Article 8 argument, a reliance which can no longer hold good.

Council.[58] Under that type of approach, factors such as the regulatory regime, the nature of the contract between the parties, the nature of the provider (whether, for example, they are a commercial organization or not), direct receipt of public funding, are all relevant to the decision. On that basis, it would be unlikely that this jurisdiction would extend beyond social housing landlords. However, it is to be noted that the question whether the 1998 Act caught a private landlord housing a homeless household was expressly left open in *YL* itself.[59]

Nevertheless, although the factor-based approach is now established as the test, its applicability in the range of cases in which proportionality would otherwise become relevant remains uncertain. The Supreme Court in *Pinnock* explicitly left this open, noting that there were arguments both ways.[60] The question is whether the 1998 Act has horizontal as well as vertical application, so as to be applicable between purely private parties; the answer hinges in part on the role of the court as a core public authority, which cannot act in a way which is incompatible with Convention rights.[61] Although the Supreme Court referred to *Belchikova v Russia* (App No 2408/06, 25 March 2010) as an example of where, possibly, the ECtHR had considered a matter between two private parties in relation to the Article 8 right, the better decision on this (arguably) is *Zehentner v Austria* (App No 20082/02, 16 July 2009) in which the ECtHR intervened in a forced judicial sale between two private parties (an occupier and her plumber and other creditors) over a small debt.[62] It was the act of the forced judicial sale, like the act of ordering possession against an assured shorthold tenant, which was significant.[63]

Less clear, however, are cases of possession without the interference of judicial process. In the *Horsham Properties* case (receiver selling property over the heads of the mortgagors), the 1998 Act was deployed without thought. A factor of potential significance in relation to mortgage lenders is the extent of public funding/ ownership of the bank or building society – it may matter, for example, at least as a relevant factor, if your mortgage came from (say) the publicly owned part of Northern Rock as opposed to a lender without any public ownership or funding. On the flip side of that coin, though, is the fact that these institutions remain public companies, or mutuals, seeking and obtaining commercial rates of return by virtue of contracts. The owner/mortgagee also has their own right to their possessions, including property,[64] which balances against the Article 8 rights of the occupier.[65]

---

[58] [2008] 1 AC 95.

[59] At [85], Lord Mance. Local authorities can use the private rented sector to discharge their obligations to homeless households (s. 193(5) & (7AA)) given the satisfaction of certain conditions; the Localism Act 2011 contains provisions to extend this right in certain circumstances.

[60] At [50].

[61] s. 6(3)(a).

[62] [2009] ECHR 1119.

[63] See also *Ghaidan v Godin-Mendoza* [2004] 3 WLR 113, where the 1998 Act was deployed between two private parties.

[64] See below.

[65] A point also made by the Supreme Court in *Pinnock*, at [50].

Debate 2

Peaceful enjoyment of possessions

Article 1 to the First Protocol (A1P1) to the European Convention contains the following rights:

> **Article 1**
> Every natural or legal person is entitled to the peaceful enjoyment of his possessions. No one shall be deprived of his possessions except in the public interest and subject to the conditions provided for by law and by the general principles of international law.
> The preceding provisions shall not, however, in any way impair the right of a State to enforce such laws as it deems necessary to control the use of property in accordance with the general interest or to secure the payment of taxes or other contributions or penalties.

Properly, this provision contains three rights, the first being general; the second sentence of the first paragraph and the second paragraph are particular instances of interference with the right to peaceful enjoyment of property; and the latter two are therefore construed in light of the general principle in the first sentence of the first paragraph.[66] There are two particular legal issues which are considered in this section in relation to this provision: adverse possession and shared ownership. They are both of some difficulty, although one has been resolved (adverse possession) and the other remains an open question (shared ownership). Before that discussion takes place, we provide a broad summary of the basic principles in this Article.

SUMMARY

A number of points can be made about this Article, both generally and specifically in this context:

a. The definition of 'possessions' is broad and includes rights flowing from the identification of an item as property (such as the right of alienation), assets and other claims, such as those based on a legitimate expectation.[67]
b. The ECtHR usually proceeds by examining whether there has been a breach of the second or third rights before considering the general right.[68]
c. As regards 'deprivation', the ECtHR appears to look at the substance of the matter – so, for example, a successful claim of adverse possession was not a 'deprivation' of ownership rights but regulated questions of title; rather, that system involved a 'control of use' and fell within the second paragraph.[69]
d. An interference with the peaceful enjoyment of possessions

---

[66] *Pye v UK* (2008) 46 EHRR 1083, at [52]; *Sporrong & Lonnroth v Sweden* (1982) Series A No 52, at [61].
[67] *Marckx v Belgium* (1979) Series A No 31, at [63]; *Pye v UK* (2008) 46 EHRR 1083, at [61].
[68] *Id.*
[69] *Pye*, at [66].

...must strike a 'fair balance' between the demands of the general interest of the community and the requirements of the protection of the individual's fundamental rights....in particular, there must be a reasonable relationship of proportionality between the means employed and the aim sought to be realised by any measure depriving a person of his possessions.

In determining whether this requirement is met, the Court recognises that the State enjoys a wide margin of appreciation with regard both to choosing the means of enforcement and to ascertaining whether the consequences of enforcement are justified in the general interest for the purpose of achieving the object of the law in question.

...

94. Compensation terms under the relevant legislation are material to the assessment whether the contested measure respects the requisite fair balance and, notably, whether it imposes a disproportionate burden on the applicants. In this connection, the Court has already found that the taking of property without payment of an amount reasonably related to its value will normally constitute a disproportionate interference and a total lack of compensation can be considered justifiable under Article 1 of Protocol No. 1 only in exceptional circumstances.[70]

e. A failure to offer compensation is not necessarily determinative that the rights have been breached.[71]
f. The 'margin of appreciation' is particularly wide in the context of the 'public interest' and in housing, when aimed at 'securing greater social justice in the sphere of people's homes, even where such legislation interferes with existing contractual relations between private parties and confers no direct benefit on the State or community at large'; indeed, the width of the margin is such that the ECtHR will respect the state's position on the public interest 'unless that judgment be manifestly without reasonable foundation'.[72]
g. Finally, it is significant to note that the ECtHR arrogates jurisdiction to itself even if the primary dispute is between two private parties, but where the proper application of the law engages the rights.[73]

ADVERSE POSSESSION

In Chapter 6, we considered the law on adverse possession. The question for the ECtHR in *Pye v UK* was as to the compatibility of that law operating prior to the Land Registration Act 2002 with A1P1. Having accepted as 'inescapable' that Pye's loss of their beneficial interest in land was a possession for the purposes of

---

[70] *Jahn v Germany* [2004] ECHR 36 at [93]-[94], 'Recapitulation of the relevant principles'; see also *James v UK* (1986) Series A No 98, esp at [54], noting that compensation does not, however, guarantee a right to 'full' compensation.
[71] *Jahn* itself (context of reunification of Germany).
[72] *James*, at [46]–[47].
[73] See, in particular, the discussion in *Pye*, at [75].

A1P1, the question turned on whether the loss of that interest was disproportionate bearing in mind the failure to compensate them for that loss. In turn, this depended on whether the specific right engaged was the deprivation of user or the loss of control (the second sentence and the second paragraph respectively). It was held that the Limitation Act 1980 was part of the regulation of property rights, which controlled the use of land, and was not intended to deprive Pye of their ownership.[74] That distinction was important because, as opposed to deprivation of use, where the matter is considered to be one of loss of control, compensation is not a relevant criterion to weigh in the balance:

> The Court would note, in agreement with the Government, that a requirement of compensation for the situation brought about by a party failing to observe a limitation period would sit uneasily alongside the very concept of limitation periods, whose aim is to further legal certainty by preventing a party from pursuing an action after a certain date.[75]

The question, then, was whether the law on adverse possession provided a 'fair balance' between the public interest and the individual's interests. They held that it did so. Their reasoning was, first, that the UK had a wide margin of appreciation; the limitation of action rules were 'logical and pragmatic'; the companies knew or ought to have known about the legislation; during the limitation period, they had procedural protection (after all, they could have brought a claim for possession based on the Grahams' occupation qua trespasser); although the financial loss to Pye was considerable and the benefit to the Grahams correspondingly considerable, this fell within the margin of appreciation; and that limitation periods must apply regardless of the amount of the loss/gain: 'The value of the land cannot therefore be of any consequence to the outcome of the present case'.[76]

In a sustained critique of the ECtHR's decision, Fox O'Mahony and Cobb argue that the court drew on '... a variety of jurisprudential techniques to reposition the doctrine of adverse possession within a less morally contentious framework than that found within UK political discourse ...'.[77] Their argument was that fault and hardship to the squatter was found by the court to be irrelevant; rather the court regarded Pye's failure to act as blameworthy so that their hardship was a necessary and not unreasonable consequence. The Court, on their analysis 'de-moralised' the issue, so that adverse possession was '... a mere bureaucratic tool and, as such, downplayed its redistributive implications.'[78] One might say, then, that the court

---

[74] At [66]. For similar reasoning, see *Horsham*, n.57 above, the reasoning for which is unconvincing at best.

[75] At [79].

[76] At [84].

[77] L. Fox O'Mahony & N. Cobb, 'Taxonomies of Squatting: Unlawful Occupation in a New Legal Order' (2008) 71 *MLR* 878, 903.

[78] At 902.

actually reinforced the notion of possession as central to property law and that the 'de-moralisation' was, in fact, the property lawyer's traditional analysis.[79]

SHARED OWNERSHIP

The position in respect of shared ownership is rather more difficult – for discussion about the models of shared ownership, readers are referred to Chapter 4. Absent Article 8, the question is whether a rigid insistence by the provider on a mandatory ground for possession, or (indeed) a discretionary ground, which gives rise to a court order for possession within a certain period, is incompatible with A1P1.[80]

Such a question might have arisen in *Midland Heart v Richardson*,[81] but was not developed in that case. Its facts are nevertheless instructive. Ms Richardson bought a 50 per cent stake in the property on a conventional SO basis – long lease – without a mortgage. She paid £29,500. In 2003, her ex-partner was imprisoned and Ms Richardson was forced to leave the property having received threats. She moved in to a women's refuge. Rent arrears built up. By the time of the possession claim, there were about 16 months' rent arrears (approx. £1,941), which increased to around £3,000 at the date of the hearing. Ms Richardson tried unsuccessfully to sell the property (which had been vandalized in her absence). By that time, the property was worth approximately £151,000. In 2005, Midland Heart sought possession on the basis of a mandatory ground for possession based on rent arrears (Ground 8).

The arguments deployed for Ms Richardson to defeat the claim relied principally on property law devices – it was argued that there were two tenancies crafted out of the single formal long lease, an assured tenancy and a long lease; and that there was a trust of the freehold – but these devices were properly rejected by HHJ Gaunt QC in the Birmingham County Court.

Bright and Hopkins, in their discussion of this case, found alternative property law arguments, based on resulting and constructive trusts or proprietary estoppels, to be similarly wanting on the facts of this case at least.[82] The outcome, though, was that Ms Richardson lost not just her £29,500 but also her share of the increase in value of the property – she lost everything (although it is reported that Midland Heart offered an ex gratia payment of £29,500, less the rent arrears and costs of repair[83]). As HHJ Gaunt QC put it:

> That all said, I have found this case troubling. Miss Richardson has had a rough ride in life and has now lost what is probably her only capital asset. Moreover, she lost it in proceedings brought at a time when, to the know-

[79] See R. Kerridge & A. Brierley, 'Adverse Possession, Human Rights and Land Registration: And They All Lived Happily Ever after?' (2007) *Conv* 552; and, subsequently, *Ofulue v Bossert* [2009] Ch 1.

[80] See D. Cowan, 'A Ticking Time Bomb' (2011) 161 (7467) *NLJ* 729.

[81] Birmingham Civil Justice Centre (ChD), 12 November 2007.

[82] S. Bright and N. Hopkins, '*Richardson v Midland Heart Ltd*: Low Cost Home Ownership – Legal Issues of the Shared Ownership Lease' [2009] *Conveyancer and Property Lawyer* 337.

[83] At [24]; See <http://nearlylegal.co.uk/blog/2008/09/shared-ownership-midland-heart-with-benefit-of-transcript/>

ledge of the housing association, she was actively seeking to sell the house to pay off her debts and the housing association was itself involved in that process. I must say that I find the stance taken by the housing association strange in the circumstances and I have not received any adequate explanation. There may, of course, be many facts and matters in the background that I know not of and so I do not intend to be unduly critical. I simply comment on the timing.[84]

The interference with the shared owner's possessions through the claimant's successful claim is not at issue under A1P1; what is at issue is whether that interference is disproportionate to the owner's financial stake in the property. It is the equivalent of forfeiture *without* relief (and the ECtHR has shown itself willing to interfere where a state's act stops short of expropriation[85]), but the framing of the issue is only about the expropriation of the buyer's financial stake and probably not about their interest in the property.

That having been said, though, it is the combination of the failure of the state to regulate this point beyond the Housing Act 1988, combined with the lack of compensation to the buyer, which frames this issue within the terms of A1P1. There is perhaps here an issue around compatibility, which may well be resolved by a proportionality hearing, but, even so, if the possession claim results in the loss of possessions without compensation for no justifiable reason, then A1P1 must be at issue. It seems indisputable that, as opposed to the way in which the ECtHR considered the limitation rules in *Pye*, we are dealing with a deprivation of possessions in these cases. In any event, whether this argument is framed as deprivation or loss of control, the appropriate balance and justification needs to be made. While that is axiomatic in the 'normal' tenancy relationship, it is less clear in shared ownership cases where this form of forfeiture, in effect, operates.[86] Ms Richardson's case is instructive in this regard – she lost £29,500 (or £75,500, if you account for the uplift in the property market) because of rent arrears of around £3,000. The rent arrears, on the facts of the case, arose because of the refusal of the housing benefit authority to pay both for her place in the refuge and for the shared ownership rent for more than 52 weeks. It was clear, on any reading of the case, that she could not and would not return to the SO property because of her fears for her personal safety (and no doubt was cast on their genuineness).

In summary, then, shared ownership cases represent a potentially fruitful ground for the further consideration of A1P1.

CONCLUSIONS

This chapter demonstrates that certain cherished principles of property law require re-balancing in light of the direct implementation of the principles of the

---

[84] At [23].

[85] *Sporrong*, n.66.

[86] Although see *James v UK* (1986) Series A No 98, and the admissibility decision in *DiPalma v UK* (1988) 10 EHRR 149.

European Convention in UK law. It can no longer be said that unencumbered property rights, on their own, are sufficient to maintain a claim when the interposer occupies property as their home and raises a defence based on Article 8. The precise parameters of this new jurisdiction as yet are unclear and it may well be that purely private entities, such as private landlords and private tenants, mortgage lenders and receivers, will be caught up in this new jurisdiction. Similarly, although A1P1 may well provide the basis for an assumption that property law is consonant with that Article, given the wide margin of appreciation, the boundaries of that particular jurisdiction remain to be fully appreciated.

Further Reading

D. Cowan and C. Hunter, '"Yeah but, no but": *Pinnock* and *Powell* in the Supreme Court' (2012) 75(1) *MLR* 78.

R. Kerridge & A. Brierley, 'Adverse Possession, Human Rights and Land Registration: And They All Lived Happily Ever after?' [2007] *Conv* 552.

A. Latham, 'Talking without Speaking, Hearing without Listening? Evictions, the Law Lords and the European Court of Human Rights' [2011] *Public Law* 730.

I. Loveland, 'A Tale of Two Trespassers: Reconsidering the Impact of the Human rights Act on Rights of Residence in Rented Housing' [2009] *European Human rights Law Review* 148 (pt 1), 495 (pt 2).

9

LAW, EQUALITY AND HOUSING

INTRODUCTION

In the previous chapter we explored the interaction between human rights norms and property law. This chapter considers the relationship between property and what we refer to as 'equalities law' under the Equality Act 2010 (EA), which forms one further part of our human rights framework.[1] That Act was designed to consolidate, and in places expand, the complex and fragmented Acts of Parliament, statutory instruments and case law which had developed previously to address discrimination and inequality in society.

Some of the most well-established protections now afforded by the Act address discrimination in property, though this field has been relatively overlooked in legal scholarship compared, for example, to fields like employment.[2] The purpose of this chapter is to consider the role played by protections against discrimination relating to property under the Act in tackling the particular problem of unequal access to housing. Housing is a basic human need, and so it is unsurprising that discrimination and inequality in the sale, rental, or management of residential premises both reflects and exacerbates wider forms of socio-economic exclusion tied to the characteristics now protected by the Act.

Understanding the causes and consequences of discrimination and inequality in housing provision can be complex, as can identifying the appropriate role that law should play in addressing unequal access to residential premises. Our aim here is to consider the interaction between rights and interests in housing, as they are recognized by property law, contract, and landlord and tenant legislation, and the changing form and function of this developing equalities agenda. In doing so, the

---

[1] Note that the European Convention on Human Rights (ECHR) and Human Rights Act 1998 also require equal treatment in the protection of the other Articles of the Convention under Article 14, which has had some influence on the approach to equality and housing in the UK: see *Ghaidan v Godin-Mendoza* [2004] 2 AC557. See also the discussion of Article 14 in Equality and Human Rights Commission, *Human Rights at Home: Guidance for Social Housing Providers* (EHRC, 2011).

[2] See, though, the following law-focused studies on race and housing: D. MacKay, *Housing and Race in Industrial Society: Civil Rights and Urban Policy in Britain and the United States* (Croom Helm, 1977); M. MacEwan, *Housing, Race and Law: The British Experience* (Routledge, 1991).

chapter considers the Equality Act in its wider policy context, while taking a closer look at some of the specific rules through which the Act's aims are implemented.

The first section outlines the present legal framework under the Equality Act and its impact on housing, before examining one field of enquiry and debate that has become synonymous with discrimination and inequality in the housing context: the role played by race and ethnicity in unequal housing outcomes in the UK. That is Debate 1. The second section then considers two recent debates that have emerged in this area. Debate 2 relates to the implicit private/ public binary which underpins equalities law in the housing context and, more specifically, the distinction drawn by the law between the acceptable sphere of 'private' prejudice (even on protected grounds), and the unacceptable sphere of 'public' discrimination. Debate 3 relates to the scope of disability discrimination in housing (especially the challenges to landlords posed by the concept of 'disability-related' discrimination and the duty to make 'reasonable adjustments'). The chapter concludes by evaluating the important future role of transformative 'equality work' – that is, the mechanisms in the Act which move beyond the negative proscription of discrimination in the housing context and instead encourage the adoption of a more strategic approach to addressing structural disadvantages in the housing market – through the work of the Equality and Human Rights Commission (EHRC), the public sector Equality Duty, and the concept of 'positive action'.

Debate 1

Has equalities law successfully addressed racial inequality in housing?

The EA extends the principle of non-discrimination across the fields of work, education, service provision, public functions and premises. Part 4 prohibits:

> direct and indirect discrimination,[3] harassment and victimization,[4]
>
> in the disposal, withholding of permission to dispose, and management[5] of premises,
>
> on grounds of race, sex, sexual orientation, gender identity, disability, and religion and belief (although not all these characteristics are equally protected).[6]

---

[3] EA 2010, ss. 13 and 19.

[4] EA 2010, ss. 26 and 27.

[5] The concept of premises is left undefined by the Act. However, previous legislation has explicitly defined 'premises' to include 'land' more generally: see Race Relations Act 1976, s. 78(2). On the basis of this old definition the meaning of premises is likely to be interpreted to include both buildings and other types of land.

[6] Though note that these protections have not been afforded consistently across all the protected characteristics. One example is the lack of protection from harassment on grounds of sexual orientation and religion and belief in the fields of service provision or premises: EA 2010, ss. 29(8), 33(6), 34(4) and 35(4).

Disposal includes sale, rental (whether the landlord is a private individual or organization, a local authority or a housing association), and the granting of any other right to occupy premises.[7] In relation to disability, the Act also prohibits 'disability-related' discrimination in the disposal, withholding of permission to dispose, and management of premises, and requires landlords and property managers to make certain reasonable adjustments in relation to premises to avoid a disabled person being placed at a substantial disadvantage in the use of those premises.[8] Not all forms of accommodation fall within Part 4 of the Act. Short-stay, non-residential arrangements, such as occupation of hotel rooms or B&B accommodation for travellers and holidaymakers, are classified instead as falling within Part 3, relating to services and public functions,[9] as is the provision of accommodation for the purpose only of exercising a public function or providing a service.[10]

Before exploring the rules prohibiting discrimination in more detail, the wider policy context in which the provisions of the Act relating to non-discrimination and premises were originally formulated are of importance as they provide the basis for understanding the Act's provisions. The approach of equalities law in this area was shaped primarily by the politics of race and housing in the post-war period.[11] When economic migrants began to arrive in the 1950s from the 'New Commonwealth', especially the Caribbean, to alleviate the chronic post-war shortage of labour at that time, they were met in many instances by hostility, discrimination and even violence at the hands of the indigenous white population. Race, racism and race relations were prominent political issues for successive governments, leading to state-led efforts to integrate the new arrivals, while strengthening immigration controls to placate the indigenous population. The use of legal measures to control discriminatory conduct was first mooted following the race riots which erupted in Notting Hill and Nottingham in 1958,[12] though it was 1965 before the first Race Relations Act was enacted, which outlawed direct race discrimination in prescribed public accommodations, such as hotels, restaurants and public transport. Furthermore, the Act was generally perceived at the time as a 'token venture',[13] not least because it did nothing to address the endemic problem of race discrimination in the provision of housing.[14]

Calls for further protections in this field had grown following the publication of several studies which provided ample evidence of the inequality and

---

[7] EA 2010, s. 28(3) and (4).

[8] EA 2010, s. 20 and sch. 4.

[9] EA 2010, s. 32(3)(a).

[10] EA 2010, s. 32(3)(b).

[11] P. Goulbourne, *Race Relations in Britain since 1945* (Macmillan, 1998); P. Sarre, D. Phillips & R. Skellington, *Ethnic Minority Housing: Explanations and Policies* (Avebury, 1989). Race is used here as it is in the Equality Act, which defines it to include race, ethnicity and nationality.

[12] P. Sooben, *The Origins of the Race Relations Acts* (Warwick Research Papers Series, 1991).

[13] H. Street, G. Howe and G. Bindman, *Anti-Discrimination Legislation* (PEP, 1967) p. 63.

[14] B. A. Hepple, 'Race Relations Act 1965' (1966) 29(2) *MLR* 306.

discrimination faced by ethnic minorities in the housing market.[15] Immigrants typically lived in the oldest and poorest quality private rented or owner-occupier housing, in the most deprived parts of the inner cities; few were housed by local authorities, and when they were it was often in pre-war stock rather than new-build council housing. While poverty and other factors contributed to the poor housing outcomes of immigrants within the private sector it was clear that discrimination also shaped racial inequalities. Unequal treatment on grounds of race was deliberate and overt across the sector. Landlords openly discriminated, with 'No Coloureds' or 'Whites Only' often added to advertisements for properties; estate agents enabled their clients' prejudices; racial stereotypes informed the financial assessments of mortgage providers; and property developers imposed colour bars on the assumption that white households would only buy homes in all-white estates.[16] In respect of council housing, the primary difficulty faced by newly arrived immigrants was often their inability to meet the length of residency requirements imposed by many council allocation policies,[17] illustrating that racial inequality in housing could be exacerbated as much by the disadvantages arising from the application of ostensibly neutral rules, as by racial prejudice, bias or stereotyping.

The Race Relations Act 1968 outlawed direct discrimination (or less favourable treatment of a person on grounds of their race) in the disposal and management of premises, whether publicly or privately owned, following the recommendations of the Race Relations Board[18] and the independent Street Report.[19] However, although the Act ensured that the most blatant forms of race discrimination in the private sector were addressed,[20] the law still lacked teeth. It would take another eight years before the Race Relations Act 1976 extended protection for the first time against indirect forms of discrimination, or those facially neutral rules which disproportionately affected ethnic minorities, and granted individuals the power to bring claims under the Act before the courts themselves (so liberating them from the bureaucratic conciliatory mechanisms of the Race Relations Board). The 1976 Act also established the Commission for Racial Equality (CRE), which was designed to take a more strategic approach to race discrimination and inequality. During the course of the 1980s and 1990s the CRE carried out a series of formal investigations into housing providers and ancillary services such as estate agents (some involving named organizations and others more general in scope). These investigations indicated that while some progress towards race equality in housing was being made, the 1976 Act had not, in and of itself, eliminated discrimination by providers. For example, one early named investigation by the CRE of Hackney

---

[15] E. Burney, *Housing on Trial: A Study of Immigrants and Local Government* (Cambridge University Press, 1967); J. Rex and R. Moore, *Race, Community and Conflict: A Study of Sparkbrook* (Oxford University Press, 1967); W. Daniel, *Racial Discrimination in England* (Penguin, 1968).

[16] Daniel, n.15.

[17] Rex and Moore, n.15.

[18] M. Bonham Carter, *Report of the Race Relations Board for 1966–67* (RRB, 1967).

[19] Street, Howe and Bindman, n.13.

[20] N. McIntosh and S. Smith, *The Extent of Racial Discrimination* (PEP, 1974).

Borough Council in 1984 revealed that black applicants were consistently allo-cated housing of inferior quality to white applicants, due in part to stereotyping by housing officers in their appraisals during home visits.[21] The CRE's non-named investigation into discrimination in the private rented sector in 1990 concluded that one in five accommodation agencies discriminated on grounds of race in the letting of residential properties through subtle processes such as racial steering.[22]

More recently, there has been evidence of a 'differentiation in the housing experiences' of ethnic minorities, meaning rapidly improved housing outcomes for some, while 'in all tenures ethnic minority groups remain in a worse situation than whites in relation to housing quality, over-crowding, concentration in disad-vantaged areas and levels of segregation'.[23] Differentiation has been caused by the upward mobility of the most well-established ethnic minority groups, coupled with the 'minority ethnicization' of social housing which, since the 1980s, has been residualized as a tenure of last resort. This exacerbates the poor housing outcomes of certain ethnic minority households who are now disproportionately reliant on the sector.[24]

Much less clear is the role still played by race discrimination in (re-)produc-ing racial inequality in housing. One reason is that, since the 1990s, there has been a dearth of new empirical research on the existence of discrimination within the housing market, especially by the CRE, and its successor the Equality and Human Rights Commission (EHRC). This makes it difficult to evaluate the extent of discriminatory practices in the sector today.[25] While social landlords are more aware than ever of the need to address inequality in housing provision, the complexity of 'institutional racism' means that direct and indirect discrimination are likely to persist.[26] As such, the conclusion that as '[t]here is no recent research providing evidence of discriminatory practices [in the social sector] it is fair to assume that these practices have been eliminated' seems premature.[27] Racial preju-dice and stereotyping almost certainly still lead to deliberate unequal treatment in the private housing market today, although the scale and form of this discrimin-ation needs further formal investigation, and the current high demand for rented

---

[21] Commission for Racial Equality, *Race and Council Housing in Hackney* (CRE, 1984); see further M. Bryan, 'Discrimination in the Public Provision of Housing: The CRE Report on Housing in Hackney' [1984] *Public Law* 194. See also the now classic academic study on housing officer discretion: J. Henderson and V. Karn, *Race, Class and State Housing: Inequality and the Allocation of Public Housing in Britain* (Gower, 1987).

[22] Commission for Racial Equality, *Sorry, It's Gone: Testing for Racial Discrimination in the Private Rented Sector* (CRE, 1990).

[23] V. Karn and D. Phillips, 'Race and Ethnicity in Housing: A Diversity of Experience' in P. Bhikhu, P. Sanders and T. Blackstone, *Race Relations in Britain: A Developing Agenda* (Routledge, 1998).

[24] C. Hamnett and T. Butler, 'The Changing Ethnic Structure of Housing Tenures in London, 1991–2001' (2010) 47(1) *Urban Studies* 55.

[25] See the specific criticisms levelled at the lack of research in Karn and Phillips, n.23, 130–31.

[26] D. Phillips, 'The Rhetoric of Anti-Racism in Public Housing Allocation' in P. Jackson (ed.), *Race and Racism: Essays in Social Geography* (Routledge, 1987) p. 213.

[27] D. Manley and M. van Ham, 'Choice-Based Letting, Ethnicity and Segregation in England' (2011) 48(8) *Urban Studies* 3125, 3129.

housing in areas like London may well increase the opportunities for landlords, sellers and their agents to discriminate against minority ethnic communities.[28]

The legal protections afforded under Part 4 of the Equality Act were conceived originally to address the inequalities in housing outcome faced by ethnic minorities in the post-war period. These anti-discrimination measures had significant limitations. First, evidence since the enactment of such protections in the mid-1970s suggests that direct and indirect forms of race discrimination in the housing market will inevitably continue across all tenures regardless of legal prohibitions, especially as discrimination in housing is often well-hidden and thus difficult to prove, and enforcement is invariably sporadic.[29] Second, improving the housing outcomes of ethnic minorities requires not only equal opportunity within the housing market, but also equality in areas such as education and employment, and the elimination of racial harassment and violence, all of which shore up the socio-economic disadvantages which still dictate the housing choices available to ethnic minorities. Third, achieving more equal housing outcomes for ethnic minorities means not only addressing direct or indirect forms of race discrimination, but overcoming the wider structural problems within the housing market, such as the ongoing residualization of the social rented sector. In other words, tackling racial inequality in the housing context must entail more than merely outlawing discriminatory conduct. We consider how other measures contained in the Equality Act might encourage a more strategic, joined-up approach to addressing inequalities in housing in the final part of this chapter.

CONTEMPORARY DEBATES: THE CONTOURS OF ANTI-DISCRIMINATION LAW IN HOUSING

This section shifts the focus from the history and policy context of the principle of non-discrimination in the housing context to more recent debates over the appropriate scope of the protections afforded in this area. The enforcement of the principle of non-discrimination has divided opinion since it was introduced into law by the Race Relations Acts. It is often challenged, in the housing context and elsewhere, as an incursion on the interests of others, either because critics wish to preserve the freedom to act on their personal distaste for particular protected groups, or because they view the rules imposed by legislation as too costly or challenging to satisfy. The two case studies considered below have been selected to illustrate how these tensions have played out in the field of discrimination and housing. The first case study explores the small premises and private disposal exemptions which continue to permit certain forms of direct discrimination in relation to the privacy of the home. The second case study considers the shifting scope of the protections afforded to disabled people in the housing context in recent years, in light of the concerns of (primarily social) landlords over the effect

---

[28] Karn and Phillips, n.23, 144.

[29] See, for example, S. Halliday, 'Institutional Racism in Bureaucratic Decision-Making: A Case Study in the Administration of Homelessness Law' (2000) 27(3), *Journal of Law and Society* 449.

on housing management of disability-related discrimination and the landlord's duty to make reasonable adjustments.

Debate 2

Public versus private space: the incursion of equalities law into the 'home'

The general prohibitions relating to the disposal and management of premises under the EA are subject to two important exceptions. The first is known as the small premises exemption, which permits a person to discriminate against someone who shares any protected characteristic except for race, where this relates to the disposal, management or occupation of premises in which the person also lives, and which can house a maximum of two other households, or a maximum of six other individual occupants.[30] The second is the 'private disposal' exemption. This permits discrimination in the disposal of property by an owner who occupies the premises as a home, and on grounds of sexual orientation, or religion and belief, in relation to permission to dispose,[31] so long as the disposal is carried out in private. 'Private' means that the owner does not use the services of an estate agent or publish an advertisement regarding the disposal.[32] Versions of the exemptions also extend to the duty to make 'reasonable adjustments' for disabled people.[33] The small premises and private disposal exemptions have an established pedigree, included as they were in the first protections from discrimination in housing under the Race Relations Act 1968.[34] They were modelled on exemptions found in some US civil rights law of the time.[35] Importantly, however, they were both abolished in the context of race discrimination in 2003 to comply with the EU Race Directive,[36] an inconsistency considered in more detail below.

In February 1965, the Home Secretary presented a memorandum to the Cabinet setting out his proposals for the first Race Relations Act. This document provides an important insight into the role played by conceptions of the 'private' in shaping the scope of the legislation:

> [D]iscrimination on grounds of race or colour should be penalised if it is practised in places to which the public have access – in particular in hotels, restaurants, public houses, places of entertainment or recreation and public transport vehicles. There is not much evidence of discrimination in such places now; but it is indefensible if it should occur and I think it is

---

[30] EA, sch. 5, para. 3.
[31] EA, sch. 4, para. 1(4).
[32] EA, sch. 5, para. 1(2).
[33] EA, sch. 4, paras 2 and 4.
[34] RRA 1968, s. 7.
[35] Laws in Alaska and Minnesota included neither exemption: see Street, Howe and Bindman, n.13.
[36] Race Relations Act 1976 (Amendment) Regulations 2003/1626, regs 23(2)(b) and 24.

right to prohibit it. We cannot, I feel, go further and deal (for example) with the refusal of landladies to take coloured lodgers – which leads to a lot of complaint – without interfering unjustifiably with the rights of the individual.[37]

The paradigmatic landlady and her refusal to house ethnic minority lodgers personified the potentially problematic impact of anti-discrimination laws on private freedoms. The problem was implicitly constructed, in the words of the Street Report of 1967, as an issue of 'intimate personal proximity',[38] and the concern that the landlady who offered rooms to lodgers might be forced to share her home with those towards whom she held deeply felt objections. It was also a scenario that seems to have formed the basis for the government's initial refusal to outlaw discrimination relating to premises until 1968, even after acknowledging that this form of discriminatory conduct had led to significantly more complaints in practice than discrimination in public accommodations, which were actually outlawed by the 1965 Act.

In the end, the government was persuaded by the stark evidence of widespread race discrimination in the housing market to extent the scope of the Race Relations Acts to premises in 1968, although it still included the small premises exemption to address the problem of the landlady and the ethnic minority lodger.[39] However, new fears emerged about the impact of the proposed law, which had shifted from the problem of shared residence in small premises to the sale of homes by owner-occupiers.[40] In this regard, the Street Report noted two issues: 'that owner-occupiers fear ostracism by their neighbours who feel that house values will be lowered if coloured residents move into an area',[41] and the view that 'the home is so fundamental an aspect of the citizen's financial and domestic arrangements that it should not be the subject of legal regulation'.[42] The issue vexed the Cabinet to such an extent that it was referred to the Home Affairs Committee in December 1967 for further consideration and recommendations.[43] The Committee recognized that sales by owner-occupiers were 'a highly sensitive area'; it noted the concern that 'public opinion might be affronted by complaints against white home-owners who were exercising a legitimate freedom to dispose of their own property and were not actuated by racial prejudice', but where the house owner had chosen to sell to a white person rather than a black person.

---

[37] Cabinet Office, *Memorandum from the Minister for Home Affairs: Racial Discrimination and Incitement to Racial Hatred*, C(65)23, 17 February 1965 (unpublished, available at <www.nationalarchives.gov.uk>).

[38] Street, Howe and Bindman, n.13, p. 83.

[39] Ibid, p. 85.

[40] Cabinet Office, *Cabinet Conclusions*, CC(67)74, 21 December 1967 (unpublished, available at <www.nationalarchives.gov.uk>), Minute 2.

[41] Street, Howe and Bindman, n.13, p. 85.

[42] Ibid, p. 86.

[43] Cabinet Office, *Memorandum from the First Secretary of State. Race Relations Legislation*. C(68)12, 8 January 1968 (unpublished, available at <www.nationalarchives.gov.uk>).

The Home Affairs Committee concluded by a majority that sales by owner-occupiers should stay within the ambit of the legislation, primarily on the ground that:

> From the point of view of the immigrant community housing is where discrimination hurts most. Nearly 50 per cent of houses in England and Wales are in the hands of owner-occupiers, and what we do here will be regarded as a touchstone of the Government's sincerity. The whole philosophy of the Bill and its educative effect would be greatly weakened if the owner-occupier were excluded.[44]

It was surprising, then, that the 1968 Act included a 'private disposal' exemption at all. This was not, of course, a general exemption for sales of owner-occupied homes; instead, it excluded only those transactions taking place without advertising or estate agents. However, it did grant a level of protection to the owner-occupier which the Committee had not sanctioned, suggesting that a compromise was struck – at the eleventh hour – between the perceived need to protect the freedom to dispose of private property (the home), and the interest of immigrant communities in equal access to homes through purchase. It achieved this by pushing discriminatory sales behind closed doors, and outside the (visible) mainstream marketplace.

The small premises and private disposal exemptions were included in the Race Relations Act 1968 on the ground that non-discrimination 'should fall short of certain personal and private relationships'.[45] However, the Report also recognized that 'in the end the drawing of such a line will be governed by personal and political choice'.[46] The political choice that in practice shaped the exemptions is clear: the private sphere (in which discrimination was apparently permissible) was aligned more or less with the home. The exemptions were as much strategic as they were principled measures, designed to allay public concerns over the legislation, when these objections might have otherwise jeopardized the Act as a whole at a time when the Labour government was highly sensitive to growing hostility to racial integration. However, it was a settlement which would have considerably more far-reaching consequences for the scope of equalities law over the next forty years. From 1968, the exemptions were presumed (by the state) to be legitimate, and incorporated automatically by drafters into each new raft of equalities legislation. Yet these exemptions remained contentious, primarily because they imply that the interest of the home owner in treating another person less favourably on grounds of a protected characteristic – for reasons of prejudice or otherwise – has more value than the interest in being protected from discrimination because the act relates to the home, even though discrimination is arguably as wrong and as harmful in this context as any other.[47]

---

44 Ibid, 1.

45 Street, Howe and Bindman, n.13, p. 64.

46 Ibid, p. 64.

47 For criticism of the small premises exemption in the US context, see J. Walsh, 'Reaching Mrs. Murphy: A Call for Repeal of the Mrs. Murphy Exemption to the Fair Housing Act' (1999) 34 *Harv CR-CL L Rev* 605. We consider further recent criticisms of the small premises exemption as it applies to disability, when we consider the protections afforded to disabled people by the Equality Act in more detail below.

It was only at the outset of the twenty-first century that the exemptions were revisited. In 2000, the Council of the European Union enacted the Race Directive, which extended protection from discrimination on grounds of race under European law to include 'access to and supply of goods and services which are available to the public, including housing'.[48] The Labour government implemented the Directive by amending the 1976 Act by regulation, concluding initially that this could be achieved by partially restricting the small premises exemption to meet the terms of the Directive.[49] However, the final regulations abandoned both exemptions altogether in relation to race alone.[50] The EA adopted the same approach, with the result that race, the characteristic which formed the basis for the earliest justifications for the exemptions, is now – ironically – the only characteristic excluded from the exemptions in modern equalities law. When the Joint Committee for Human Rights reviewed the Equality Bill in 2009, it concluded that the exemptions as they are currently formulated strike 'an appropriate balance between protecting the right to equality and the right to privacy and freedom of association'.[51] It gave no further justification for this view, nor did it grapple with the inconsistency that presently exists between race and other equality characteristics.[52]

Nevertheless, more recent struggles over the scope of the principle of non-discrimination support the need for a shift towards a more restrictive approach. First, the small premises exemption was criticized by the Disability Rights Taskforce, leading to the incorporation of a power allowing the executive to amend or remove it (see discussion of disability discrimination below).[53] Second, the deployment of the home as a protected private sphere has been challenged successfully in relation to the related paradigm of discrimination by Christian B&B owners against gay couples. Following proposals in 2007 to introduce the first equality protections for gay people in the provision of goods and services many Christian B&B owners

---

[48] Council Directive 2000/43/EC of 29 June 2000, implementing the principle of equal treatment between persons irrespective of racial or ethnic origin.

[49] Department of Trade and Industry, *Towards Equality and Diversity – Implementing the Employment and Race Directives* (DTI, 2003) p. 31; Department of Trade and Industry, *Equality and Diversity: The Way Ahead* (DTI, 2003) p. 43 (limiting exemption to those premises where landlord shares facilities).

[50] Race Relations Act 1976 (Amendment) Regulations 2003/1626, regs 23(2)(b) and 24. Note that the government actually only removed the exemptions in relation to race, ethnic or national origins (which were grounds formally covered by the Directive) but not colour or nationality (which were further grounds under the RRA 1976 but were not covered by the Directive). The EA addressed the obvious irrationality of distinguishing between these different heads of discrimination by going on to outlaw the exemptions across the Act's extended umbrella concept of 'race'.

[51] Joint Committee on Human Rights, *Legislative Scrutiny: Equality Bill*, 26th Report of Session 2008–09 HL Paper 169 (HMSO, 2009).

[52] Perhaps once again change will be instigated by the EU, where proposals for a new Equal Treatment Directive are being debated: see European Commission, *Proposal for a Council Directive on Implementing the Principle of Equal Treatment between Persons Irrespective of Religion or Belief, Disability, Age or Sexual Orientation* (2 July 2008). This will impose non-discrimination in the fields of goods, services and premises on grounds of sexual orientation, age, disability and religion and belief, and – like the Race Directive before it – may offer a future opportunity for the UK government to abolish the exemptions when transposing the law by regulation.

[53] EA, sch. 5, para. 5.

had argued that they should be protected from the new law on grounds of privacy because their B&Bs were also their homes (the small premises exemption could not apply as B&B owners are deemed by law to be service providers). However, the government concluded that they should not be exempt. It argued instead that when a B&B owner uses his or her home for business purposes, these purposes bring the property out from the otherwise protected private sphere of owner-occupation and into the public arena of commerce and profit-making.[54] The government took this view even though the arguments by B&B owners were the same in principle as those arguments accepted in relation to race and the small premises exemption in 1968. The government's position was affirmed in a recent case in which the defendant B&B owners contended *inter alia* that they should be able to refuse to allow gay couples to share double rooms on human rights grounds. The owners drew once again on the rhetoric of home and private property rights to defend their position using Article 8 of the European Convention, but the argument was rejected.[55] This alignment of equalities law with equal opportunity in the commercial market, while open to criticism for reducing the significance of non-commercial discrimination and inequalities,[56] raises important questions about whether the values of owner-occupation, the home and private property are sufficient to vindicate the landlady or the home seller when they discriminate for financial gain under the small premises or private disposal exemptions.

Autobiographical note

Neil reflects on (safe) space and LGBT equality

The 'Pink Triangle' is home to Newcastle upon Tyne's gay scene. Like other scenes across the country, and the world, the Triangle developed away from the city centre proper, as a (relatively) safe space where gay men, lesbians, bisexual and transgender people could meet each other and socialize. Significantly (and not uncontroversially), gay scenes are established on commercial terms, organized around bars, clubs and restaurants which serve a gay clientele.

As a gay man living in Newcastle I've had a complicated relationship with the scene. Arriving for the first time in the city, and knowing practically no one, it was indispensible as a ready-made social hub which would not have been available so straightforwardly to a straight person in the same predicament. However, I like others am wary of the exclusions that

---

54 Department of Communities and Local Government, *Getting Equal: Proposals to Outlaw Sexual Orientation Discrimination in the Provision of Goods and Services: Government Response to Consultation* (DCLG, 2007), p.13.

55 *Hall and Preddy v Bull and Bull* [2011] EW Misc 2 (CC), para 38. The decision has since been confirmed by the Court of Appeal: [2012] EWCA Civ 83.

56 N. Cobb, ' "Gay Couple's Break Like Fawlty Towers": Dangerous Representations of Lesbian and Gay Oppression in An Era of "Progressive" Law Reform' (2009) 18(3) *Social and Legal Studies* 333.

operate invariably within a commercially orientated social space, in which income can dictate one's ability to participate.

Over my six years in Newcastle I've also become aware of changes to the scene's demographics. As LGBT people have become more visible and accepted, the scene itself has become something of a tourist destination, with hen parties (particularly popular in Newcastle) descending on the Triangle in droves on Friday and Saturday nights.[57] The result is occasional gawping at best, and mockery or abuse at worst. My lesbian friends usually find things more difficult than me, as approaching a straight woman in the mistaken belief she is gay can lead sometimes to serious altercations.

I have a feeling that the increasing presence of straight people on the scene is partly to blame for its rapid contraction in recent years,[58] though responsibility must also go to the rise of the internet, punitive bar prices, and the increasing acceptance of gay and lesbian people within Newcastle's mainstream night-time economy (transgender people still fare much less well).

One response to the problem of straight tourism has been to impose door policies barring straight people from entry (though I suspect that many gay establishments continue to encourage straight tourism for purely commercial ends). However, it was a surprise for many LGBT people to discover that the extension of equalities law to sexual orientation meant that it is now *prima facie* illegal discrimination on grounds of sexual orientation to operate LGBT-only venues.

Some flexibility remains: government guidance notes that 'a gay bar would still legitimately be able to turn away customers who they believed might be disruptive, or might wish to enter the bar to cause trouble.'[59] I have since wondered too whether it would be possible to justify LGBT-only door policies as positive action under the Equality Act, to support the need of LGBT people to have access to a safe space in which to express themselves without fear of judgement or ridicule.

Intuitively, though, I think it's probably right that it should not be possible to refuse entry to gay establishments simply on the ground that a person is (perceived to be) straight, not least because blanket rules of this kind lead inevitably to arbitrary door policies as bouncers are granted the authority to decide who is 'visibly' gay or not. But the wider debate from which this legal issue springs – the changing face of gay scenes like Newcastle's Pink Triangle and what it means to those who use them – highlights the complex relationship between (safe) space, commerce,

---

57 P. Hensher, 'Please Keep Out of Gay Bars and Clubs', *The Independent*, 25 June 2002.
58 I. Herbert, 'Are Hen Nights to Blame for Hard Times in Manchester's Gay Village?' *The Independent*, 11 February 2006.
59 B. Cohen, 'Government Tells Gay Bars to Let in Straights', PinkNews.co.uk, 27 February 2006.

> equality and the power to exclude, at a time when LGBT people in
> Newcastle and elsewhere are emerging from the shadows of the ghetto.

Debate 3

Equality versus regulation: controlling the consequences of disability

Part of the work of the EA was to consolidate and update the protections granted to disabled people by the Disability Discrimination Act 1995 (DDA) and amending legislation. The social model of disability contends that the inequality experienced by disabled people is not caused by their condition but by the failure of society to accommodate the effects of that condition adequately.[60] For this reason, the EA – like the DDA before it – imposes more demanding duties to accommodate difference than the concept of 'indirect discrimination', which traditionally serves this purpose in relation to other characteristics. First, as well as direct and indirect discrimination, the Equality Act also prohibits 'disability-related' discrimination in relation to the disposal, permission to dispose or management of premises. This is defined as less favourable treatment of a disabled person where the the other party 'knows or ought to know' of the disability, for a reason 'arising as a consequence' of the person's disability, unless it is a 'proportionate means to achieve a legitimate aim'.[61] Second, landlords (and property managers) are under a duty to make certain 'reasonable adjustments' when asked to do so by a disabled occupier if, without that adjustment being made, the occupier would be placed at a 'substantial disadvantage' in relation to the use of the premises when compared to a person without the relevant disability.

The protection from disability-related discrimination has had important implications for social housing management.[62] The effects of disability can sometimes make it difficult, if not impossible, for a disabled person to adhere to the terms of a tenancy agreement. For example, a tenant may engage in conduct due to mental illness which negatively affects the quality of life of other residents, or the tenant might not be able to pay the rent because of physical incapacity arising from disability. Landlords may wish to take steps to respond to that behaviour by evicting the tenant, or subjecting the tenant to other unwanted treatment (for example, to subject that person to an anti-social behaviour order, or evict them from the property) to address problematic behaviour caused by disability. That might be in line with their published policies on anti-social behaviour and obligations to the tenant's neighbours, or on the basis that the tenant's failure to pay the rent poses a threat to the landlord's financial viability. The question raised by the EA is whether such steps will (and should) amount to unlawful discriminatory

---

[60] M. Oliver, *Understanding Disability: From Theory to Practice* (Palgrave Macmillan, 1996).

[61] EA, s. 15.

[62] See, generally, N. Cobb, 'Patronising the Mentally Disordered? Social Landlords and the Control of "Anti-Social Behaviour" Under the Disability Discrimination Act 1995' (2006) 26(2) *Legal Studies* 238.

treatment under the legislation. This question is – at its core – one aspect of a wider debate regarding the appropriate balance to be struck between the interests of the disabled person and society, when the effects of a disability have a negative impact on others.

Understanding the balance now enforced by the Equality Act requires consideration of the difficulties that arose when disability-related discrimination was applied under the DDA. The concept of disability-related discrimination under the DDA was significantly different from the current position and was viewed by some as striking this balance too far in favour of the disabled person.

The problem was twofold. First, the old law was couched in terms that meant any negative treatment, such as eviction, relating to a disability was *prima facie* illegal. This was because to establish less favourable treatment the law required that the landlord's response to the disabled person should be compared with the response that would be given to someone who was not disabled, and did not behave in the same way.[63] Less favourable treatment could only be justified by a narrow list of reasons for the treatment specified by the Act: that the treatment was necessary in order not to endanger the health or safety of the disabled person or another; that the disabled person was incapable of entering into an enforceable agreement, or of giving informed consent; or, where the treatment related to the use of a benefit or facility, that the treatment was necessary in order for the disabled person or the occupiers of other premises in the building to make use of the benefit or facility.[64] If no such justification was established the landlord would be powerless to proceed with the less favourable treatment. The second problem was that disability-related discrimination seemed to occur under the terms of the Act even if the landlord did not know, and had no reasonable way of knowing, that the problematic behaviour was caused by a disability.[65]

It was these concerns that encouraged the intervention of the House of Lords in *Malcolm v Lewisham London Borough Council*.[66] The majority were desperate to recalibrate the DDA to expand the powers of landlords to respond to the problematic behaviour that could arise from disability. In doing so, they effectively neutralized the concept of disability-related discrimination by deciding that, to establish less favourable treatment, the landlord's response to the disabled person's problematic behaviour must be compared with the response the landlord would have made to someone who was not disabled, but engaged in the same conduct (e.g. anti-social behaviour or non-payment of rent). The result of this reasoning was that punitive responses to behaviour arising from a disability would never be less favourable treatment, if the landlord would have responded in the same way to the same behaviour if carried out by a non-disabled person. Thus, the majority concluded that, to amount to discrimination, the claimant's disability must

---

[63] *Clark v Novacold* [1999] IRLR 318.
[64] DDA, s. 24(3).
[65] *Manchester City Council v Romano and Sumari* [2005] 1 WLR 2775.
[66] [2008] 1 AC 1399.

'motivate' the actions of the landlord,[67] which by definition would require the landlord to be fully aware of the existence of the disability when the negative treatment was carried out.

Malcolm illustrates the unresolved tensions behind the protection of the disabled from disability-related discrimination, in terms of the difficult balance that equalities law is expected to strike between the interests of disabled people and others. In the case of social housing management the question is whether, and if so when, a landlord should be entitled to take action to respond to conduct related to disability which has a negative impact on the landlord or other people, such as neighbours of the disabled tenant. The DDA was designed to limit the situations in which it was permissible to subject a disabled person to less favourable treatment, in order to encourage society to accommodate the effects of disability as far as possible. However, for the House of Lords, the limited grounds on which less favourable treatment could be justified under the Act were simply too inflexible to allow landlords (and others) to balance effectively the interests of disabled people with the interests of those affected by those disabilities. Moreover, the liability of those who were unaware of the disability imposed a duty on even those who could not reasonably be expected to have identified the disability and taken it into consideration. The concept of discrimination introduced by the EA was formulated to respond to these concerns.

The EA imposes liability on landlords only if they knew or ought to have known about a disability at the time at which they carried out activity otherwise prohibited by the Act.[68] This requirement protects landlords if they were unaware of the condition, but requires them to take at least reasonable steps to find out whether conduct is disability-related, which should encourage them proactively to investigate possible links between problem behaviour and a disability protected by the legislation before acting against a tenant. The Act also reinstates the pre-*Malcolm* approach by which any and all negative treatment arising from a disability must be justified before it can be permitted. However, the grounds for justification have shifted from the prescribed list in the DDA to a more broad-brush approach using the well-established human rights concepts of proportionality and legitimate aims.

While the EA approach maximizes flexibility, it is less certain that it will protect sufficiently the interests of disabled people. The new system of justifications grants a wide discretion to courts to decide on the right balance between the interests of disabled people and wider society. However, the difficulty with the new scheme is the lack of clarity it provides about the ambit of the protection from disability-related discrimination, and the inevitable concern that the courts will tend towards defending the interests of others over and above those of the disabled. There is, perhaps, still something to be said for the approach under the original DDA, by which specific justifications were defined by statute. As

---

[67] [29].
[68] The approach adopted by Baroness Hale in *Malcolm*: [87].

Baroness Hale indicated in her dissent in *Malcolm*, the DDA was not as inflexible as might have first appeared, because it made special provision for the executive to enact further statutory regulations setting out additional grounds on which discrimination would be justified.[69] The strength of this system compared to the broad discretion now granted to the courts is that further justifications would be formulated within a more democratic process and after appropriate engagement with those affected which, one might argue, would better suit the complex policy questions that shape the scope of discrimination in this field.

The duty to make reasonable adjustments – as it applies to the housing context – has also undergone significant changes under the EA. The Act now imposes a specific duty on landlords (including managers of property) to take reasonable steps to alter 'a provision, criterion or practice' or provide an 'auxiliary aid' if requested to do so by a disabled tenant, if the provision, criterion or practice, or the absence of the auxiliary aid, puts the disabled person at a 'substantial disadvantage' in their 'enjoyment' of the property or their 'use of a benefit or facility' related to the property.[70]

In much the same way as the concept of disability-related discrimination, the principle of reasonable adjustment poses difficult questions about the appropriate balance that should be struck between the interests of the disabled tenant in having their disability accommodated in this way, and the interests of others, such as the potential costs of auxiliary aids (for example, a landlord being required to carry out interior decorating),[71] and the impact on neighbours (for example, a tenant being allowed to keep a noisy dog).[72] In interpreting similar terms under the DDA, the courts adopted a cautious approach to the duty, leading for instance to the Court of Appeal's conclusion that 'enjoyment of premises', means 'to live in the premises in an ordinary lawful way as any other typical tenant would live in them; enjoyment of premises does not mean deriving pleasure from them';[73] and, moreover, that 'the right to enjoy the premises is dictated by the terms of the lease itself. That right cannot exceed what the letting entitles the tenant to do.'[74]

In practice the scope of the duty – and the balance it strikes between the interests of the disabled and others – will be dictated primarily by the interpretation of whether it is 'reasonable' to implement an adjustment. On one hand, the EA appears to have reformulated the new duty in favour of the disabled person, by requiring only that the occupier should experience 'substantial disadvantage' in the enjoyment of premises or use of a benefit or facility (rather than the more onerous requirement under the DDA that it should be 'impossible or unreasonably difficult'). In future, cases like *Beedles*, in which the Court of Appeal found that poor interior decoration resulting from the inability of an epileptic tenant

---

[69] DDA, s. 24(5).
[70] EA, s. 20 and sch. 4.
[71] *Beedles v Guinness Northern Counties* [2011] EWCA Civ 442.
[72] *Ashley v Drum Housing Association* [2010] L&TR 117.
[73] *Beedles v Guinness Northern Counties* [2011] EWCA Civ 442.
[74] *Ashley v Drum Housing Association* [2010] L&TR 117.

to carry out the decorating as required by his tenancy agreement did not make it 'impossible or unreasonably difficult' to enjoy the premises, may well be decided differently under the 'substantial disadvantage' test.[75] However, one can imagine the courts may still try their best to protect landlords from the financial impact of, for example, the transfer of a contractual repair obligation from landlord to tenant. That the cost of the duty to landlords is likely to be at the forefront of the minds of judges is illustrated by the *Beedles dictum* that the cost implications of an adjustment requested by a disabled person can legitimately be taken into account when courts evaluate what is 'reasonable'.[76] This indicates not only that judges are likely to apply the law with one eye on the economics of accommodating disability in housing, but also that the broader question of who should pay – the state, the landlord, or the disabled person – will be fiercely contested before the courts. The power granted to the executive under the EA to make further regulations defining in more detailed terms the scope of the reasonable adjustments duty could either challenge or compound judicial resistance to the duty and the burden it imposes on landlords, depending on the commitment of future governments to accommodating disabled people.[77]

CONCLUSIONS: BEYOND 'NON-DISCRIMINATION' AND TOWARDS 'EQUALITY WORK'

The primary focus of the discussion in this chapter has been the principle of non-discrimination and the appropriate scope of that principle in the property and housing context. There is more to equalities law, however, than the protections from discrimination considered so far. The enforcement of non-discrimination cannot hope to achieve substantive equality for minority communities in housing, because these laws can never eliminate discrimination on their own; because improving housing outcomes requires connections to be made between housing and inequalities in other areas such as education or employment; and because inequality in housing is caused as much by wider structural factors – for instance, institutional racism – as it is by specific discriminatory acts or practices. For these reasons, under the Act several measures move beyond equality law's more established concern with non-discrimination towards a more strategic concern with transformative *equality work*: provisions aimed at encouraging public and private bodies to promote equality positively, rather than merely refraining from discriminatory acts. This final section considers what role equality work might play in alleviating unequal housing outcomes, in three areas: the work of the central co-ordinating responsibilities of the Equality and Human Rights Commission (EHRC) for promoting equality in housing (and other fields covered by the Act); the Public Sector Equality Duty imposed by section 149 of the Act; and the power

---

[75] [2011] EWCA Civ 442.
[76] Ibid, at [27].
[77] EA, s. 22.

granted by the Act to take positive steps to address the structural disadvantages of specific communities by discriminating in their favour.

Since it was established in October 2007, the EHRC has taken on the strategic remits of the Commission for Racial Equality, the Equal Opportunities Commission and the Disability Rights Commission, and has been given additional responsibilities regarding discrimination in the areas of age, sexual orientation, gender identity, and religion and belief.[78] Like its predecessors, the EHRC was designed to facilitate a more strategic approach to discrimination and inequality (together with its new remit for human rights promotion). It is empowered to support individual claims of discrimination, to act as an intervener in appellate cases on equalities law (but not to bring claims itself), and to carry out 'investigations' into alleged discriminatory practices by named persons, and 'inquiries' focused more generally on non-named performance in fields or sectors. There has been a long history of investigations and inquiries by the CRE into race discrimination and inequality in the housing market. Between 1980 and 1990, the CRE carried out several investigations into estate agencies, property developers, local housing authorities and housing associations, which shone a spotlight onto the problem of continued non-compliance with equalities law across the housing sector.[79]

Over the last two decades, no investigations or inquiries into the housing sector have been carried out by either the previous commissions or the EHRC. Instead, their equality work in this field has focused almost entirely on the release of guidance and codes of practice to housing providers.[80] This seems to give support to the accusation that previous commissions were 'too timid in their enforcement work',[81] especially in relation to named investigations into private sector organizations, due in part to the 'cowing effect' of judicial controls on named investigations, arising from at least one CRE investigation into council housing.[82] In response, the CRE and other commissions 'tended to err on the side of extreme caution in deciding whether to launch formal investigations'.[83] The EHRC appears to be no more 'tough-minded', as some had hoped,[84] in its approach to enforcement in the housing sector, even though its named investigation powers have been strengthened. Moreover, the 'political and judicial disquiet'[85] which met previous efforts by the CRE to carry out named investigations does not explain the continued reluctance to carry out more general non-named inquiries into discrimination

---

[78] For an overview and discussion, see C. O'Cinneide, 'The Commission for Equality and Human Rights: A New Institution for New and Uncertain Times' (2007) *ILJ* 141.

[79] See e.g. Commission for Racial Equality (1984), n.21.

[80] See, for example, Commission for Racial Equality, *Statutory Code of Practice on Racial Equality in Housing – England* (CRE, 2006). Equality-related guidance on housing (although in this case relating to Article 14 of the European Convention) has been issued recently by the Equality and Human Rights Commission: n.1.

[81] O'Cinneide, n.78, 152.

[82] *R v CRE*, Ex p *Hillingdon* LBC [1982] AC 779; see also *In re Prestige* [1984] ICR 473.

[83] O'Cinneide, n.78, 149.

[84] Ibid, 162.

[85] Ibid, 149.

in the housing sector.[86] The lack of investigations or inquiries suggests that initial fears that the EHRC would adopt an even more 'excessively placatory and "soft touch" approach' than previous commissions were well-founded.[87] The reluctance of the EHRC to carry out named investigations or general inquiries into discrimination in housing is likely to be reinforced by the swingeing cuts to the EHRC's budgets – apparently running at 68 per cent – imposed as part of the Coalition Government's austerity measures.[88]

The aim of the Public Sector Duty is to encourage public bodies to 'mainstream' equality work throughout their core business by requiring these bodies to give 'due regard to the need to eliminate unlawful discrimination, harassment and victimisation; advance equality of opportunity between different groups; and foster good relations between different groups'.[89] Specific duties were imposed recently, to flesh out the General Duty in England, requiring public authorities 'to publish information' demonstrating compliance with the Duty, and prepare and publish 'one or more equality objectives' every four years, which are 'specific and measurable'.[90] In principle at least, the duties have the potential to encourage a more strategic and structural approach to discrimination and inequalities in housing. Both duties are imposed on the Department for Communities and Local Government, local authorities, and the social housing regulator, while registered housing associations are subject to the general duty when carrying out public functions, as 'hybrid' authorities. Each of these organizations will be expected therefore to integrate equality work when creating housing policy, or in the allocation, management and other regulation of all forms of housing.

However, it may be more difficult in practice to realize the potential of the duties in the field of discrimination and inequality in housing. First, the scope of the duties suggests that in many cases it will be a struggle to keep housing outcomes at the forefront of the equality work of relevant authorities. With obligations owed across all protected characteristics, and an obligation under the specific duties recently released in England to formulate only 'one or more' equality objective every four years, national government departments and local authorities with their various other functions may not have the time or inclination to focus on housing (though this may be less of a problem for the social housing regulator, whose core business is oversight of all social renting). Second, while it remains possible to challenge specific policies and decision in the courts under the terms of the General Duty,[91] case law suggests that success in this area is likely to depend on evidence of inadequate consultation or a failure by an authority to

---

[86] The last general housing inquiry was carried out in the private rented sector in 1990: CRE, op. cit. n XXX.

[87] O'Cinneide, n.78, 147.

[88] P. Curtis, 'Cuts Will Clobber Equality and Human Rights Commission, Claim Staff', *Guardian*, 8 February 2011.

[89] EA, s. 149.

[90] Equality Act 2010 (Specific Duties) Regulations 2011/2260.

[91] See, for example, in the housing context, but under the previous disability equality duty, *Pieretti v Enfield LBC* [2010] EWCA Civ 1104.

consider the equality implications of the decision or policy at all: 'at best [section 149] will ensure public and hybrid authorities are willing to listen with an open mind'.[92] In law at least, no particular outcome will be required, and the authority will retain the final word. Much will depend instead on the capacity of individuals and organizations, including the EHRC, to hold authorities to account through the democratic process. For this reason, the specific duties require authorities to 'publish information' about how the duty is being met, and armed with this data it is expected that authorities will be held to account in the political sphere for their equality work. The problem with this approach, of course, is the lack of specificity regarding the information that must now be published by bodies to satisfy the specific duties. The Coalition was worried that too much regulation would overburden authorities in a time of recession,[93] but, without more, accountability under the duty may be illusory in practice.

The final provision of the EA which could support a more far-reaching strategic approach to inequality in housing is the concept of 'positive action', which permits discrimination by individuals and organizations in the housing context if it is a proportionate way to address the structural disadvantage and inequality of particular communities or groups.[94] The CRE previously suggested in its *Guidance on Race Equality in Housing* that landlords might consider taking positive action under the terms of the race equality duty by:

> developing temporary hostel accommodation catering especially for newly-arrived Somali refugees, who may have needs arising from shared traumatic experiences; or sheltered housing schemes for Chinese elders; or by providing wardens and carers who speak a particular Asian language; or by meeting certain dietary and religious requirements.[95]

There are obvious examples of specific housing needs across the range of disadvantaged groups now covered by the EA – such as social housing for young LGBT people, or supported accommodation for those with specific medical conditions like HIV/AIDS – which will also almost certainly be justifiable under the current terms of the positive action provisions.

Positive action is a power not a duty, unlike, for instance, the positive duty on landlords to make reasonable adjustments for disabled people. Permitting discrimination in order to address disadvantage is also politically sensitive, suggesting as it does the special treatment of certain groups. For these reasons, housing managers in the public sector may be reluctant to engage in positive action for fear of possible public resistance. One need only consider the EHRC's

---

[92] J. Halford and S. Khan, 'Equality Act Will Pressure Authorities to Listen' *Law Society Gazette*, 28 April 2011. See generally *R (Luton Borough Council) v Secretary of State for Education* [2011] EWHC 217 (Admin).

[93] Compare the approach of the outgoing Labour government: Government Equalities Office, *Equality Bill: Making it Work: Policy Proposals for Specific Duties A Consultation* (GEO, 2009).

[94] EA, s. 158.

[95] Commission for Racial Equality (2006), n.80, para. 2.41.

recent commission of independent research into the allegation that immigrants receive preferable treatment compared to the indigenous white population in social housing allocation to recognize that social landlords may face a backlash if they use the discretionary power of positive action to provide services tailored to meet the needs of unpopular groups.[96] A further problem with positive action is that, as considered above, taking positive steps to meet specific group needs can be costly, and so – in this time of austerity – housing providers may be less able or willing than before to offer tailored housing services to particular groups. As such, the potential for positive action to challenge structural inequalities in a meaningful way will depend in large part on the resources invested in equality objectives across the housing sector. Like the future role of the EHRC, and the effectiveness of the public sector equality duty, the success of positive action will depend primarily on the priority given by the state to investment in equality work in an increasingly fraught economic climate.

Further Reading

N. Cobb, 'Patronising the Mentally Disordered? Social Landlords and the Control of "Anti-Social Behaviour" Under the Disability Discrimination Act 1995' (2006) 26(2) *Legal Studies* 238.

Commission for Racial Equality, *Statutory Code of Practice on Racial Equality in Housing – England* (CRE, 2006).

D. Cowan, 'State Support for Housing Ethnic Minority Households: Spatial Segregation and Ghettoisation?' in J. Murphy (ed.), *Ethnic Minorities, their Families and the Law* (Hart, 2000).

B. Hepple, *Equality: The New Legal Framework* (Hart, 2011).

V. Karn and D. Phillips, 'Race and Ethnicity in Housing: a Diversity of Experience' in P. Bhikhu, P. Sanders and T. Blackstone, *Race Relations in Britain: A Developing Agenda* (Routledge, 1998).

A. Lawson, *Disability and Equality Law in Britain: The role of Reasonable Adjustment* (Hart, 2008).

---

[96] J. Rutter and M. Lattore, *Social Housing Allocation and Immigrant Communities* (EHRC, 2009).

10

MORTGAGES AND SECURITY INTERESTS IN LAND

INTRODUCTION

One of the most familiar land transactions within the popular consciousness – and the most crucial for anyone who has bought their home with the support of a bank or building society loan – is the mortgage. Mortgages are the bread-and-butter transactions which have enabled over 70 per cent of the UK's population to become home owners. In the period that has followed the housing market crisis that began in 2007, the impact of what began as a sub-prime lending crisis in the US has affected hundreds of thousands of UK home owners who have been unable to keep up repayments on their mortgages and have been threatened with – or experienced – repossession. National repossession statistics dating from 1990 highlight the cyclical nature of mortgage repossessions, with the number of properties taken into possession rising from 43,900 in 1990 to a high point of 75,500 in 1991 (the high point of the previous housing crisis); then falling off to a low of 8,200 in 2004, before beginning a gradual climb from 14,500 in 2005 to 47,900 in 2009.[1] 2010 figures showed a drop to 36,300, and although 2011 has shown signs of tepid economic recovery, the housing and mortgage market remains bruised.

Of course, statistics on mortgage possession orders made only tell part of the story of mortgage default. About half of mortgage orders throughout the period 1990 to 2011 were suspended,[2] although the percentage of orders suspended varies in inverse proportion to the number of possession orders made – from a low of 47 per cent in 1990 rising to around 60 per cent in the mid-1990s, and then falling again to 46 per cent in 2009. Against a backdrop in which over-indebted owner-occupiers face heightened levels of risk in relation to default and repossession, the courts who administer these orders seem more likely to suspend the order (so allowing the borrower a further opportunity to resolve their own personal financial crisis) in a more benign economic climate than in periods of

---

[1] For statistics, see Ministry of Justice website, Mortgage and landlord possession statistics, Possession data from 1990 to 2001; available online at <http://www.justice.gov.uk/publications/statistics-and-data/civil-justice/mortgage-possession.htm>.

[2] Ibid.

crisis when – it might be thought – the cause of the default is much more clearly attributable to the wider economic recession than the personal default of the individual borrower.

This chapter explores the key features of the mortgage market as it relates to property law by examining the core provisions of mortgage law, bankruptcy law and mortgage market regulation as they have been developed and applied in the contemporary context. This discussion will revolve around a core tension, between the use of domestic property as security and its function as an owner-occupied home. These competing uses (which echo the tensions discussed in Chapter 3) constitute the defining legal debate surrounding the use of property as security, which concerns how and where the balance should be struck between the protection of creditors' interests in the property as security (with the implications that this is presumed to have for the availability of credit to home owners) on the one hand, and the occupier's interest in the property as a home, on the other.

When the term 'occupier' is used in this context it usually refers to the owner-occupier, although mortgage repossessions often also affect private sector tenants. This dimension has been notable in the most recent crisis, as growing numbers of private landlords have defaulted on their mortgages, potentially leading to repossession for their tenants.[3] The position for such a tenant depends on whether the lease is binding on the landlord's lender (usually the case where the landlord has a 'buy-to-let' mortgage), where the lender has given permission for the property to be let, or where the tenant's occupation pre-dates, and so takes priority over, the grant of the mortgage or the landlord's purchase of the property. If the tenancy is not binding on the lender, recent developments under the Mortgage Repossessions (Protection of Tenants etc.) Act 2010 have shored up the position of the tenant to some extent, by ensuring that tenants will be made aware of the repossession action at an earlier stage,[4] and have the opportunity to apply to the court for a postponement of up to two months.[5] In exercising its discretion to order such a postponement, the factors to be considered by the court include the circumstances of the tenant, as well as any breach of terms by the tenant.[6]

The chapter will begin, however, by charting the development of the mortgage market, as driven by the political ideology of home ownership and expansion of owner-occupation, including for low-income households. That provides the backdrop to Debate 1 with which this chapter engages. Debate 2 concerns the appropriate level of consumer protection at the point of sale of the mortgage product. Debate 3 concerns the appropriate level of occupier protection at the point of crisis. The terminology here is important because it reflects the different ways in which we think about

---

[3] See Shelter, Citizens' Advice, Crisis, CIH, *A Private Matter? Private Tenants – the forgotten victims of the repossession crisis* (March 2009), available online at <http://england.shelter.org.uk/professional_resources/policy_library/policy_library_folder/a_private_matter_-_private_tenants_the_forgotten_victims_of_the_repossessions_crisis>.

[4] The lender must send a notice to the tenant or occupier in advance of the possession hearing, followed by a second notice in advance of any eviction.

[5] Mortgage Repossessions (Protection of Tenants etc.) Act 2010, s. 1(2).

[6] Mortgage Repossessions (Protection of Tenants etc.) Act 2010, s. 1(5).

the individual at different moments in their housing pathway: they are consumers at one point, occupiers at another. Furthermore, this is played out against an ideological backdrop that badges home buyers (subject to a mortgages) as 'home owners' from the outset, and an experiential reality that can leave these 'owners' in a precarious legal position if they default on debt payments.

Debate **1**

The functions of owner-occupied land: security interest or home?

One of the perennial great debates of property law, particularly brought to the fore in times of housing market crisis, is the inevitable tension between the use of property as security to leverage a loan (in some cases, the loan which has enabled the purchaser to acquire the property) and the function of the property as a home for the (owner-) occupier. The emergence of two competing paradigms surrounding the role and functions of owned housing is a further example of the more general debate relating to property for use and exchange. When it comes to mortgages and other forms of secured lending, the context for these different modes of thinking about owner-occupied property, its functions and its meanings was fundamentally altered by the deregulation of the UK's mortgage market in the 1980s. That process significantly broadened the range of situations in which borrowers may leverage their owned housing asset to include not only conventional acquisition mortgages and second mortgages, but also 'flexible mortgages' and financial products which enable the release of equity for older owners (including equity release/reverse mortgages, home reversion plans, and sale and rentback).[7]

The upsurge in mortgage-based financial products which enable the use of the home as security, combined with government policies which not only facilitate but encourage and rely on such transactions in the neoliberal 'wealth-fare' state,[8] has heightened the tensions between the competing functions of owned property as security in financial transactions, on the one hand, and as the owner-occupier's home on the other. Susan Smith has described owned homes as 'a hybrid of money, materials, and meanings',[9] and it is this context which provides the backdrop for

---

[7] See L. Fox O'Mahony, *Home Equity and Ageing Owners: Between Risk and Regulation* (Hart Publishing, 2012). Note that although home reversion plans, and sale and rentback, are collectively categorized by the Financial Services Authority (with conventional mortgages and other forms of secured lending) as 'regulated home finance activities' (<http://fsahandbook.info/FSA/html/handbook/PERG/2/Annex2>), they do not, in fact, involve using the property as security, but a sale of the property to the finance provider, with a lease back to the occupier on terms.

[8] The term 'wealth-fare state' reflects the shift from public provision of welfare to the neoliberal expectation that citizens, particularly owners, will self-provide for their own financial needs by leveraging their housing wealth: see S. Parkinson, B. Searle, S. Smith, A. Stokes and G. Wood, 'Mortgage Equity Withdrawal in Australia and Britain: Towards a Wealth-Fare State?' (2009) 9(3) *European Journal of Housing Policy* 363.

[9] S. Smith, 'Owner-Occupation: At Home with a Hybrid of Money and Materials' (2008) 40(5) *Environment and Planning A* 520, 521.

financial transactions that use the owned home as security. Smith explored the tensions this has created in her research into the changing character of housing assets, the owned home, and perhaps owner-occupiers themselves, as households shift towards deliberate strategies of 'banking on housing'; as property-holding citizens become asset-accumulating investors; and as the growing fungibility of housing wealth stimulates an 'ethically charged encounter between the governance of housing and the micropolitics of home'.[10]

Autobiographical note

On the power of the lender

One of my most brilliant friends reminded me the other day about the trick that property law plays on us. It makes us think that we are 'home owners' when, in fact, we are nothing of the sort. My friend loves their home – it's funky and in a cool part of the city. They are about to go abroad for a couple of years and decided that they would rent out their home for that period so that they could come back to it. They wanted to do it properly and got in touch with their lender to tell it of their plan (although apparently some letting agents said that notification was unnecessary). Their lender said that the only way they would consent to the rental would be if my friend's mortgage (currently at a pretty good fixed rate) was moved to a different product at a much higher rate of interest (which would make renting it out effectively uneconomical). One possible outcome is that my friend will have to sell the much-cherished funky home.

As my friend remarked to me, 'it makes you realize, doesn't it?' Indeed, it does; if we go 'by the book', we find out just how disempowered we are in our own homes by the need for, and existence of, this thing called a mortgage. It's property law's most brilliant confidence trick because you only recognizes it really when certain life-changing moments occur and you are, like my friend, stuck in the middle.

The transformation of housing discourse in Britain in recent decades has been so significant that it is easy to forget that, until the 1970s, the paradigm of housing as home was clearly dominant.[11] To the extent that owned housing was also viewed as an investment asset, it was with a view to providing a resource for inheritance for the next generation. The paradigms of housing as home and housing as inheritance have, however, been displaced in recent decades through a combination of increased political expectations that owners will liquidate and spend their housing wealth, the development of new financial products to enable housing wealth to

---

[10] Ibid.

[11] C. Hamnett, M. Harmer and P. Williams, *As Safe as Houses: Housing Inheritance in Britain* (Paul Chapman, 1991) p. 150.

be released, and the gradual normalization amongst owners of, first, the paradigm of housing as investment, and latterly, housing as investment-to-spend.

The first stage in this development can be charted as the role of the acquisition mortgage in enabling and supporting the expansion of owner-occupation as the tenure of choice for lower middle-class, and latterly low-income, households.[12] In the 1970s, Lord Diplock described the 'emergence of a property-owning, particularly a real-property-mortgaged-to-a-building-society-owning democracy'[13] which linked the availability of credit for home ownership with the idea of citizenship associated with owning property, discussed in Chapter 1. The expansion of ownership has many significant implications for the mortgage lending context, including the emergence of a line of argument that creditors must be protected and their interests afforded priority in legal contexts. The basis for that argument was that the expansion of home ownership was dependent on creditors' willingness to lend. A circuitous form of reasoning developed, maintaining that if creditors were not protected by the law in the event of debtor default, this would adversely affect the availability of credit, which would ultimately harm the consumer.[14] From a social perspective, the expansion of low-income ownership also exploded the myth that the status of owner could be viewed as providing a reliable indication of socio-economic wellbeing. In turn, that raises questions about the extent to which owners (or, more accurately, buyers who remain subject to a mortgage, often for decades, before becoming unencumbered owners) can be viewed as autonomous consumers, free of the structural constraints that inhibit financial decision-making concerning credit.[15]

Following on the heels of the increased availability of acquisition mortgages to expand the ownership sector, there was also, from the 1980s, a growing market in the use of the owned home as an asset to raise additional (non-acquisition) finance, often to fund business ventures and through the vehicle of the second mortgage. The reasons for taking a second mortgage (which generally ranks second in priority behind the first, acquisition, mortgage) vary, but can include repairs/maintenance/improvements to the property as well as securing business finance against the (often family) home. Interest rates on second mortgages are usually higher than those for acquisition mortgages, reflecting their second

---

[12] See R. Burrows and S. Wilcox, *Half the Poor: Home-owners with Low Incomes*, (Council of Mortgage Lenders Research Report, 2000), which demonstrated that half of the population categorized as 'living in poverty' in the UK are now home owners.

[13] *Pettitt v Pettitt* [1970] AC 777, 824.

[14] In a Parliamentary debate concerning practices of pro-creditor priority in legal decision-making, Lord Templeman claimed that: 'No one has great sympathy for lenders or banks…[but] the point is that at the end of the day it is the borrower who pays, unless there is some speedy and efficient method of conveyancing': 437 HL Deb (5th Series) col 650 (15 December 1982). This reasoning is questioned in L. Fox, *Conceptualising Home: Theories, Laws and Policies* (Hart Publishing, 2006) p. 88ff.

[15] These constraints are linked to the reality of the choices that are available to any individual consumer, so that the freedom to make choices between options that are seen as as 'bad', 'terrible', and 'disastrous' (A. Sen, 'Markets and Freedoms' in A. Sen (ed.), *Rationality and Freedom* (Belknap, 2002) p. 515) cannot be viewed as substantive freedom, but only 'process freedom'; J. Purdy, 'A Freedom-Promoting Approach to Property: A Renewed Tradition for New Debates' (2005) 72 *Univ Chicago L Rev* 1237, 1260).

place in priority and so their greater riskiness. There has also been a long debate concerning the desirability of using the owned home – particularly a family home – to secure business liabilities. On the one hand, the owned home has been identified as a crucial source of finance for small business entrepreneurs; yet there has also been some debate surrounding the desirability of encouraging the use of the home – particularly a *family* home – as security against business debts.[16]

While the courts have appeared to support the use of the owner-occupied home as security for non-acquisition debts,[17] some commentators have argued that the risk involved in such a venture is too great, and that the interest of the family in preserving their home outweighs the arguments in support of facilitating credit transactions. Barlow, for example, argued that: '[w]hile restricting the availability of the family home as an easy means of securing business credit and reducing its attractiveness to lenders…are consequences…which commercial vested interests may oppose',[18] the use of the family home as security for non-acquisition credit should not be encouraged.[19] The paradigm of housing as investment to spend emerged from the 1980s as a result of the financial deregulation of the UK's mortgage market,[20] including the development of a new generation of flexible mortgage products.[21] This (dominant) paradigm supported a particular, politically driven, type of market in which housing wealth was viewed as 'fungible' (or spendable), and legal subjects are presumed to fit the investor model of legal rationality. Indeed, the growing use of flexible mortgages to enable owner-occupiers to have easy and ongoing access to their housing equity throughout the life of the mortgage led Smith to conclude that wealth that is tied up in the owned home is not only a financial investment with a view to capital appreciation, but is also regarded as 'more "spendable" now than it will ever be again'.[22]

The behavioural changes within the home-owner/mortgagee population that have enabled property as security to assume this dominant position within our psyches were shaped by a political discourse which had become increasingly explicit in the designation of owned housing as an investment asset-to-spend, and in the expectation

[16] See, for example, A. Barlow, 'Rights in the Family Home – Time for a Conceptual Revolution?' in A. Hudson (ed.) *New Perspectives on Property Law, Human Rights and the Home* (Cavendish, 2003).

[17] For example, in *Barclay's Bank plc v O'Brien* [1994] 1 AC 180, 188, Lord Browne Wilkinson described an 'important public interest viz, the need to ensure that the wealth currently tied up in the matrimonial home does not become economically sterile', to which Lord Oliver added that: 'If the rights secured to wives by the law render vulnerable loans granted on the security of matrimonial homes, institutions will be unwilling to accept such security, thereby reducing the flow of loan capital to business enterprises. It is therefore essential that a law designed to protect the vulnerable does not render the matrimonial home unacceptable as security to financial institutions': ibid).

[18] Barlow, n.16, 75.

[19] Ibid.

[20] S. Smith, 'Risky Business? The Challenge of Residential Mortgage Markets' (2005) *Housing Finance International* 3–8.

[21] S. Smith, J. Ford and M. Munro with R. Davis, *A Review of Flexible Mortgages* (Council of Mortgage Lenders, 2002).

[22] S. Smith, 'Banking on Housing: Speculating on the Role and Relevance of Housing Wealth in Britain', Paper prepared for the Joseph Rowntree Foundation Inquiry into Home Ownership 2010 and Beyond (2005) 11; available online at <http://dro.dur.ac.uk/71/1/Smith_speculating.pdf?DDD14>, p2.

that this newly spendable wealth would be used to support welfare needs, both after retirement and throughout the life-course.[23] The practices surrounding property as security are intimately linked to the broader political discourse of the citizen-consumer. Neoliberal policies based on privatization and individual responsibility heighten expectations that older owners will take responsibility for their own lives (their biographies) by planning for the future, including strategies to ensure financial well-being after retirement and into old age. Meanwhile, liberal legal perspectives characterize the subject of (particularly private) law as an autonomous individual who takes responsibility for his own actions and choices and whose free and equal moral agency must be respected by holding him to those choices, no matter how bad they are.[24] Modern citizen-consumers (to operate as full political and legal risk subjects) are expected to participate in financial transactions secured against their owned homes, to operate as informed consumers in the credit market, and to engage with the risks that are inherent to the deregulated mortgage market. Those who are successful in doing so are rewarded with capital growth, improved lifestyles and financial security; but those who are not are often required to bear their own losses in this game of winners and losers.

This model of the home owner as an autonomous consumer – and all the expectations that go with that in relation to their ability to make good financial decisions and the relative lack of protection they are afforded through property law, compared to creditors – is challenged by arguments highlighting the inequalities surrounding opportunities for people to construct their own lives. Research has shown that the ability to be a self-responsible, autonomous consumer is limited by structural social factors (for example, education and access to information).[25] More recently, the financial crisis that began with a housing market recession in late 2007 has provided a cogent reminder of the vulnerabilities of many home-owning consumers to default and repossession, as well as highlighting the link between individual, micro-level mortgage defaults and the macro-economic recession.

One consequence of the most recent housing market crisis is the shift in attitudes towards the idea of responsibility in mortgages and other secured lending transactions. While the neoliberal political landscape which established dominance in the UK from the late 1980s emphasized the individual self-responsibility of the owner-occupier as an autonomous consumer – including responsibility to bear the losses of default and repossession – there are indications that political,

---

[23] 'Homes not just places to live, they are also assets'; and the aims of widening home ownership include 'enabling more people to share in increasing asset wealth': Office of the Deputy Prime Minister, 'Homebuy: Expanding the Opportunity to Own', Consultation Paper (Office of the Deputy Prime Minister, 2005).

[24] See, for example, R. Dworkin, *Sovereign Virtue: The Theory and Practice of Equality* (Harvard University Press, 2000).

[25] See, for example, S. Lash, 'Reflexivity and Its Doubles: Structure, Aesthetics, Community' in U. Beck, A. Giddens and S. Lash (eds), *Reflexive Modernisation: Politics, Tradition and Aesthetics in the Modern Social Order* (Sage, 1994), where he uses the example of a 'ghetto mother' to ask 'just how "reflexive" is it possible for a single mother in an urban ghetto to be?... just how much freedom from the "necessity" of "structure" and structural poverty does this ghetto mother have to self-construct her own "life narratives"?'(p. 120).

policy and legal thinking is shifting to allow a greater role for lender responsibility, through more rigorous management of product risk and consumer risk, and for state responsibility through the institutions of law.[26] The Financial Services Authority (FSA) moved from a 'light-touch' approach to regulating general standards of lender behaviour to more prescriptive product regulation, increased lender responsibility for affordability and suitability, and a re-balancing of decision-making responsibilities between borrower and lender. There is evidence of a shift towards greater lender responsibility for the affordability of the transaction for the individual consumer, such that 'lenders would be required to look beyond their own interests and take the mortgagor's interests into account. No longer can lenders be self-interested players within the neo-liberal market model.'[27]

In tracing the evolution of this debate through recent developments in mortgage law, this chapter considers the treatment of both creditors and borrowers under what might be termed conventional property law (the statutes and cases that determine when and why mortgages can be enforced by creditors) and the regulatory jurisdiction of the then Financial Services Authority and the Office of Fair Trading. The discussion is organized along the life-course of the mortgage: from the regulations surrounding creation of the mortgage at the point of sale, to provisions governing the point of crisis when a debtor defaults and the creditor seeks to realize the security.

Debate 2

What level of consumer protection is appropriate at the point of sale?

A conventional mortgage is primarily intended as a financial services contract, backed by proprietary securitization: in the normal course of events, the mortgagor will repay the loan to discharge the mortgage, and the securitization of the home provides an enforcement strategy which the creditor will only seek to use as a last resort in the event of default.[28] The validity of the mortgage transaction is determined according to conventional property law principles relating to enforceabil-

---

[26] For a discussion of this shift, see S. Nield, 'Responsible Lending and Borrowing: Whereto Low-Cost Home Ownership?' (2010) 30(4) *Legal Studies* 610, for analysis of the concepts of responsible lending and borrowing in home finance and the impact of the 2009 Turner Review on the concept of lender responsibility (Lord Turner, *The Turner Review: A Regulatory Response to the Global Banking Crisis* (FSA, 2009); online at <http://www.fsa.gov.uk/pubs/other/turner_review.pdf>); the Turner Review was commissioned to look into the lessons from the financial crisis for the FSA).

[27] Nield, n.26, 629.

[28] See L. Whitehouse, 'The Mortgage Arrears Pre-Action Protocol: An Opportunity Lost' (2009) 72(6) *Modern Law Review* 793, criticizing the Civil Justice Council's Pre-Action Protocol for merely encouraging, rather than compelling, lenders to view repossession as a last resort. The idea that repossession should be a last resort is also promoted by the FSA in its statement of policy and practice concerning possession actions under regulated mortgages: The Mortgages and Home Finance: Conduct of Business sourcebook (MCOB) 13.3.2E(1)(f) (available online at <http://fsahandbook.info/FSA/html/handbook/MCOB>), as part of its policy of treating customers fairly.

ity: the core of the mortgage transaction is a valid contract between borrower and lender, with terms detailing the agreement relating to repayment, accompanied by the creation of a securitized interest over the property in favour of the mortgagor. The legal framework within which this transaction takes place was largely set in the 1925 legislation, and the policy agenda in pursuit of alienability. In contrast to the pre-1925 position, the 1925 legislation set the scene for modern mortgage law by changing the legal structure of the mortgage transaction to recognize its function as a financial services contract with back-up securitization, rather than an outright transfer of the property.[29] This approach was further reinforced when the LRA 2002 provided that mortgages of registered land can now only be created by the use of a charge,[30] although the charge has the same effect as creation of a proprietary interest.[31]

While the conveyancing aspects of the mortgage transaction have been heavily influenced by the alienability agenda of the 1925 legislation (reinforced by the LRA 2002), equity historically intervened in the mortgage transaction to protect the mortgagor from unconscionable transactions. More recently, the Financial Services Authority and Office of Fair Trading put in place regulatory systems to ensure that the creditor meets standards of (procedural) fairness at the point of sale. Equitable intervention – which included the equitable right to redeem the mortgage and recover unencumbered title to the property;[32] a bar on clogs on the equity of redemption, which make it prohibitively difficult to redeem the mortgage;[33] careful regulation of collateral advantages in favour of the mortgagee;[34] and the application of the historic unconscionable bargain doctrine, which offers relief against certain unfair transactions where the terms of the mortgage are oppressive.[35] These equitable doctrines ensure a minimal standard of fairness in the creation and terms of mortgage contracts, although – in the case of the unconscionable bargain doctrine – the fairness bar is set at a relatively low level.[36]

Second, mortgages fall under the jurisdiction of the Consumer Credit Act 1974 (as amended by the Consumer Credit Act 2006), which empowers the court to strike down a bargain where the credit relationship was 'unfair' due to the terms, the way the terms are exercised, or resulting from 'any other thing done (or not done) by, or on behalf of, the creditor (either before or after the making of the agreement or any related agreement)'; although there is limited evidence that the

---

[29] LPA 1925, s. 85(1).

[30] LRA 2002, s. 23(1).

[31] LPA 1925, s. 87.

[32] *Thornborough v Baker* (1675) 3 Swans 628.

[33] *Samuel v Jarrah Timber* [1904] AC 323; *Jones v Morgan* (2001) Lloyd's Rep 323.

[34] *Bradley v Carrit* [1903] AC 253; *Kregliner v New Patagonia Meat Co* [1914] AC 25.

[35] *Multiservice Bookbinding v Marden* [1979] Ch 84; *Nash v Paragon Finance* [2001] EWCA Civ 1466; *Paragon Finance v Pender* [2005] EWCA 760.

[36] It is not sufficient that the transaction is objectively harsh, unreasonable or foolish, and there must be misconduct on the part of the defendant – see for example, *Boustany v Piggott* (1995) 69 P&CR 298, 303, Lord Templeman.

courts are prepared to exercise this power except in the most exceptional circumstances.[37] Limited protection is also provided for borrowers under the Unfair Terms in Consumer Contracts Regulations 1999, which withdraw binding effect from any unfair term, although the standards of fairness applied by the courts under these Regulations still fall some way short of the standards expected by the FSA.[38]

Finally, conventional first mortgages, which are regulated by the FSA, are subject to a series of rules and guidance relating to the promotion of mortgages, advising and selling standards, disclosure rules (including the mortgage key facts information and health warning concerning the possible consequences of default), responsible lending practices, rules relating to charges and practices for dealing with customers in arrears and in repossession.[39] The FSA approach to regulating conventional mortgages has come under scrutiny following the most recent housing market crisis and recession, and the FSA published its own *Mortgage Market Review*[40] as well as a more general review of its approach to regulation (the Turner Review).[41] These reviews have come at a moment when the image of 'owners as self-responsible consumers',[42] consistent with a neoliberal, market-led ideology which opposed stronger government intervention in macro-financial markets, has been widely challenged in the wake of the global financial crisis.[43] While much of the debate that has followed the crisis in the UK has focused on macro-prudential strategies to restore and maintain confidence in the stability of financial

---

[37] CCA 2006, s 140A(1). In *Khodari v Al Tamimi* [2008] EWHC 3065, the court held that the high costs of the loan were balanced against the credit risk to the lender; while in *Nine Regions (T/A Logbook Loans) v Sadeer*, Bromley County Court, 14 January 2009, the court held that since a last resort loan was of higher risk for the lender, it naturally attracted a higher interest rate (in this case, 384.4 per cent APR), and so did not give rise to an unfair relationship. Although the court did find an unfair relationship in *Barons Finance Ltd v Olubisi*, Mayor's and City of London Court, 26 April 2010, Claim No: 7BB82089, the facts of that case were quite extreme – the agreement had not been properly executed, the interest rate on the loan was 3.5 per cent per month calculated on a day-to-day basis of the balance outstanding each month, and there had been flagrant breaches of the Consumer Credit Act and the 1983 Consumer Credit (Agreements) Regulations, and the loan was made in circumstances in which the borrower desperately needed to obtain the loan in order to stave off possession proceedings (the loan took place 2 days before the date fixed for the possession hearing).

[38] In a 2008 review of awareness of, and compliance with, the Unfair Terms in Consumer Contracts Regulations, and the use of the Regulations to secure an appropriate level of consumer protection, the FSA claimed that, while it expects firms to be proactive in reviewing all their contract terms and other firms' undertakings, firms need to do more to ensure that their terms are drafted fairly: FSA, *Fairness of Terms in Consumer Contracts: A Visible Factor in Firms Treating their Customers Fairly*, (FSA, 2008); online at <http://www.fsa.gov.uk/pubs/other/consumer_contracts_report.pdf>; para. 3.5.

[39] See FSA Handbook, Mortgages and Home Finance Conduct of Business Sourcebook (MCOB); online at <http://fsahandbook.info/FSA/html/handbook/MCOB>.

[40] FSA, *Mortgage Market Review* (FSA, 2009); online at <http://www.fsa.gov.uk/pubs/discussion/dp09_03.pdf>.

[41] Lord Turner, n.26.

[42] See Nield, n.26, for analysis of the concepts of responsible lending and borrowing in home finance and the impact of the Turner Review on the concept of lender responsibility; and our discussion of legal subjects as responsible risk-takers in Chapter 4.

[43] See R. Tomasic, 'Beyond "Light Touch"' Regulation of British Banks after the Financial Crisis' in I. MacNeil and J. O'Brien (eds), *The Future of Financial Regulation* (Hart Publishing, 2010).

institutions,[44] both Reviews focused on irresponsible lending as a key factor giving rise to the crisis. This has resulted in a series of regulatory initiatives which suggest a stronger commitment towards lender responsibility in the conventional mortgage market, through affordability checks, better quality product information and arguments for minimum product standards.[45] This reflects a changing perspective on the capabilities of consumers as financial and legal subjects, and, while initial indications suggest that this shift in approach may be carried forward by the new Financial Conduct Authority (FCA),[46] it remains to be seen how far the developing regulatory regime will go in adopting an interventionist and pre-emptive philosophy towards responsible lending as well as addressing issues of product risk in unfair mortgage terms.

Debate 3

What level of occupier protection is appropriate at the point of crisis?

The crucial distinguishing factor between secured and unsecured credit is that, in the event of default on repayments, and in addition to the borrower's personal obligation to repay the loan,[47] a mortgagee may also seek to enforce its proprietary security over the property. Where the property is owner-occupied, this brings the property's dual functions as a securitizing asset and a home into conflict. The principal remedies available to the mortgagee in such circumstances are possession and sale of the property. This section will consider the balance struck by conventional property law between the roles of the property as security and as housing and home.

First, however, the conduct of the mortgagee in acting to recover possession of owner-occupied property has come under fresh scrutiny. The FSA has attempted to govern the arrears management practices of regulated mortgage lenders. In addition to the rules concerning the arrears management strategies of lenders, the creditor is required to market the property for sale as soon as possible, and obtain the best price that might reasonably be paid,[48] and to make reasonable efforts to re-negotiate with customers who are in financial difficulties,[49] including considering whether to extend the term of the mortgage.[50] In July 2010, the FSA fined one

---

[44] The Government's 2009 White Paper, HM Treasury, *Reforming Financial Markets*, Cm 7667, (London: TSO, 2009); online at <http://news.bbc.co.uk/1/shared/bsp/hi/pdfs/08_07_09_markets.pdf>, focused on four key objectives: dealing with firms deemed too big to fail; strengthening the UK's regulatory institutional framework; identifying and managing systemic risk at a macro-level; and learning and applying the lessons of the current financial crisis.

[45] See Nield, n.26.

[46] The successor to the FSA – see FSA, *The Financial Conduct Authority: Approach to Regulation* (London: FSA, June 2011); online at <www.fsa.gov.uk/pubs/events/fca_approach.pdf>.

[47] *Bolton* v *Buckenham* (1891) 1 QB 278.

[48] *FSA Handbook*, MCOB, 13.6.1; online at <http://fsahandbook.info/FSA/html/handbook/MCOB/13/6>.

[49] MCOB 13.3.2A, online at <http://fsahandbook.info/FSA/html/handbook/MCOB/13/3>.

[50] MCOB 13.3.4A.

mortgage provider £630,000 for poor treatment of some customers facing mortgage arrears,[51] although sector-wide compliance remains exposed to the uneven uptake of guidance and good practice, and in some cases compliance with rules, across the industry.

Mortgagees are also encouraged to follow the procedural guidelines set out in the Mortgage Arrears Pre-Action Protocol.[52] These sought to encourage greater communication between borrowers and lenders, to ensure that lenders act 'fairly and reasonably' in the event of arrears, and avoid repossession except as a last resort. It has been argued, however, that the Pre-Action Protocol is inadequate due to its reliance on good practice, which has already proven ineffective in this context,[53] and which leaves borrowers 'vulnerable to inconsistent and potentially adverse treatment at the hands of lenders'.[54] Although the FSA has put its weight behind the development of good practices amongst lenders, research has shown that there are considerable issues of non-compliance by firms with the arrears rule,[55] particularly where the borrower is vulnerable, for example, because of an impaired credit history.[56] The issues of forbearance and the balance struck between the interests of the creditor in the property as security and the occupier's interest in the property as a home continues to provoke debate in the UK, as repossession rates remain high and political pressure to protect the apparently innocent owners who have defaulted on their mortgages in the context of the financial crisis remains extant.[57] The proposals set out in this paper included closing the loophole by which out-of-court possession can be obtained without the consent of the borrower.

For the time being, however, it remains possible for a lender to take possession of a property when the borrower defaults on repayments.[58] While it is usual for a mortgagee to seek a court order for possession, this is not always strictly necessary[59] where the lender is able to take peaceful possession without a court order.[60] Although the practice of taking possession without a court order is uncommon in

---

[51] <http://www.fsa.gov.uk/pages/Library/Communication/PR/2010/120.shtml>.

[52] Available at <http://www.justice.gov.uk/civil/procrules.fin/contents/protocols/prot_mha.htm>.

[53] L. Whitehouse, n.28.

[54] Ibid, 812.

[55] FSA, *Mortgage Effectiveness Review: Arrears Findings*, Research Report, (FSA, 2008); available online at: <http://www.fsa.gov.uk/pubs/other/mer_report.pdf>.

[56] See FSA, 'FSA Reiterates Call for Firms to Treat Customers Fairly in Current Market Conditions', online at <http://www.fsa.gov.uk/pages/Library/Communication/PR/2008/087.shtml>.

[57] In March 2011, the Ministry of Justice issued a consultation on reforms to the civil justice system in England and Wales which included discussion of alternative dispute resolution, 'pre-action dispute management' and debt recovery and enforcement: Ministry of Justice, *Solving Disputes in the County Courts: Creating a Simpler, Quicker and more Proportionate System*, CP6/2001, Cm 8045 (TSO, 2011).

[58] The immediate right to possession 'as soon as the ink is dry' is usually excluded by the mortgage deed for as long as payments are being made: *Birmingham Citizens BS* v *Caunt* (1962)Ch 883.

[59] *Ropaigealach v Barclay's Bank plc* [2000] QB 263; *Horsham Properties Group Ltd v Clark* [2009] 1 WLR 1255.

[60] Both the Criminal Law Act 1977 and the Protection of Eviction Act 1977 impose criminal sanctions against the forcible eviction of residential occupiers.

owner-occupied homes, it is more common in relation to buy-to-let properties.[61] Some concerns have been expressed about the potential for lenders to make increasing use of the inherent right to possession as they become more aware of the possibility of avoiding section 36.[62] If the lender does apply to the court for an order for possession, the court has only limited discretion to intervene on behalf of the occupier who wishes to stay in their home. The court's inherent equitable jurisdiction to adjourn possession proceedings is limited to a very short time – probably no longer than 28 days – to allow the mortgagor to find the money to pay arrears. While the statutory power to delay repossession of property that includes a dwelling-house under section 36 of the Administration of Justice Act 1970 is considerably more significant, it is also limited to cases in which '... it appears to the court that in the event of its exercising the power the mortgagor is likely to be able within a reasonable period to pay any sums due under the mortgage ...'.[63]

The conditions for the exercise of this discretion are strict, based on the debtor's financial ability to make good on arrears within a 'reasonable time' – taking as a starting point the whole remaining term of the mortgage[64] – while continuing to meet installments as they fall due.[65] The opportunity to spread the arrears over a longer period appeared to favour the owner-occupier's interests in the property as a home over the enforcement of the creditor's right to possession. This was tempered, however, by the strong emphasis placed on 'detailed analysis of present figures and future [budget] projections',[66] requiring the owner-occupier to establish their financial credibility if they are to persuade the court to adjourn the possession proceedings.[67] In any event, section 36 can provide no more than interim relief where temporary financial straits have led to the accrual of arrears; the owner-occupier must demonstrate their financial credibility to ensure such interim relief; and the courts have become progressively less likely to tolerate repeated applications for relief. The prospect of employment for the borrower is not necessarily to be equated with the prospect of payment of the mortgage installments.[68] Thus, while the function of the property as housing and home is clearly recognized, the mortgagee's interest in recovering possession once the borrower is in default continues to dominate. It also remains somewhat arbitrary that access to the section 36 protection is dependent on whether the mortgagee has been able to recover possession without a court order.

---

[61] Council of Mortgage Lenders, *Mortgage Remedies (Possession and Sale) Review Response by the Council of Mortgage lenders to the Ministry of Justice's Initial Review* (14 January 2009) at <www.cml.org.uk/cml/filegrab/MortgageReviewQuestionsforStakeholdersdraftresponse-FINAL.pdf?ref=6248>, para. 3.

[62] S. Greer, 'Urgent Review' (2009) 159 *NLJ* 254.

[63] Administration of Justice Act 1970, s. 36(1).

[64] *Cheltenham & Gloucester Building Society v Norgan* [1996] 1 WLR 343.

[65] Ibid.

[66] *Norgan*, above, Waite LJ; *Bristol & West Building Society v Ellis* (1996) 73 P&CR 158 (CA).

[67] See also *Cheval Bridging Finance Ltd v Bhasin* [2008] EWCA Civ 1613.

[68] *Halifax Plc v Okin* [2007] EWCA Civ 567.

The primary purpose of recovering possession is to facilitate sale of the property, capitalizing the financial asset represented by the home, so that the mortgagee can recover the value of the loan. The procedure to achieving sale depends on the method by which the mortgage was created, the nature of the mortgagor's default, and the nature of the ownership interest(s) in the property (sole ownership or jointly owned property). The most straightforward method for a mortgagee to achieve sale is through an out-of-court sale under sections 101–103 of the Law of Property Act 1925, which incorporates an automatic power of sale in the mortgagee for all mortgages created by deed.[69] Certain conditions must be satisfied before this power of sale arises (the legal date of redemption must have passed; this is set by the mortgage terms, usually a relatively short time after the mortgage is granted) and become exercisable (when *one* of the three conditions set out in section 103 of the Law of Property Act 1925 has been satisfied).[70] The ease with which a mortgagee can achieve sale through this route reflects the pro-purchaser policy of the 1925 legislation, and represents a powerful remedy for the mortgagee once the borrower is in default. Furthermore, in cases where the mortgagee is able to achieve possession without a court order, the out-of-court sale route presents an opportunity for the mortgagee to recover possession of mortgage property and realize its capital value without the mortgagee having any opportunity to defend the action in court.

This potentially raises issues under the right to respect for home in Article 8 of the Human Rights Act 1996, as it enables the mortgagee to dispossess occupiers from their homes without any recourse to adjudication concerning the proportionality of the decision to take possession. While a successful Article 8 case is yet to be made in these circumstances, the court appears to have implicitly accepted that the private nature of the dispute does not preclude the raising of the human rights arguments in this context.[71] As the decisions of the Supreme Court in *Manchester City Council v Pinnock*[72] and *London Borough of Hounslow v Powell*[73] have begun to embed the proportionality test under Article 8 within domestic UK law, there is arguably greater scope for challenging procedures which allow an occupier to be evicted by a mortgagor without the due process of a court hearing.

Efforts to close the loopholes of out-of-court repossession and sale have also been brought through political avenues. For example, in 2009, Andrew Dismore MP (Chair of the Joint Committee on Human Rights) introduced a Ten-Minute Rule bill entitled 'Home Repossession (Protection) Bill' which proposed amending the Law of Property 1925 to require mortgagees to obtain the court's permission before exercising the power of sale, where the mortgaged land consists of

---

[69] Law of Property Act 1925, s. 101(1)(i).

[70] These conditions are that either (a) notice requiring payment has been served on the mortgagor and default has continued for three months after service of the notice; (b) interest is in arrears for two months or more; or (c) there has been a breach of any other mortgage provision or LPA provision, other than a covenant for payment of mortgage debt or interest.

[71] See *Horsham Properties Group Ltd v Clark* [2009] 1 WLR 1255.

[72] [2010] 3 WLR 1441.

[73] [2011] 2 WLR 287.

or includes a dwelling-house. That Bill did not reach its second reading.[74] The link between financial crises and initiatives to shift the balance of mortgage law towards the protection of the occupier is also clear. An earlier attempt to close these loopholes dates back to the previous housing market crisis in 1991, when the Law Commission made recommendations (which were not implemented) that the mortgagee's rights in respect of possession and sale should be exercised only in good faith and for the purposes of protecting or enforcing the security;[75] and that the artificiality of the two-stage test should be abandoned in favour of one test involving 'enforceable events' defined to allow sale only where the mortgagor has failed to keep to the original repayment bargain, or where the mortgagee's security is otherwise threatened.[76]

There are alternatives to out-of-court sale. Section 91 of the Law of Property Act allows the mortgagee to apply to the court for sale of mortgaged property, and the court may in its discretion direct that the mortgaged property be sold. When judicial sale is requested under section 91, the court has an unfettered discretion to order sale, notwithstanding the objections of any parties. It has been suggested that '[i]n exercising its discretion the court is not limited to considering financial matters, but can also take into account social considerations',[77] although the case law supporting this proposition involved requests by occupiers to *proceed* with sale against the wishes of the banks, rather than to *prevent* sale of the property.[78] Finally, any creditor holding a security interest in co-owned land can apply for sale of the property under the Trusts of Land and Appointment of Trustees Act 1996 and, as demonstrated in Chapter 3, the courts have, to date, followed a strong pro-sale policy under sections 14 and 15. The overall picture, when it comes to mortgage enforcement, is that the present arrangements strongly favour the property as security function over property as housing and home.

CONCLUSIONS

This pro-creditor bias – which has its origins in a political and economic agenda in favour of alienability and support for the creditors whose financial backing has enabled the growth of owner-occupation – continues to come under fresh political challenges in the context of the financial crisis. This is hardly surprising, in light of evidence concerning the public (as well as private) costs when mortgage repossessions reach critical levels,[79] not only for borrowers and lenders but also for insurers, central government, local government, housing market institutions,

---

[74] <http://services.parliament.uk/bills/2008–09/homerepossessionprotection.html>.

[75] Law Commission, *Transfer of Land: Land Mortgages*, Law Com No 204 (Law Commission, 1991), paras 3.4, 7.3.

[76] Ibid, paras 7.7, 7.8. These proposals were taken up by the Northern Ireland Law Commission in its 2010 Report on *Land Law* (NILC 8), available online at <http://www.nilawcommission.gov.uk/index/completed_projects-2/land-law-reform/report_on_land_law_nilc_8__2010.htm>.

[77] Fisher & Lightwood, *Law of Mortgages* (Elsevier, 11th edn, 2002) para. 21.8.

[78] *Polonski v Lloyd's Bank Mortgages Ltd* (1997) 31 HLR 721; *Palk v Mortgage Services Funding plc* [1993] Ch 330.

[79] See Fox, pp. 109–22.

labour market institutions and health services. Indeed, since the impact of widespread foreclosures in the US sub-prime mortgage market triggered the current global economic crisis, it is difficult to underestimate the economic, as well as political, social and personal effect of loss of the securitized home through mortgage repossession actions.

There was a history of government-sponsored mortgagor safety nets in the UK in the twentieth century, although these were significantly eroded under the Thatcher governments of the 1980s. Those safety nets were revived under subsequent Labour governments, but their provision became increasingly privatized within the neoliberal mantra of self-responsibility and self-provision. The provision of safety nets for home owners facing payment problems, and legal policies that seek to value the occupier's interest in their home, perform similar functions as they attempt to ameliorate the risks that are inherent to market-led housing consumption. Historically, government-funded support for home owners took two main forms: mortgage interest tax relief, and the safety-net provisions which entitled mortgagors to claim assistance with their mortgage costs when their income level fell below a specified amount. Although provision for mortgage interest tax relief was established before World War II, the significance of this tax exemption grew as a result of the sheer volume of home- owning households, and as house prices began to rise significantly, from the 1970s. It was just as the proportion of home owners seeking to claim mortgage interest tax relief was beginning to turn it into a widespread and significant welfare support that the government took steps to limit its availability. The decline in mortgage interest tax relief provision began in 1974, when relief was withdrawn for mortgage debts over £25,000; further reductions were made in 1991, until this head of tax relief was finally abolished in 2000. The principal form of state safety-net provision for home owners, introduced in Britain under the National Assistance Act 1948, was aimed at mortgagors who became unable to meet their repayments due to unexpected loss of income. However, in a significant policy departure from 1995, Income Support for Mortgage Interest (ISMI) was restricted in various ways, including restrictions in when assistance could be claimed, and the total loan amount covered.

The privatization of safety nets for mortgage borrowers meant that debtors are now expected to protect themselves through private insurance policies, such as Mortgage Payment Protection Insurance (MPPI), Critical Illness Insurance (CI), Permanent Health Insurance (PHI), and Unemployment Insurance (UI), as well as drawing on personal savings, reserves through flexible mortgages or from employee benefits. It is only when these avenues of relief are exhausted that the residual role of Income Support for Mortgage Interest (ISMI) comes into play.[80] The decline in state-sponsored provision for home-owning households advances the neoliberal agenda and ideological commitments towards self-responsibility, although research has shown that take-up on these self-provided safety-nets has

[80] J. Ford, D. Quilgars, R. Burrows, D. Rhodes, *Homeowners Risk and Safety-Nets: Mortgage Payment Protection Insurance (MPPI) and Beyond* (Office of the Deputy Prime Minister, 2004) p. 4.

been low and does not provide a robust form of protection.[81] Having said that, though, steps were taken in 2008 to re-introduce ISMI, by way of recognition of the failure of MPPI (and its misselling).[82]

The links between welfare support and safety nets, on the one hand, and the legal frameworks governing the enforcement of mortgages in the event of default, on the other, were explicitly recognized in a House of Commons debate that followed the decision in *Williams and Glyn's Bank Ltd v Boland*,[83] when one member rejected a proposal to strengthen the legal protection afforded to occupiers with the suggestion that: 'If the Government want to do something to help owner-occupiers in this regard…they should withdraw their proposals to cut back mortgage relief for those who are unemployed …'[84] This underlines the implicit trade-off between welfare policies and legal policies, in the sense that the existence of welfare protections for occupiers might be regarded as mitigating the tendency to overlook such interests within the property law framework.

The role of government rescue schemes for mortgagors facing payment difficulties made a decisive return to the policy agenda following the most recent housing market crisis. The UK government set in place a number of such schemes following the 2008 downturn, including a Mortgage Rescue Scheme (MRS), designed to provide a structured exit from home ownership for vulnerable households who would otherwise have been entitled to homelessness assistance; and the Homeowners Mortgage Support (HMS), which provides support to lenders to encourage greater levels of forbearance for up to two years for borrowers unable to access other support. While initial evaluations suggest that the MRS has been deemed a qualified success, HMS has proven more problematic, although it has had an indirect benefit to the extent that it has encouraged lenders themselves to offer greater degrees of forbearance.[85]

Finally, there are some moves towards providing greater levels of mortgagor protection within the property law framework, although it remains too early to say whether these will be successful. In June 2010, a Secured Lending Reform Bill was presented to Parliament as a Private Members Bill, but lapsed on 30 March 2012. Proposals in this Bill included amendments to provide for the Secretary of State (by regulations) to abolish the right of a mortgagee to obtain peaceable re-entry of a property and to prescribe maximum penalties that may be imposed on a mortgagee who peaceably re-enters a property;[86] as well as provision for the

---

[81] See J. Ford, R. Burrows and S. Nettleton, *Home Ownership in a Risk Society: A Social Analysis of Mortgage Arrears and Possessions* (Policy Press, 2001); Ford, Quilgars, Burrows, and Rhodes,.

[82] For discussion, see J. Ford, J. Bretherton, A. Jones, and D. Rhodes, *Giving up Home Ownership: A Qualitative Study of Voluntary Possession and Selling because of Financial Difficulties* (DCLG, 2010), esp. para. 3.30–3.31.

[83] [1981] AC 487.

[84] Mr Nicholas Brown, MP, HC Standing Committee Official Report, Session 1985–6, Vol X, (21 May 1986), p. 3.

[85] Ford, Bretherton, Jones and Rhodes, n.81 esp. para. 3.30–3.31. <http://www.communities.gov.uk/documents/housing/pdf/1648140.pdf>.

[86] Cl 2.

Secretary of State to ensure that a possession order is not made by the court on the application of a mortgagee unless the court is satisfied that the mortgagor has received an adequate opportunity to raise any counterclaim, set-off or other defence that may be available against the mortgagee, and the court has determined the merits of any such defence.[87] Finally, it would have allowed for provision to confer on the court power to vary terms of the mortgage (the rate of interest, the schedule of payments, or the value of payments) where it appears just to do so.[88] These amendments were intended to aid *all* mortgagors in financial difficulty – not merely owner-occupiers; clause 4 would broaden the court's discretion under section 36 of the AJA to remove the restriction to 'dwelling houses'.

The Bill was designed to encourage a rescue culture within the banking industry by embedding a framework to support forbearance, and closing the loopholes that have allowed some mortgagees to enforce their security aggressively, without giving the mortgagor any opportunity to defend the proceedings in a court. This move was consistent with the discourse of greater lender responsibility in the regulatory context. It may transpire that this most recent moment of 'crisis' in the housing market and wider economy will effect significant shifts in the philosophical orientation of property law;[89] as yet, any lasting impact remains to be seen.

Further Reading

J. Ford, J. Bretherton, A. Jones, and D. Rhodes, *Giving up Home Ownership: A Qualitative Study of Voluntary Possession and Selling because of Financial Difficulties* (DCLG, 2010).

L. Fox, *Conceptualising Home: Theories, Laws and Policies* (Hart Publishing, 2006).

S. Nield, 'Responsible Lending and Borrowing: Whereto Low-Cost Home Ownership?' (2010) 30(4) *Legal Studies* 610.

L. Whitehouse, 'The Mortgage Arrears Pre-Action Protocol: An Opportunity Lost' (2009) 72(6) *MLR* 793.

L. Whitehouse, 'Making the Case for Socio-Legal Research in Land Law: Renner and the Law of Mortgage' (2010) 37(4) *Journal of Law and Society* 545.

---

[87] Cl 3.

[88] Sch. 5; see <http://services.parliament.uk/bills/2010–11/securedlendingreform.html>.

[89] N. Davidson and R. Dyal-Chand, 'Property in Crisis' (2009) 78 *Fordham L Rev* 1607.

11

COHABITATION: RIGHTS TO THE HOME

INTRODUCTION

Nowhere in the law of property is the tension between the theme of rationality and the emotional dimensions of property more exposed than in the question of whether a non-owning cohabitant is entitled to a share of (or interest in) their co-lived property; and, if so, the quantification of that share or interest. That is the fundamental issue tackled in this chapter, which focuses on the rights of cohabitants in their homes.[1] It is in many ways *the* Great Debate of our time, masking doctrinal, procedural and broad socio-legal issues. Those issues highlight the problematic nature of property law's rational search for intention when the parties themselves may not have expressed it. The first flush of love leads people to do extraordinary things without thought; it is only when, inevitably, that love turns to bitterness and hatred, or, more mundanely, the cohabitants part company, that the issues for property law arise. It is at that latter point that property law requires the re-construction – or, perhaps, the better word is translation – of events around the tools provided by property law: the constructive trust and proprietary estoppel.

That this is an *interdisciplinary* issue almost goes without saying, but it also highlights what we have referred to as the 'destination' nature of property law within the legal canon. It is where property law meets family law and trusts law, each vying for supremacy.[2] It is where socio-legal and feminist critique often meets property law. It is where empirical socio-legal research exposes the fallacies inherent in the assumptions of property law. It is where the uncertainty at the roots of the doctrines creates considerable practical problems, and also exposes the fallacy of rationality in law. As Bettina Lange explains, law 'others' emotion in the pursuit of rationality:

> [E]motions are considered as potentially anarchic, unbounded, and associated with a lack of control. Therefore when lawyers have discussed the role

---

[1] We do not here deal with the rights of married couples and civil partners, which are governed by different legislative principles.

[2] For an interesting discussion of the different ways of thinking and procedural interaction, see A. Bottomley, 'Production of a Text: *Hammond v Mitchell* [1991] 1 WLR 1127' (1994) 2(1) *Feminist Legal Studies* 83.

of emotions in legal processes they have emphasized the importance of containing them. The 'messy individuality' of emotions is contrasted with hard and fast 'categorical rules'. Thus, lawyers' construction of emotion as 'other' distances emotion not just from cognition but also from normative processes. This again is different from sociologists' understanding of emotions.[3]

And, notwithstanding numerous Law Commission projects and proposals for reform, successive governments have failed to address these conflicts through legislation, not wanting to touch the 'hot potato' for fear of undermining the supposed naturalness and better associations of marriage and civil partnership. The blood that has been spilt – that may be hyperbole, but the area rouses strong emotions – by judges, academics, and policy-makers, together with the trees that have been mercilessly cut down to enable them to develop their positions, could so easily have been resolved by Parliamentary intervention. Scotland has done so and the Law Commission made reform proposals which, to a certain extent, mirrored and extended the Scottish position.[4] Most recently, the 2010 Coalition Government has refused to implement the Law Commission's proposals during this Parliament.[5]

It is no wonder, given the level of dissatisfaction amongst the experts with the current state of the law, that there is also considerable confusion in the public domain, including amongst members of the legal profession. Study after study has found that non-owning and part-owning cohabitants believe in a set of laws which have no foundation in *the* law. So, for example, the myth of common law marriage (that cohabitants somehow 'become' the equivalent to married couples over an unspecified period of time, and thus gain the same rights as married couples) remains prevalent – in one large-scale survey, just under six in ten of cohabiting couples believed in the common law marriage.[6] There is also considerable evidence of *diversity* of practice amongst cohabitants as to how they arrange their finances and, at a qualitative level, the influence of interactional settings.[7]

In this chapter, we isolate four Great Debates. The first two are doctrinal. Debate 1 concerns the principles by which cohabitants can establish an interest in their home. Debate 2 concerns the principles by which, if a cohabitant has successfully established an interest in their home, the law assesses that interest. The purpose of

---

[3] B. Lange, 'The Emotional Dimension in Legal Regulation' (2002) 29(1) *Journal of Law and Society* 197, 199.

[4] Family Law (Scotland) Act 2006; Law Commission, *The Financial Consequences of Relationship Breakdown*, Law Com No 307 (TSO, 2007). In addition, a Private Members' Bill introduced into the House of Lords by Lord Lester, the Cohabitation Bill, did not survive the Parliamentary process, but offered a further alternative vision.

[5] HL Deb, 6 September 2011, Col WS18.

[6] A. Barlow, C. Burgoyne, E. Clery and J. Smithson, 'Cohabitation and the Law: Myths, Money and the Media' in A. Park, J. Curtis, K. Thompson, M. Phillips, M. Johnson, E. Clery (eds), *British Social Attitudes: The 24th Report* (Sage, 2008) p. 40.

[7] See, in particular, G. Douglas, J. Pearce and H. Woodward, *A Failure of Trust: Resolving Property Disputes on Cohabitation Breakdown*, Report of a Study Funded by the ESRC (Cardiff Law School, 2007).

our discussion of these debates is to isolate certain schemas of this doctrinal law – the way it thinks about why people do things and the sort of evidence by which the cohabitant can establish their interest and its extent. In those two debates, we draw attention also to the apparent differences and similarities between constructive trusts and proprietary estoppel. That leads into Debate 3: are constructive trusts and proprietary estoppel different and, more to the point, does it matter? Debate 4 takes a step back from that heavy-duty doctrinal law and draws on the broader literature in this field, theoretical and empirical, to demonstrate that law's rationality and assumptions have little empirical foundation. Although the development of the doctrinal law in this area was, in part, designed to come to terms with the empirical reality of large-scale cohabitation, it has done so through rational doctrines which cannot account for that lived experience.

Autobiographical note

On writing ...

When one begins a book project like this with other people, the first thing we do is to split it up. Who is going to take primary responsibility for which chapter? We carved this book up in that way and, although each of us has edited the others' work, it is still pretty obvious (to us, at any rate) who wrote which bit. At the carve-up, I got lumbered with this chapter. At the time, I wasn't hugely bothered but subsequently I just couldn't get round to it. I procrastinated and, when the commissioning editor came asking, there was a great excuse: 'we're expecting *Jones v Kernott* any day now'. But, by mid-November, I couldn't ignore it any longer: *Jones* was out. I'd blogged about it. The chapter had to be written although my computer tells me that it took another month before it was done. But, well, the original draft was wobbly and the reviewer picked up on the uncertainty inherent in the chapter, as well as kindly pointing out how it could be fixed. The reviewer isn't responsible for this final version but they helped it on its way.

The thing is, I love writing and particularly about tricky inter- or multi-disciplinary things. Most of all, though, I need to care about something before I write about it. Writing is emotional and my style, if there is one, reflects that experience. But this chapter was just a step too far. The hesitation was not induced by the fact that there is so much written about this subject by incredibly clever people, with some of whom I disagree both expressly and by implication. It's just that, although I appreciated how the law had developed, I have absolutely no faith in it at all; in fact, I regarded it as intellectually moribund.

The starting point of the approach taken by law to human motivation seems so banal, monochrome, one-dimensional, irrelevant to lived experience, and requires subjective opinion which merely exposes the prejudice/s of the speaker. It ignores the complicated narratives of the

> parties, fixes on certain matters which may have been an afterthought (if they gave any thought to it or its implication), and, despite the (sometimes) best intentions of the judges to do 'the right thing', the law just is plain stupid.
>
> What finally galvanized me and made me care enough to write this chapter was its links with a parallel project concerning a focus on legal technique and technicality as a resource for socio-legal studies. I also found much rich literature that reflected on the law from the outside, with which I have far more empathy than that produced by those insiders. So, I cared again, and found that I passionately cared, and hope that some of that passion rubs off in this chapter.

Debate 1

What are the principles by which a cohabitant can establish an interest in their home?

This is the foundational doctrinal question. What parties should rationally do is to set out in writing at the outset what type of interest they each have in the property and (hopefully) the extent of that interest. That was the expectation and hope of the Law of Property Act 1925. If that is done, and done properly (in the sense that it complies with the formalities), that document will bind the parties subject to the application of limited equitable doctrines (such as rectification and mistake).[8] There are many examples of the most learned judges throwing their hands up in the air and wondering why people do not adopt this rationalist solution to avoid costly litigation. Perhaps the best example of this is the comment of Ward LJ:

> I ask in despair how often this court has to remind conveyancers that they would save their clients a great deal of later difficulty if only they would sit the purchasers down, explain the difference between a joint tenancy and tenancy in common, ascertain what they want and then expressly declare in the conveyance of transfer how the beneficial interest is to be held because that will be conclusive and save all argument. When are conveyancers going to do this as a matter of invariable standard practice? This court has urged that time after time. Perhaps conveyancers do not read the law reports. I will try one more time: ALWAYS TRY TO AGREE ON AND THEN RECORD HOW THE BENEFICIAL INTEREST IS TO BE HELD. It is not very difficult to do.[9]

---

[8] *Goodman v Gallant* [1986] 2 WLR 236; the formalities are contained in LPA 1925, s. 53(1)(b).
[9] *Carlton v Goodman* [2002] EWCA Civ 545 at [44].

Since 1998, HM Land Registry has had a form TR1, which allows parties to express the nature of the trust by which they share the beneficial ownership. Box 10 enables parties to say how they hold the property and in what shares, but it is not compulsory to complete this box. Where it has been done, this simple process would avoid many subsequent legal disputes, although it may also leave the parties dissatisfied.

There are potentially two legal doctrines involved when disputes arise – the constructive trust and proprietary estoppel. These are similar but there are differences, at the very least terminological (holding off debate for now about their substantive and procedural assonance and/or dissonance). We will take each in turn.

But first, there is a preliminary question which we must clear out of the way. Why use the constructive trust, and not the resulting trust? Despite considerable evidence from some quarters of a desire to use the resulting trust[10] – which, in essence, entitles a paying party to the return of their money as a matter of rebuttable presumption and, in its absence, a property right – it is now crystal clear that the resulting trust has only a residual value where the parties are in some sort of commercial relationship with each other (as lovers and business partners or just business partners). That is because, in essence, the resulting trust is just too blunt an instrument because of its single-minded financial focus – as Baroness Hale pithily observed: 'The law has indeed moved on in response to changing social and economic conditions'.[11] In her joint judgment with Lord Walker in *Jones v Kernott*,[12] they make clear that it is these social and economic conditions which make problematic the enquiry, inherent in the resulting trust, into who paid for what; and render inappropriate the discriminatory presumption of advancement which could be used to undermine the presumption of the resulting trust.[13] As Lord Hoffmann put it in *Stack v Dowden*,

> [C]ohabiting couples are in a different kind of relationship. The place where they live together is their home. Living together is an exercise in give and take, mutual co-operation and compromise. Who pays for what in regard to the home has to be seen in the wider context of their overall relationship. A more practical, down-to-earth, fact-based approach is called for in their case. The framework which the law provides should be simple, and it should be accessible.[14]

---

[10] See, for example, W. Swadling, 'The Common Intention Trust in the House of Lords: An Opportunity Missed' (2007) 123 *LQR* 511.

[11] *Stack v Dowden* [2007] 2 AC 432, [60].

[12] [2011] UKSC 53, [24].

[13] The presumption of advancement was a method of rebutting the presumption of the resulting trust. In certain cases and in certain relationships (e.g. wife to husband but not vice versa), equity presumed a gift, as opposed to a resulting trust. The presumption of advancement is to be abolished by Equality Act 2010, s. 199.

[14] [3].

Quite so, but one might remark that the framework we have been left with is anything but simple and accessible. In any event, we are left, in most cases, with the choice of the constructive trust or estoppel.

CONSTRUCTIVE TRUST

It is now established that the first question to be addressed is how legal title is held.[15] What this establishes is a presumption. Where legal title to the property is vested in one party, the presumption is that that party has sole beneficial ownership as well. Where legal title is vested in both cohabitants, the presumption is that they intend that each of them is to have an interest in the property. To put these propositions another way, that vesting of legal title establishes a common intention. The question is how, in cases of sole ownership, that presumption or common intention can be rebutted.

That rebuttal can be demonstrated, in broad terms, by a common intention between the cohabitants that they hold the property differently from that initial presumption, and they acted in some way on that different common intention. Common intention on its own is never enough because that would be the equivalent of a mere promise; but common intention is an essential ingredient.

Common intention

On the question of common intention, the law divides into two or, possibly, three parts. Common intention may be express or inferred; the law is currently in a state of flux as to whether, at this stage of the inquiry, it is appropriate to impute a common intention. The significance of this inquiry and the basis for the common intention is that the quality of acts of detriment required by the non-owning cohabitant are, or are likely to be, different as a matter of law. It is, therefore, essential to get a handle on what is meant by these different types of intention. Again, the law is in a state of flux here, but there is some common ground.

The classic description of the express common intention was provided by the judgment of Lord Bridge in *Lloyds Bank v Rosset*:[16]

> The first and fundamental question which must always be resolved is whether, independently of any inference to be drawn from the conduct of the parties in the course of sharing the house as their home and managing their joint affairs, there has at any time prior to acquisition, or exceptionally at some later date, been any agreement, arrangement or understanding reached between them that the property is to be shared beneficially. The finding of an agreement or arrangement to share in this sense can only, I think, be based on evidence of express discussions between the partners, however imperfectly remembered and however imprecise their terms may have been.

---

[15] *Stack.*
[16] [1991] 1 AC 107, 132.

There is no disagreement about this category, although there is an oddity. The oddity is that, in some cases, the courts derive an express common intention when clearly there was not one. In these cases, the owner partner generally provides a misleading explanation about why the non-owning partner is not on the title to the property – 'it will affect your divorce settlement', 'you are under age', or 'it will affect your taxation liability'.[17] On the face of it, there can be no meeting of minds between the parties; but the courts construct the common intention by making the point that, if the bar was gone, then the parties would have been joint owners; or to put the point another way, but for the excuse, the parties would have been joint owners.

However, the difference between the inference and the imputation is central. The starting point is the description of both provided by Lord Neuberger in *Stack v Dowden*:

> An inferred intention is one which is objectively deduced to be the subjective actual intention of the parties, in the light of their actions and statements. An imputed intention is one which is attributed to the parties, even though no such actual intention can be deduced from their actions and statements, and even though they had no such intention. Imputation involves concluding what the parties would have intended, whereas inference involves concluding what they did intend.[18]

If we leave to one side for the moment the question of from what the inference is to be drawn, the distinction between these two types of intention appears to be essentially a difference of emphasis. An inference is derived from the facts and explains the actions of the parties only on the basis that the non-owner is to get a share in the property (or not). An imputation puts thoughts into the minds of the parties which were never there in the first place but, judged objectively, concluding what they would have intended had they given their minds to the question.

At the moment, it is settled law that a common intention can be inferred.[19] What remains unsettled is the fact-base from which one can infer that intention. In *Rosset*, Lord Bridge said that, as he read the authorities, it is at least doubtful whether anything other than direct contributions to the purchase price or mortgage payments would be sufficient.[20] We must, however, treat that comment with caution (as, indeed, it was expressed). In *Stack*, for example, Lord Walker noted that the comment was 'certainly consistent with many first-instance and Court of Appeal decisions, but I respectfully doubt whether it took full account of the views (conflicting though they were) expressed in *Gissing [v Gissing]*'.[21] And, as Baroness

---

[17] *Grant v Edwards* [1986] Ch 638; *Eves v Eves* [1975] 1 WLR 1338; *Hammond v Mitchell* [1991] 1 WLR 1127.

[18] [2007] 2 AC 432, [126].

[19] *Rosset*, 132–33.

[20] 133.

[21] [1971] AC 886 , [26], citing the speeches in *Gissing* of Lord Reid [1971] AC 886 at 896G–897B and Lord Diplock at 909 D-H.

Hale put it in *Stack*, Lord Bridge's comment may well have 'set that hurdle rather too high in certain respects'.[22]

We must, therefore, turn to the case of *Burns v Burns*, which has been treated as something of a *cause célèbre* in the clamour for reform.[23] As will be seen, we take rather different messages from the case. Mr and Mrs Burns were not married but lived together for 17 years. They had two children together. The home was bought by Mr Burns and in his name. Mrs Burns cared for the children and, only when they were old enough, did she start to earn any money (about £60 per week from her driving instructor business), which was combined with the housekeeping allowance paid to her by Mr Burns. She bought a few bits and pieces around the home and re-decorated it completely a couple of years before they split up. She paid some of the bills, but this was out of money given to her by Mr Burns.

The Court of Appeal were split on the outcome, but the majority were clear that there was insufficient evidence from which one could infer a common intention. They wrote off her non-financial contributions to the household as being irrelevant to the enquiry. However, the majority also seemed to be clear about the types of expenditure from which the common intention could be inferred. Fox LJ said:

> If there is a substantial contribution by the woman to family expenses, and the house was purchased on a mortgage, her contribution is, indirectly, referable to the acquisition of the house since, in one way or another, it enables the family to pay the mortgage instalments. Thus, a payment could be said to be referable to the acquisition of the house if, for example, the payer either (a) pays part of the purchase price or (b) contributes regularly to the mortgage instalments or (c) pays off part of the mortgage or (d) makes a substantial financial contribution to the family expenses so as to enable the mortgage instalments to be paid.
>
> But if a payment cannot be said to be, in a real sense, referable to the acquisition of the house it is difficult to see how, in such a case as the present, it can base a claim for an interest in the house.[24]

May LJ added that, for a common intention to be inferred, there needed to be some '"real" or "substantial" financial contribution towards either the purchase price, deposit or mortgage instalments by the means of which the family home was acquired'.[25] Whether that expression of real or substantial referred back to the earlier part of the paragraph in which that sentence appeared, where he had accepted the significance of indirect payments, is unclear.

Be that as it may, it is already clear that Lord Bridge's reading was narrow. Yet, if we take a moment to think about indirect payment, it does not seem to be the

---

[22] [63].

[23] For discussion and critique, see A. Bottomley, 'From Mrs Burns to Mrs Oxley: Do Co-Habiting Women (Still) Need Marriage Law?' (2006) 14(2) *Feminist Legal Studies* 181.

[24] [1984] 1 Ch 317, 329.

[25] At 345.

answer at all; in fact, it also seems quite perverse. Remember that Mrs Burns was given a housekeeping allowance into which she put her own income as well. Mr Burns did not really need her to pay the bills so that, in fact, her indirect contributions were neither here nor there. This is the fallacy of that debate – it only 'works' when there is already financial equality or the owning partner *needs* the resources of the non-owning partner. The indirect contribution line, then, misses the point in some cases.

The real point is the failure (or refusal) to accept the relevance of non-financial contributions. One might say that this refusal is doctrinally justified because it is not related to the actual purchase of the home or because one does such acts (such as childcare, housework, DIY) not out of a desire to obtain an interest in the property but out of love, affection, and, perhaps, because it is the norm.[26] And, Bottomley asks, 'Should we support or defend the development of an area of law which allows the play of a figure of woman/victim and privileges women who can be ascribed within the wife/mother role?'.[27]

And now we come to the question of whether one can impute a common intention at this stage. In the earliest House of Lords decision developing the application of the constructive trust in this context, *Pettitt v Pettitt*,[28] the Law Lords divided on the question, and the majority seemed to settle uneasily on the proposition that the intention could not be imputed. In the subsequent case, *Gissing v Gissing*, there was an uneasy truce. Lord Diplock, who in *Pettitt* had advocated the use of imputation, can be read as making the same point in his speech in *Gissing*, simply replacing the word 'impute' with 'infer'.[29]

The description by Baroness Hale and Lord Walker in *Jones v Kernott*[30] of the different reasoning of the House of Lords in *Gissing* summarizes the general expression of dissatisfaction with that decision:

> ...it may be worth pointing out that their Lordships' speeches were singularly unresponsive to each other. The only reference to another speech is by Viscount Dilhorne (at p 900) where he agreed with Lord Diplock on a very general proposition as to the law of trusts. The law reporter has managed to find a ratio for the headnote (at p 886) only by putting these two propositions together with some remarks by Lord Reid (at p 896) which have a quite different flavour. We can only guess at the order in which the speeches were composed, but [certain passages from] Lord Reid's speech, ...,

---

26 See, for example, *Rosset*, 127–28.

27 A. Bottomley, 'Self and Subjectivities: Languages of Claim in Property Law', (1993) 20(1) *Journal of Law and Society* 56, 60. The question derives from Bottomley's reading of the text in *Eves v Eves* [1971] 1 WLR 1338. The discussion of the ideology of the victim by Kristin Bumiller in *The Civil Rights Society: The Social Construction of Victims*, (Johns Hopkins Press, 1989) has particular power in this context.

28 [1970] AC 777.

29 Lord Walker, in *Stack*, makes this point: 'But for the substitution of the word 'infer' for 'impute' the substance of the reasoning is, it seems to me, essentially the same (although worked out in a good deal more detail) as Lord Diplock's reasoning in *Pettitt v Pettitt*, when he was in the minority' ([20]).

30 [2011] UKSC 53.

suggest that Lord Reid had read Lord Diplock's speech in draft, and thought that it was about 'an imputation of a deemed intention'.[31]

It is clear that Lord Walker and Baroness Hale believe that the time may well have come to roll back these decisions and accept that a common intention at this stage can be imputed. The groundwork has been laid for that development in *Stack*.[32]

It may well be that we are arguing over nothing. As we shall see, in *Jones v Kernott*,[33] the majority of the Supreme Court argued that there was considerable overlap between the concepts. But the resistance to imputed intentions seems ingrained into the property lawyer's psyche. Furthermore, if accepted, difficult questions remain about what types of factors or acts can give rise to such an imputation.

Detriment

When it comes to proving detriment, inferred common intention cases are the easiest – the facts which give rise to the inference also provide the detriment. It is express common intention cases which are the most difficult. The test which seems most useful is that propounded by Nourse LJ in *Grant v Edwards*, where he said that

> The difficulty is caused, I think because although the common intention has been made plain, everything else remains a matter of inference. Let me illustrate it in this way. It would be possible to take the view that the mere moving into the house by the woman amounted to an acting upon the common intention. But that was evidently not the view of the majority in *Eves v. Eves* [1975] 1 WLR 1338. And the reason for that may be that, in the absence of evidence, the law is not so cynical as to infer that a woman will only go to live with a man to whom she is not married if she understands that she is to have an interest in their home. So what sort of conduct is required? In my judgment it must be conduct on which the woman could not reasonably have been expected to embark unless she was to have an interest in the house. If she was not to have such an interest, she could reasonably be expected to go and live with her lover, but not, for example, to wield a 14-lb. sledge hammer in the front garden. In adopting the latter kind of conduct she is seen to act to her detriment on the faith of the common intention.[34]

So, the type of conduct required is conduct out of the norm. The use of the '14-lb. sledge hammer' is because the Claimant in *Eves* did precisely that while pregnant. It does not really take too much thought to appreciate the inherent fallacy in this test. If one is looking for conduct outside the norm, then one needs to

---

[31] *Stack*, [28].
[32] Lord Walker, [20]-[21]; Baroness Hale, [60].
[33] [2011] UKSC 53.
[34] [1986] Ch 638, 648.

have an appreciation of the norm from which one can make that judgment. One needs to ask why the person did the act in question and, suspending reality for a moment, assume that there is one single motivation as, it seems, the courts do. So, in *Rosset*, even if there had been a common intention, Mrs Rosset had simply not acted outside the norm. Her activities (assisting and managing builders) were constructed by Lord Bridge as follows:

> It was common ground that Mrs Rosset was extremely anxious that the new matrimonial home should be ready for occupation before Christmas if possible. In these circumstances it would seem the most natural thing in the world for any wife, in the absence of her husband abroad, to spend all the time she could spare and to employ any skills she might have, such as the ability to decorate a room, in doing all she could to accelerate progress of the work quite irrespective of any expectation she might have of enjoying a beneficial interest in the property. The judge's view that some of this work was work 'upon which she could not reasonably have been expected to embark unless she was to have an interest in the house' seems to me, with respect, quite untenable.[35]

Furthermore, and in any event, Lord Bridge said that Mrs Rosset's acts were 'so trifling as to be almost de minimis', and would not have supported any claim if there had been the clearest common intention.[36]

PROPRIETARY ESTOPPEL

By contrast with the contestation over constructive trusts, the principles in relation to proprietary estoppel seem relatively simple. In essence, what is required is an assurance by one party on which the other party relies to their detriment. Sometimes, instead of the assurance, that party simply stands back while the other acts to their detriment in reliance on facts which they believe.[37] That is something of a reduction of three rather different types of case, which all have an element of mistake underpinning them: imperfect gift (common mistake), standing by (unilateral mistake) and common expectation (a 'flavour' of mistake or misprediction).[38] Perhaps the unifying element is 'unconscionability' – as Lord Walker suggested, 'If the other elements appear to be present but the result does not shock the conscience of the court, the analysis needs to be looked at again'.[39]

---

[35] At 131. As Bottomley aptly puts it, 'What is required is not only labour which can be valued, but labour which can be dissociated from any wifely role and in which it can be proved that the woman specifically directed the activity towards ownership rather than simply use of the property. We are drawn back to forms of specific thinking which seem at variance not only with women's socio-economic activities but with the very way in which they think them': A. Bottomley, n.27, 65; see also A. Bottomley, n.23, especially at 207.

[36] Ibid.

[37] *Ramsden v Dyson* (1866) LR 1 HL 129.

[38] [2008] 1 WLR 1752, [63].

[39] [2008] 1 WLR 1752, [92]; see also M. Dixon, 'Confining and Defining Proprietary Estoppel: The Role of Unconscionability' (2010) 30(3) *Legal Studies* 408.

The concepts are flexible, but within boundaries. As Lord Walker memorably put it in *Yeoman's Row v Cobbe*:

> [E]quitable estoppel is a flexible doctrine which the court can use, in appropriate circumstances, to prevent injustice caused by the vagaries and inconstancy of human nature. But is not a sort of joker or wild card to be used whenever a Court disapproves of the conduct of a litigant who seems to have the law on his side. Flexible though it is, the doctrine must be formulated and applied in a disciplined and principled way. Certainty is important in property transactions.[40]

The usual requirement is that the assurance must be 'clear and unambiguous', but this is context-specific – so, in *Thorner v Major*, the representor was '… a very taciturn farmer, given to indirect statements, [who] made remarks obliquely referring to his intention with regard to his farm after his death'.[41] On the other hand, in *Yeoman's Row v Cobbe*, the context of a commercial transaction between two experienced property business people, which was not properly formalized, was accepted as binding in honour only, and for which some of the terms remained to be negotiated, told against an estoppel arising. It now also seems to be the case that a representation about how property is to be left on death is sufficiently certain, even if the shape of the property changes. Thus, in *Thorner*, the apparent promise concerned a farm on the Mendips, but over time parts were sold and bought. That was neither here nor there for the House of Lords because the subject matter was the farm; it was, therefore, certain.[42] Finally, the criteria for raising the estoppel are interactive, so that a particularly clear representation will result in a lowering of the threshold for the detriment and reliance elements;[43] and, it should be added, the acts of detrimental reliance are for the representee to take from the representation (irrespective of whether the representor meant their words to be taken that way).[44]

Perhaps the classic example of the operation of proprietary estoppel occurred in *Crabb v Arun DC*.[45] Crabb owned some land and the council owned a lane by the side of that land. Crabb needed another point of access to part of his land and negotiated an oral agreement with the council for that access point from their lane. No formal agreement was completed. Crabb nevertheless acted on that agreement, setting new gateposts in concrete next to the land, and sold off a part of the land. The council then uprooted the gatepost and refused rights of access from their lane, leaving Crabb's property effectively landlocked. The Court

---

[40] [2008] 1 WLR 1752, [46].

[41] [2009] 1 WLR 776, [80], Lord Neuberger.

[42] [18], Lord Scott. He notes that, if the representor were to have sought to sell the farm before his death, it would have been possible for the representee to establish a claim through estoppel and to consequential relief, as in *Gillett v Holt* [2001] Ch 210.

[43] *Gillett v Holt* [2001] Ch 210.

[44] *Thorner*.

[45] [1976] Ch 179. Although the context of the case is non-domestic, it provides a useful example and examination of the key concepts involved in proprietary estoppel claims.

of Appeal held that it would be inequitable for the council to rely on their strict legal rights. In principle, of course, they could act in the way they did because no formal agreement had been signed and thus no title had passed to Crabb. However, the Court held that their conscience was affected and granted a right (the access point) to Crabb by way of a proprietary estoppel.

Debate 2

What principles does the law use to assess the remedy?

Once the Claimant has surmounted the first hurdle, the next question is the extent of the interest to which the Claimant is entitled. Once more, there is a degree of uncertainty, although recent cases have provided some clarification. The analysis is once again split between the constructive trust and proprietary estoppel.

CONSTRUCTIVE TRUST

The same two starting presumptions apply here, viz. if the property is held by one person, the assumption is that they are the sole beneficial owner; if the property is held jointly, the assumption is that they hold the property as joint owners, 50:50. The basis for that proposition is that 'equity follows the law',[46] although there are significant policy reasons for this outcome, most notably certainty.[47] The onus is on the Claimant to prove that they are entitled to more, and the principles regarding quantification are the same whether one is dealing with a joint names or a sole name case.[48] There are suggestions that it is only very rarely that that starting point is capable of being displaced. As Baroness Hale put it in *Stack v Dowden*:

> This is not a task to be lightly embarked upon. In family disputes, strong feelings are aroused when couples split up. These often lead the parties, honestly but mistakenly, to reinterpret the past in self-exculpatory or vengeful terms. They also lead people to spend far more on the legal battle than is warranted by the sums actually at stake. A full examination of the facts is likely to involve disproportionate costs. In joint names cases it is also unlikely to lead to a different result unless the facts are very unusual.[49]

Yet it is also the case that in both *Stack* and *Jones v Kernott*,[50] the Supreme Court did engage in that process so that it remains unclear what facts are 'very unusual'. It is the plurality of relationships and individual decisions made which suggest that there is no particular norm, a point to which we return below.

---

46 *Stack*, [54], Baroness Hale.
47 *Jones*, [19], Baroness Hale/Lord Walker, where it was noted that this is not a 'slavish' application of that equitable maxim.
48 [65].
49 [2007] 2 AC 432, [68]; see also *Jones*, [19]–[22].
50 [2011] UKSC 53.

It is now crystal clear that quantification depends on the common intention of the parties. That is the guiding principle. There is a degree of consensus as to the type of common intention: one can look to express, inferred, *or* imputed common intention. That is the clear outcome of both *Stack* and *Jones*. The issue lies in how one operationalizes the difference between inferred and imputed intention, and, indeed, whether it matters or not. Let us start with the conclusion, which is summarized by Baroness Hale and Lord Walker, and about which there can be no disagreement:

(1) The starting point is that equity follows the law and they are joint tenants both in law and in equity.

(2) That presumption can be displaced by showing (a) that the parties had a different common intention at the time when they acquired the home, or (b) that they later formed the common intention that their respective shares would change.

(3) Their common intention is to be deduced objectively from their conduct: 'the relevant intention of each party is the intention which was reasonably understood by the other party to be manifested by that party's words and conduct notwithstanding that he did not consciously formulate that intention in his own mind or even acted with some different intention which he did not communicate to the other party'.[51] Examples of the sort of evidence which might be relevant to drawing such inferences are given in *Stack v Dowden*.[52]

(4) In those cases where it is clear either (a) that the parties did not intend joint tenancy at the outset, or (b) had changed their original intention, but where it is not possible to ascertain by direct evidence or by inference what their actual intention was as to the shares in which they would own the property, 'the answer is that each is entitled to that share which the court considers fair having regard to the whole course of dealing between them in relation to the property'.[53] In our judgment, 'the whole course of dealing... in relation to the property' should be given a broad meaning, enabling a similar range of factors to be taken into account as may be relevant to ascertaining the parties' actual intentions.

(5) Each case will turn on its own facts. Financial contributions are relevant but there are many other factors which may enable the court to decide what shares were either intended (as in case (3)) or fair (as in case (4)).[54]

The same reasoning process should also apply in sole name cases.

The Supreme Court in *Jones* differed as to the breadth of inference. The facts of *Jones* are relatively simple. The parties were in a relationship in which they had two children. They bought a house in their joint names in 1985. In 1993, Mr Kernott left. At this stage, all parties agreed that the property was to be shared

---

[51] *Gissing v Gissing* [1971] AC 886, 906, Lord Diplock.
[52] at [69].
[53] *Oxley v Hiscock* [2005] Fam 211, para. 69, Chadwick LJ.
[54] *Jones*, [52].

50:50. After leaving, Mr Kernott stopped making payments to anything. In 1995, the parties cashed in a life insurance policy, which enabled Mr Kernott to buy another home to live in. In 2007, he asked for his half share of the former family home. In the meantime, Ms Jones had been making all payments for the home and children. There was no express agreement between the parties as to whether, after 1993, the parties had altered their intentions as to the shares in which they held the property. The question seemed to be whether, if one could not infer a common intention in these circumstances, one could impute such an intention.

For Lord Walker and Baroness Hale, however, this was a case of inference. They make the important point that an imputation is not such an unusual approach in law:

> Whenever a judge concludes that an individual 'intended, or must be taken to have intended,' or 'knew, or must be taken to have known,' there is an elision between what the judge can find as a fact (usually by inference) on consideration of the admissible evidence, and what the law may supply (to fill the evidential gap) by way of a presumption. The presumption of a resulting trust is a clear example of a rule by which the law *does* impute an intention, the rule being based on a very broad generalisation about human motivation.[55]

Furthermore, '... while the conceptual difference between inferring and imputing is clear, the difference in practice may not be so great. In this area, as in many others, the scope for inference is wide. The law recognizes that a legitimate inference may not correspond to an individual's subjective state of mind.'[56] This line of argument was followed by Lord Collins, who pointed out that 'what is one person's inference will be another person's imputation'.[57] On this point, there was a difference of opinion – Lords Kerr and Wilson found that the case depended on 'fairness', an imputation from the facts.[58] Both preferred a clear demarcation between an inference and imputation.

Nobody, however, disagreed on the outcome. Ms Jones was entitled to 90 per cent of the property. This could be inferred (Lord Walker/Baroness Hale, Lord Collins) from the sale of the life insurance policy in 1995, when 'a new plan was formed' by the parties.[59] That was not a finding of fact made by the judge, but one that would have been open for him to make. Lords Kerr and Wilson reached the same result on the basis of fairness/imputation. As Lord Kerr put it, '...the bare facts of his departure from the family home and acquisition of another property are a slender foundation on which to conclude that he had entirely abandoned whatever stake he had in the previously shared property'.[60]

---

[55] [29].
[56] [34].
[57] [65].
[58] Although it is fair to say that Lord Kerr was not overly enamoured by the concept of 'imputation': [74].
[59] [48].
[60] [76].

This still leaves the question of when it will be appropriate to upset the starting presumption. The answer seems to be that it depends on the facts of the case. In *Stack*, the parties had been in a relationship for 27 years and had four children. Mr Stack had made direct and unquantifiable payments to the purchase of the home and had done work to it (he was a builder). They had both looked after the home and the children. The judge's original finding had been that they should share 50:50 in the proceeds. The House of Lords disagreed, awarding Ms Dowden 65 per cent. They upset the starting point by looking principally at the way the parties organized their finances – separately from each other and without joint savings[61] – and noted that Ms Dowden had paid the capital up front to the purchase so that Mr Stack had contributed to the mortgage payments. This was, therefore, a 'very unusual' case – as Baroness Hale put it, 'There cannot be many unmarried couples who have lived together for as long as this, who have had four children together, and whose affairs have been kept as rigidly separate as this couple's affairs were kept'[62].

PROPRIETARY ESTOPPEL

The interest that the successful Claimant may obtain in the property through proprietary estoppel is extremely flexible. It might be said that, ordinarily, the remedy should follow the representation – the Claimant obtains their expectation loss. If the representation is that the Claimant will be 'given' the house, then that should ordinarily be the remedy.[63] This was the outcome in, for example, *Pascoe v Turner*.[64] However, that analysis, while doctrinally appropriate in that equity perfects the gift through estoppel, does not reflect the authorities. Indeed, in *Pascoe* itself, the ratio for requiring the transfer of legal title to the representee was based on the Court of Appeal's view that '... the equity cannot here be satisfied without granting a remedy which assures to the respondent security of tenure, quiet enjoyment, and freedom of action in respect of repairs and improvements without interference from the appellant'.[65] The conduct of the representor had been ruthless, and the remedy was designed to protect her from future manifestations of that ruthlessness, as well as enable her to finance any major repairs by way of loan.[66] Similarly, in *Crabb v Arun DC*,[67] Mr Crabb obtained his expected

---

[61] As Baroness Hale, at [90], said, 'This is not a case in which it can be said that the parties pooled their separate resources, even notionally, for the common good. The only things they ever had in their joint names were Chatsworth Road and the associated endowment policy. Everything else was kept strictly separate'.

[62] *Stack*, [92].

[63] See, for example, *Jennings v Rice* [2003] 1 P & CR 8; *Yeonman's Row v Cobbe*, at [4], Lord Scott; see also, S. Moriarty, 'Licences and Land Law: Legal Principles and Public Policy' (1984) 100(3) *LQR* 376; J. Dewar, 'Licences and Land Law: An Alternative View' (1986) 49(6) *MLR* 741; for further discussion, see S. Gardner, 'The Remedial Discretion in Proprietary Estoppel' (1999) 115(3) *LQR* 438; and S. Gardner, 'The Remedial Discretion in Proprietary Estoppel Again' (2006) 122(3) LQR 492.

[64] [1979] 1 WLR 431.

[65] At 438.

[66] At 438–39.

[67] [1976] Ch 179.

easement by way of proprietary estoppel, but the court's approach to the remedy was rather different.

Scarman LJ, in *Crabb*, analysed the grant of the easement as the 'minimum equity to do justice to the [Claimant]'.[68] It is that approach to remedy which seems to have characterized the development of the law in this area, although that approach also has considerable discretion and uncertainty attached to it. It is also not hugely helpful. It is sometimes framed, in more modern vein, as equity seeking a proportionate outcome.[69] The problems to which these approaches give rise are exemplified by *Gillett v Holt*.[70] This was a case in which Mr Holt promised Mr Gillett his entire farming business on Holt's death. The relationship lasted an extended period. The underlying promise was simple; but the actual farming business was complicated, the acts of detriment in reliance took place over a lengthy period, and involved a number of separate properties, and also a series of transactions after the parties had fallen out. Robert Walker LJ set out to find the maximum extent of the equity so as to form a basis for identifying the minimum, with the observation that 'The court must look at all the circumstances, including the need to achieve a 'clean break' so far as possible and avoid or minimise future friction'.[71]

All of this seems unsatisfactory as it is not conducive to certainty or, indeed, a principled jurisdiction. It seems clear, however, that the remedy is tailored to the facts. The need for a clean break, as best as possible, is clearly a relevant criterion. Equally, the remedy needs to be realistic. There is no point giving effect to a representation where the outcome is unachievable. It may well be, therefore, that a proprietary claim may give rise to a personal remedy (such as the payment of money to satisfy the equity), or, indeed, to no remedy at all (as the extent of the equity has already been satisfied).[72] From *Sledmore v Dalby*, Gardner identifies seven possible factors affecting the remedy if one has to pass over the expectation criterion: '(i) the claimant's expectation, but also proportionality with her detriment; (ii) the parties' conduct; (iii) the need for a clean break; (iv) alterations in the defendant's assets and circumstances; (v) the effect of taxation; (vi) other claims on the defendant or his or her estate; (vii) possible other factors'.[73] Gardner's position is that the role of this jurisdiction is to rectify unconscionability, which '..., can be understood as the extent to which the defendant's role in the claimant's detrimental reliance upon her expectation makes it right to hold the defendant responsible for it. Addressing this is a reasonably well-defined aim, such that a judge can work to it as the law's agent.'[74] Bright and McFarlane, by slight contrast,

---

[68] At 198.

[69] E.g. *Sledmore v Dalby* (1996) 72 P & CR 196, 208–9.

[70] [2001] Ch 210.

[71] At 237.

[72] See, for example, *Burrows v Sharp* (1993) 23 HLR 82; *Baker v Baker* (1993) 23 HLR 408.

[73] Gardner, 2006, n.63, 494.

[74] At 506. He also notes certain problems in relation to the factors identified, not least that they are not necessarily related to detrimental reliance and also because different judges' 'positions remain unstated', at 507.

argue for a restrictive approach to a proprietary remedy, on the basis that the key ingredient should be the Claimant's reliance.[75] A proprietary remedy should only ensue, on this argument, if that protects the Claimant's reasonable reliance. As yet, there is no answer to this question. Our preference is for Gardner's proffered solution as this seems more in tune with an explanation of the *outcome* of most of the cases.

Debate 3

Are constructive trusts and proprietary estoppel different and, more to the point, does it matter?

Let us start with two propositions by way of answering the first part of this question. The first is that the constructive trust (or, at least the type considered above) arises as a result of the common intention regarding the *acquisition* of the property; in principle, proprietary estoppel is not so limited and can arise at any stage. If you think in terms of venn diagrams, it is the fried egg one, with estoppel the whole egg and constructive trust the yolk bit. The second proposition is that a constructive trust arises by the acts of detrimental reliance, whatever they may be; the estoppel, however, in principle, only arises when a judge so pronounces.[76] As regards the latter point about estoppel, that seems to follow from the flexibility of the remedy – it may not give rise to a proprietary right at all. There is a legislative corrective in relation to registered land for the protection of the person claiming the right to estoppel 'for the avoidance of doubt' – the equity by estoppel 'has effect from the time the equity arises as an interest capable of binding successors in title ...'.[77] Lord Scott, in *Thorner*, suggests a third proposition, that the inheritance cases (like *Gillett*, for example) are better explained by way of constructive trust but this seems to have been based more on instinct than grounded doctrine.[78] However one frames it, then, there are (or seem to be) differences between the two doctrines.

Nevertheless, there is considerable discussion in the cases about the overlap. Browne-Wilkinson V-C, in *Grant v Edwards*, suggested that they are 'closely akin' and 'they rest on the same foundation and have on all other matters reached the same conclusions'.[79] Lord Walker, who, in *Yaxley v Gotts*,[80] had found similar crossovers, nevertheless resiled from the view that they should be unified in *Thorner*:

---

[75] S. Bright & B. McFarlane, 'Proprietary Estoppel and Property Rights' (2005) 64(2) *CLJ* 449.

[76] See P. Ferguson, 'Constructive Trusts – A Note of Caution' (1993) 109(1) *LQR* 114; cf P. Matthews, 'The Words Which Are Not There: A Partial History of the Constructive Trust' in C. Mitchell (ed.), *Constructive and Resulting Trusts* (Hart, 2009) pp. 55–7; B. McFarlane, 'Proprietary Estoppel and Third Parties after the Land Registration Act 2002' (2003) 62(4) *CLJ* 661.

[77] LRA 2002, s. 116.

[78] [2009] 1 WLR 776, [20]; see also *Re Basham* [1986] 1 WLR 1498, 1504.

[79] [1986] Ch 638, 656; see also *Yaxley v Gotts* [2000] Ch 162, 177.

[80] *Yaxley v Gotts* [2000] Ch 162, 177, Robert Walker LJ.

Proprietary estoppel typically consists of asserting an equitable claim against the conscience of the 'true' owner. The claim is a 'mere equity'. It is to be satisfied by the minimum award necessary to do justice..., which may sometimes lead to no more than a monetary award. A 'common intention' constructive trust, by contrast, is identifying the true beneficial owner or owners, and the size of their beneficial interests.[81]

Why the fuss? It seems that the principal problem, quite apart from the doctrinal differences, lies in section 2 of the Law of Property (Miscellaneous Provisions) Act 1989. That section expresses Parliamentary intention regarding the required formalities for the sale or disposition of an interest in land. Constructive trusts (as well as resulting and implied trusts) are exempted from those strict requirements.[82] Estoppel is not so exempted. In *Yaxley v Gotts*, where only proprietary estoppel was pleaded, it was argued that public policy prevented estoppel from getting round the section 2 formalities. As Robert Walker LJ put it in that case: 'If an estoppel would have the effect of enforcing a void contract and subverting Parliament's purpose it may have to yield to the statutory law which confronts it, except so far as the statute's saving for a constructive trust provides a means of reconciliation of the apparent conflict'.[83] On the facts, he was able to find a constructive trust as well, so there was no problem for him. Beldam LJ (who was the Law Commission Chair at the time the report which led to the 1989 Act was under consideration by that body) was less concerned and (naturally) referred to the Law Commission report which assumed the continued availability of proprietary estoppel to defeat a claim, even where there had been no compliance with the section 2 formalities.[84]

However, in *Yeoman's Row*, Lord Scott suggested

My present view, however, is that proprietary estoppel cannot be prayed in aid in order to render enforceable an agreement that statute has declared to be void. The proposition that an owner of land can be estopped from asserting that an agreement is void for want of compliance with the requirements of section 2 is, in my opinion, unacceptable. The assertion is no more than the statute provides. Equity can surely not contradict the statute.[85]

In *Thorner*, Lord Neuberger said:

[A]t least as at present advised, I do not consider that section 2 has any impact on a claim such as the present, which is a straightforward estoppel claim without any contractual connection. It was no doubt for that reason that the respondents, rightly in my view, eschewed any argument based on section 2.[86]

---

[81] *Stack*, [37].
[82] s. 2(5).
[83] At 175; Clarke LJ agreed with him on this point, at 181.
[84] At 190–91.
[85] [29].
[86] [99]; see also *Anderson Antiques v Anderson Wharf* [2007] EWHC 2086 (Ch).

In neither case was the point particularly argued. It leaves us with four possible solutions: estoppel cannot get round section 2 plain and simple; estoppel can where the same facts would give rise to a constructive trust; estoppel can where the parties are not seeking to create a 'contractual connection'; estoppel is unaffected by section 2.[87] In the only subsequent case to date, Bean J preferred the latter interpretation.[88] That probably is the best interpretation because of the second proposition above – until a judge formalizes the remedy, there is no estoppel and, therefore, nothing on which section 2 can 'bite'. It is to be noted that, if the first proposition is correct, then proprietary estoppel would, in most circumstances, be of extremely limited practical utility.

Debate 4

Do the foundations of the doctrinal law correlate with empirical findings?

It is easy to get caught up in hard, doctrinal law. Given that it is under-developed and there are many outstanding questions, it is both interesting and thought-provoking stuff. But we should also take a step back and consider whether the foundations of that law actually correlate with lived realities. We are referring here to the empirical assumptions of the law – for example, Baroness Hale's assertion that the facts in *Stack v Dowden* were very unusual.[89] The simple answer to the question is 'not really'. Indeed, the development of the law in this area is characterized by its inability to cope with the plurality of circumstances by which ordinary people live and manage their lives. The findings of qualitative studies in this regard are particularly illuminating. As Barlow and Smithson put it, 'our analysis [of their data] shows that there was often a surprising ability to separate off the emotional or social commitment from a sense of legal and financial commitment which might be expected to accompany it'.[90] More directly, Douglas, Pearce and Woodward directly attack the empirical basis for Baroness Hale's claim that the facts of *Stack* were very unusual – as they put it,

> …there is little clear correlation between other features of relationships and the way the couple organised their finances. … [their] study also found cohabitants to be more likely than not to keep their finances separate, with two-thirds of [their] sample only operating sole bank accounts. Even among couples who owned their home in joint names, fewer than half operated joint bank accounts. … This all suggests that keeping money separate – or pooling it – does not necessarily provide reliable evidence of the parties'

---

[87] See generally, Dixon, n.39, who argues that unconscionability provides the answer.
[88] *Whittaker v Kinnear* [2011] EWHC 1479 (QB), [30].
[89] [2007] 2 AC 432.
[90] A. Barlow and J. Smithson, 'Legal Assumptions, Cohabitants' Talk and the Rocky Road to Freedom' (2010) 22(3) *Child and Family Law Quarterly* 328.

intentions, and it may not be at all easy for practitioners to identify cases which have sufficiently 'unusual financial arrangements to justify attempting to displace the heavy presumption emphasised in *Stack v Dowden* that equity follows the law in determining beneficial interests.[91]

The findings of Douglas, Pearce and Woodward provide particular pause for thought. Theirs was a small-scale qualitative study – which included cohabitants, conveyancers and family solicitors – but the findings demonstrate not just the variety of different pressures involved when cohabitants buy or mortgage a home, but also the antipathy of different elements of the legal profession towards each other. It is particularly notable, for example, that cohabitant property issues are routed by firms to their family departments, which (by definition) are not as aware of the *civil* procedure applicable to these claims, which are different from family procedural rules including (most importantly) regarding costs.[92] Few of the couples in this study had made written agreements relating to their property, although most had made wills; but the agreements '... had as much potential to exacerbate as to clarify issues' and their understandings of ownership at the time of purchase were hazy.[93] Separate legal advice was generally not sought (or suggested).

But one of the key findings of the study concerns the power of the emotions, which led to many of their sample not questioning arrangements, and doing things (like ticking a box to indicate joint ownership) on the basis that it would otherwise be embarrassing (as one cohabitant participant put it, '*It was explained to me that I could protect my extra contribution – but she was pregnant, sitting there next to me – you just don't do that*'[94]). Conveyancing solicitors were generally complicit in these power issues. As the researchers put it, 'One conveyancer summed up the attitude of purchasing clients in a nutshell: *Normally they just want the keys and to know when they're moving in. The legal aspects of it, they don't really think about*'.[95] The cohabitants' views as to the types of principles which should be relevant to the resolution of their disputes (contribution/compensation, need, honesty/honour, strict legal entitlement) were necessarily reflected by the law and practice. One conclusion expressed is damning:

> The legal construction of property ownership does not reflect any lay conception of cohabiting partnerships. The concepts used in property law do not reflect matters which are likely to appear relevant and important to clients, or the way they have lived their lives together. Furthermore, the law brings together and treats as the same issues which from a practical 'client'

---

[91] G. Douglas, J. Pearce and H. Woodward, 'Cohabitants, Property and the Law: A Study of Injustice' (2009) 72(1) *MLR* 24, 37–38; see also A. Barlow, C. Burgoyne and J. Smithson, *The Living Together Campaign – An Investigation of its Impact on the Legally Aware Cohabitants* (Ministry of Justice, 2007); R. Tennant, J. Taylor and J. Lewis, *Separating from Cohabitation: Making Arrangements for Finances and Parenting*, DCA 7/06 (DCA, 2007).

[92] Paras 7.20–7.27.

[93] Paras 5.8–5.9.

[94] Para. 5.12.

[95] Para. 5.28.

point of view are quite different, while conversely separating and treating differently issues which, as experienced practically, seem very similar to the lay person.[96]

Further, 'the way in which property is owned may not reflect the parties' understandings, what they feel to be fair, or what can practically be achieved'.[97] In any event, getting the evidence together to justify a claim was likely to be unrealistic.

One conclusion that one might draw is that the law has got some way to go before it catches up with everyday life. However, the research makes a number of more wide-ranging points about the organization of the profession: the lack of knowledge of cohabitants about their entitlements (and, more so, the mis-knowledge[98]); the difficulty of knowing with any degree of certainty what principles are, so that bargaining in the shadow of the law becomes impossible; and the significance of everyday interactions, including the shame (or stigma) attached to claiming or acting contrary to expectations.

CONCLUSIONS

There is not much more to say than appears in the previous paragraph. The doctrinal law is confused and confusing, it lacks much by way of principle and application, and there are outstanding gaps. It is entirely ridiculous that some 40 years after the leading case of *Pettitt*, we are still searching for principle, but that is the doctrinal position. The lack of Parliamentary leadership in this area is also entirely lamentable – if it was apathetic, it would be perhaps more understandable – and there is a desperate need for somebody, anybody, to grapple with the really difficult issues.

Further Reading

A. Barlow, C. Burgoyne, E. Clery and J. Smithson, 'Cohabitation and the Law: Myths, Money and the Media' in A. Park, J. Curtis, K. Thompson, M. Phillips, M. Johnson, E. Clery (eds), *British Social Attitudes: The 24th Report* (Sage, 2008).

A. Bottomley, 'Self and Subjectivities: Languages of Claim in Property Law' (1993) 20(1) *Journal of Law and Society* 56.

A. Bottomley, 'From Mrs Burns to Mrs Oxley: Do Co-Habiting Women (Still) Need Marriage Law?' (2006) 14(2) *Feminist Legal Studies* 181.

G. Douglas, J. Pearce and H. Woodward, 'Cohabitants, Property and the Law: A Study of Injustice' (2009) 72(1) *MLR* 24.

P. Matthews, 'The Words Which Are Not There: A Partial History of the Constructive Trust' in C. Mitchell (ed.), *Constructive and Resulting Trusts* (Hart, 2009).

---

[96] Para. 6.38.

[97] Para. 6.43.

[98] There is a reminder here of the analogy drawn by Ewick and Silbey of legal consciousness developing like whale song: P. Ewick & S. Silbey, *The Common Place of Law: Stories from Everyday Life* (University of Chicago Press, 1999) p. 44.

12

CONCLUSIONS: WHAT IS THE POINT OF PROPERTY?

We have spent some time in this book identifying some of the flaws in the conventional law of property, in particular through the lens of the five themes of property identified in Chapter 1: alienation, citizenship, exclusion, rationality, responsibility and space. In this conclusion, we reflect on our journey by way of extended observations on the limits of property in law. We do not seek to repeat our call to arms in the introduction here, and nor is what follows a manifesto or suchlike; what we offer here are merely some personal observations to which we collectively mostly sign up.

Our opening observation is significant for us as teachers. If this book has sought to do one thing, it is to exhort our colleagues and students to go beyond the doctrine, to see the real in real property, and not to slavishly follow others' agendas for conventional analysis. The simple thing, of course, is to stick with what we know, what we were taught, and to limit ourselves accordingly. In doing so, we fear that we fall into the trap laid for us by our teachers and others, so that we end up subscribing to what we regard as the rationality errors of property law, its liberal emphases on alienation, its circuits of inclusion masquerading as citizenship, its assumptions about (and individualization of) responsibility, and its carving up of space. It is the apparently mundane, taken-for-granted, everyday life of property law which, perhaps paradoxically, means that we miss the variety of experiences of the everyday – as Delaney observes, we need to investigate '... *how* unremarkableness (particularly the unremarkableness of mundane power) is produced and maintained'.[1]

We forget that there is a public dimension to private law (or, as Annelise Riles puts it, 'there is nothing inherently public or private about legal technicalities'), and we forget that the real in property is unreal, lacking in both empirical validity and credibility. Indeed, we see many parallels between our rather mundane book about property law and Riles' ethnographic study of collateral in global financial markets. Part of Riles' study concerned the use of legal techniques, which are means and not ends (although lawyers regard them as instrumental in achieving

---

[1] D. Delaney, *Nomospheric Investigations: The Spatial, The Legal and the Pragmatics of World-Making* (Routledge-Glasshouse, 2010) p. 48 (emphasis in original).

their desired ends), and she argues that law is seen as a tool in this process. She goes on:

> This deceptively simple cultural reality deserves a bit more attention. The notion of law as tool assumes that the user of the tool is completely in control of the purpose, process, and outcome of the tool's use. It assumes that the legal tool is really nothing but collateral knowledge, on the way to achieving certain stated objectives, defined in other terms. But legal tools…are more interesting than this. They sometimes, mysteriously, overtake their users. And the 'users' (perhaps we dare say 'collaborators with') of such tools are neither completely aware, nor completely unaware, of the agency of 'their' tools. Again, it is one of those collateral realities that lies under the radar, and yet in plain view for all to see. … [W]e are dealing with something more mysterious and profound: in the 'meantime', the means often occlude the ends and overtake the instrument's user. There are intriguing political possibilities in this too-often-unacknowledged technical reality.[2]

Our perspectives on property law, which in places appears fixed and barely changed, has similarly drawn attention to the agency of these tools, and the truths which they expose. So, our point (like Riles) is not to throw the baby out with the bathwater, but that we should take legal technicality on, on its own terms, and seek to expose its truths and hidden assumptions. So, for example, if we think about the figure of Mrs Burns (see Chapter 11), our analysis of the injustice to her is that, on the facts and without an express common intention, the methods of inferring a common intention were of no use to her because of the financial imbalance between herself and Mr Burns. This is a slightly different way of telling that story, in which the public and private merge in legal technicality, the key point being not that we have no way of quantifying her contributions (which is, of course, true; it is the end of legal technicality) but that, even if we did, it would have been unlikely that she would have been able to demonstrate that inference. By way of further example, our analysis of the apparently paradigmatic shift from a trust for sale to a trust of land in Chapter 3 demonstrates that the shadow of the past bears heavily, and so the sub-title of that chapter might have been 'change but no change'.

Our second observation, linked to that, is that we often have a blinkered analysis where our focus remains within the conventional boundaries of property law. And our conventional focus on rights and entitlements to property – the metaphors of property law – make us miss a trick because we lose sight of the phenomena of property, and we miss out on seeing the thing or the asset itself.

In particular, we argue that the presentation of property law as apparently 'neutral' is wrong-headed. In our apparent need for conventional principle, we forget that there is a shared human need to *use* property. That use is the basis for all human activities, yet the principles by which this use is governed tend to be

---

[2] A. Riles, *Collateral knowledge: Legal Reasoning in Global Financial Markets* (University of Chicago Press, 2011) p. 229.

abstracted from the reality of human experience. The presentation of the subject of property as apparently neutral (which is, of course, a political statement in itself) suggests that the priorities of legislators and courts are not driven by values; or as if those values are incontestable. What this book has demonstrated is that the orientations of property law – and the patterns of property use and access to property that are shaped by that law – are not neutral but directed by specific (if sometimes unarticulated) policy goals. Those policy goals – especially a particular, pro-purchaser, commercialist ethos – live on despite apparent shifts in use and values (Chapter 3).

The particular policy driver which those goals have facilitated has been the shift towards 'home ownership', discussed in Chapter 2. This is regularly presented as the natural desire of the population, which is facilitated by housing policy.[3] However, the alternative story that might be told is of differentiated citizenship among such home owners. In her extended analysis of the right of council tenants to buy the flat they rent on long leaseholds, Helen Carr makes this same point:

> [T]here seems to have been an assumption that home-ownership in whatever form and however extended would convey these inherent qualities [capital growth, independence, responsibility], offering them equally to all who acquired its status… [T]he stratification that is inherent in private ownership [is demonstrated by] its limits as a mechanism of economic and social inclusion.[4]

She goes on to add a biting critique of the assumption of equivalence between citizenship and home ownership:

> What concerns me is that for the Right to Buy lessees, the citizenship that the democratization of home-ownership offers may be as conditional as the flawed welfare citizenship that it replaces, and that the risk of impoverishment appears disproportionately high. The stretching of home-ownership by extending it to those occupiers of inner-city tower blocks, whilst at the same time minimizing their autonomy, reveals what is frequently obscured, namely, that private ownership is stratified, a site 'where very unevenly distributed power is exercised'.[5]

Our point, as with Carr, is that the apparent neutrality of property law obscures this differentiated citizenship.

Our third observation is that, as we have argued, property law is a destination subject; it needs to remain flexible, perhaps normatively open, not siloed in some foundational subject backwater subject to professional demands. The study of the reception of the Article 8 proportionality defence to mandatory possession claims in Chapter 8 provides an example of the way in which a blinkered property law

---

[3] See HM Government, *Laying the Foundations: A Housing Strategy for England* (DCLG, 2011) esp. ch. 2.

[4] H. Carr, 'The Right to Buy, the Leaseholder, and the Impoverishment of Ownership' (2011) 38(4) *Journal of Law and Society* 519, 539–40.

[5] Ibid, 541.

analysis (*Qazi*) was dragged, kicking and screaming, into a pragmatic compromise, in which property and human rights were balanced – with the edge firmly in favour of property (*Pinnock* and *Powell*). The same analysis can be applied to equality issues. There is, in one sense, a natural inclination to avoid these issues in conventional property law, but, as we have demonstrated in Chapter 9, the interface between public and private in property is brought to the fore, in this case by reference to the 'paradigmatic landlady'.

The effect of placing rights and entitlements at the centre of property analysis is – as Kate Green memorably argued – that the 'needs of property owners, self-interested and rational individuals in the market place, override the needs of those who are different: weaker or poorer, or in a different way defined as Other'. In his analysis of South African cases in which residential occupiers were evicted by the state for the purposes of economic development, van der Walt observed that 'the hierarchical domination of ownership' prioritizes certain types of claim, rooted in contractual and proprietary rights, so that:

> [E]ven when contextual factors enter the equation, courts' professional tendency to enforce the law of eviction 'normally', 'neutrally' or 'objectively' will more often than not still privilege the protection of stronger rights and result in more or less mechanical eviction of unlawful or weak occupiers who are unable to prove legal occupation rights that are strong enough to trump the owner's right.[6]

Some property scholarship has challenged this emphasis on rights and entitlements from within: for example, the Cornell School of Progressive Property[7] argues for a re-distributive approach to property rights and entitlements on the basis that our shared commitment (as human beings) to the values of 'life and human flourishing, the protection of physical security, the ability to acquire knowledge and make choices, and the freedom to live one's own life on one's own terms',[8] implicates moral and political conceptions that require property law to promote that human flourishing. This type of 'strong property rights' stance[9] seeks to address issues of justice and equality through a more just allocation of rights and entitlements in property. We (the authors) might fall out over whether this is 'progressive' or, indeed, 'modern', but the important point is that we need to explore alternatives to the narrow doctrine.

Such approaches can be contrasted with alternative approaches which rely not on challenging capital/commercial agendas through property rights *per se*, but on non-property entitlement approaches (for example, by arguing for greater

---

[6] A. van der Walt, *Property in the Margins* (Hart, 2009) p. 73.

[7] G. Alexander, E. Peñalver, J. Singer and L. Underkuffler, 'A Statement on Progressive Property' (2009) 94 *Cornell L Rev* 743.

[8] Ibid.

[9] For an extensive illustration of the insights to be gained through considering alternative perspectives to the 'strong property rights' paradigm, and arguing for a wider notion of what can be considered worthy of recognition as property interests, see van der Walt,.

recognition of home interests, protection of occupation, giving content to the idea of a right to housing, or other human rights strategies). Yet, as the discussion in Chapter 8 has shown, the application of human rights arguments to counter commercialist ideologies is not straightforward. Indeed, at a time when the human rights movement itself is at risk of being subverted by the recognition of 'human' rights for corporate and profit-making entities,[10] the reluctance of domestic English courts to give meaningful effect to the right to respect for home under Article 8 in domestic eviction cases provides a sharp contrast to the recognition of a corporation's right to 'home, family and private life' in the course of competition proceedings brought against it.[11]

Fourth, in our introduction to Chapter 2, we meandered a little, wondering what property law might look like if it was recast as a law of place or the law of the home. It would, of course, be forced to shed its rationality commercial cloth, and take the empirical as the starting point. It would also be more humanistic, more emotional, without denying the importance of other actors (like documents and other artefacts of the legal, reducing to objects on the land like trees and hedges[12]). This seems to be the direction of much property scholarship, which is both at the margins and at the cutting edge. It would require a reconfiguration of conventional understandings to allow for the significance of place and space; it would recognize that the public and the private merge, and emerge '... acknowledge[ing] that the site of regulation may shift from the national, local or individual level to a more amorphous scale, delineated on an ad hoc basis by developers, local authority officials or regulators'.[13] It would require us to think about belonging and propriety, and the ways in which law structures power relations, including resistance.[14]

Our final observation is that the effect of the narrow focus on rights and entitlements in property law is that the human context and consequences of the dispute are often excluded from the adjudicative process. Some interests or claims – for example, the (subjective, emotional) claim of the property-less to housing and/ or home – are not conceptually suited to the absolute standards required of legal

---

[10] See M. Addo, 'The Corporation as a Victim of Human Rights Violations' in M. Addo (ed.) *Human Rights Standards and the Responsibility of Transnational Corporations* (Kluwer, 1999) p. 187 (supporting this development); M. Emberland, *The Human Rights of Companies: Exploring the Structure of ECHR Protection* (Oxford University Press, 2006); cf. A. Grear, 'Challenging Corporate "Humanity": Legal Disembodiment, Embodiment and Human Rights' (2007) 7(3) *Human Rights Law Review* 511.

[11] See *Société Colas Est and Others v. France* (2004) 39 EHRR 17, at [41] in particular, where the European Court held that, 'Building on its dynamic interpretation of the Convention, the Court considers that the time has come to hold that in certain circumstances the rights guaranteed by Article 8 of the Convention may be construed as including the right to respect for a company's registered office, branches or other business premises'.

[12] See, for example, the important work of I. Braverman, '"The Tree Is the Enemy Soldier": A Sociolegal Making of War Landscapes in the Occupied West Bank' (2008) 42(3) *Law and Society Review* 449; or the high hedge as actant in anti-social behaviour, as to which see the Anti-Social Behaviour Act 2003, pt 8.

[13] A. Layard, 'Shopping in the Public Realm: A Law of Place' (2010) 37(3) *Journal of Law and Society* 412, 414.

[14] For a classic such study, or series of studies, see D. Cooper, *Governing out of Order: Space, Law and the Politics of Belonging* (Rivers Oram Press, 1998).

frameworks of rights and entitlements. Even where the court expresses sympathy with the apparently weaker party – who does not have the benefit of strict legal rights to secure their claim to property – the rhetoric of rights and entitlements functions to suggest that property law (and those who apply it) lacks power to change the harsh realities of society, so placing the problems under adjudication beyond judicial power or jurisdiction.[15] A particular example of this can be found in the context of shared ownership and sale and rentback transactions, discussed in Chapter 2, where the court becomes literally powerless in the face of its own self-created doctrine.

The vocabulary with which we allow claims to be articulated within property law, and the centring of rights and entitlements in legal methodologies, determine whether we can even recognize an issue or outcome as a problem to be addressed. Furthermore, policy analysts recognize that 'facts are things that never speak for themselves, they require an interpreter'.[16] Property lawyers are the interpreters of the anecdotal experiences of everyday life but they also make worlds in their translations. This is a fairly basic legal method point, of course; it is how to answer a problem question in a way, but the practice of translation is to objectify, de-emotionalize, and prescribe relevance to certain facts based on collages of various legal artefacts.[17] What matters to the real-life participants in the drama is less relevant: 'What matters here is what matters to the professional nomospheric technicians in their practical tasks of making (legal) sense'.[18] We recognize that, in scrutinizing conventional interpretations of property law, and seeking to open up the possibility of alternative interpretations, we are similarly 'agents of technocratic form',[19] or nomospheric technicians, but this only emphasizes the significance of the generic role as academic. It also emphasizes the ambition of the task that awaits us. This is the way Valverde describes the task:

> In order to avoid sociological reductionism and better understand the 'how' of legal mechanisms, analyses need to be simultaneously inside and outside law, simultaneously technical and theoretical, legal and socio-legal. Doctrinal 'technicalities' would be as important in such a study as sociological analyses of power effects.[20]

There we have it: an ethnographic task as a way of doing property/place/home law.

---

[15] T. Ross, 'The Rhetoric of Poverty: Their Immorality, Our Helplessness' (1991) 79 *Georgetown Law Journal* 1499, 1509.

[16] W. Parsons, *Public Policy: An Introduction to the Theory and Practice of Policy Analysis* (Edward Elgar, 1995) p. 87.

[17] See D. Delaney, *Nomospheric Investigations: The Spatial, The Legal and the Pragmatics of World-Making* (Routledge-Glasshouse, 2010) ch. 6; and see G. Douglas, 'Cohabitation and Conveyancing Practice: Problems and Solutions' (2008) 72(5) *Conv* 365.

[18] At 163.

[19] See A. Riles, 'A New Agenda for the Cultural Study of Law: Taking on the Technicalities' (2005–6) 63(4) *Buffalo Law Review* 973.

[20] M. Valverde, 'Jurisdiction and Scale: Legal "Technicalities" as Resources for Theory' (2009) 18(2) *Social and Legal Studies* 140.

INDEX

1925 legislation, the 41–60, 85

access 135, 136, 144
adverse possession 17, 50, 94, 104, 119,
     122–5, 145, 159, 160–2
alienability 46, 47, 52, 59, 103,
     194, 200
alienation 45, 56, 58, 67, 159
   theme of 2, 4–7, 9, 19, 49, 55, 226
amenities 132, 134
anti-discrimination 170–1, 172
anti-social behaviour 177–9
arrears 39, 70, 76, 162, 163, 195, 196,
     197–8
assets 30, 37
   homes as 190
   land as 45, 46, 51, 52–4, 55
   property as 28, 49–50, 56, 189, 196
assured shorthold tenancies 63, 66, 67–8,
     72, 79, 80, 82, 83
assured tenancies 39, 76
authorized schemes 79–81
autonomy 13, 14, 16, 27
auxiliary aids 180

bankruptcy 55–6, 187
belonging, sense of 3, 9, 230
beneficiaries 45, 101, 102
binaries 18
borrowers
   see mortgagors
boundaries 3, 8–9, 18, 124, 136
building societies 6, 25
burdens 97–8, 99, 130, 137–8, 139, 140,
     141–2

bureaucratization 88, 90–2, 93, 94, 96,
     98, 103–5
business finance 190–1

cadastral mapping 85–7
capital 4, 6, 19, 25, 27, 28
capitalist economic structures 7
cartography
   see mapping
certainty 5, 11, 93, 104, 215, 216, 225
certainty rule 71
chain information 91
choice 12–13, 14–15, 144
circulation of property 6
citizenship 53, 190, 228
   theme of 2, 7–8, 226
claims, stale 108
Coalition government
   and cohabitation 205
   and equality 183, 184
   and shared ownership 36
   and squatting 108, 111, 112, 113, 114,
        115, 118
coercion 142
cohabitation 204–25
collateral 226–7
colonialism 86–7
commercialism 48–9, 127, 229–30
Commission for Racial Equality 168, 182,
     184–5
commodification
   of housing/property 64, 103, 125, 127
   of land 17, 41–5, 47, 59, 132
   of loan documents 19
commonhold 31, 133–4, 136, 137, 141

common intention 209–13, 217, 221, 222
   express 209–10, 213–14, 217
   imputed 210, 212, 217, 218
   inferred 210, 213, 217, 218, 227
commons land 121
communities
   gated 10, 133–4, 136
   indigenous 119–20
   minority 170, 181
community, the wider 15, 16–17, 108,
      118–19, 121
compatibility (with ECHR) 149, 160, 162
compensation 160, 161, 162
Conservative party 31, 66, 111, 116
constructive trusts 204, 206, 208–14,
      216–19, 221–3
consultations
   on e-transfers 98
   on land registration 138
   on squatting 108, 111, 113, 114,
      115–16, 118
consumer protection 187, 193–6
consumers 78, 188, 190, 192, 195
contracting parties 71
contracts 24, 194
conversion, doctrine of 53–5, 57, 59
conveyancing 43, 108, 194
   electronic 90–92, 96, 105
   simplifying/improving 4, 5, 41, 88, 95, 104
co-operatives, mutual 82
co-ownership 42, 46, 51–8, 69, 75, 96–7
costs 224
council housing 27, 28, 168, 182
   see also social housing
covenants
   binding 135
   implied 68
   leasehold 129, 132
   negative 130
   positive 129–30, 138
   restrictive freehold 128, 129–30, 132,
      133, 137–44
creditors 45, 194, 196, 200
   interests of 52–3, 55, 187, 190, 197
   protection for 190
curtain principle 89

decent homes standard 32
deeds 89, 91
defaulting (mortgage) 186–7, 188, 190,
      192, 197, 198, 202
defeasibility 89
democracy 7, 13, 134, 180, 184
   property-owning 8, 190, 228
deposits 79–81
deprivation 159, 160, 161, 162
deregulation 188
detriment 209, 213–14
   reliance in 215, 220, 221
disability 166, 167, 170, 177–81
   knowledge of 178–9
Disability Rights Commission 182
Disability Rights Taskforce 174
discoverability 98–103, 127, 142
discovery, doctrine of 18
discretion, of the courts 39, 52, 55, 57,
      58, 59, 82, 128, 146, 153, 162, 179,
      180, 187, 198, 200, 203, 220
discrimination 165, 166, 168, 182–3
   disability-related 166, 167, 171, 177,
      178
   justifications for 178, 179–80
   race 167–70, 172–3
disposal 167, 168, 177, 222
   private 171, 173, 175
dispositions 97–8, 100
disproportionality 155, 160, 162
disrepair claims 77–8
District Land Registries 90
documents, electronic 91
duty to sell 57
dwelling-houses 200, 203

easements 99, 127, 133, 137–44, 220
   types of 139–40, 142, 143
efficiency 90–2, 138
ejectment 82
emotions 96, 224, 230
   and homes/land/property 11, 59–60,
      64, 93, 94, 104, 204
   otherness of 204–5
empirical research 204, 206, 223–5
enclosures 135–6

enforceability 127, 137, 138, 141, 193–4
enforcement 182, 200, 202
enjoyment 7, 180–1
    quiet/peaceful 68, 78, 145
enquiries 43, 44, 98–9
entitlement 227, 229, 230–1
environmental law 130, 131–2
environmental protection 119
equality 12, 165–84, 229
    and disability 177–81
    LGBT 175–7
    racial 166–71
Equality and Human Rights Commission
    (EHRC) 166, 169, 181, 182, 185
equality impact assessments 116
equality work 181–5
Equal Opportunities Commission 182
equitable doctrines 194
equity 194, 216, 217, 219, 220, 222
equity's darling 42, 70
estate 21–40, 42, 43, 44
    see also possession
estoppel
    equitable 215, 221
    proprietary 204, 206, 208, 209, 214–16,
        219–23
    tenancies by 73
ethics 117–22, 123, 131
ethnicity 166
ethnic minorities 168–70
eviction 33, 63, 65, 82, 152, 153, 155,
        177, 178, 230
    unlawful 62, 68, 83
evidence, documentary 43
exceptional categories 68–9, 72, 74
exceptional circumstances 55–6
exchange value 45, 46, 47–8, 49–50, 54,
        56, 57, 59, 96, 128, 188
exclusion 3–4, 7, 135, 136, 144
    rights of 124, 127
    theme of 2, 8–11, 67, 226
exemptions 66, 111, 122
    private disposal 170, 171, 173, 175
    small premises 170, 171, 172–5
expenditure 140
expense 44

factor-based approach 158
failure to leave 110, 111, 112
fairness 78–9, 138, 141, 142, 194, 197,
        217, 218
feudal system 23–4, 121
finances, of cohabitants 208, 219, 223–4
Financial Conduct Authority (FCA) 196
financial contributions 211, 217
financial crisis 19, 27, 186, 192, 195–6,
        197, 200, 201
financial markets, global 226
Financial Services Authority (FSA) 33, 34,
        193, 194, 195, 196–7
forbearance 197, 202, 203
forfeiture clauses 79
franchise, the 7
freeholders 30–1
freeholds 23, 30
functions of a public nature 157

gateway defences 149–53, 157
geography 17–18
good faith 78, 108, 124, 200
goods, public 135–6
governance 1, 63, 189
    private 133–9
    public 129–30
    self 10, 135
    of use rights 129–30, 133–9
government, idea of 9

harassment 62, 68, 83
'highly exceptional' test 153
holiday lets 67
homelessness 112, 113, 118, 125
home owners 1, 10, 192
home ownership 1, 3–4, 8, 22, 36, 186,
        190, 224, 228
    defensive 9–10
    emotional dimension of 59–60
    promoting 25–7, 36
    purpose of 56–7
    understandings about 27–8
    see also co-ownership; owner
        occupation; ownership; shared
        ownership

homes 1–2, 7
  as assets 190
  businesses as 175
  characteristics of 10–11, 26, 27
  emotional attachment to 11
  equalities law in 171–7
  law of 21–2
  loss of 152
  meanings of 46, 52, 56, 104
  preservation of 64
  property as 102, 188–93, 196, 197, 198, 200
  purposes of 55, 59–60
  rights to 145, 204–25
  as security 201
  use as 118
houses 59–60, 104
  see also homes; housing; property
housing 64, 189, 200
  affordable 37, 118
  allocation of 113, 185
  and discrimination/equality 165–84
  as an investment 190, 191–2
  local authority 26–7, 28
  see also council housing; social housing
housing associations 36–7
housing benefit 67
Housing Law Practitioners
    Association 116–17
housing market
  crisis 109, 115, 186–7, 188, 192, 195, 200, 202, 203
  discrimination in 172–3
housing need 112, 118
housing policy 22, 24–5, 27, 31, 36–7, 183, 228
housing wealth 189–90, 191–2
human flourishing 16, 229
human rights 123, 145–64, 228, 230
  to respect for one's home 146–52, 199
human rights movement 230

immigrants 168, 185
immigration 167
imperialism 86–7
inclusion 8, 135, 226, 228

Income Support for Mortgage Interest
    (ISMI) 201, 202
incompatibility 147, 158, 161
incumbrances 97–8, 99
individualism, liberal 13, 16, 49
industrial revolutions 127, 132
inequality 8, 13–14, 75, 77, 121, 165, 166–71, 183, 185
  see also equality
inheritance 189, 221
injunctions 109
insecurity 9–10
  see also security
inspections 43–4, 98, 100
insurance policies 201–2
insurance principle 89
insurance, private title 104
integrity 153–4
intention 65, 68, 72–7, 204
  see also common intention
interest holders 98–9, 100
interests
  balancing 179, 180, 197
  beneficial 4, 53, 54, 56, 96–7, 160, 207, 214, 222, 224
  of cohabitants 204, 205–6, 207–16
  community 118–19, 135
  conflicts of 128
  in co-owned land 54–5
  creation of 97
  of creditors 52–3, 55, 187, 190, 197
  of debtors 55
  of disabled people 179, 180
  emotional 96
  equitable 42, 43, 44, 45, 53, 89, 99–100, 102
  in housing 165
  individual 119, 161
  informal 105
  in land 57, 138, 141, 222
  legal 42, 89, 91, 99
  of occupiers 55, 197
  'on the ground' 89
  overriding 33, 89, 96, 98–103
  of owner-occupiers 198
  ownership 125

interests – *continued*
  in possession 57
  proprietary 89, 194
  of purchasers 88
  reduced categories of 44
  registrable 97–8
  registration of 44, 96
  of squatters 108
  subjective 96
  subsidiary 42, 89, 98, 142
  third-party 91, 96, 127–44
  transfer of 53, 65, 92, 97, 207
  unregistrable 44–5
  vulnerable 98–103
interpretation 231
interventions 77, 129, 158, 178, 182, 194
investigations
  into discrimination 168–9, 182–3
  see also title, investigation of
irremovability 107

judicial review 151, 153, 154
jurisdiction 40
justice 123, 229
  distributive 15
  interpersonal 13
  social 13, 121

knowledge 225

Labour party 31, 66, 173, 174, 201
land
  as an asset 45, 46, 51, 52–54, 55
  bureaucratization of 88, 90–2
  as a commodity 17, 41–5, 47, 59, 132
  control of 127–44
  emotional attachment to 104
  as a home 46
  ideas of 93–4
  interests in 89–90
  Navajo concept of 120
  owner-occupied 188–93
  as property 47
  as space 94
  transfer of 41, 42, 44, 45, 46, 49, 51,
    54, 88, 95, 96, 97, 101, 138, 142, 194

  trust of 38
  unregistered 91, 97, 98, 142
  use of 94, 127–44
land certificates, paper 91
Land Charges Register 89
land law 41–60
landlordism 84
landlords 62, 64, 157
  behaviour of 79
  duties of 77–8, 171, 177, 180, 181, 184
  private 62, 158, 187
  relationships with tenants 62–4, 65, 66,
    67, 74, 83–4
  social 32, 62, 156, 158, 169, 170–1, 185
  treatment of disabled tenants
    by 177–81
land owners 89, 108
  power of 135–6
  private 116–22, 128, 131, 141
  responsibilities of 116–22
land ownership 85–9, 120, 137
  duties of 17, 140
  freehold 134
  philosophy of 93, 94
  private 131–3
Land Register 89–90, 95–6, 99, 103
land registration 42, 44, 50–1, 85–105,
    123–4, 127, 137, 141, 142
  modernization of 96, 104
  practical/technical changes 93, 96–103
  systems 85–9, 91, 98
  Torrens-style 85, 105, 123
Land Registry 90–1, 104, 107, 123, 208
law and geography 17–18
law, as a tool 227
Law Commission 56, 57, 88, 110, 114–15,
    123, 138, 140, 142, 200, 205, 222
law, doctrinal 144, 205, 206, 207, 223–5,
    231
leaseholders 25, 30, 31–2
leaseholds 23–4, 31
  characteristics of 29–32
  long 22, 29–32, 38–9, 40
leasehold system, private 132
Leasehold Valuation Tribunal 31, 32
leases 30, 61–84, 97, 99

legal analysis 51
legal consciousness 29
legal fictions 23–4
legal mechanisms 40, 135, 231
legal profession 224–5
legal realism 13
legal relations 15, 72
legal subjects/persons 12–13, 15
legal techniques 226
lenders
    see mortgage lenders
lending, irresponsible 196
liberty 14
licence agreements 73
licences 64, 65, 75, 77, 149–50
limitation 161, 162
local authorities 83, 131, 152, 155–6
logic 11–12, 46, 49
loss of control 161, 162

management, premises 167, 168, 177
mapping 9, 18, 85–9
margin of appreciation 160, 161
market ethos 58
marriage 205
material attachments 94
media, the 109, 111, 115–16
minor interests 97, 99–100
mirror principle 89, 98
mistake 207, 214
moral agenda 116–17, 122, 124–5
mortgagees
    see mortgage lenders
mortgage interest 65
mortgage interest tax relief 201
mortgage law 187, 194
mortgage lenders 158, 196–200, 202
    power of 189, 199
    responsibilities of 193, 196, 203
mortgage market
    deregulation of 188, 191–2
    regulation of 187, 193, 195
mortgage payments 210, 211, 219
mortgages 5–6, 19, 25, 33–4, 38, 186–203
    enforcement of 200, 202
    types of 33, 187, 188, 190–1, 194–5

mortgagors 198, 199, 202
mutual benefit 130

Nearly Legal blog 116–17
necessity, squatting as 112
need, social 108
neighbours 128, 133, 179, 180
neoliberalism 8, 12, 16, 25–6, 108, 125,
    188, 192, 193, 195, 201
neutrality 13, 227–8
non-discrimination 170, 181–5
non-financial contributions 211–12
non-owners 210
non-ownership 25
non-property 229
non-registration 89
Northern Ireland Law Commission 51,
    52, 124–5
notice 98
    constructive 42–4
    doctrine of 5, 43
notices 96
    to quit 81, 148, 152
nuisance 130–1, 133

obligations 49, 62, 69, 71, 77–8, 127, 133,
    137, 138, 141, 142, 156
occupation 43, 51, 99, 108
    actual 100–1, 102
    adverse 110
    unauthorized 116
    unlawful 107–26
occupiers 188
    legal 110–11, 114
    protecting 187, 196–200
    unauthorized 149
Office of Fair Trading 78, 193, 194
orders for sale 57–8
Ordnance Survey maps 87
otherness 204–5, 228
overreaching 42, 45, 56, 101–3
over-regulation 79, 84
owner occupation 25, 26, 28, 53, 58–9,
    131, 190
    see also home ownership
owner-occupied sector 104

owner-occupiers 172–3, 186–7, 189, 191
owners 195, 228
  and adverse possession 122–5
  beneficial 216, 222
  cohabiting 210, 211–12
  joint 210, 216, 223
  protection for 114
  self-help for 110–11
  use of violence by 110
ownership 1–2, 6, 67
  beneficial 107, 208, 209
  see also co-ownership; co-ownership;
    home ownership; land ownership;
    property ownership

payments, indirect 211–12
pedestrianism 4
penalties 80–1
place 17, 18–19, 135
  attachment to 148
  law of 21–2, 230
  meaning of 87
  as space 103, 104
planning law 128, 130, 131–2
point of sale 193–6
police 116, 125
policy, government
  agenda 49, 50, 144, 194, 202
  on discrimination 167, 170, 180, 184
  on gated communities 134, 136
  goals 11, 12, 47, 51, 228
  on home ownership 2, 53, 200, 228
  on land ownership 39–40, 49, 101,
    108, 128
  on land/property law 41–2, 46, 47, 50,
    54
  on mortgages 184, 188, 199, 201
  on occupation 101
  and over-regulation 79
  on property as capital 49, 52, 53, 54
  on shared owners 38
  on squatting 111, 113–17, 118, 124
  and theme of alienation 49
  on welfare 15
  see also housing policy
political agenda 119, 124

political ideologies 104–5
politics
  of citizenship 7–8
  of private renting 66, 84
  of race and housing 167
  of squatting 115–17
positive action 166, 184–5
possession 43, 49, 82, 86, 91, 103, 109,
    123–4, 149
  exclusive 68, 72, 73–4, 75
  loss of 39
  mandatory rights to 145–58, 161, 228
  material 93–6
  right to 198
  taking/obtaining 40, 80, 197–8
  see also adverse possession
possession orders 63, 65, 109, 146, 148,
    149, 152, 161, 197
possessions 159
postponement of sale 52
precedent 147
pre-emption 38
prejudice, private 166, 170
premises
  see housing; property
presumption 209, 218, 219, 224
  in favour of sale 51, 52–3, 55, 57
pretences 69–70, 75–7
private law 12, 127, 128, 130–1, 134, 144,
    226
private parties 158, 162
private rented sector 75, 84, 187
  failure of 25, 26
  over-regulation of 79
  regulation of 83
  see also landlords, private
private sphere 171–7
privatization 27, 134, 135–6, 192, 201
privity of contract 65, 130
professionalism 33
profits à prendre 128, 136–7, 138
property 1, 7, 11, 15, 44, 56, 87, 120, 194,
    198, 199, 221
  as an asset/commodity/wealth 28,
    49–50, 56, 103, 196
  emotional dimension of 93, 94, 204

property – *continued*
  empty 114, 115, 118
  as home 102, 110, 188–93, 196, 197,
    198, 200
  as a metaphor 2–3
  private 45–51, 127, 136, 141
  purchase price of 210, 211, 219
  real 17, 52, 53, 54, 104, 119, 125, 190,
    226
  as security 188–93, 196, 197, 200
  social context/dimension of 15, 93–94,
    96
  theories of 16
property law 22, 131, 136, 139–40, 141,
    148
  and cohabitation 204–25
  critiques of 204
  as destination subject 2, 204, 228
  emotional dimension of 11
  frameworks 41–5, 230–1
  and human rights 145–64
  key themes of 1, 2, 19
  and mortgages 202
  reforming 4–5
property ownership 15, 32, 48–9, 224–5
property rights 74, 83, 86, 103, 121, 135,
    136, 145–6, 147, 156, 162, 227, 229,
    230–1
property rights thesis 148–9, 150, 155–6
proportionality 146–7, 152, 153, 155,
    156, 157, 162, 179, 199, 220, 228
propriety 17
protected characteristics 173, 183
public bodies, duties of 183–4
public funding 36, 37
public housing 4, 6, 7
  see also council housing; social housing
public interest, the 118–19, 127–8, 130,
    132, 135, 159, 160, 161
public law 127, 128, 130–1, 144, 149,
    154, 156
public ownership 158
public sector equality duty 166, 181,
    183, 185
public sphere 171–7
purchasers 42–5, 88, 89, 97, 99, 141–2

protection for 56, 100, 101
responsibilities of 98–9

race 166
Race Relations Board 168
racism, institutional 169, 181
rationality 46, 103, 128
  abstract 93–6
  deep 11, 14, 16
  economic 12–13, 14, 47, 49,
    119, 128
  legal 191, 206, 230
  move towards 104–5
  theme of 2, 11–14, 49, 93, 204, 226
reason 11–12
reasonable adjustments 166, 171, 177,
    180, 181
reasonableness 128, 149, 150, 197
rectification 207
registration
  see land registration; title, registration
    of
relationships
  between landlords and tenants 62–4,
    65, 66, 67, 74, 83–84
  between neighbours 128
  between property and community 16
  between users and land 93
reliance 215, 220, 221
remedies 216–21
rent 75–6
  failure to pay 177–8
  market 67
  regulation/control 65
renting 3–4, 22, 72–3
repossessions 186–7, 192, 197, 200–1
  out-of-court 197–8, 199–200
rescue schemes 202
residence, length of 151, 152
responsibilities 108, 128
  of conveyancers 207, 224
  of land owners 116–22
  of mortgage lenders 193, 196, 203
  of purchasers 98–9
  state 116–22
  of tenants 62–3

responsibility
  individual 192, 226
  theme of 2, 14–17, 226
restrictions 96–7, 98
restrictive freehold 127
rights 42, 44, 64–81, 83, 132
  absolute 145, 155, 156
  of access 121, 124
  acquisition of 8
  communal/collective 121–2
  corporate 230
  to defend one's home 10
  equitable 42, 89
  of exclusion 124, 127
  to housing 7–8
  in housing 165
  indigenous 119–20
  in/over land 21, 133–9
  of land owners 108
  of leaseholders 31
  of occupation 100, 149
  to possession 145–58, 198
  to possessions 158
  proprietary 64–5, 116–17,
    133, 221
  of re-entry 79
  to respect for one's home 230
  right to buy, the 8, 30, 31–2
  to roam 128, 131, 136
  of way 136–7
  see also human rights; property
    rights
risk 186, 193, 196
rural commons 135–6

safety nets 201–2
sale and rentback 22, 33–5
sale of property
  see housing market
Secured Lending Reform Bill 202–3
securitization 19, 193–4, 196, 201
security 10, 27, 39, 71, 88, 91, 108, 200
security of tenure 65, 66, 67, 74
segregation 134
self-governance 10
self-help 110–11, 125

self-interest 13, 17, 128, 132
self-responsibility 201
service charges 32
sham, doctrine of 69–70
shared ownership 22, 36–7, 38, 40, 145,
    159, 161–63
simplification 5, 104, 138
social housing 4, 8, 32, 37, 149, 154, 158,
    170, 183, 184, 185
  management 177, 179
  and shared ownership 36, 37
social landlords
  see landlords, social
'social', the 20
sovereignty 10
space 103, 104, 135
  law of 230
  public versus private 171–7
  safe 175–7
  theme of 2, 17–19, 226
squatters 50, 51, 108, 109, 112, 113,
    122–5, 161
  criminalization of 108, 110, 111, 112,
    109–17, 118, 122, 125
status of moveability 63, 83
stereotypes, racial 168, 169
stewardship 17, 116–22, 123, 125
substantial disadvantage 177,
    180, 181
surveillance 64

taxation 134
tenancies 24, 33, 67, 70, 73, 82
  determining 81–3, 148, 152
  for life 71–2
  see also assured shorthold tenancies;
    assured tenancies
tenancy agreements 61–4, 69–79, 177
tenancy law 61–4
tenants 24, 30, 187
  with disabilities 177–81
  information for 79–80
  joint 69, 82, 217
  relationships with landlords 62–4, 65,
    66, 67, 74, 83–84
  rights and responsibilities of 62–3

tenure 21–40, 48
  doctrine of 21, 23
  hierarchy of 27, 28
  terminology of 28–9
  transforming 24–9
term 68, 70–2
  void 70, 71
terms 77, 78
  unfair 78–9, 194–5, 196
terra nullius 86
time delays 44
title 89, 91, 107, 108, 209
  acquisition of 122–5
  certainty of 5, 93, 104
  clean/good 43–4, 51, 89
  investigation of 5, 42, 43, 89, 91, 92
  registration of 42, 85–9, 90–2, 93, 95,
    104, 142
  successors in 129–30, 137, 140, 142,
    221
  transfer of 90, 92, 219
topography 86, 87–8
tourism 176
transactions 13–14, 15, 49, 51, 69, 97,
    101, 105
  commercial 104, 215, 220
  electronic 90–2
  facilitation of 11, 13, 46, 89, 90, 91,
    94, 103
  overriding 100, 102
  private 12
  registering 85, 89
  sale and rentback 33, 34–5, 220
  see also mortgages
transmissibility 143

treatment, less favourable 178–9
trespass 109, 110, 111-12, 123
trust 63, 64
trustees for sale 52
trusts
  and co-ownership 44, 51
  implied 51
  of land 45, 46, 56–8, 96–7, 227
  resulting 208
  for sale 46, 51, 52–4, 56–7, 59, 227
  statutory 107
  see also constructive trusts
truth 65

uncertainty 44, 220
unconscionability 33, 194, 214, 215, 220
urban commons 135, 136
urbanization 129–30
use
  immediate 114–15
  of land 101, 102, 108
  unlawful 107
use value 46, 47–8, 49–50, 54, 56–7, 59,
    128, 188, 227–8
  deprivation of 113–14, 116

value 4, 47–8
values 4, 13–14, 27, 45–51, 228
violence 110
volition 141, 142
vulnerability 112, 156, 192, 197, 202

waiting lists 37
welfare 13, 192
welfare state, the 8